7/95

WITHDRAWN

 St. Louis Community College

Forest Park
Florissant Valley
Meramec

Instructional Reso
St. Louis, Missouri

The Superpower Space Race

An Explosive Rivalry
through the Solar System

The Superpower Space Race

An Explosive Rivalry through the Solar System

Robert Reeves

Plenum Press • New York and London

Library of Congress Cataloging-in-Publication Data

Reeves, Robert.
    The superpower space race : an explosive rivalry through the solar
system / Robert Reeves.
        p.   cm.
    Includes bibliographical references and index.
    ISBN 0-306-44768-1
    1. Outer space--Exploration--United States--History. 2. Outer
space--Exploration--Soviet Union--History. 3. Astronautics and
state--United States--History. 4. Astronautics and state--Soviet
Union--History. 5. Space probes.   I. Title.
TL789.8.U5R44   1994
327.1--dc20   94-28240
                                                                   CIP

ISBN 0-306-44768-1

© 1994 Robert Reeves
Plenum Press is a Division of Plenum Publishing Corporation
233 Spring Street, New York, N.Y. 10013-1578

Printed in the United States of America

To Mary,
the one who makes
my universe complete

SPACE RACE LOG
Mission Summary between the USSR and the USA

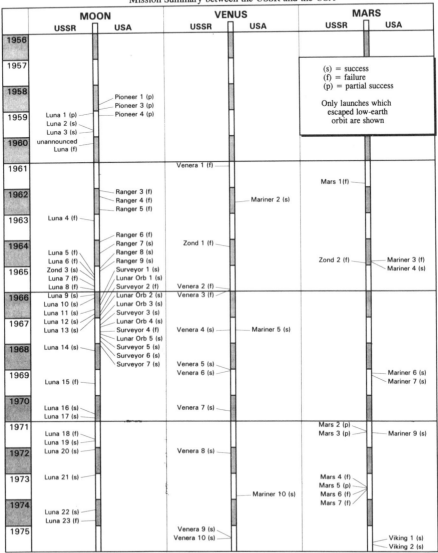

	MOON		VENUS		MARS	
	USSR	USA	USSR	USA	USSR	USA
1956						
1957					(s) = success	
1958		Pioneer 1 (p)			(f) = failure	
		Pioneer 3 (p)			(p) = partial success	
1959	Luna 1 (p)	Pioneer 4 (p)			Only launches which	
	Luna 2 (s)				escaped low-earth	
	Luna 3 (s)				orbit are shown	
1960	unannounced					
	Luna (f)					
1961			Venera 1 (f)			
					Mars 1(f)	
1962		Ranger 3 (f)		Mariner 2 (s)		
		Ranger 4 (f)				
		Ranger 5 (f)				
1963	Luna 4 (f)					
1964		Ranger 6 (f)	Zond 1 (f)			
		Ranger 7 (s)				
	Luna 5 (f)	Ranger 8 (s)			Zond 2 (f)	Mariner 3 (f)
	Luna 6 (f)	Ranger 9 (s)				Mariner 4 (s)
1965	Zond 3 (s)	Surveyor 1 (s)				
	Luna 7 (f)	Lunar Orb 1 (s)	Venera 2 (f)			
	Luna 8 (f)	Surveyor 2 (f)				
1966	Luna 9 (s)	Lunar Orb 2 (s)	Venera 3 (f)			
	Luna 10 (s)	Lunar Orb 3 (s)				
	Luna 11 (s)	Surveyor 3 (s)				
1967	Luna 12 (s)	Lunar Orb 4 (s)	Venera 4 (s)	Mariner 5 (s)		
	Luna 13 (s)	Surveyor 4 (f)				
		Lunar Orb 5 (s)				
1968	Luna 14 (s)	Surveyor 5 (s)				
		Surveyor 6 (s)	Venera 5 (s)			
		Surveyor 7 (s)	Venera 6 (s)			Mariner 6 (s)
1969	Luna 15 (f)					Mariner 7 (s)
1970	Luna 16 (s)		Venera 7 (s)			
	Luna 17 (s)					
1971	Luna 18 (f)				Mars 2 (p)	
	Luna 19 (s)				Mars 3 (p)	Mariner 9 (s)
1972	Luna 20 (s)		Venera 8 (s)			
1973	Luna 21 (s)				Mars 4 (f)	
					Mars 5 (p)	
				Mariner 10 (s)	Mars 6 (f)	
1974	Luna 22 (s)				Mars 7 (f)	
	Luna 23 (f)					
1975			Venera 9 (s)			Viking 1 (s)
			Venera 10 (s)			Viking 2 (s)

SPACE RACE LOG
Mission Summary between the USSR and the USA

	MOON		VENUS		MARS	
	USSR	**USA**	**USSR**	**USA**	**USSR**	**USA**
1976	Luna 24 (s)					
1977						
1978			Venera 11 (s) Venera 12 (s)	Pioneer-Venus 1 (s) Pioneer-Venus 2 (s)		
1979						
1980						
1981			Venera 13 (s) Venera 14 (s)			
1982						
1983			Venera 15 (s) Venera 16 (s)			
1984						
1985			Vega 1 (s) Vega 2 (s)			
1986						
1987						
1988					Phobos 1 (p) Phobos 2 (p)	
1989				Magellan (s)		
1990						
1991						
1992						
1993						Mars Obs (f)
1994		Clementine (?)				
1995						

Preface

The moon is in orbit a mere cosmic stone's throw away from earth. Venus, the second planet from the sun, is our closest planetary neighbor, while Mars circles the sun just outside earth's orbit. Despite the relative proximity of these neighbors to our home world, the distance between us has proved to be an immense barrier to learning the true nature of our solar companions. The moon is so close we can telescopically stare inside its deep craters, yet it remains just beyond reach as we now lack the rocket capability to transport visitors from earth to our natural satellite. Venus is surrounded by a thick, opaque atmosphere that hides its surface from human eyes and Mars, even when its orbit brings it closest to earth, remains a mere speck in a telescope.

After the dawn of the space age, rocketry allowed us to fill in part of the void in our knowledge of these nearby worlds. Starting in 1958, the United States and the Soviet Union sent Pioneer and Luna probes to the moon. Soon after, Mariner, Venera, and Mars robot explorers revealed the secrets of nearby mysterious planets, bit by tantalizing bit. Thanks to the explorations carried out by these intricate and wondrous machines, we have seen much of what has been hidden from us since time began. Within the span of a human generation, centuries of cosmic ignorance has been stripped away.

The purpose of this book is to chronicle the history of the American and Russian unmanned exploration of the inner solar system. Such a history must be both scientific and political: while the space explorations were scientific in intent, they became also a focal point in the political power struggle between the United States and the Soviet Union from the late 1950s to the 1970s. The rocket exploration of the moon and inner planets not only was man's first venture into space but also represented a cold war battleground—both nations fought for supremacy in the space race.

U.S. civilian space efforts have always been openly presented by the U.S. news media and are a matter of public record. The Soviet space program, however, had been traditionally kept a state secret, cloaked from the rest of the world. Eventually new political thinking in the Soviet Union, initiated by Mikhail Gorbachev's policy of "glasnost", or openness, reversed the policy of silence: planetary explorations became remarkably open and well publicized. The political collapse of the Soviet Union has brought further revelations about secret space exploits. The scope of this book, therefore, is a historical review of the trials and triumphs of these explorations from their birth at the height of the cold war to the present state of international cooperation between the superpowers.

Personally, I love facts and figures about the space program. The study of space exploration, yields, by its very nature, technical data by the pageful. It is easy, however, to choke on too much data—I resist including *too much* in this history. All spacecraft data, mission summaries, and results presented are openly gathered from published technical and scientific sources. Other data on Russian missions are gathered from public releases by TASS (the official news agency of the Soviet government); *Pravda*, *Izvestia,* and *Krasnaya Zvezda* newspapers; Radio Moscow; and personal interviews. All measurements of weights and distances are presented in both metric and standard form. All times relating to U.S. missions are given in Eastern time while those for Russian missions are given in Moscow time.

Acknowledgments

To complete any research or creative endeavor, an author relies on the generous help of many other persons. This space history is no exception. I would like to thank the following people who aided me in the preparation of this book:

- My wife, Mary, and son, Jeffery, for helping me find the time to prepare this manuscript and still have a family life.

- My friend, Don Sheron, who reviewed early drafts of the manuscript and showed me that it was possible for me to write a book such as this.

- Fellow astronomer and friend, Ron Dawes, whose drawings of Soviet spacecraft are featured in this book.

- Mars specialist Jeffrey D. Beish and space historian Fritz Bronner for reviewing later drafts of this book.

- My literary guardian angel, Melicca McCormick, whose suggestions and guidance were invaluable in making this book a source of personal pride.

- Dr. Alan Stern from Southwest Research Institute for guidance toward the proper sources for illustrations.

- Mary Noel Black from the Lunar and Planetary Institute, Mike Gentry from the Johnson Space Center, Edgar M. Cortright from the Langley Research Center, Susan Brough from the TRW Space and Electronics Group, and Emery Wilson from the Hughes Aircraft Company for supplying the illustrations used in this book.

- Astronomer and photographer Dick Mischke for allowing me to use his wonderful darkroom to prepare the illustrations used here.

Contents

Introduction

Today, we aim telescopes and spaceships at the shining orbs in the sky that we call the moon and planets. In the modern quest for knowledge, it is easy to forget that over the span of human existence, it has only been a mere wink of an eye since the time we revered these celestial wanderers as gods. Now, we revere the moon and planets not because they represent deities, but because they propel human imagination, compelling us to make exciting explorations on a grand scale in pursuit of scientific knowledge.

However, our motivations to pursue even such noble endeavors are not immune to basic human failings. Perhaps more important than a sincere desire to make a scientific quest, it was politics, nationalistic pride, and ultimately money which first propelled us to the moon, then led us to abandon that celestial outpost prematurely and attempt further, more glorious explorations deeper in space. This book is the story of the U.S. and Russian race to reach into the solar system and reap the scientific fruits of this competition.

*　　*　　*

In the late 1950s the obscure and mysterious Soviet space program became politically and scientifically intertwined with the first American attempts to launch space probes toward other worlds. The scientific reach into space became part of the propaganda war between the U.S. and the U.S.S.R. This was a marvelous time. Just months after the birth of the space age, when the first Russian Sputnik appeared, spaceships from earth were sent out toward the moon. The push of cold war politics gave these explorations an added urgency.

The explorations which have followed over the next several decades have been staggering to the average person. Before the space age, we were taught that the moon was an airless, inhospitable world beyond our reach, that Venus was a featureless, unknown world and that Mars might harbor some form of life. The modern gush of data about these previously mysterious worlds has been hard to assimilate. Seemingly in the blink of an eye, information about many new celestial bodies has been thrust upon us, unveiling new and completely alien environments, new topographies, strange and unusual atmospheres, and hundreds of new geographic features to map and name.

This book, however, is more than the history of the rocket exploration of the inner solar system. It is a reflection of my lifelong fascination with two subjects: the spacecraft exploration of other worlds, and the nature of the other planets in our solar system. Several decades ago, both these other worlds and the Soviet scientists trying to reach them, were very good at hiding their secrets, and secrets have always fascinated me.

SETTING THE STAGE

The timing of our initial steps into space has to be viewed against the backdrop of world politics during the two decades following World War II. As we shall see, early exploration of space was irrevocably linked to the cold war, the Russian need for pomp and glory, and the propaganda used by Soviet Premier Nikita Khrushchev to further his political aims.

I grew up during the worrisome postwar times when Nazi and imperial Japanese aggression was crushed, only to be replaced by global conflict between the ideals of western democracy and the communist world. Like many others born after the war, my very upbringing took place under the shadow of the U.S. struggle against Communism. At that time, decades before the collapse of the Iron Curtain and emergence of Russia as a political and scientific ally, the Soviet Union was seen as a formidable opponent, bent on world domination. Relations between the United States and the Soviet Union continually bordered on the hostile. Total military preparedness and the constant specter of espionage punctuated the terrible balance of power maintained between the western world and communist dictatorships. Only the most idealistic dreamers dared envision a time when a Russian president might attend church and when the United States would consider its former opponent an ally.

I was raised in a military family and was transferred to many locations during my childhood. The period of the Korean conflict found me living in Lisbon, Portugal. While living in that European country in the early 1950s, fear of the militaristic, unknown Soviet giant to the east was something even a 6-year-old could feel.

After the Korean hostilities were over, my family was transferred back to the United States, settling at Presque Isle Air Force Base in Maine—a jet fighter base assigned to protect the United States from Soviet bombers. To leap from sunny Portugal to the incredible winter cold of Maine was a numbing shock. Equally shocking were some of the activities introduced to me in American schools. Inspired by fear of the unknown lurking behind the Iron Curtain, we practiced air raid drills in school and were taught that when the Soviet bombers came, we had to "duck and cover." While traumatic to many children, these drills made me curious about the mysterious enemy behind the closed borders of the Soviet Union.

My youth was not entirely spent in morbid anticipation of the red menace. By 1956 my family had moved to Macon, Georgia. Some of my fondest childhood memories are from the time I was in the fourth grade. I spent hours in the library of the Alexander IV grade school. Here, I entered the world of space, reading about astronomy and the plans for future space exploration. I was fascinated by the prospect of space travel in the near future.

A SUDDEN CHANGE IN HISTORY

The first artificial earth satellite, Sputnik, appeared in the heavens on October 4, 1957, when I was only ten years old. Sputnik created a political firestorm all over the world. The new Soviet star streaking through the heavens implied the Soviet Union was far more technically advanced than the free world believed. If the Russians were capable of launching a satellite before the Americans, perhaps they were capable of launching intercontinental ballistic missiles (ICBMs) at the west as well. Compounding the fear was the constant anti-American propaganda rhetoric issued by Khrushchev. I remember the political cartoons in the Macon newspaper showing the moon-faced Khrushchev, two months after the Russian satellite success, mocking the west as the first American Vanguard satellite fell back to the launch pad in flames.

One could sense the national air of anxiety caused by the upstart Soviet satellite. After the United States' well-publicized plans for orbiting the world's first artificial satellite, the Soviets had usurped the glory of western science by orbiting a spacecraft with more than ten times the mass of the planned American satellite. Worse, Sputnik crossing overhead sent a clear message to the many countries who were no longer shielded from the threat of sudden Soviet attack by wide oceans. Sputnik reinforced the fear that the Soviet Union could reach the United States in thirty minutes with nuclear destruction. An angry Congress reacted sharply to Sputnik by escalating American strategic missile programs and spurring the missile race by starting a program to extend militarization into outer space.

In addition to the constant threat of conflict with the Soviets, Sputnik accelerated the war in the realm of science. Sputnik was seen as a scientific and intellectual challenge for American scientists to meet and exceed. Even to a child as young as I, the implication was clear. The exploration of space was going to accelerate because of the sudden Soviet emergence in the cosmos. I saw this new prospect of space exploration as nothing less than wondrous.

But what of the mysterious Soviet space program? How was it developed and by whom? While there was a flood of information about American space plans, I had not read anything about the Soviet project. What were their plans? What did their rockets look like? Who developed them? The secrecy fascinated me.

KHRUSHCHEV GAMBLES, RUSSIA LOSES

Sputnik blazed into orbit around the earth, marking the beginning of the space age. Khrushchev repeatedly stated then that the existence of the Russian satellite proved that the Soviet system of government, economy, and education was better than ours because the west was failing in its space efforts. To the Soviets, success in space meant to socialist superiority on earth. Khrushchev loved the attention gained by Sputnik. The space achievement gave his image international clout that was lacking before. However, Sputnik gave the false impression that the Soviet space program was broader and more far reaching than it really was. While the Russians did possess boosters with great power compared to American rockets, this and Khrushchev's dictatorial power to order space flights was their only strength in the space race. Soviet secrecy effectively hid just how restricted the Soviet space effort actually was. The flashy and headline-grabbing spectacle of the first satellite, coupled with Khrushchev's pomp and rhetoric, gave the impression that their space effort was much larger than was actually the case. With extensive secrecy hiding the truth, the west did not realize that there were few Soviet rockets available and that there was no effective Soviet ICBM force. The American public believed in the political football known as the "missile gap"—the perceived notion that the Soviet Union possessed many more strategic missiles than the west—when in fact the opposite was true.

However, with Sputnik circling overhead, Khrushchev garnered more of a world reaction to his space propaganda than he initially bargained for. Instead of a stunned, paralyzed reaction in the west, which would have underscored a Soviet propaganda triumph, Khrushchev saw the American political and industrial giant awaken with a roar. History has shown one thing to be true: Americans are at their best when times are at their worst. Just as Pearl Harbor shocked and galvanized America into military action, Sputnik awakened and propelled America into scientific action. As we responded to this challenge, talented teachers were sought, universities were expanded, research facilities built, and a new generation of scientists was trained in response to the sudden need for high technology—for the present and the future.

The Russians, on the other hand, chose the simplest space technology they had available at the time in order to get the job done quickly. This gave Khrushchev quick space results that he could parlay into propaganda triumphs, but it was also a reflection of the technically primitive state of Russian research and development in electronics and space systems. The powerful rocket which enabled the first Russian spacecraft to leave earth was both a blessing and a curse. It was a blessing in that it allowed missions to be quickly flown using heavy, unsophisticated, off-the-shelf electrical components and scientific instruments, but it was a curse in that it did not force the development of lightweight miniaturized instruments and electronic devices.

In the long run Soviet science would suffer because of the lack of research and development to create miniaturized electronic devices and the accompanying technological breakthroughs in computer and communications technology. While western society benefitted directly from the byproducts of space research, Soviet society did not. The western standard of living improved dramatically because of the electronics, communications, computers, data processing, and hundreds of other advances developed to serve the American space program. In this respect, Khrushchev's rush to create propaganda backfired, while in contrast the long-term commitments of the U.S. benefited western society.

FAMILY HISTORY FOCUSES HISTORICAL PERSPECTIVE

Born to a family with a long-standing involvement in aviation, I saw the exploration of space as a natural extension of the activities my family had engaged in for the past fifty years. My grandfather, Col. Vernon L. Burge, began his aviation career as a balloon pilot in the Army Signal Corps at the turn of the century. When the Army entered the aviation era, my grandfather was a mechanic on the Army's first airplane, a Wright flyer. Soon, he became the first enlisted pilot in the military. Shortly before World War I, he became an officer. My family's involvement in military aviation meant that famous people such as Billy Mitchell, Charles Lindberg, and Jimmy Doolittle were spoken of as family friends. Our participation in aviation continued with my father who was an airline captain and with my stepfather who was one of the last of the sergeant pilots in the Air Force following World War II.

This rich aviation heritage, unfortunately, stopped with me. Poor eyesight restricts my aviation adventures to flying solely for enjoyment. However, my eyes never let me fail to see the importance of space exploration or the role of the cold war in accelerating the exploration of space.

My grandfather was a genuine historical figure in early aviation. His personal military keepsakes and stories about early aviation history that have been passed down three generations showed me the importance of preserving history. As the space age unfolded, I felt the need to preserve part of this new era of history. My self-imposed station in life as a space historian can be traced back to that exciting time of the birth of the space race between the United States and the Soviets. My attraction to the secrecy of the Soviet program led me to collect everything I could get my hands on related to the Soviet space efforts. This collection now covers the space programs of all nations and has grown until it now totals several tons of materials.

BEGINNING MY COLLECTION OF HISTORY

In the spring of 1961, I was fourteen and lived on a ranch near Cotulla, Texas, about halfway between San Antonio and the Mexican border. Here, away from bright city lights, I was able to see the night sky in its natural dark glory for the first time. There, in south Texas, an incident occurred that would forever rivet my attention on the exploration of the planets.

We acquired a new horse at the ranch where I was living. For some reason, there was no trailer available to transport the animal from Cotulla to the ranch about 20 km (12 mi) away. The easiest solution was simply to ride the horse from town to the ranch.

As we wanted the horse to be on the ranch early on a Saturday, I departed town long before sunrise. A last quarter moon dimly illuminated the deserted two-lane Texas highway that led to the ranch. At about 5 A.M., as I slowly made my way down the road, I saw a brilliant star rise. I realized it was my old astronomical friend Venus, now appearing as the morning star.

With little to do except keep the horse moving down the highway until I reached the ranch gate, my thoughts drifted to the shining planet above the eastern horizon. I was aware that the first Soviet probe, Venera, had been launched toward Venus several months before, but signals from the probe had ceased shortly after launch.

Now, as my horse trotted along under the Texas moon, I realized the significance of this spacecraft approaching its target. I hung on the thought of it—Venera was just days away from passing this brilliant beacon in the sky. I was struck by the magnitude of the event. An object from earth, fashioned by mankind, was approaching another planet for the first time.

It did not matter to me that the craft was made by our communist enemy, or that its instruments had failed and it was a dead hulk speeding along a predestined course. What mattered was that it was there—millions of kilometers from earth—approaching this beautiful diamond in the sky which so fascinated me. At that moment, I realized that mankind had truly reached beyond our earth, and I was witness to the vanguard of planetary exploration.

After that, I realized I was fortunate to be born just at the right time during man's long existence on this planet. I was witness to the first explorations of other worlds and old enough to grasp the significance of man's initial steps away from our home planet.

The old Soviet Union, by its very nature, liked to keep secrets. As the space race progressed, information and hard facts about its space ventures were hard to obtain. At the same time, volumes of propaganda extolling the virtues of the Soviet system were hard to avoid each time another Soviet space triumph splashed across the headlines. For more than three decades I have searched for cracks and leaks in the cover of secrecy surrounding Soviet space efforts. At the same time, I have carefully collected everything I could find about the American push into the cosmos. This passion has continued throughout my adult life.

If you are as spellbound as I am by the exploration of other planets, and if the mysteries of the early Soviet space program arouse your curiosity as they did mine, then I invite you to come with me and relive one of the most remarkable periods in human history.

PURSUING THE ANCIENT GODS

Our moon, circling the earth every month, is the most recognizable celestial object other than the sun. For millennia humans have watched and wondered as this silvery sphere slowly slipped through its phases, blossoming into a brilliant beacon which lights the night, then fading away again.

Throughout antiquity, the moon has often been perceived as a deity and has been the driving force behind thousands of legends and a recurring theme in the folklore of all people and cultures. The Incas of Peru thought that silver was a gift to mankind in the form of the moon's tears. Eskimos thought of the moon as a male spirit so potent that a woman could become pregnant by drinking water which had been illuminated by moonlight. In our western heritage the moon is embodied as Diana, or Luna, the Roman goddess of animals and hunting. Even the Latin verb *lucere*, or to shine, gives us the name "lunar."

Even deprived of the status of a god, the moon remains fascinating. Its cycles across the sky gave us our earliest calendars. Eclipses have both terrified and thrilled generations. The moon's influences on ocean tides have affected mariners and commerce for centuries. Modern observational astronomy also had its origins with the charting of the motions of the moon. The Greek scientist, Aristarchus of Samos, recognized that the moon and sun were independent bodies in space. In the third century, he made the first crude measurements of celestial distances, determining that the sun was twenty times as far away from earth as the moon. While Aristarchus's figures were in error, his calculations were remarkable for their time.

OLD MOON, NEW MOON

The proximity of this natural satellite makes the moon the most studied of all celestial objects. Modern lunar studies date from 1610 when Galileo published "Siderius Nuncius" (the Sidereal Messenger). This work presented a record of the first detailed telescopic observations of the moon and included his studies of the height of lunar mountains which he measured by comparing the first and last rays of the sun to reach their tops. Galileo also noted the moon's libration, or rhythmical monthly rocking and nodding motion caused by its elliptical orbit. This motion allows an earth-bound observer to eventually see a total of fifty-nine percent of the moon's surface.

However, as with observers today, Galileo was frustrated by his inability to see the moon's far side. The moon's rotation matches its orbital period and, within the limits of libration, always presents the same face toward earth. The hidden side of the moon became a powerful force in drawing human attention toward lunar exploration.

Over the past centuries, observations from earth have progressively improved our understanding of the moon. Its diameter was established to be 3476 km (2160 mi), making it the solar system's second largest natural satellite relative to its parent body. The moon's elliptical orbit was calculated to lie at a mean distance of 384,392 km (238,861 mi). Temperatures on its airless surface have been measured, varying from a noontime high of 101 degrees Centigrade (214 °F) to a night time low of −155 degrees Centigrade (−247 °F). Features on its surface as small as 400 m (1/4 mile) have been accurately charted. The broad dark areas on the moon were originally thought to be oceans by observers using early crude telescopes. Improved optics showed these areas to be smooth plains. However, the origin of the thousands of craters dotting its surface was hotly debated for decades. Some theorists thought they were caused by meteor impacts while others assumed they were of volcanic origin.

While modern science uncovered much about the moon, the most intriguing questions remained unanswered. What was the moon made of and how was it created? No single theory could be proved or disproved by observations from earth. Was the moon created as a double planet along with the earth? Was the moon gravitationally captured by the earth after it was created elsewhere, or did it split off the earth after our world was formed at the birth of the solar system? These questions could only be answered when men from earth traveled to Luna and examined it up close.

THE EVENING STAR

The brilliant planet Venus has captured our imagination for thousands of years. Shining so brightly that it casts a nighttime shadow, Venus is known by many names. It has been called the "mystery planet" and the "enigma planet" because its secrets have been hidden from us for centuries; it has also been called the "veiled planet" and the "cloud-shrouded planet" because of its perpetual, enveloping cloud cover. Venus has even been called earth's twin planet or sister planet because it is a near match to our home world in size and mass. No one who gazes at the beauty of Venus punctuating a colorful twilight can escape the attraction of this celestial neighbor.

We know that Venus attracted the attention of ancient civilizations. In 1700 B.C., the Babylonians named Venus "Ishtar," the earth Mother and the goddess of love and the reproductive forces of nature. During the reign of King Ammizaduga, they charted the celestial motions of the planet on clay Venus Tablets which survive to this day. To the Phoenicians, Venus was Astarte, the goddess of fertility and sexual love. The Chinese called the bright planet "Tai-pe," or the Beautiful White One. Sicilian observers called it "Cytheria," but regarded it as the goddess Aphrodite, or Venus, just as it is known in our culture. The Romans gave Venus its current name and associated the planet with their goddess of love and beauty. In the western hemisphere ancient observations of Venus were also recorded on Mayan codices (ancient writing tablets). However, centuries of observation revealed few facts about our inner planetary companion.

Reflecting seventy-one percent of incoming sunlight, Venus is the brightest starlike object in the sky. Venus orbits the sun every 224.7 days in a nearly circular orbit. With an average orbital radius of 108.2 million km (67.2 million mi), Venus is closer to the sun than the earth. Due to the positions of the earth and Venus, we can see Venus in either the evening sky or the morning sky; from our perspective on earth, Venus never travels further than 48 degrees of angular distance in the sky from the sun. Because of this double apparition, the ancient Greeks thought Venus was two separate bodies, naming them "Phosphoros" (the morning star) and "Hesperos" (the evening star).

SCIENCE ATTACKS VENUSIAN SECRETS

In 1610, the first of Venus' secrets was exposed when Galileo turned a telescope toward it. He saw the planet as a featureless white globe that underwent phase changes like earth's moon, sometimes looking like a thin crescent while other times appearing round and ball-shaped. Little else was known about Venus until 1761 when the Russian astronomer Mikhail

Lomonosov observed the planet cross the face of the sun during a solar transit. As the planet traversed the sun, he noted that Venus had a halo. Lomonosov correctly concluded that he was seeing sunlight illuminating a thick atmosphere.

In 1891 the Italian astronomer Giovanni Schiaparelli, who first observed canals on Mars, discovered what appeared to be canals on Venus as well. He further suggested that the Venusian day was equal to its orbital period of 225 earth days. Six years later Percival Lowell confirmed Schiaparelli's rotation figure and claimed that he too had seen the Venusian canals—an oddly incorrect claim considering the planet's total cloud cover hid the surface. Using radar to penetrate the cloud mantle, modern astronomers have determined the true rotation of Venus to be a slow retrograde motion taking 243 days, a close match with the 19th century observations.

But just how similar, or dissimilar, is the veiled planet to our own world? The permanent layer of clouds enveloping Venus limited the true nature of the planet to the realm of speculation.

In the early 20th century Venus still presented the same image to earth that Galileo saw almost 300 years before: a brilliant, silvery sphere apparently lacking a moon. For decades, the inability to see the surface of the planet led to wild conjecture concerning what lay under the mysterious clouds. Some envisioned plants and animal life flourishing in steaming alien swamps. Others thought the planet was completely covered with an ocean. A very few even dared to predict that the planet was covered with a dry, blisteringly hot desert. For all its brilliance, over the centuries Venus remained a beautifully elusive, unknown world.

Only after rocket propelled probes began the exploration of space did Venus grudgingly surrender it's long-guarded secrets. Before the invasion of spacecraft from earth, no one ever dreamed the planet could be the nightmarish, inhospitable hell that Venus would prove to be.

From the 1960s to the 1980s, startling discoveries became commonplace as Venus came under increasing scrutiny by spacecraft. Venus had traditionally been called earth's twin because of the two planets' similar size, mass, and average density. In reality, this comparison breaks down and it becomes all too apparent that these similarities are merely superficial. The more that was revealed of our inner neighbor, the more we realized that Venus was far from the twin of earth imagined in romantic visions. Indeed, Venus seems to be the the exact opposite of the life-nurturing planet earth.

THE ELUSIVE RED PLANET

Mars is distinctive as it shines in the sky because of its reddish color caused by oxides, or rust, in the Martian soil. Millennia ago, Mars' reddish hue attracted the interest of the ancients who associated the planet's color with blood. Mars, because of this color, has traditionally been deified in almost all ancient civilizations as the god of war. Our modern name for the fourth planet from the sun is derived from the Roman god of war, Mars.

Circling outside the orbit of earth, Mars maintains an average distance of 228 million km (141 million mi) from the sun and takes 687 earth days to complete one revolution. Earth, traveling faster around the sun overtakes Mars every twenty-six months. This close approach is called the "opposition of Mars" because the planet is then directly opposite the sun as seen from earth. The elliptical shape of the orbit of both earth and Mars causes a cyclic period of near and far oppositions at roughly seventeen year intervals. Mars can pass as close as 56 million km (35 million mi) to earth, then move into unfavorable oppositions that eventually position Mars 101 million km (63 million mi) from earth before repeating the cycle.

Even at its closest approach to earth, Mars jealously guards its secrets. The planet is 6794 km (4422 mi) in diameter, or about twice the diameter of earth's moon. However, even at its closest, when Mars becomes a reddish beacon in the sky outshining all the planets except Venus, it is still 140 times more distant than our moon. This presents a telescopic target only 25 arc seconds in diameter. This scale renders the planet about the size of a quarter viewed from 150 m (492 ft). Equating this to our moon, the telescopic image of Mars is no bigger in apparent scale than an average crater on the moon.

At such a small scale, understanding the nature of Mars took centuries. Galileo observed the planet with his primitive telescope and saw it as featureless. The first recognizable feature on the planet was not seen until 1659 when the Dutch physicist Christian Huygens recorded a triangular dark spot that we have since named "Syrtis Major." Just seven years later, Italian astronomer Gian Cassini noted the white polar caps and estimated Mars' rotation to be 24 hr, 40 min. By the 1780s, improvements in telescopes allowed England's William Herschel to chart the seasonal advance and retreat of the polar caps and to measure the tilt of Mars' poles at about 30 degrees. Other astronomers interpreted the dark markings on Mars as oceans. These interpretations led us to perceive Mars as more earthlike and inviting.

MARS SPARKS THE HUMAN MIND

Detailed observations of earth's moon in the 1800s had shown there was little likelihood of intelligent beings inhabiting that sphere. Hopes of life on other worlds then focused on Mars. In 1869 Italian observer Father Pierre Angelo Secchi noted streak-like markings on Mars while producing the first color sketches of the planet. He called them "canali," or channels, probably to maintain the contemporary convention that dark areas on Mars were named after bodies of water.

The particularly close opposition of 1877 was a cornerstone year in Martian studies. That year Giovanni Schiaparelli, an observatory director in Milan, decided to limit the confusion over names of Martian features. Contemporary maps had multiple names for the same object, with many features named after observers. Schiaparelli chose, instead, to standardize the naming of Martian features by using historical and mythological names from the Mediterranean world. In 1877 he designated sixty-two permanent markings based on his observations of Mars. This convention of naming telescopically discovered features after mythological features is still in use today and the list has expanded to nearly six hundred features.

American astronomer Asaph Hall used the 1877 opposition to settle, once and for all, the question of whether Mars had a moon. Tired of reading the assumption that Mars had no moon, he decided to look for one. After several weeks of effort using the 26-inch telescope at the Naval Observatory in Washington, D.C., he was rewarded with the discovery of two tiny moons. Hall named the faint moons "Phobos" and "Deimos," after "Fear" and "Terror," the horses which drew the chariot of the Roman god of war.

Our perception of Mars took an even more earthlike slant in 1877 when English astronomer Nathaniel Green identified white clouds extending far above the surface. The idea that these were composed of life-nurturing water was reinforced by Schiaparelli's inadvertent popularization of the most infamous of all Martian lore: canals. Though Father Secchi had previously seen straight channel-like features a decade before Schiaparelli, as had several other well-known observers, Schiaparelli, known to be a skilled observer, saw more of them and maintained Secchi's convention of calling then canali. Schiaparelli also discussed them more than other observers, which lead to their notoriety. Mistranslations of the term "canale," and its plural "canali," into the literal English "canal" led to a scientific argument about the existence of Martian canals which spanned the next half century and beyond. Because no two people have the same eye–mind coordination, some observers readily saw canals while others did not. In 1894 in America, Percival Lowell founded the observatory bearing his name at Flagstaff, Arizona. He eventually identified over five hundred canals, though not all were visible at any one time. Lowell fueled the controversy over the existence of water on Mars by popularizing the idea of life on Mars, arguing that straight canals could only have been built by intelligent beings. Regardless of whether the canals were real, the controversy had been seeded in the public's mind and the observed canals were often seen as proof of the existence of intelligent beings on Mars. The collective public desire for the canals, and their implication of beings on Mars, to be real was so deep-seated that it profoundly influenced literature and the direction of Martian scientific studies for decades. But for all the interest in the canals and life on Mars, no conclusive proof could be found to positively establish that either existed.

MAN UNCOVERS THE REAL MARS

In the early 20th century, the continuing perception that Mars was earthlike propelled imaginations. Mars' atmosphere was known to be thinner than earth's, but was thought to be habitable. The low temperature extremes seemed no lower than the hostile polar regions of our planet. Observations had shown that equatorial regions darkened as the polar caps receded, leading to speculation that melting polar snows fed thirsty vegetation, causing the surface to darken. Thus, long before the earliest space probes, Mars became a much desired target for human exploration.

The ancient celestial gods had lured us across the voids between earth and the moon, Venus, and Mars. After thousands of years of wonder and speculation, today's generation lives during the unique period of time when mankind has at last perfected a means to travel to other worlds. These early explorations have shown that much of what we once thought about our moon and other planets is wrong. But the sustained lure of the cosmos has drawn us back to these worlds and, while we did not find what we expected, the real worlds in space have proved even more bizarre and fascinating than we ever dared imagine.

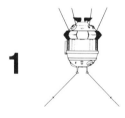

1 The Challenge of the Moon

To fly to the moon—to explore the tantalizingly close, yet so far away alien world that circles the earth—has from early in the twentieth century been a dream nurtured by science fiction writers and pursued by a handful of visionary scientists. In the decade after World War II, the development of military missiles gave the potential for lunar flight. When the U.S. Air Force and Army branches began testing long-range ballistic missiles in the mid-1950s, few realized how soon cold war politics and scientific competition with the Soviet Union would be propelling lunar dreams to reality.

In response to the first Russian satellite, Sputnik, the U.S. Air Force and Army both planned technically challenging and daring lunar flight programs. However, fate reserved the first lunar success for the Soviet Union: their Luna 1 probe escaped earth's gravity a mere fifteen months after Sputnik. The Russian moon flight quickly escalated the political and scientific stakes in the space race.

BEFORE LUNA

The Russian space flight theorist Konstantin Eduardovich Tsiolkovsky wrote in 1929:

> The conquest of the solar system will not only give us energy and life... but will give us spaciousness... We may say that man on earth commands two dimensions, the third is limited, that is, propagation up and down is impossible at this time. When the solar system is conquered, man will have three dimensions.[1]

Soviet scientists took Tsiolkovsky's writing to heart, particularly a young aeronautical designer named Sergei Pavlovich Korolyov. He dreamed of perfecting craft, like those envisioned by Tsiolkovsky, that would allow humankind to travel freely in the third dimension—indeed, even to the moon and planets. Even while Stalinist political turmoil and the subsequent "Great Patriotic War" with Germany in the 1940s destroyed normal life in Russia, Korolyov never lost sight of his ideal: the possibility of space flight. After the war, Korolyov's enthusiasm and technical expertise eventually catapulted him into leading the early Russian military missile and spaceflight program where he was able to pursue his dream of flight to other worlds.

After World War II, other scientific awakenings also nudged America down the path toward the moon. The International Geophysical Year (IGY), an unprecedented 18-month international cooperative effort to be carried out between July 1957 and December 1958 to explore the earth and space above it, had its beginnings at a humble location. The scientific event was conceived in 1950 at a gathering of physicists who met at the house of Dr. James Van Allen in Silver Spring, Maryland. Present, among others, were the eminent physicists Lloyd Berkner, S. Fred Singer, J. Wallace Jouce, and Englishman Sydney Chapman. Together, they discussed ways of coordinating high-altitude research around the world.

In the following years, the IGY was formalized by the International Council of Scientific Unions into an international cooperative scientific event. In all, 5000 scientists from 54 cooperating nations were to explore the earth and space on an unprecedented scale. In 1954, the IGY organizing committee asked the United States and the Soviet Union to use their developing rocket programs to send instruments to altitudes that balloons could not reach. That request would, in the course of three short years, explode into the space race between the U.S. and U.S.S.R. As both nations perfected powerful military rockets, the spirit of scientific cooperation spawned by the IGY would give way to a scientific showdown between the two superpowers. The exploration of space became embroiled in nationalism and cold war propaganda.

MILITARY DEVELOPMENTS AWAKEN LUNAR DREAM

Back in the U.S.S.R., Korolyov now headed the fledgling Soviet rocket enterprise as the anonymous chief of the secret Korolyov design bureau. Here, he was finalizing the design which became the first long-range Russian military rocket, the R-7 ICBM. In the mid-1950s Korolyov realized that the R-7, with its 491,000 kg (1,082,655 lb) of thrust, was capable not only of launching nuclear warheads, but earth satellites as well, and with the addition of a modest upper stage, it could reach the moon.

Korolyov knew the R-7, affectionately known as "semyorka," or "old number seven," was a poor weapons system. The big rocket needed hours of preparation before launch, leaving it vulnerable to attack. But he also knew it would make a marvelous space launcher. After all, it was the conquest of space, not weapons systems, that drove him. The perfection of semyorka as a weapons delivery system was just a means to an end. His aim was to satisfy Premier Nikita Khrushchev's desire for rockets, then use them for space exploration.

Other Russian scientists also began to think of rocket flights to earth's celestial neighbor. In an address to the World Peace Council in Vienna delivered on November 27, 1953, academician Alexander Nesmeyanov, then president of the U.S.S.R. Academy of Sciences, stated: "Science has reached a state when it is possible to send a stratoplane to the moon, to create an artificial satellite of the earth."[2]

It was clear that the academy was thinking about reaching the moon. In April 1955, the academy established the Commission on Interplanetary Communications. Among the members of the new elite science group were Leonid Sedov, P.L. Kapitsa, and V.A. Ambartsymian. Half a year later, Yuri S. Khlebtsevich proposed in the November 1955 issue of the magazine *Nauka i Zhizn* (*Science and Life*) that a remote-controlled television-carrying "tankett-laboratory," or a robotic self-propelled tank-tracked vehicle, could be sent to the moon using a rocket weighing several hundred tons. In 1956 the Committee for Interplanetary Research was also established within the Academy of Sciences. At the same time, mathematicians Mstislav Keldysh, V.A. Yegorov, and Khlebtsevich calculated over 600 possible trajectories to the moon.

DREAMS AND REALITY MERGE

As early as 1956, Korolyov had sought permission from Kremlin chiefs to use the R-7 to launch a large satellite before the Americans could loft their effort for the IGY, the tiny Vanguard satellite. By 1957 Korolyov had also outlined to close associates his plans to impact a probe on the moon and even photograph its hidden side. His deputy, Semyin Kosberg, designed a 5000-kg (11,025-lb)-thrust upper stage for semyorka which could propel a small spaceship to the moon. Mated to the R-7, this additional stage gave birth to the SL-3 Luna booster.

As Korolyov and his engineers became convinced their creation could reach the moon, well-known Soviet astronomers such as Alla G. Massevich, N.P. Barabashov, V.V. Sharonov, and A.A. Mikhailov were brought into the program. The astronomers were astonished that rocket travel to the moon was going to be possible so soon. Korolyov drew on their expertise in order to explore how the hidden side of the moon could be photographed.

By mid-1957 test launches of the R-7 had shown that a flight to the moon was feasible. Members of Korolyov's design bureau calculated flight paths to the moon and around it with a return back to earth.

The United States in 1957 also slowly but methodically readied its entry into the space age. The American Vanguard satellite program was nearing initial flight testing at Cape Canaveral. Although managed by the Navy, Vanguard was basically a civilian scientific rocket program and, thus, had low priority compared to military ICBM war rocket development that was spurred by cold war tensions. Vanguard's slow progress reflected this low priority.

BIRTH OF THE SPACE AGE

After Korolyov successfully tested the R-7 in the summer of 1957, Khrushchev rewarded him by finally granting permission to use the newly developed rocket to lift into orbit a scientific satellite. A massive, one-ton geophysical observatory satellite was on the drawing boards at Korolyov's design bureau, but could not be prepared for launch before the annual October anniversary of the Bolshevik Revolution. Instead, a smaller, spherical, "preliminary satellite" was quickly developed.

When the satellite was launched on October 4, 1957, Khrushchev was totally unprepared for the astounding world-wide reaction. The satellite, Sputnik, appeared during a tense time in the cold war. The memories of the Berlin blockade, Stalin's horrors, and Khrushchev's violent 1956 crushing of the Hungarian revolution left the world wary and watchful of Soviet actions; now, the technical and scientific victory of Sputnik was a great blow to American world prestige. Khrushchev quickly realized the tremendous power and propaganda value inherent in such space shot spectaculars, and ordered more. Sputnik 2 followed a month later carrying a live passenger, the dog Laika. The original one-ton observatory satellite eventually followed as Sputnik 3.

While not unexpected by the American government and space science establishment, Sputnik was a complete shock to the American public. The average American regarded the Russians as little removed from peasants and incapable of such technical feats. The initial yet-to-be-launched Vanguard test satellite weighed only 1.47 kgs (3.25 lbs) and seemed puny in comparison to the robust 83.6-kg (184-lb) Sputnik. In the ensuing political and social turmoil following the appearance of the Soviet satellite, leading U.S. space scientists realized that a grand space science plan must be formulated quickly to salvage American scientific honor. Not only was the "space race" thrust upon us, but the "prestige race" quickly followed as well.

MOON PLANS FORMULATED

Just three weeks after Sputnik, William Pickering, director of Caltech's Jet Propulsion Laboratory (JPL), declared that it was "imperative" for the nation to regain scientific and political stature in the world through a significant technical advance over the Soviet Union. He further warned that Sputnik implied the Soviet Union could soon send flights to the moon. Pickering stated that it was "essential" to demonstrate that the United States had a similar capability. With JPL's years of experience in perfecting Army missile systems, Pickering felt the Laboratory had a unique blend of theoretical and technical capability to perform such a mission.[3]

Pickering went on to detail a workable lunar program designated "Project Red Socks" and sought Defense Department approval for JPL to embark on a series of nine rocket flights to the moon. Red Socks was to use existing solid-fueled upper stage rocket components developed by JPL for the Army's Reentry Test Vehicle (RTV) program. The RTV components had been developed to test scale models of the warhead-carrying nose cone of the single-stage Jupiter missile. When these upper stages were adapted to the Jupiter missile, the resulting booster was capable of reaching the moon. Plans called for an initial 6.8-kg (15-lb) payload to be sent around the moon in June 1958. Additional launches would scale up between January 1959 and the end of 1960 to send 54.5 kgs (120 lbs) into orbit around the moon. To propose such a far reach into space before America even attempted its first satellite launch was a bold stroke, but Pickering felt that national interests dictated such daring action.

Although Army officials were enthusiastic about Pickering's proposal, their Pentagon superiors wanted to involve the Air Force in lunar plans. Red Socks, based on Army missile equipment, was dismissed. Pickering, however, would eventually see a portion of the Red Socks idea revived. Two years later, the JPL-developed, solid-fueled RTV upper stages, mated to an Army Jupiter missile, would loft the first U.S. moon probe to escape earth.

The shock of the first Sputnik was compounded a month later when the 500-kg (1100-lb) Sputnik 2 carried a live animal into orbit on November 3, 1957. In the nationwide response to the political and scientific pressure of the Sputniks, it became obvious that the Air Force would make a decision in early 1958 about sending a probe to the moon. Every major aerospace manufacturer and science institution in the United States had its own idea on how best to reach the moon, but, because of its missile expertise, the task of sorting out lunar proposals fell to the Defense Department. These were evaluated by the newly formed Advanced Research Projects Agency (ARPA), headed by former General Electric Company executive Roy Johnson. His deputy, Rear Admiral John E. Clark, jokingly recalled that in 1958, everyone in the country had his or her own idea on how to reach the moon except the Fanny Farmer Candy Company, and he expected their proposal any minute.[4] In all, over two hundred serious lunar proposals poured in.

Because Russia had yet to launch a rocket to the moon, a lunar mission had great appeal as a means to "beat the Russians" in space. Thus, ARPA investigated a number of schemes to quickly get a small American instrument package to the moon. One inexpensive proposal given serious thought was Farside II, a balloon-borne, five-stage, solid-fueled rocket assembled from existing components. The first stage was a cluster of four Sergeant rockets, the second stage was a single Sergeant, the third was a cluster of three Vanguard third stages, the fourth was a single Vanguard third stage, and the fifth was a scaled-down Sergeant. The prime contractor for this proposal, a subsidiary of Ford called Aeronutronic Systems, was so confident of success that it offered to bear one quarter of the expected $3 million expense.

Other missile manufacturers championed their hardware to carry our flag to the moon. Martin Company proposed their Titan missile, Convair pushed their Atlas, North American Aviation touted a modification of the canceled Navajo booster. Aerojet General proposed a five stage, solid-fueled moon rocket to be called Aerobee-M built, of course, by Aerojet.

OPERATION MONA TARGETS THE MOON

In January 1958 the Air Force, on the strength of a Rand Corporation report, had all but committed to a moon flight program using the 68,025-kg (150,000-lb)-thrust Thor IRBM as a booster. Thus, as the new year arrived, America scrambled to answer the challenge of the Sputniks. The Navy had tried and failed to orbit a Vanguard satellite and the Army was nearly ready to attempt a satellite shot of its own, but the Air Force was already looking toward the moon.

America finally responded to the two Russian satellites by launching its first Explorer satellite on January 31, 1958. Although it flew four months after Sputnik, the little American satellite made up for its tardiness with the profound discovery of radiation belts surrounding the earth. This phenomenon was discovered by instruments designed by Dr. James Van Allen, and thus became known as the Van Allen radiation belts.

On March 27, 1958, a mere two months after Explorer's launch, Secretary of Defense Neil McElroy announced the green light for ARPA's lunar program. It called for a two-pronged assault on the moon by both the Air Force and the Army using proven, existing rockets. These programs were to be part of the American contribution to the world IGY effort. The Air Force was directed to prepare three moon probes launched by a combination of the Thor IRBM and Vanguard upper stages. The Army was to prepare two probes using the 68,025-kg (150,000-lb)-thrust Jupiter IRBM paired with JPL's RTV upper stages. These combinations of rockets resulted in the Air Force's Able 1 booster and the Army's Juno 2.

The beauty of the ARPA plan was that it utilized existing rocket systems, allowing a lunar launch effort to proceed quickly. Both the Thor and Jupiter missiles had achieved a degree of reliability in test flights, and were available as production line items from Douglas Aircraft and the Chrysler Corporation.

Space Technology Laboratories—the manager of the Air Force's ballistic missile program, and the Jet Propulsion Laboratory—long an Army contractor, were designated to work with the Air Force and Army in developing their respective lunar probes. Collectively, the ARPA moon program was known as "Operation Mona." To the public however, the American moon shots were simply known as "Pioneer."

Many unknowns plagued the ambitious project. The 27-m (90-ft) tall three-stage Able rocket had never been flown before. The navigational tolerances for achieving lunar flight called for maximum performance from the rocket and left no room for error. The entire Operation Mona moon probe effort was so full of first-time unknowns that the director of ARPA, Roy Johnson, stated the project would be counted a success if it placed scientific instruments within 80,000 km (50,000 mi) of the moon.[5]

To complicate things further, a spacecraft had never before been tracked at lunar distances. ARPA was not even sure if the data from a successfully launched probe could be recovered at such distances. To improve the odds of success, a giant tracking network was quickly set up with sensitive antennae spread around the world. In addition to antennae in Massachusetts, New Hampshire, and Florida, new tracking facilities were built in Hawaii and Singapore. Even the giant 76-m (250-ft) radio telescope at Jodrell Bank, England, was brought into play to ensure around-the-clock reception of a probe en route to the moon. This network was completed just seventeen days before the first Pioneer launch in the summer of 1958.

RUSSIA ALSO AIMS FOR THE MOON

Back in the U.S.S.R., with Korolyov's initiative, the first Soviet Luna probes were also conceived. One was a lunar impact mission which was to explore near-moon space en route to a free-fall crash on the lunar surface. The other was a photographic probe which was to circle behind the moon and relay photographs of the hidden side. Later efforts would include soft landing craft to explore the surface.

Most western observers had expected the Soviets to try for the moon early in 1958. Instead, however, there was a half-year-long lull in Soviet space activity after Sputnik 2. Though this puzzled analysts of the Russian space program at the time, the reason for the six months of apparent inactivity can now be easily understood. In 1958, secrecy and security surrounding the Soviet space effort cloaked the truth from world view. The first two Sputniks were the result of the dedicated efforts of a very small band of technicians headed by Sergei Korolyov. Unlike the infant American space program which, in 1958, quickly ballooned into a broad-based effort to reach the moon, the Soviet program remained for the most part a "one-man" operation.

When the Russians learned of the American moon plans, their attention also turned to our nearest celestial neighbor. Now, with Khrushchev's blessing, Korolyov was concentrating on moon shots instead of earth-orbiting Sputniks. But, in spite of his enthusiasm, he could only accomplish so much within a given period of time. Korolyov was stretched thin. He was simultaneously the Chief Designer of Rocket-Cosmic Systems, the technical director of the space flights and the deputy chairman of Goskomissiya—the State Commission for the Organization and Execution of Space Flight.

Outside the Soviet Union, Korolyov remained anonymous and Russian space enterprises were classified a strict state secret. Official public references to him ceased in the early 1950s. Other more internationally prominent Russian scientists were thought to be the directors of Soviet space programs. Many thought academician Anatoly Blagonravov was the "Father of Sputnik" and that Professor G.A. Chebatarev was in charge of lunar missions. In the United States, however, the names of dozens of U.S. moon program officials became household words.

By summer of 1958, Soviet scientists openly hinted that their moon rocket had been perfected. No credit was given to Korolyov or Kosberg, but scientists A. Ilyushin and V. Lensky wrote in the newspaper *Izvestia*: "Our rocketry is capable at any time of overcoming the second cosmic barrier (escape velocity) by adding to the speed of the original (Sputnik) rocket, which was 18,000 mi per hr, one more stage which would produce a speed of over 25,000 mi per hr."[6] In other words, the upper stage for the SL-3 was ready for the moon.

PIONEER PROBES ASSEMBLED

Many American engineers had thought that preparing a moon flight in just five months was impossible. But brilliant planning and coordination by General Bernard Schriever, the head of the Air Force's Ballistic Missile Division (BMD), ensured that when authorization was received, the Air Force would be ready to respond quickly. Several other factors helped the Air Force. To go to the moon, the Thor missile needed no modification and the Vanguard upper stages were already developed. Additionally, Thor launch facilities already existed at Cape Canaveral. The only missing element was the Pioneer probe itself and the means to track it.

The Air Force Pioneers were prepared by the Space Technology Laboratories (STL) at Redondo Beach, California. Built as the heaviest American space probe to date, the 38-kg (83.8-lb) craft were amazingly sophisticated and versatile considering they came into being at the genesis of the space age. All three probes were designed to spin like a top for stability in space. They were built around a 1360-kg (3000-lb)-thrust, solid-fueled rocket motor from the Falcon air-to-air missile. This rocket was not to help blast to Pioneer toward the moon, but to slow it down once it got there. The Air Force was not content to shoot Pioneer past the moon or even to hit the moon. In a heroic stroke, the Air Force instead chose the hard route—Pioneer was going to orbit the moon.

The STL moon probes took the shape of two end-to-end cones resembling a child's toy top, 45 cm (18 in) high and 74 cm (29 in) wide. These first lunar trailblazers carried 18 kg (39.6 lb) of basic instruments to chart the temperature, number of micrometeors, and the radiation environment near the moon. The most exciting instrument by far was the 875-g (14-oz) lead-sulfide infrared scanner. As the probe looped behind the moon, its spinning motion would allow the scanner to image successive strips of the surface, thus returning a crude facsimile image of the hidden far side.

In all, fifty-two industrial and technical teams totaling more than 3000 people were gathered to complete the first three Pioneer missions. The fruit of their labors would be a spacecraft-booster combination containing 300,000 pieces—all of which had to work for the lunar mission to succeed.

The Army's versions of the lunar probes were much simpler and were prepared by JPL in Pasadena, California. These two Pioneers were to fly past the moon, not orbit it. The Army's 5.9-kg (12.9-lb) gold-covered fiberglass, cone-shaped spacecraft stood 58 cm (23 in) high and measured 25 cm (10 in) across its base. White thermal control stripes painted on the cone gave it the appearance of an elongated merry-go-round canopy. The pointed spike at the tip acted as an antenna. For stability in space, the Army Pioneers were rotated at 400 revolutions per min (rpm) at launch. To achieve this, the Pioneer and all three upper stages atop the Jupiter missile were mounted on an electrically driven turntable which spun the entire assembly. In order to scan the moon with their instruments, the Army Pioneers were to reduce their spin to 6 rpm about 10 hours after launch by deploying twin 7-g (0.25-oz) weights on 1.5-m (5-ft) wires. These weights slowed the Pioneer's spin much the same way spinning ice skaters slow down by extending their arms.

The only instrument planned for the tiny probe was a simple single-shot camera which was to photograph the far side of the moon. A photocell was to detect the bright moon as the craft passed and snap the shutter at the proper moment. Automatically developed onboard, the wet negative would then be scanned by a miniature facsimile device and transmitted to earth.

After the first Explorer satellite made the unexpected discovery of earth's Van Allen radiation belts, JPL determined Pioneer's film would be fogged by radiation. Another photo system was then prepared consisting of a slow-scan television camera and a lightweight tape recorder to store the image and play it back to earth.

JPL used its own tracking facilities to listen to its Pioneers. The Laboratory's 26-m (85-ft) tracking antenna at Camp Irwin at Goldstone, California, became the anchor station for a world-wide tracking network. Other listening facilities were located in South Africa and Singapore.

Both the Air Force and Army Pioneers had no ability to alter their course as later deep space probes would. The early moon rockets barely possessed enough power to loft the lightweight probes, much less apparatus for a course correction. The first Pioneers were "shoot-and-hope" affairs with their ultimate trajectory totally dependent on the booster.

RUSSIAN RUMORS

By June 1958 rumors of an attempted U.S.S.R. moon shot gone astray began to filter out of Russia. According to some sources, the SL-3 booster had exploded at liftoff and caused considerable damage but no casualties. Such rumors only served to inflame the urgency of work on Operation Mona. Having launched three satellites which dwarfed American spacecraft, the Soviets were viewed as having the rocket capability to reach the moon at any time. The Russians' technical trouble offered some consolation to American rocketeers who were in a feverish rush to prepare their first moon launch by mid-summer.

Other rumors told of an incredible Russian plan to loft a nuclear bomb to the moon. The plan, these rumors claimed, was to photograph a nuclear explosion on the lunar surface for propaganda purposes. The prestigious trade magazine *Aviation Week* even reported that the nuclear mission to the moon had been attempted shortly after the launch of the first Sputnik.[7] In reality, this rumor had its origin with Operation Baikal, a Soviet military test conducted in February 1956. Operation Baikal involved the successful test firing of an R-5 IRBM missile, known in the west by the code name of "Shyster," which carried a live nuclear warhead. By the time fragments of information about this highly secret rocket test and nuclear detonation sifted down to western intelligence, it was associated with anticipated Soviet moon shots. American space planners had also toyed with the idea of sending nuclear devices to the moon. However, the idea of exploding atomic bombs on the moon drew a storm of scientific criticism and any thoughts of actually attempting such a stunt were quickly dropped by both the Russians and the Americans.

DESTINATION: MOON

By mid-summer STL had completed the Air Force's Pioneers, the world-wide tracking network was finished, and, at Cape Canaveral, the Thor-Able booster was ready. Only the laws of physics stood in the way of America's first launch to the moon. The flight could occur only during a brief few days each month when the moon would be positioned where the Thor-Able could reach such a distant destination. Extensive calculations had shown that, to arrive at the point where the moon would be along its orbit 2.6 days after Pioneer's launch, the probe would have to liftoff at 8:14 A.M., August 17, 1958.

In the days prior to the launch, Thor Number 127 and its Able upper stages had been stacked on Pad 17-A. The rocket was then nestled inside a 10-story, 400-ton mobile service structure called a gantry. In a weather-tight room high in the gantry, the Pioneer itself was pieced together atop its third stage booster. As Pioneer was assembled, technicians in surgical gowns, gloves and masks bathed each section in powerful ultraviolet light to sterilize it. In case Pioneer accidentally hit the moon, no earth germs were to contaminate the lunar surface.

Some questioned the need for such sterilization. Because there was only a slim chance of actually hitting the moon. However, the Rand Corporation raised some scientific concerns when its studies had concluded that uncontrolled lunar experimentation could contaminate the lunar surface and negate the validity of later searches for life.

Dr. Harold Urey, Caltech's respected lunar scientist, disagreed. He said even if we contaminated a square km of the moon, there would still be

30 million more square km available for experimentation. Besides he added, the harsh lunar vacuum, heat, and radiation environment would kill any earth microbes which survived the impact.[8] For now, however, caution and scientific reason prevailed. The early Pioneers would be sterilized.

Looking back from our vantage point in history, we see that just twelve years later, Urey's assumptions would prove wrong. Fortunately, no scientific damage was done to the moon, but the tenacity of life to cling to existence was underestimated. Earth microbes hitch-hiking on spacecraft eventually did survive for years on the moon in spite of our best efforts to isolate our natural satellite from our germs.

OFF TO THE MOON

Finally, all was complete. The 5-month crash project involving 3000 people to get Pioneer's 300,000 parts together paid off. Just 4 minutes past the target time, but still within launch tolerance, the engine on Thor Number 127 roared into life. The Able 1 booster lifted off at 8:18 A.M. and climbed perfectly into the Florida morning sky.

Just half a year after launching its first satellite, America was on the way to the moon. Indeed, for the first time, a man-made machine was trying to step off the home planet for good with Pioneer which was to make a one-way trip. Hopes of reaching another world grew while Pioneer gained altitude, America was answering the scientific challenge of the Russian Sputniks.

Then, 77 seconds after launch, all was lost. A bearing froze in a propellant turbopump feeding the Thor's rocket engine, with disastrous results. The motor blew itself apart and shattered the moon rocket at 15,000 m (50,000 ft) altitude. The flaming pieces took 123 seconds to plunge into the Atlantic ocean. During the heartbreaking fall, scientists listened to the radio signal from the Pioneer probe. The spacecraft had survived the explosion and refused to die until it struck the ocean.

Since it never reached space, the Pioneer was not numbered. However, in honor of the first attempt to reach another world, modern nomenclature designates the launch as Pioneer 0.

In the aftermath of the first Pioneer's flaming end, American engineers asked the disturbing question: why had the Russians not tried for the moon? The 1324-kg (2919-lb) Sputnik 3 launched the previous May had demonstrated that the Russians had a booster capable of lifting a moon probe with ten times the mass of Pioneer. With that thought in mind, engineers at Cape Canaveral rushed to ready the next probe for launch on September 14, 1958.

That event was not to occur, however. As important as the moon flights were to the nation's interests, they did not have priority over national defense. The next Thor rocket, Number 128, was removed from Operation Mona and diverted to Project Bravo. This program was to determine the feasibility of using the Thor-Able as a military ICBM. This project delayed the next moon launch by one month. While expecting a Russian moon shot to upstage them at any time, American officials set October 11, 1958 for the next Pioneer attempt. The one-month delay gave the Russians an open opportunity to reach the moon without American competition. Though unknown to American observers, the Russians did, indeed, seize this opportunity.

COSMIC DEPARTURE POINTS

All American lunar and planetary launches have originated from the Eastern Test Range located at Cape Canaveral, Florida, under full publicity and public scrutiny. All Russian flights have originated from their cosmodrome at Tyuratam. Although the launches are now open to foreigners, for decades these missions were clandestinely launched. The location of the Russian space launch site was a state secret until 1961.

In the summer of 1957 the secret Russian launch site was located by western intelligence on photographs made during an American U-2 reconnaissance aircraft overflight of Kazakhstan. The Soviets did not admit the existence of the launch site and the Central Intelligence Agency (CIA) did not publicly admit they knew of its location. However, a name had to be chosen to identify the location within U.S. Government circles. The photo data were corollated with the best maps of that region available at the time. These were Nazi maps prepared in 1939 by Mil-Geo, the geographic division of the German army during World War II. Dino Brugioni, the chief CIA information officer, chose the name Tyuratam for the closest town shown on these maps. In the native Kazakh language, the name means "arrow burial ground."[9] Within official Soviet circles, the launch site was known by the less romantic code name of "Tashkent 50," the official postal mailing address of the secret rocket base.[10]

Tyuratam was repeatedly photographed by U-2 spy planes, but, starting in 1961, the Soviets insisted that their space facility was located near the town of Baikonur, 375 km (233 mi) northeast of Tyuratam. The Soviets maintained the ruse for the next 31 years, and by sheer usage of the misnomer, Baikonur became the internationally accepted name of the Russian spaceport. In the summer of 1992, when Kazakhstan became an independent nation, the name of the rocket base was officially changed to Tyuratam.

RUSSIANS ALSO REACH FOR THE MOON

As rumors and speculation about Russian moon plans swept the world, Korolyov and his team of scientists completed the development of the SL-3 booster and the first of its lunar payloads. As those preparing the Pioneers feared, Korolyov's team made three secret moon launch attempts from Tyuratam beginning in the early fall of 1958. All three were planned as lunar impact missions. They were never announced and remained a state secret.

On the afternoon of September 23, 1958, the first Russian moon probe mimicked America's Pioneer when the SL-3 Luna booster failed catastrophically 92 seconds after launch. However, it was difficult to keep such a historic effort completely secret, even in the Soviet society. While the first Russian moon probe lay shattered on the steppes of Kazakhstan, distorted versions of the first Russian moon launch leaked out.

As the first anniversary of Sputnik 1 arrived, the Moscow rumor mill again went into high gear. Soviet sources said a payload about the size of Sputnik 2 would be launched toward the moon "in the near future" and that preparations were being carried out "energetically."

THE MAGNIFICENT FAILURE

At Cape Canaveral, other energetic preparations were also concluding. With the delay of Project Bravo behind them, technicians prepared Thor Number 130 for the second American lunar attempt. This time, celestial alignments dictated a liftoff at 4:47 A.M., October 11.

Liftoff came just seconds after the appointed time. The rocket climbed perfectly into the starry Florida night. Hundreds of technicians and newsmen held their breath as it passed the 77-sec point in the flight which proved fatal to Pioneer 0. This time all was well. The booster continued to fire for a full 160 sec, delivering the best performance of any Thor to date. The Able second stage then thrust Pioneer further into the darkness. Finally, the third stage unleashed its brief but furious burst of energy and lofted the probe into deep space. Now officially christened Pioneer 1, the little spacecraft soared upwards to heights never before attained. For all appearances, this time America really was going to the moon.

But incredibly, Pioneer 1 failed to reach its goal. The plan had been to boost the probe to a velocity of 10,744 m (35,250 ft) per sec. This speed was not enough to escape earth's gravity, but was enough to reach the moon where the probe could fire its retrorocket and enter lunar orbit. A number of minor discrepancies together robbed Pioneer 1 of the precious final nudge of velocity to make it all the way to the moon. The rocket's aim turned out to be 2.1 degrees too high, the second stage shut down prematurely, and the third stage was skewed slightly in the wrong direction when it fired. These left Pioneer 1 approximately 251 m (825 ft) per second short of the velocity needed to reach the moon. The only recourse was to fire all eight of Pioneer's vernier rockets. These were small solid-fueled rockets which could be fired in pairs to slightly adjust the probe's velocity if needed. However, they could only add a total of 48 m (160 ft) per sec to the velocity. Pioneer 1 was doomed to loop 113,830 km (70,700 mi) into space before beginning its drop back to earth.

One final option remained. If the probe's retrorocket could be fired at apogee, its highest point above earth, Pioneer would enter a huge elliptical orbit above earth, never approaching closer than 32,000 km (20,000 mi). But even this option was lost because of Pioneer's erring trajectory. The probe was now at an odd angle to the sun and its internal temperature dropped to near freezing. Because of the cold, the rocket's electrical ignition relay refused to close. At 11:46 P.M., October 12, Pioneer ended its life as a streak of flame above the South Pacific as it slammed into the atmosphere.

Even without reaching its celestial goal, Pioneer 1 did much to improve the sagging image of American space exploration. During its 43-hr flight into uncharted space, Pioneer had achieved the highest velocity of any spacecraft and attained an altitude 25 times greater than ever reached before. The probe also measured newly discovered radiation belts above 4000 km (2500 mi) and made the first direct measurements of the earth's magnetic field. In a little known experiment, Pioneer was also the first communications satellite. The Air Force used the probe as an active repeater to relay signals from one side of the globe to the other. Pioneer 1, a failed moon probe, was thus known as the "magnificent failure."

ANOTHER SOVIET ATTEMPT

Unknown to those furiously preparing Pioneer 1, another lunar countdown was also underway on the far side of the world. The rumors of a new Russian lunar shot again had some seeds of truth. When the American Pioneer 1 lifted off for the moon on October 11, Korolyov explained to his technicians that if they worked all night and launched the next day, their Soviet probe could beat Pioneer to the moon.

As it turned out, the Soviet attempt fared worse than Pioneer. While the American probe fell back after lofting one third the way to the moon, the Soviet booster exploded 100 seconds after liftoff. An investigation determined both Russian lunar failures to date had occurred because adding the upper stage to the R-7 rocket raised the booster's center of gravity, thus setting up resonance vibrations which tore it apart just as a singer's high-pitched voice can shatter a crystal glass.

Officially, Soviet sources said nothing about plans to reach the moon, but according to rumors circulating in Moscow, two different types of lunar payloads were being prepared. One would impact the moon and another would loop around the moon and return to earth. Professor Vitaly Bronshtien, a scientific advisor to the Moscow Planetarium, speculated in a Polish magazine about the instruments to be carried by the two moon probe designs. He stated that one would determine the moon's mass, study the moon's conductivity of heat and electricity, and measure the lunar magnetic field. The second probe would carry a television apparatus to view the far side of the moon.[11] Looking at the Lunas in retrospect, Bronshtien was remarkably accurate.

FINAL THOR-ABLE FAILS

The third and last of the Thor-Able-powered Pioneers thundered up from Cape Canaveral at 2:30 A.M., November 8, 1958. After a flawless liftoff, Thor Number 129 dazzled observers as it climbed above an unusual ground mist and barreled through a low-level cloud deck. The Thor's brilliant flame illuminated the eerie scene with an orange glow.

After the Thor first stage performed perfectly, the second stage took over. Not wanting a repeat of Pioneer 1's premature second stage cutoff, ground control would signal the Able stage to shut down at the proper velocity. With this accomplished just under 5 minutes after liftoff, the solid-fueled third stage was left to complete Pioneer 2's journey to the moon. But, as on previous tries, the moon eluded Pioneer.

For some unknown reason, the third stage never ignited. After separating from the second stage, it remained inert, arcing upward with Pioneer 2 to an altitude of 1550 km (963 mi) before plummeting back to earth. The end came 41.2 min after launch when, some 12,000 km (7500 mi) from Cape Canaveral, Pioneer 2 incinerated above east central Africa.

THE ARMY'S TURN

After Pioneer 2 was burned into cosmic dust, the lunar torch was passed from General Schriever's Ballistic Missile Division to the Army Ballistic Missile Agency. The next two moon shots were now in the hands of the same team which launched America's first Explorer satellite. General John Medaris headed the Army team with the popular and charismatic German emigré Wernher von Braun as the chief technical advisor. William Pickering headed JPL's contribution, providing the upper stages and the moon probe.

The moon race, however, was not now entirely the Army's show. After NASA was created in October 1958, it inherited the Pioneers from ARPA. But in its infancy, the new civilian space agency was little more than a spectator watching the Army and JPL moon program continue under its own inertia. When the Army booster lifted off from Cape Canaveral with "NASA" emblazoned on its side, the agency was still just a national figurehead for space exploration.

But NASA was already looking toward future programs. Turning to the same USAF-STL team which lofted the first moon probes, NASA investigated the possibility of mating the upper stages from the Thor-Able to the giant 176,415-kg (389,000-lb)-thrust Atlas ICBM to launch Venus probes weighing nearly 136 kg (300 lb).

While NASA planned for the future, the Army pondered a more immediate problem. Pioneer 1 had discovered evidence of intense radiation at altitudes greater than the Explorer satellites could reach, and scientific concerns again changed the payload of the little Army probes. The first Pioneer had only traveled one-third of the way to the moon. Now, a crucial question needed to be answered. Was the radiation field local to the earth or did it extend all the way to the moon, or even beyond? The very ability to send men to the moon balanced on this question. To find out, the lunar far-side imaging experiment was dropped. In its place, two Geiger-Mueller tubes were to register radiation levels between earth and the moon.

The new Pioneer was to measure radiation at different energy levels. One detector had a saturation point of 10 roentgens per hr, the other 100 roentgens per hr. The camera shutter trigger mechanism from the previous photographic payload was retained as an engineering test. When Pioneer passed within 32,000 km (20,000 mi) of the moon, the photocell would signal earth. To prevent the bright earth from activating the mechanism, a hydraulic timer switched on the device 20 hr after launch when the probe was expected to be 225,000 km (140,000 mi) from earth.

On December 6, 1958, all was ready for the Army's first lunar attempt. The date was the ominous first anniversary of America's humiliating Vanguard disaster when our first satellite launch collapsed in flames while two Russian Sputniks circled overhead.

Unlike the first three Pioneers, the 23-m (76-ft) tall Juno 2 booster did not rest high on an impressive launch stand with a flame trench below. Pad 5 was little more than a simple metal frame resting on flat concrete. The Army rocket seemed to sit directly on the ground; its appearance belied the fact that here rested the lunar hopes of American scientists and a chance for U.S. prestige to spring back from the embarrassment of a year before. Perhaps Pad 5 would bring the Army luck. The previous January, the same launch site had sent our first Explorer satellite up to meet the Sputniks.

At 1:45 A.M., the countdown reached zero and the Juno 2 ignited. Smoke and flames burst out in all directions, obscuring the stubby rocket as it slowly rose. Then Pioneer 3 was up and away toward the moon. For a time it appeared the Army would again redeem American space efforts.

But this was not to be. The Juno was supposed to climb at an inclination of 68 degrees while its main engine burned for 179.8 sec. Soon it became apparent the booster was climbing at between 71 and 71.5 degrees inclination. At this rate, Pioneer 3 would miss the moon by too wide a margin for the photo-trigger to work. Then came Pioneer 3's death knell: The main engine exhausted its fuel 3.7 seconds too soon and flamed out.

Although the upper stages performed flawlessly, they could not make up the 316 m (1037 ft) per sec velocity shortfall caused by both the trajectory error and the premature engine shutdown.

The Juno's push was sufficient to zoom Pioneer 3 some 107,264 km (66,654 mi) into space before it lost its battle with earth's gravity. The Army's first moon probe lived for 38 hr, 6 min, then flamed like a meteor as it burned in the atmosphere over French Equatorial Africa.

Although not a lunar success, Pioneer 3 vindicated the decision to remove the photographic equipment and substitute radiation detectors. The probe confirmed a radiation belt around the earth at 4800 km (3000 mi) altitude and discovered a second radiation belt 11,250 km (7000 mi) beyond the first.

RUSSIAN MOON ACTIVITY INCREASES

Just two days before the American Pioneer 3 left for the moon, the third 1958 lunar launch took place at Tyuratam. This time, on December 4, the launch seemed normal until the SL-3 core stage engine failed after 245 seconds of flight. As usual, the Russian failure remained a state secret while the hapless Pioneer 3 lived its brief life in full world view.

Then, just after New Year's day in 1959, the Soviets hurled a scientific bombshell. Radio Moscow proclaimed the beginning of a new age for human exploration: "On January 2, 1959, a cosmic rocket was launched toward the moon. The launching again demonstrates to the world the outstanding achievements of Soviet science and technology."[12] The startling announcement heralded Luna 1, the world's first spacecraft to reach what the Soviets called the "second cosmic speed," or escape velocity. On their fourth attempt, a Russian probe had slipped the bonds of earth's gravity.

The 361-kg (797-lb) Luna 1, called "Mechta" (The Dream) by the Soviets, was launched at about 8:00 P.M., Moscow time, January 2, 1959. Thirty-four hours later, at 5:59 A.M., January 4, Mechta passed within 5955 km (3728 mi) of the moon. Streaking onward at 2.45 km (1.52 mi) per sec relative to earth, Mechta remained in contact for 62 hr until its batteries gave out at 9:00 A.M., January 5, while 500,000 km (373,125 mi) from earth.

Mechta was supposed to have collided with the moon but missed and entered a 446-day solar orbit. Preliminary calculations showed this orbit ranged from 146.4 million km (91.5 million mi) to 197.2 million km (123.25 million mi) from the sun. In this orbit, the probe would approach the earth every 5.43 years.

According to Alexandre Ananov, the Russian founder of the International Astronautical Federation, Mechta's booster imparted an excess of velocity, causing the lunar miss. Other Soviet announcements confused the issue, stating that Mechta's mission all along was to fly by the moon. That Mechta was indeed targeted to impact the moon was finally confirmed in the summer of 1961 when cosmonaut Yuri Gagarin admitted this in a letter to the magazine *Soviet Lithuania*. Decades later, in the April 11, 1989 issue of *Pravda*, cosmonaut Georgi Grechko also confirmed that designers had intended Mechta to hit the moon. At the time, he was an engineer in the Korolyov design bureau and was in a position to know the truth about Mechta.

The historic probe was a 1.2-m (4-ft) diameter polished aluminum-magnesium sphere with a 1-m (3.3-ft) magnetometer boom and with four symmetrically placed rod antennae protruding from one hemisphere. The spent carrier rocket weighed 1111 kg (2449 lb), which together with the probe, put a combined mass of 1472 kg (3246 lb) into solar orbit.

Mechta was powered by silver-zinc and mercury-oxide batteries and carried a variety of instruments including a magnetometer, two piezoelectric micrometeor detectors, cosmic ray and plasma detectors, and internal pressure and temperature-measuring instruments. These devices were mounted in a framework attached to the probe's lower hemisphere.

Scientific data were transmitted in 50.9-sec bursts at 19.993 MHz. The probe received signals from earth at 183.6 MHz. In addition, the final stage booster rocket transmitted cosmic ray data to earth in 81.6 seconds bursts at 19.995 MHz and 19.997 MHz. Listeners at the Moscow Planetarium were able to tune in Mechta by using short-wave radio equipment.

A significant scientific result of Mechta's flight was detection of a zone of intensive radiation between 5 and 6 earth radii altitude. This supplemented previous measurements of the outer Van Allen radiation belt which surrounds the earth.

Both Mechta and its booster carried a commemorative 9 × 15 cm (3.5 × 6 inch) "imperishable plaque" reading "U.S.S.R., January 1959" in Cyrilic engraving.

TRACKING MECHTA

Soviet deep space tracking capabilities were crude in 1959. To help pinpoint the location of the cosmic rocket as well as study the properties of translunar space, a spectacular experiment was prepared by well-known Soviet astronomer Professor Iosef Shklovsky. A quartz clock timer released 1 kg (2.2 lb) of sodium from Mechta's booster at 3:57 A.M. on January 3 while approximately 120,000 km (75,000 mi) from earth. The sodium evaporated in 6 seconds and fluoresced in sunlight for 5 min, creating a 650-km (400-mi)-diameter artificial comet which was visible in the constellation Virgo from earth's eastern hemisphere. The spectacle was a propaganda coup, leaving no doubt that Mechta was real.

Still, many American officials remained skeptical about the probe. Evidence outside the Soviet Union about Mechta's existence was still sketchy and some officials openly speculated about Russian fraud. Long-range radars in Turkey which tracked suborbital shots from Russia's Kapustin Yar missile base did not detect Mechta's liftoff from Tyuratam. Only a single U.S. tracking station in Hawaii received any indication that a Soviet launch had taken place on January 2, but at that time the nature of the launch was unknown. The Pentagon learned of the Russian moon launch only when it came across wire service news tickers as the story broke in the world press.

American tracking stations tried to tune in Mechta but only NASA's Jet Propulsion Laboratory reported any success. Even they were unable to get a precise fix on the craft because its signals were too weak and unsteady. By the time JPL's Goldstone tracking station acquired Mechta's signals on January 4, the craft had already passed the moon. Other facilities also tried but found they were hearing signals from other earth radio stations or rebroadcasts by Radio Moscow.

LUNAR POLITICS AND ONE-UPMANSHIP

In a patriotic rush, Soviet scientists hailed Mechta as the "tenth planet," but in reality it was considered an artificial asteroid. The Russians nicknamed the probe "Lunik" and the popular name caught on. For several years afterward, the word Lunik was synonymous with any moon probe.

Maximizing every propaganda opportunity, Radio Moscow made no mention of previous failures or the fact that the craft missed its intended lunar target. Soviet propaganda rhetoric was broadcast in a dozen languages. It hammered the theme that Mechta was the result of "the creative toil of the whole Soviet people [in] the development of Socialist society and in the interests of all progressive mankind."[13] Other propaganda efforts included issuing postage stamps commemorating the first three Sputniks and an artist's conception of Mechta's rocket.

Premier Nikita Khrushchev touted the spectacular space achievement to an attentive world press by noting that Soviet scientists "are the first in the world to map out the way from the earth to the moon." Khrushchev also said he felt "like hugging the man who has produced this, the first cosmic rocket, a new victory for the Soviet Union."[14] Whether Korolyov ever received his hug is not noted in history.

At a time when cold war tensions were high, the Russian moon flight was a demoralizing blow to American space scientists whose efforts to reach the moon had failed four times. To needle U.S. scientists further, Mechta produced a salvo of impressive statistics. Pioneers 1 and 3 each reached only a third of the way to the moon before falling back to earth. Their masses paled in comparison to Mechta which was heavier than all the American space probes to date combined. The Pioneers had fallen about 1000 km (620 mi) per hr short of reaching escape velocity while Luna actually had too much velocity. A final insult to the American efforts was the fact that the Russian rocket's trajectory was three times more accurate than the trajectories of the Pioneers.

In spite of the lunar miss, the moon flight caught the world's imagination and gave Russia the image of being the leader in space exploration. Mechta provided the political impetus to direct the U.S. space program into an almost moon-only objective in a "race to the moon" with the Soviets. Politics and international prestige were now more important objectives than the acquisition of scientific data.

American officials lamented their lack of powerful boosters to compete with the seemingly giant Russian moon rocket. But already on the drawing boards was the answer to Mechta's rocket. American aerospace industries were furiously developing the Agena and Centaur upper stages which in time would loft American probes to the moon and planets.

"ME TOO"

In spite of the efforts made by both the Air Force and Army, the Russians had beaten America to the moon. Each country had made four lunar attempts and Russia was lucky when its fourth shot passed the moon while America's fourth try fell back to earth. Russian space prestige reached an all-time high.

Operation Mona had one chance left to recoup American scientific honor. At 1:45 A.M., March 3, 1959, that time had come. The Army's Juno 2 again sprang to life and soared into space. Less than 4 minutes after liftoff, the spacecraft was on course. After a year of hard effort, ARPA's Operation Mona had succeeded in sending a spacecraft toward the moon. But the momentous occasion was anticlimactic as it passed the moon and followed in the shadow of Mechta to become the second artificial planet. For that reason, Pioneer 4 was tagged the "Me Too" probe as it followed Luna 1 around the sun.

Pioneer 4 had escaped earth forever, but its path was not the one chosen by scientists. Because of slight velocity and aim errors, Pioneer would not pass the moon within the desired 32,185 km (20,000 mi). The moon-detecting photo trigger was the only thing affected by the 60,000 km (37,300 mile) miss, but it would have been more satisfying if Operation Mona's final flight had passed near the moon.

Nearly two days after launch, Pioneer 4 passed the moon's orbit while travelling 7225 km (4490 mi) per hr relative to earth. On its way out into the solar system, the probe relayed important radiation data. Pioneer 4 showed that beyond the Van Allen belt out to lunar distances, radiation was low enough for humans to travel safely to the moon.

Eighty-two hours after launch, Pioneer 4's batteries faded and its last whisper was heard by the Goldstone tracking station as the probe receded beyond 663,000 km (412,000 mi). The silent probe then slipped into a 397.75-day solar orbit that ranged from 147.6 million km (91.7 million mi) to 173.7 million km (108 million mi) from the sun.

OPERATION MONA CONCLUDES

Von Braun and Pickering basked in the public attention given the U.S. space program following Pioneer 4's flight. But the achievement was bittersweet. Mechta had been first to get near the moon and, well into the second year of the space age, America was still playing "catch-up" with Russian space efforts.

Ironically, Operation Mona had been a total lunar failure. Not one scrap of new information about the moon had been aquired. However, in the fledgling days of the space age, the very act of trying to get to the moon brought invaluable engineering experience. The high flight of Pioneer 1 and the solar orbiting Pioneer 4 were vital to U.S. prestige and showed America could respond to the scientific and propaganda challenges of its cold-war adversary. Operation Mona's race for the moon with the Russians had set into motion what would become a series of lunar explorations which would continue until men walked on the moon ten years later. In this respect, Operation Mona was an unqualified success.

As the first American lunar efforts concluded in the spring of 1959, the next phase began. Substituting the larger Atlas ICBM for the Thor, NASA and the Air Force prepared the Atlas-Able booster to send the next generation of heavier Pioneers to the moon in late 1959. Because Mechta had missed its target, the Russians had not actually reached the moon yet. If luck prevailed, America still had a chance to claim the moon prize.

The Soviets tried again for a lunar impact mission on June 16, 1959, but the second stage guidance failed and the booster was intentionally destroyed when it strayed off course. The attempted launch was never announced although U.S. intelligence reports, later, confirmed an unsuccessful Soviet lunar attempt in mid-1959.

SOVIETS REACH THE MOON

Then came the galvanizing event everyone feared would come. On the evening of September 12, Radio Moscow interrupted a program of popular music and announced a TASS bulletin: "A second successful launching of a cosmic rocket took place in the Soviet Union today. The last stage of the rocket, having exceeded the second cosmic speed of 11,200 m per sec, is flying toward the moon."[15]

At 3:30 P.M., September 12, the 390-kg (868-lb) Luna 2 was launched from Tyuratam into a direct-ascent trajectory toward the moon. Before the rocket's precise trajectory was known, the Soviets hedged their bets when announcing the flight. In the Russian language, the preposition "k," pronounced "kuh," means both to and toward. Thus, the launch announcement was not clear about the mission's planned outcome.

Later, while Luna 2 was still in flight, the Soviets refined the announcement to say that it would impact the moon near the junction of the Sea of Serenity, the Sea of Tranquility, and the Sea of Vapors. The probe, the first object to strike another celestial body, was aimed squarely between the Man-in-the-moon's eyes.

Luna 2's instruments were basically identical to those carried by Mechta the previous January. However, the new probe's radio systems were improved to prevent the weak signal and poor reception which plagued Mechta.

The probe transmitted on frequencies of 19.993, 19.997, 20.003, 39.986, and 183.6 MHz. Luna was heard by a large number of amateur radio stations in Europe and Asia and, this time, American tracking stations had no problem tuning in the moon-bound craft. The Soviets still had no world-wide tracking facilities and officials requested that tape recordings of Luna's signals be mailed to the address of "Moscow, Cosmos."

About 6 hours after launch, Luna 2's final stage repeated the sodium release artificial comet experiment. The cloud was released at 9:39:42 P.M., at an altitude of 141,615 km (88,000 mi), and was seen in the constellation of Aquarius, but the event was not visible in the U.S. A number of observatories in the U.S.S.R. observed it for 5 to 6 min at a brightness equal to a fourth magnitude star.

Luna entered the moon's gravitational field about 5 hours before impact. The pull of lunar gravity slowly accelerated the probe to 3315 m (10,877 ft) per sec. Then, some 33.5 hr after launch, Luna 2 streaked down at 30 degrees from vertical and stuck the moon east of the Sea of Serenity between the craters Archimedes and Autolycus. The impact was about 800 km (500 mi) from the visible center of the moon at 30 degrees north along the lunar meridian.

When Luna hit the moon, Radio Moscow broke off its programming. After a period of silence, the Communist theme "Internationale" was played and the announcer began: "At 00:02:24 Moscow time, the second Soviet cosmic rocket reached the surface of the moon..."[16] This was a time to be carved into the record of history. Luna was the first craft from earth to reach the moon.

BRITISH TRACK LUNAR STRIKE

At the time of Luna's launch, the giant radio telescope at Jodrell Bank in Manchester, England, was bouncing radar signals off the planet Venus. The Jodrell Bank director, Bernard Lovell, was preparing to play in an English cricket match when word of the launch arrived. Lovell later joked that on hearing about the Soviet moon flight, he pressed on with important duties: He played his cricket game while Luna sped away from earth. After all, the moon would not rise at Jodrell Bank for several more hours.[17]

Later in the evening, when the moon rose above the English horizon, the Air Force BMD-STL team which was at Jodrell Bank to track the American Pioneer moon probes helped Lovell track Luna using coordinates supplied by two teletype messages from the Soviets. At one point during a trans-Atlantic phone call with U.S. tracking facilities, American technicians expressed disbelief that Jodrell Bank was receiving loud, strong signals from Luna. Lovell held the telephone up to a loudspeaker so the Americans could hear Luna's signals for themselves.

Luna's instruments measured earth's radiation belts as the probe ascended from the earth. Luna investigator Professor Sergei Vernov reported detecting not just the one known radiation belt surrounding earth, but two belts. The upper belt stretched to 9 earth radii altitude while the most intense radiation was at 4 radii altitude. Vernov also stated that at 15,000 km (9300 mi), there are 700 times more trapped radiation particles than there are at 400 km (250 mi). Above 60,000 km (36,000 mi), Luna reported that cosmic radiation was "negligible," only two particles per sec per cubic cm.

While Luna traveled to the moon, it detected less than 100 gas molecules per cubic cm of space. Approaching the moon, it registered an increase in ionized gases at a 10,000-km (6000-mi) altitude. This led the Soviets to wonder if the moon had a tenuous ionosphere.

Luna detected no lunar magnetic field down to an altitude of 55 km and also found no lunar radiation belt. The lack of a magnetic field led American lunar expert Gerard Kuiper to reason that the moon's core must be solid and not molten like earth's. However, Harold Urey, a professor at the University of California, speculated that the moon may well have a liquid molten core. Its slow rotation rate, he claimed, does not move the core fast enough to create magnetism.[18] Western scientists later criticized the design of Luna's magnetometer, claiming it was a 13-year-old outdated design more suited to terrestrial magnetic measurements.

Nikolai Barabashov, director of Kharkov Observatory, reported in the newspaper *Trud* that scientists at Kharkov Observatory "observed a certain light effect at the moment of the Soviet lunar rocket's impact on the moon... exactly where it was predicted to occur." Other Soviet astronomers claimed to have telescopically observed the impact of the Luna probe and its booster. Astronomer Dr. Kiril Stanyukovich stated that some observers saw the dust cloud thrown up by Luna's impact while others saw the cloud's shadow.[19] This claim is refuted today since the larger Saturn S-4B Apollo booster impacted ten years later without being visually detected.

MORE LUNAR POLITICS

Many people, including governmental leaders in the U.S., refused to believe that Luna 2 had impacted the moon. They assumed the Soviets were incapable of such a technical feat. Some suggested that Luna 2 carried a clock timer to shut off the signal, simulating a lunar hit. This naive view was refuted by tracking information gathered by the Jodrell Bank radio telescope in England. The 76-m (250-ft) diameter instrument positively established Luna 2's velocity increase near the moon by Doppler tracking and confirmed the lunar impact. When the signals ceased, the radio telescope was pointed directly at the moon.

Other U.S. government officials displayed reactions which can best be classified as "sour grapes." Critics of the U.S. space program said the Russians succeeded in reaching the moon with Luna 2 while our astronauts and their wives succeeded in reaching the cover of *Life* magazine.

Academician Leonid Sedov said the new Luna carried several versions of a commemorative "imperishable plaque." To show that Soviet science had conquered the remote and unattainable, the devices were designed to survive impact and scatter Soviet medallions on the moon. Within Luna was a 90-mm (3.5-inch) diameter ball made up of 72 pentagonal sections, each of which displayed the coat of arms of the Soviet Union and had the inscription "The Union of Soviet Socialist Republics, September 1959." The rocket stage carried a similar ball 150 mm (6 inch) in diameter. Luna also carried a steel ribbon attached to a steel ball which had the inscription within it.

The launch of Luna 2 came just three days before a state visit to the U.S. by Soviet Premier Khrushchev. When he met with President Eisenhower, Khrushchev gleefully presented him with replicas of the commemorative medallions carried by Luna 2. Khrushchev told Eisenhower: "We have no doubt that the excellent scientists, engineers and workers of the U.S.A. who are engaged in the field of conquering the cosmos will also carry your pennant over to the moon. The Soviet pennant, as an old resident, will then welcome your pennant, and they will live there together in peace and friendship."[20]

Khrushchev's visit had a strange effect on Congressional investigations into why the U.S. did not succeed in sending a craft to the moon before the Russians. Congressional members wasted no time in leaving Washington before Khrushchev arrived, and, thus, delayed any hearings on the matter until later in the year.

When Luna 2 struck the lunar surface, it concluded the first chapter in man's exploration of the moon. Pushed by cold-war politics and national pride, a messenger from humanity had reached our natural satellite a mere fifteen months after the space age began. Russia had won a lunar battle, but the war was far from over. As yet, no one in their wildest dreams imagined that, as a result of the race between the Pioneers and the Lunas, men from earth would voyage to the moon just ten short years later.

2 Reaching for the Moon

AMERICA PREPARES NEXT LUNAR VOLLEY

As the American lunar effort continued in late 1958, preparations began for the initial U.S. planetary explorations. However, in January 1959, the success of Mechta threw a monkey wrench into NASA's plans to explore Venus. The Russian moon probe created such a political sensation that two Venus orbiters to be launched by Atlas-Able rockets were dropped from the immediate plan and were retargeted toward lunar orbit out of political expediency.

The new Pioneers were still simple spin-stabilized probes but they were giants compared to the previous tiny American lunar craft which could be cradled in one's arms. Measuring 1 m (39 in) in diameter, the new spherical aluminum-skinned craft had grown to 169 kg (373 lb). Four solar "paddles," each a half-meter (18 in) square and containing 2200 solar cells, extended on hinged arms from the spacecraft's equator in order to charge nickel-cadmium batteries. These appendages gave the craft the nickname "paddle-wheel satellite." Scientific instruments on the new Pioneers included a television scanner to image the far side of the moon, radiation detectors, a magnetometer, and micrometeor detectors. The new Pioneers were also the first lunar probes with a liquid-fueled propulsion system to adjust their velocity in space.

Work continued throughout the summer of 1959 to ready the first Atlas-Able lunar launch. Each rocket stage had a fifty percent chance of failing and the reliability of the complex spacecraft itself was unknown. Thus, scientists gave the moon flights only a ten percent chance of success.

Just ten days after Luna 2 struck the moon, the new moon probe's Atlas booster underwent a crucial test. As was standard practice before committing the Atlas to flight with a payload, the vehicle's engines were test-fired on the launch pad to verify their reliability. On September 24, 1959 such a test took place with disastrous results. The Atlas exploded and destroyed the probe, ending any hope of quickly following Luna 2 and imaging the moon with a more advanced American spacecraft. As the debris was cleared from the shattered launch pad, a grim stage had been set for the rest of the Atlas-Able Pioneer program.

RUSSIA LOOPS THE MOON

Less than a month after striking the moon, the Russians made another startling announcement. At 1:00 P.M., October 4, 1959, Radio Moscow broadcast: "Attention, attention, dear Comrades! Listen now to the signals coming from the cosmos, from the third cosmic rocket launched today." What followed sounded like a raspy violin playing the A note above middle C.[1] The source of the signals, Luna 3, had been launched by an SL-3 booster on the second anniversary of Sputnik, lifting off from Tyuratam at 5:00 A.M.

Jodrell Bank also heard the signals for 20 min, then they abruptly shut off. The Soviets announced the new moon probe would transmit for two to four hours per day on command from earth. As the Soviets lacked a world-wide tracking network, the Luna only transmitted while in view of Soviet territory.

Early announcements were vague about Luna 3's objective, but unofficial news reports were quite specific. Georgi Duboshin, head of the celestial mechanics department of Moscow's Sternberg Astronomical Institute stated that the probe would photograph the far side of the moon.[2] It was not until October 19, over two weeks after launch, when the Soviets had the pictures in hand, that official sources admitted that Luna had indeed accomplished this.

A HIGHLY SOPHISTICATED SPACECRAFT

Luna 3 was a short cylinder, 120 cm (47 in) in diameter and 130 cm (51 in) long with dome-shaped ends. Pressurized to 1.35 atm, it had a mass of 278.5 kg (614 lb). On both ends were portholes for the cameras and sun and moon seekers to view their targets. Luna 3 was the first Russian spacecraft powered by solar cells and was also the first to be three-axis-stabilized using a system of gyroscopes and gas jets which were located on the end opposite the camera.

Luna's cameras used a 200-mm (8-in) focal length f/5.6 wide field lens and a 500-mm (20-in) focal length f/9.5 narrow field lens. Small scale images were 10 mm in size on the film and showed the entire moon while large scale were 25 mm. Exposures varied from frame to frame to insure good contrast.

Photographs were made on heat resistant 35-mm photographic film which was protected from cosmic rays. The film was automatically developed shortly after exposure by an apparatus designed to work in weightlessness. A facsimile system then scanned the film at various resolutions up to 1000 lines per frame. This is twice the resolution of broadcast television. Telemetery and photographs were transmitted at 39.986 megahertz and 183.6 megahertz through redundant radio systems.

FLIGHT AROUND THE MOON

At 6:16 P.M., October 6, 1959, the probe passed south of the moon at an altitude of about 7000 km (4350 mi). Many people held the misconception that Luna 3 orbited the moon, but actually it was a satellite of the earth which used a very unusual orbit to be in the right place at the right time. Because of concerns over the ability to transmit the far side images over large distances, it was decided not to let Luna 3 escape earth's gravity. Instead, it would stay in a highly elliptical orbit returning close to earth, allowing better reception.

The trajectory carried Luna 3 under the southern portion of the moon; then lunar gravity lofted the probe back over the moon where it returned to earth over the north pole, allowing Soviet tracking stations to follow the craft. As Luna approached the earth, it eventually became circumpolar; that is, it did not go below the tracking station's horizon all day. This unusual looping trajectory was accomplished solely by the booster rocket's accuracy because Luna 3 had no course correction ability.

FIRST PHOTOS OF THE MOON'S FAR SIDE

In flight, Luna 3 rolled to even out solar heating. When photography was started, its spin was stopped by gas jets and photoelectric sensors oriented the spacecraft to point its cameras toward the moon. When photography ended, the spacecraft rolled again to control internal temperatures.

Photography began at 6:30 A.M., October 7, while the probe was 65,200 km (40,000 mi) from the moon, and continued for 40 min while

Luna 3 receded another 3200 km (2000 mi) from the moon. Thirty percent of the moon visible from earth was also in the view as a reference. Luna 3 photographed seventy percent of the far side not visible from earth. Unfortunately, the apparatus using the long-focus lens jammed.

Facsimile transmission of the images began the next day while Luna was still beyond the moon. Because there were only a few watts of power allocated to the radio system, it was designed to transmit the images slowly at great distances and more quickly closer to earth. Over the translunar distances, the strength of Luna's signal when it reached earth was about 100 million times less than that of ordinary television.

The first four attempts to transmit the photos at great distances were unsuccessful because radio static washed out the images. The receiving station in the Crimea then undertook special measures to eliminate all possible sources of man-made radio interference. On the fifth attempt, as Luna moved closer to earth, two usable images were received. In all, seventeen photos were finally transmitted to earth on October 18, but even the better images were fogged and streaked by radio interference. On October 22, both radio systems failed, preventing photo retransmission on following orbits.

Luna's earth orbit ranged from 40,671 to 469,306 km (25,273 to 291,627 mi), inclined 76.8 degrees with a period of 15.3 days. The orbit was unstable because perturbations resulting from solar gravity were pushing it closer and closer to earth. It was thought that upon reaching the 13th perigee, or closest point to earth, after 198 days in space, Luna 3 ran into the earth's atmosphere on May 19, 1960, and burned up. However, in 1961, a silent mystery spacecraft was tracked in a retrograde, or backward, orbit. Some analysts concluded that Luna had survived and was the mystery satellite.

HISTORIC FIRST LOOK

The initial lunar far side photos were a public sensation. However, due to the crude equipment available, the images were of poor quality. The need for wide area coverage on the first far-side photo mission dictated that the moon be fully illuminated, resulting in flat, low-contrast lighting. The images had the same approximate quality as daguerreotypes taken of the moon's near side in the 1840s. After enhancement, gross features could be identified on nine frames out of seventeen received. A single far-side photograph, released to the presses of the world on October 27, 1959, was really a three-photo composite.

The far side proved different than the near side in that there were fewer mare regions, as the flat dark plains we see on the near side of the moon are known. Conversely, there were more craters on the far side. Only two dark mare areas were visible. One which was 300 km (185 mi) in diameter was named "Mare Moscovise" (Moscow Sea) and the other "Mare Desiderii" (Dream Sea). Other recognizable features were named after famous writers, scientists, and philosophers such as Thomas Edison, Louis Pasteur, and Konstantin Tsiolkovsky.

American reaction to Luna 3 was markedly quieter than that which greeted Luna 2. Soviet authorities, however, continued to play up their latest achievement. Some in the west claimed that the far side photos were fakes and a propaganda hoax. These skeptics were proved wrong in less than a decade. The later Zond 3 probe and the American Lunar Orbiter photo reconnaissance craft showed the same features seen in Luna 3 images.

MORE RUSSIAN MOON FLIGHTS PREPARED

Six months after the Luna 3 success, the Soviets again tried to launch two 300-kg (661-lb) photographic lunar probes. These were to fly closer to the moon and take higher resolution photographs. The power of the transmitters aboard the new probes was doubled to correct the photo transmission problem which nearly caused Luna 3 to fail.

The first flight on April 15, 1960, also using the SL-3 booster, nearly succeeded. An hour after launch, however, tracking data showed that the upper stage had shut down prematurely. The craft entered a highly elliptical orbit which would not reach the moon. The failure was kept a secret by the Soviets.

As soon as the misfire was detected, the backup spacecraft was erected on the launch pad. Time was critical since the sun would only illuminate the moon's far side on certain dates. In several days, shadow would again creep across the moon's far side and the mission would have to be delayed. Equally critical for Khrushchev was his desire for a lunar success before the May Day celebrations, just two weeks away, and the May 1960 summit meeting in Paris. What followed ranks as one of the most bizarre launches from Tyuratam.

In the afternoon, the countdown reached zero and it was time for liftoff. A group of observers, including Colonel Alexander Kashits, stood about 1.5 km (1 mile) behind the launch pad. In a recent memoir, Colonel Kashits related how after ignition, the SL-3 remained on the pad for an unusually long time. Once the booster started to slowly rise, it began to tilt over. The guidance system tried to correct the tilt, but at 150 to 200 m (500 to 650 ft) altitude, control was lost and all four of the first stage strap-on boosters separated. Two fell near the launch pad and exploded. A third rumbled on toward Kashits and his fellow observers. The men jumped into a trench as the booster roared 30 to 40 m (100 to 130 ft) over their heads. A cloud of sand blew over them just before the booster crashed and exploded some distance away. After the blast wave passed, they were showered with bits of falling aluminum. The fourth strap-on stage soon crashed nearby.

After things calmed down, Colonel Kashits and the others made their way back to the buildings on the far side of the launch pad. All the windows were blown out and the launch pad was strewn with broken glass. The SL-3 central core stage had struck close to the MIK (a Russian acronym for Assembly and Test Building) and the blast rolled all the railroad rails into a spiral. The walls of the MIK were cracked and heavy objects like safes had been thrown through the floor. The upper stage and Luna probe had flown on another kilometer ($1/2$ mi) and exploded in a salt lake.

An investigation into the disaster showed that one of the strap-on stages had misfired at launch. The booster had tried to rise with only three strap-ons firing and control was lost. Once the vehicle broke up, there was not only just one out-of-control rocket, but five, falling and crashing at random. After the dual failures, the Luna program was temporarily suspended.[3]

PIONEERS CHASE LUNA 3

Two months after the Luna 3 accomplishment, another American Atlas-Able was ready for flight, this time carrying the craft known as Pioneer P-3. Liftoff from Pad 14 at Cape Canaveral came at 2:26 A.M., November 26, 1959. Forty seconds after launch, the lunar effort came to a sad end as the 30-m (98-ft)-long booster broke up and exploded.

Analysis of the failure showed that the Atlas-Able's payload shroud, the cover which protects the probe during ascent through the atmosphere, had failed. To house the 1-m (3.3-ft) diameter spacecraft atop the Able stages, the shroud had a bulbous hammerhead shape. As the booster accelerated, the rush of air past the enlarged tip caused a partial vacuum on the outside of the shroud. The buildup of air pressure inside the shroud finally blew it apart and tore off Pioneer and its third stage.

The next Atlas-Able Pioneer would not fly for ten more months. During the lengthy delay, the probe's weight increased to 176 kg (388 lb), and the television imaging experiment was replaced by more scientific instruments. Liftoff came at 11:13 A.M., September 25, 1960. This time, the Atlas reached space and the Able stages took over. However, a fault in the oxidizer system prematurely shut down the second stage. The Pioneer and its third stage soared over the Atlantic. Forty minutes after launch, fragments crashed on farms near Zoekmekaar, in the Transvaal in what is today the Republic of South Africa.

Two months later, the final Atlas-Able lunar attempt, Pioneer P-31 lifted off at 3:40 A.M., December 14. This time, the Pioneer did not reach space. The Atlas booster pitched over and exploded 68 seconds after liftoff. The debris fell 13 to 19 km (8 to 12 mi) off Cape Canaveral in 21 m (70 ft) of water. A salvage effort was mounted to find out why the last shot of the $40 million Pioneer lunar orbiter project had also failed.

AMERICAN MOON PROGRAMS EXPANDED

At the same time the Pioneers were struggling to reach space, the next phase of American lunar exploration, an actual robotic landing, was being planned by the JPL. This effort would use sophisticated fully stabilized spacecraft capable of refining their trajectories with a small on-board rocket engine, then depositing instrument packages on the surface of the moon. In 1960, the Apollo manned lunar program was just entering its conceptual stage and the underlying goal of JPL's new lunar effort was to learn more about the moon in support of an eventual manned landing using an Apollo spacecraft. The name Ranger was suggested for the lunar probes and it quickly caught on at JPL and NASA. Five Ranger flights were approved for launch in 1961–1962 using the Atlas-Agena booster. This rocket utilized the Atlas ICBM topped with the Air Force's 6800-kg (15,000-lb) thrust Agena upper stage.

The initial design concepts of the Ranger probe were started in February of 1960 and called for the development of two types of spacecraft. The Block I would be a test spacecraft which would perform scientific investigation from an extremely elliptical earth orbit reaching twice the moon's distance. The Block II would be a two-part lunar lander. The carrier spacecraft, known as the spacecraft "bus," had two instruments which would operate until the probe crashed into the moon: a television camera and a gamma ray spectrometer to determine the chemical elements in the rocks of the moon's surface. Just prior to impact, the Block II Rangers would eject a 44-kg (97-lb) spherical landing capsule which would decelerate using a 2304-kg (5080-lb)-thrust, solid-fueled retrorocket. A seismometer and temperature probe housed in a balsawood capsule would then be rough-landed in a fashion more resembling a controlled crash. In late 1960 assembly of the Ranger hardware was near.

Responding to NASA's awakening interests in lunar science, several other JPL lunar programs were also approved by Congress in short order. A huge craft called Surveyor Lunar Orbiter was approved in May 1960. This was to be a combined orbiter-lander which would be launched by the Atlas-Centaur. When engineers developing the 13,605-kg (30,000-lb)-thrust Centaur realized in 1960 that the rocket would have a smaller payload capacity than originally calculated, the dual purpose craft was broken into its component parts. The revised Surveyor program would use the Centaur rocket to loft two versions of an advanced one-ton spacecraft toward the moon. Surveyor A was to make a controlled low-speed landing to deposit delicate scientific instruments on the surface. Surveyor B was to orbit the moon at 100 km (62 mi) and perform photographic reconnaissance and make measurements from space.

LUNAR UNKNOWNS COMPLICATE LANDER DESIGN

In the early 1960s, the question of the make-up of the lunar surface was far from solved. Was the surface hard rock or soft powdery dust? Would a craft be firmly supported or would it sink out of sight as if in quicksand? Ranger and Surveyor desperately needed to find answers in order to design the Apollo manned lander.

Many leading American specialists forwarded experimental theories about what the moon would be like. Their results were both convincing and conflicting. The more the dilemma was studied, the more it became apparent that only the first successful unmanned lander would resolve the question. Presumably Soviet spacecraft designers wrestled with the same questions.

It was known from earth-based studies that the lunar soil must be very porous. Photometric studies of lunar features showed that they brighten considerably near the full moon. This implies there is much small scale surface shadowing at less than full moon. Laboratory tests showed that the observed shadow effect was recreated by a random structure of glassy fibers, separated by several times their own thickness.

In 1955, Dr. Thomas Gold, then with the Royal Greenwich Observatory, published a paper predicting that lunar surface debris was pulverized into fine dust by billions of years of meteoric bombardment. He believed the lunar maria were really filled with soft dust which would act like an ocean, kilometers deep and any heavy object which landed on them would sink.

Using vacuum chamber tests of material with the same reflecting properties as the moon, Gold found the surface may be stirred into a loose porous structure he called "fairy castles." He predicted that lunar dust may be piled into drifts 15 m (50 ft) deep and would disastrously swallow a landing spacecraft. Some lunar observers refuted Gold's theory, but his prediction carried some weight and spacecraft planners were concerned. Only the first landing would prove or disprove Gold's ideas.

Other lunar scientists forwarded their own more optimistic theories about what could be expected when spacecraft finally arrived on our moon. The University of Arizona's Gerard Kuiper studied the shadow-casting properties of loose lunar material and concluded that the surface layer was only several inches thick. He theorized the material had a fibrous design similar to reindeer moss and would present no problem for landing.

Similar corroborating views were held by others. California astronomer David Cudaback believed the heat created by meteorite impacts would melt the material thrown up by the collisions into rock filaments which would lie smoothly like spun cotton candy. His theory was supported by radar studies of the moon. This type of surface would also pose no problems for a landing. Edward Markow of Grumman Aircraft proposed that in the lunar vacuum the heat of meteorites impacting the moon would weld sandy material into a porous and hard sponge-like rock which would also support a landing spacecraft. Other researchers championed the theory that in the lunar vacuum, fine powdered silicates would join together in a process similar to the vacuum welding of bare metals. When exposed to solar radiation this material might evolve into a form similar to solid concrete and support a spacecraft.[4]

MOON PLANS ACCELERATE

The Ranger and Surveyor programs were prepared as scientific explorations seeking answers to scientific and astronomical questions about our natural satellite. The programs also had the technological objective of gathering engineering data needed for later manned flights to the moon which would occur at some undefined date in the future. However, by summer of 1960, the fiscal reality of NASA's limited budget began to erode the funds for the Ranger effort and 100 project engineers had to be laid off. But help would soon be on the way from an unlikely source—Russia.

In October 1960 a Soviet Mars probe had failed to leave earth. In February 1961, two Venus probe attempts also rose up from Tyuratam while American planetary exploration was still on the drawing board. Clearly the Soviet space program had grand goals and the means to try for them. Then, in April, twin propaganda disasters for the United States occurred: Yuri Gagarin became the first human in space, and the Bay of Pigs invasion of Cuba failed. National honor was at stake because of perceived Russian space superiority and American political and military weakness.

The political crisis created by cold-war events and conspicuous Russian space achievements was addressed by the newly elected administration of President John Kennedy. In a major policy speech on May 25, 1961, Kennedy outlined a bold plan to resurrect the scientific and world image of the United States: send Americans to the moon and return them safely by the end of the decade. In one decisive move, the die was cast for America's lunar future.

Kennedy's lunar mandate was both a response to the Soviet space challenge and a declaration that America would be second to none in science and technology. The upshot of Kennedy's plan was that Apollo was now a crash project to achieve the political goal of beating the Russian's to a manned lunar landing. To reach this goal, the vast majority of NASA's programs would now be geared toward direct support of the manned lunar program. This included the Ranger and Surveyor projects. All stops were pulled out and the NASA budget began to grow dramatically.

Although political and monetary support for the unmanned lunar programs was expanded, there was a downside to the President's plan.

Because of the urgency of Apollo, national prestige and security now had priority over science. Ranger and Surveyor were now pathfinders for the manned landings and lunar landing technology became their goal; science was now secondary.

The Rangers faced a formidable series of technical hurdles in their development. The probes had to hold a steady attitude, or spacecraft orientation, for television photography of the moon and deployment of the landing capsule. Real-time television signals were to be sent directly from the craft across lunar distances to earth, necessitating the use of a narrow-beam high-gain antenna which must be pointed precisely toward earth. This was a major step from previous simpler spacecraft which either spun for stability or tumbled randomly. Also, the entire spacecraft had to be sterilized to prevent terrestrial organisms from contaminating alien landscapes. As the capacity of the booster rocket changed, engineers struggled to meet a constantly fluctuating allowable spacecraft weight figure. In addition, Ranger's modular concept was to be the foundation for JPL's Mariner planetary explorers, placing added pressure on the lunar project.

Another kind of headache also popped up to plague the Ranger program: the efficient management of this high-technology scientific endeavor. One sticky point was that JPL was a hybrid in the NASA organizational chart. The Laboratory was doing NASA work, but it was not staffed with NASA civil-service personnel. JPL, as part of Caltech, worked as a NASA contractor. This situation led to a strained initial relationship between the two agencies.

Many other factors complicated the Ranger program. Never before had such a sophisticated unmanned space program been initiated. As the national lunar goal gained political importance, NASA increased JPL's budget fourfold between 1958 and 1962. JPL's staff also grew to 3500 in 1962, but 60 percent of the personnel in some divisions possessed less than two years experience at JPL. Much of the work performed on the complex spacecraft had to be subcontracted to industrial firms. The desire of JPL to conduct scientific work at the moon also clashed with NASA's mandate to acquire technology to support Apollo. Perhaps the most difficult aspect of the Ranger program was developing cutting-edge technology in the pressure-cooker atmosphere created by space-race politics. All of these factors combined to place Ranger on the ragged edge of disaster before it even entered space.

RANGER TAKES SHAPE

Still, work progressed. The first two Block I Rangers were to test the craft's design while traveling beyond the moon in a highly elliptical earth orbit. As the assembly time of the Block I craft neared, their designs were frozen while the calculated payload capacity of the Atlas-Agena booster was still following a roller-coaster path. After Ranger's Block I design was locked in at 306 kgs (675 lb), the booster was found to have 74 kgs (164 lb) more capacity. Time would show that on Block II lunar landing flights, the booster's extra capacity could have been utilized by including desperately needed, mission-saving backup systems in the spacecraft.

The Block II craft carried the hard lander and its retrorocket along with a downward looking television camera to photograph the surface from 4184 to 24 km (2600 to 15 mi). The moon-bound Block II version also contained a 22.7-kg (50-lb) thrust course correction motor capable of a 44-m (144-ft)-per-sec velocity change. The Ranger basic design was so sound that it was also the prototype for JPL's Mariner planetary probes.

After President Kennedy's lunar mandate, a third series of Rangers, the Block III, was added in the summer of 1961 to directly support Apollo. Their sole objective was to do high-resolution, close-up photography of the lunar surface during a kamikaze plunge into the moon.

Rangers 1 and 2 were launched on August 22 and November 17, 1961. Their Atlas-Agenas were to boost them into extremely elliptical orbits around the earth with a 1 million-k (620,000-mi) apogee. Both Rangers reached earth orbit—just barely. The Agena stages placed them in what was supposed to be a temporary low earth parking orbit from which they would later depart for their loftier destination. However, the Agenas failed to reignite and the Rangers were trapped close to earth.

Although Rangers 1 and 2 fell short of their objectives, the national urgency of the lunar goals kept the first Block II mission, Ranger 3 on schedule for early 1962. Preparations for Ranger 3 differed from previous probes since this craft was deliberately going to strike the moon. A 1959 NASA edict stated that any craft which might strike a celestial body had to be sterilized. For the internally complicated Ranger, this presented a major headache. Alcohol wipes and lethal ethylene oxide gas could only reach part of the craft's internal mechanisms. Heat sterilization at 125°C (257°F) for 24 hr was seen as the answer.

However, sterilizing a scalpel and sterilizing a delicate electronics package were two different things entirely. In late 1961, studies began to surface showing that heat sterilization would have detrimental effects on Ranger's electronic systems. In spite of the evidence, it was decided to press ahead with the lunar flights. History would show that heat-sterilizing the Rangers may have saved the moon from catching a cold, but it killed the Ranger spacecraft by inducing electronic heat stroke.

MAIDEN LUNAR FLIGHT

Ranger 3 broke free from earth at 3:30 P.M., January 26, 1962. As the Atlas-Agena climbed before a thrilled, live, nationwide television audience, only an experienced few could tell anything was amiss. Guidance commands transmitted to the Atlas went unacknowledged as the missile's radio guidance failed. Now, under the control of the rocket's autopilot, the two Atlas booster engines burned several seconds too long, sending the vehicle higher and faster than planned. The Agena stage's guidance system was also faulty; instead of aiming Ranger 3 toward the moon's Ocean of Storms, the path would miss the moon by 32,000 km (20,000 mi), a distance beyond Ranger's ability to correct.

Still, the mission was not a total loss. By steering Ranger closer to the moon with the mid-course correction rocket, photographs of the remaining hidden part of the moon could be secured. At 2:00 A.M. the day after launch, Ranger 3 was commanded to perform the correction. To the horror of mission officials, it soon became apparent that the spacecraft was moving yet further away from the moon. A programming error inverted a sign in the computer code and Ranger was following a mirror image course to that desired.

The next day, as Ranger approached the moon, its television system was turned on and began to function. Indeed, the reference crosses imprinted on the vidicon tube were visible. At this point, however, Ranger 3 became stupid. The craft's central computer and sequencer had failed from the effects of pre-flight heat sterilization. Now, brainless, Ranger could not point its television camera toward the moon as it passed 37,000 km (23,000 mi) away on January 28 and tumbled into solar orbit.

Ranger 4 was sent on its way at 4:50 P.M., April 23 to redeem the previous effort. This time, the Atlas-Agena worked perfectly. The spacecraft was on a course so accurate that it would strike the moon without even a single correction. However, there was little time to cheer. As soon as Ranger crossed the Atlantic and rose above the horizon of the South African tracking station, it was apparent that something disastrous had happened. Only Ranger's 960 MHz tacking beacon was heard. There was no telemetry from the spacecraft indicating the probe was alive. As Ranger 4 headed moonward, it remained inert. The ravages of heat sterilization had claimed another victim as the master clock in the spacecraft's central computer and sequencer had stopped. Without the computer, Ranger was deaf, dumb, and blind. It could not respond to commands, perform its investigations, or send close-up television of the moon. One NASA official lamented that all the craft amounted to was an idiot with a radio signal.[5] Sixty-four hours after launch, at 7:47 A.M., April 26, Ranger 4 slipped behind the leading edge of the moon. Two minutes later, it plowed into the hidden side at 15.5 degrees south and 130.5 degrees west.

Ranger 4 was the first American spacecraft to hit the moon and although the press tried to put the best face possible on the mission, the fact remained that Ranger 4 was a failure.

ANOTHER EMBARRASSMENT

One final Ranger Block II lunar lander remained before attention shifted toward the Block III television missions. At 1:59 P.M., October 18, 1962, Ranger 5 rose into the overcast skies above Cape Canaveral. Public attention was drawn away from the latest moon flight by the Cuban Missile Crisis looming larger each day several hundred miles to the south. It was just as well—an hour after launch, Ranger failed again. This time it was because of a short in the computer's power-switching module which directed the flow of energy from the solar panels.

Ranger 1 and 2 had failed because of booster problems, but the lunar flights Rangers 3, 4, and 5 were all spacecraft failures. Formal investigations were launched into why the Rangers had embarassed American scientists and hurt our pride. Evidence again pointed to the deadly effects the heat sterilization procedure had on Ranger's delicate electronic brain. Additionally, the success of the mission relied too heavily on the completion of a long chain of events with failure of any one event causing the loss of the mission. The lack of redundant backup systems and the lack of flexibility to work around a single-point failure were key points in a scathing scientific indictment of the Ranger program. The Ranger Block III missions were delayed for a year while engineering and procedural changes were designed to allow Ranger to claim American lunar honor.

Even as the conduct of the Ranger program was being condemned in December 1962, additional flights were added to the program. The Block IV spacecraft were to add five additional higher resolution television reconnaissance flights while the Block V craft were to carry four more hard landers. However, the cost of modifying the Block III spacecraft in response to the three lunar failures gobbled up much of the budget allocated to the new flights.

RUSSIAN MOON PROGRAM REVIVES

In response to the awakening American lunar program, Khrushchev and Korolyov now set their sights on a Russian lunar landing. After all, it was inevitable that someday men would land on the moon. In preparation for that, it was necessary to complete a vital phase in the exploration of space: unmanned probes must precede human beings to investigate the moon's environment. In pursuit of this goal, Khrushchev was driven, as always, by the desire to demonstrate his country's technical and scientific superiority. Thus, through 1961 and 1962 Korolyov and Babakin were pushed to design a lunar lander.

While the first landers were being designed in Moscow, the same scientific debate which faced the Ranger design team raged unresolved among the Soviet design team. Was the lunar surface made up of hard material or soft powdery dust? The answer was desperately needed to design a lander lest the probe crash on hard rock or sink in loose dust. No one was willing to make a decision. Sensing the impass between members of the design team, Korolyov decreed that the design should assume the lunar surface is hard.

Legend has it that when scientists challenged Korolyov's decree, asking about who would vouch for that fact, Korolyov shot back, "Me." Taking a piece of blank paper, Korolyov wrote: "The moon's surface is hard. (signed) S. Korolyov."[6] Thus, the second generation lunar probes were to be rough landers, decelerating to a controlled crash onto what was anticipated to be a surface similar to terrestrial lava rock or stony beach sand.

From this decision, the evolving craft bore Korolyov's trademark of simplicity and austerity in design to accomplish a specific goal. The second generation Luna was composed of two modules, a ball-shaped package carrying moon-bound scientific instruments and a cylindrical carrier bus which housed a rocket engine, command and orientation devices, and radio transmitters.

DUAL PURPOSE SPACECRAFT DESIGNED FOR THE MOON

The Soviets chose to use a single craft for two objectives. The probe used a common spacecraft bus with control and propulsion equipment that could either lower instruments to a landing or place them in lunar orbit.

Unlike their Venus or Mars probe cousins, the Lunas carried no solar panels. They required only 3.5 days to reach the moon and thus drew their power exclusively from batteries, simplifying the design of the 1500-kg (3300-lb), 2.7-m (8.6-ft)-long spacecraft. The bottom portion of the spacecraft housed the rocket motor and its fuel supply. Luna's propulsion system contained a variable-thrust, single-chamber KTDU-5A engine that was capable of 4650 kg (10,250 lb) of thrust for 50 sec. Above this was a 1-m (3.3-ft)-diameter cylindrical compartment containing the main control and communications equipment. Mounted on either side of upper fuel tank were two additional "saddlebag" equipment modules, each weighing 150 kg (330 lb). Just before ignition of the retro-rocket, these saddlebag modules were jettisoned in order to lighten the spacecraft during powered descent.

The lunar landing payload was a 58-cm (23-inch)-diameter, 100-kg (220-lb) spherical capsule. The pressurized capsule carried a television-like camera to relay a panoramic photograph of the surface and instruments to measure radiation and temperature levels, and to test the chemical makeup of the lunar soil. The heavy batteries and radio equipment were placed at the bottom to lower the capsule's center of gravity and help stabilize it in an upright position after landing.

The landers were to be targeted to a point between 62 and 64 degrees west along the lunar equator. This is a magic spot on the leading edge of the moon. By aiming at this limited locale and using a 3.5-day trajectory, a descending spacecraft naturally would intercept the moon while traveling along a line perpendicular to the local lunar vertical. The craft's horizontal velocity is thus zero as it approaches the surface. This eliminates tricky navigational requirements to cancel horizontal motion, but severely limits the areas on the moon which can be investigated. During the final hour of flight, all the craft would have to do is hold a tail-first attitude parallel to the trajectory for its retrorocket to generate thrust perpendicular to the moon's surface to slow it for landing.

As the spacecraft approached the moon, a proximity sensor mounted on an extended 5-m (16-ft) arm would detect the lunar surface. This would signal the rocket motor to shutdown and a powerful spring mechanism to eject the shock-resistant landing capsule away from the area disturbed by the retrorocket blast. Shortly after touchdown, a latch would release the upper half of the lander's shell which would split into four sections like the petals of a flower. Springs would force these petals open, stabilizing the lander in an upright position.

Luna's imaging system was developed in the early 1960s by Margarita Naraeva, a young, little-known engineer who, along with a colleague, essentially worked out of a garage to independently develop the instrument on her own. The device was so successful that it was used in nearly all Soviet lunar and planetary probes for the next 20 years. The photo apparatus, a simple 1.5-kg (3.5-lb) cylindrical scanning facsimile system, popped up from the top of the lander and was covered with gold foil to reflect solar heat. Thirty-degree high panoramic photos of the local terrain would be taken from a height of 60 cm (2 ft).

SUCCESSFUL LANDING PROVES ELUSIVE

As with American attempts to reach the moon, fate seemed to present the Russians with all possible versions of failure before achieving a success. Three Luna landers would fail to reach earth orbit, two would fail to leave earth orbit, two would miss the moon completely, one would suffer retrorocket failure, and one would decelerate too soon, then crash into the moon; and one would not decelerate enough before crashing into the lunar surface.

The first of the new Luna landers took flight from Tyuratam aboard a 42-m (138-ft) SL-6 Molniya rocket on January 4, 1963. The probe never left earth orbit and the launch was not announced by the Soviets. Unofficially known in the west as Sputnik 25, it separated into three pieces which remained in orbit only overnight. A second lunar attempt on February 2, 1963, fell short of orbit and crashed into the Pacific near Midway Island.

The fourth officially announced Luna mission was launched April 2, 1963. As the craft passed over Africa, a Soviet sea-going tracking ship commanded ignition of the fourth stage, known as the escape stage, for translunar injection. The 1422-kg (3135-lb) craft was the first Soviet lunar mission launched from an earth parking orbit.

Initially, western observers thought that Luna 4's objective was to test a minimum energy trajectory to reach the vicinity of the moon. However, Khrushchev was still the political power behind the Soviet space program. His appetite for spectacular space successes must have called for a full lunar landing attempt to answer the challenge of the American Ranger probes. It is unlikely that he would have sanctioned a mere trajectory test.

Strangely enough, the Soviets did not ask the British for help in tracking the new Luna as they had in the past. However, after searching the frequency band for the craft's signal, radio telescopes at both Jodrell Bank in England and Bochum, West Germany received clear signals from the moon craft at a frequency of 183.6 MHz. A British scientist described the sound of the signals, saying they sounded like the musical tones of a pan pipe.[7]

CLUES POINT TO INTENDED LANDING

There was much fanfare in Moscow following the launch with official announcements declaring that Luna 4 was "another victory" for Soviet science. Moscow also released a postage stamp commemorating the new lunar flight.

Early in the mission, comments by Soviet scientists covered all possibilities. Depending on who spoke, Luna 4 was portrayed as another fly-by, an orbiter, a lander, and a rover. However, as Luna 4 sped toward the moon, clues began to surface as to its purpose. Soviet astronomer Nikolai Kupervich declared Luna 4 would report on the nature of the moon's surface. Additionally, Heinz Kaminski of Bochum revealed that authorities in Moscow had told him a lunar landing was imminent. Engineering and electronics expert Vladimir Siforov boldly predicted that Luna 4 would send photos of the lunar surface as well as measure lunar mountains and the depths of craters.[8]

TASS also announced: "Scientists have to clarify the physical conditions cosmonauts will meet, how they are to overcome landing difficulties and how they should prepare for a prolonged stay on the moon. The human epoch in the moon's history is beginning. There will be laboratories, sanitoria and observatories on the moon."[9]

In Washington D.C., political wags made light work of Luna 4. Reflecting on cold-war tensions between the west and Soviet forces, an anonymous quote circulating in Washington reported: "A rocket from

Russia shoots for the moon. Well, thanks to the Berlin Wall and miles of barbed wire, there's only one way out of the place."

OPTIMISM FADES

On the evening of April 4, Jodrell Bank received signals from Luna 4 for 6 hr. Then the craft attempted a course correction maneuver. Jodrell Bank reported that, several minutes later, signals from the craft suddenly stopped. Five and a half hours later the signals resumed for 44 min. Director Bernard Lovell said the observatory was attempting to analyze the signals which he characterized as more complex than those of Luna 3.

Apparently Moscow knew something had gone wrong with Luna 4. The Soviets became uncharacteristically brief in the descriptions of the mission. TASS stopped reporting that the probe was on course or that scientists were still in contact with it. Radio Moscow also canceled a special program scheduled for 7:45 P.M., on April 5 called "Hitting the Moon" and played poetry and piano music instead. Jodrell Bank received only one more 2-min burst of signals as the probe neared the moon.

Apparently the course correction was never completed and Luna 4 failed its primary mission of reaching the moon's surface. Three and a half days after launch, the craft silently passed 8529 km (5270 mi) from the moon at 4:26 P.M., April 5. It then entered a barycentric orbit, or a path around the combined center of gravity of both earth and the moon, ranging 89,782 × 692,300 km (55,800 × 434,000 mi) from earth.

After the probe passed the moon, Soviet announcements unconvincingly stated that a lunar fly-by was all that was intended. However, they also ceased all mention of getting human beings to the moon in the near term. In a general story about the moon on April 7, *Pravda* made only a brief reference to Luna 4, and, beginning April 8, no further mention was made of the shot.

NEW MOON PROBE SERIES PREPARED

In April 1963, it became apparent that the wide-area, high-resolution photo coverage of the moon would be needed for scientists to select suitable Apollo manned-landing sites. Ranger was capable of high resolution only in a limited area near the impact site, and the Surveyor B orbiters had been scrapped the previous December. Thus, a new orbiter craft was required to provide the support for Apollo. The Block IV Ranger program was canceled and the $50 million saved was used to start the Lunar Orbiter project under the management of NASA's Langley Research Center. Lockheed Aircraft Company proposed an orbiter based on its Air Force spy satellites, but on May 10, 1964, Boeing Aircraft received an $80 million contract to build five lunar orbiters. Kodak was subcontracted to provide the photographic system. The spacecraft would provide 500,000 times the high resolution photographic coverage of a Ranger impact mission.

The decision to place Langley in charge of the orbiter program was rooted in an attempt to relieve JPL of its burden. With Mariner missions to the planets and the Rangers and Surveyors preparing to go to the moon, JPL had all it could handle.

In the meantime, the revitalized Ranger Block III series was prepared for photographic close-up reconnaissance of the moon, and the Ranger Block V was retained as a backup for the Surveyor soft lander which was having expensive development troubles of its own. By mid-summer in 1963, a Ranger Block III test craft had completed 13 separate 66-hr simulated lunar flights in JPL's new 7.6-m (25-ft) thermal vacuum space chamber with only one failure. JPL was confident Ranger would not let America down again.

Retaining the same hexagonal shape and parabolic communications antenna as its predecessors, the 364-kg (802-lb) Block III craft were now equipped with an aluminum frame, unsterilized electronic brain, backup timer, redundant attitude controls, larger 60-m (197-ft)-per-sec course correction motor, double-sized solar panels and a spare battery. After America had endured six years of fruitless lunar endeavours, Ranger program managers were so intent on achieving a lunar success that they ordered the television-equipped craft stripped of all other science instruments to prevent them from affecting the success of the mission. The Block III Rangers would thus be unable to report any data about translunar and near-moon space.

The new craft's only cargo was a six-pack of two wide-angle and four narrow-angle, high-resolution television cameras. The 173-kg (381-lb) TV unit was mounted in a tapered 1.5-m (5-ft) polished aluminum tower. Two full-scan cameras returned 1152-line images while four partial scan cameras returned 300-line images. The cameras used 25-mm and 75-mm lenses to view differing areas as they fell toward the moon.

The camera-carrying spacecraft had been conceived to provide data about the lunar surface so the landing gear for the Apollo lunar module (LM) could be optimized. What Apollo would encounter was still unknown. If designed for the worst anticipated conditions, an extremely soft and quicksand-like surface, the gear could take up fifty percent of the LM's mass. If the moon's surface proved to be smooth and hard, the landing gear could take up only five percent. At a time when designers were struggling to keep the Apollo manned lander within the allowed launch weight, such information was crucial.

However, as delays pushed the first Block III launch into late 1963, the time to move forward with the LM's design had come. Plans now called for all four Block III flights to be completed by July 1964, allowing time for quick modifications to the LM if the Ranger data so dictated. But this flight schedule soon eroded as pesky electronic bugs delayed the completion of the television subsystem. It was not until January 1964 that Ranger 6 stood ready to make a suicide plunge into the lunar surface for the sake of Apollo.

RANGER 6 CONTINUES AMERICAN EMBARRASSMENT

Lifting off from Pad 12 at Cape Canaveral, Ranger 6 bored into an overcast sky at 10:49 A.M., January 30, 1964. Once again, the Atlas-Agena performed flawlessly, sending the television-laden craft on its way to the moon. The only anomaly came two minutes after launch when a telemetry signal showed that Ranger's television system had inexplicably turned on. Then, strangely, the system turned itself back off 67 seconds later.

After the Agena finished propelling Ranger away from earth, the lunar probe obediently opened its solar panels and antenna, then settled into a cruise to the moon. Telemetry showed all was well and could offer no explanation as to why the television system came to life during the launch. Everything continued to check out textbook-perfectly and the next day Ranger 6 executed a mid-course maneuver to aim toward the Sea of Tranquility.

On the morning of February 2, Ranger 6 and the American moon program prepared to meet their fate. As the moon's gravity accelerated the craft, JPL awaited the anticipated stream of lunar close-up images. Approaching within 18 min of impact, Ranger dutifully began to warm up its collection of television cameras. At minus 13 min, the images would begin.

Then, at the appointed time: nothing—monitors at JPL remained blank. No moon pictures, no lunar surface rushing up to greet the scientists. Frenzied backup commands were sent to the spacecraft and—still nothing. While Ranger's telemetry continued its strong signal, the video signal was not to be found. Repeated commands to the spacecraft brought no response. At 4:24 A.M., Ranger 6, blind as a bat, slammed uselessly into the moon.

It was horribly ironic moment. Ranger 6 had been stripped of all science instruments and had flown with the single-minded purpose of providing lunar surface imagery to support the design of the Apollo LM. Now, in the last 15 minutes of what had been a beautiful flight, the television system had failed on what was an otherwise fully functional spacecraft. To grind home the frustration, by early 1964 Apollo had no need for the data Ranger was sent to collect. The design of the LM had already been frozen prior to the flight. Any Ranger data could only confirm that the LM's current design was adequate.

As far as Apollo was concerned, Ranger 6 had been an exercise in futility. Once again, NASA, Congress, and the public railed at another lunar embarrassment. The mission represented a loss of $26 million (uninflated pre-Vietnam War dollars) and numerous investigations probed the failure. Even the fictional comic strip detective Dick Tracy got into the act. On the comic page, he traveled to the moon in a magnetically levitated spaceship supplied by Diet Smith, his Howard Hughes-like corporate mentor. There, Tracy located Ranger 6's crumpled remains. His conclusion as to why the mission embarrassed America: the cameras were never turned on.

Of course, the real-life investigations into why the failure occurred were much more complex. In the coming months, the explanation finally surfaced. It turned out that when the Atlas' booster stage separates 2 min into the flight, 67 kg (150 lb) of unburned kerosene is released into the atmosphere. This fuel, vaporized in the rocket's slipstream, is then ignited by the sustainer engine and creates a flash wave which momentarily engulfs the entire rocket. This known phenomenon is normally of no consequence to the Atlas rocket, but Ranger engineers were unaware of its potential to damage their spacecraft. The pressure of this flash had forced plasma from the burning fuel vapor past the edges of the Agena stage's umbilical door and instantaneously shorted umbilical connector pins wired through the Agena and leading to Ranger's television system. The brief connection was enough to activate the television system at the wrong time and short out critical electronics.

Ranger had failed once again, but this time scientists at JPL could take consolation in the fact that their spacecraft worked perfectly and the failure was caused by outside factors.

MORE FAILURE AND POLITICAL CHANGE

Ranger was not the only program experiencing setbacks. Back in the U.S.S.R., the lunar chase fared little better. After repeated failures of the SL-6 escape stage to leave earth orbit, Korolyov ordered a redesign of the rocket. Cosmos 21, launched November 11, 1963, was both a test of the refitted booster and a lunar fly-by mission. However, the spacecraft was not a Luna. It was, instead, a test of a Venus fly-by craft designated the MV-2. The mission was intended to photograph the remaining unseen portion of the moon's far side while testing the Venus probe. But the plan was spoiled when Cosmos 21 entered a 192 × 231 km (119 × 144 mile) orbit inclined 64.8 degrees and fell to earth after three days.

A year later, the Soviets tried to fly an improved version of the Luna lander on March 21, and again on April 20, 1964. In both cases the SL-6 booster failed to achieve earth orbit. A June 4 launch followed, this time with another test version of the MV-2 Venus probe. However, the new photographic mission to the moon's far side never reached space.

In the bloodless coup of October 1964 , Khrushchev was overthrown. Having become almost synonymous with Sputniks and moon probes, his bluster had become an expected part of the space race. To many, future Soviet space activity would seem a little bit duller without Khrushchev.

However, with Khrushchev gone, Soviet space efforts turned toward a more scientific approach. While political propaganda was still a major objective of Russian space missions, science now became a higher priority.

AN AMERICAN SUCCESS AT LAST

By now, the Ranger program seemed to have made all the mistakes possible. To allow extra time for review and modifications following the failure of Ranger 6, the next flight was deliberately delayed until the last moment before the launch complex was to be taken over by the Mariner 3 and 4 missions to Mars. This pushed the next scheduled Ranger flight into late summer 1964. Perhaps Ranger number 7 would finally receive a lucky roll of the dice.

By July 28, all was ready. The Atlas-Agena pushed forcefully into a clear Florida sky at 12:50 P.M. When the booster engines dropped away, Ranger 7's telemetry showed no anomalies. The craft had passed the barrier which had killed its predecessor. The next day, a course correction targeted Ranger 7 toward its destination on the moon's Sea of Clouds. So far, it was a textbook flight. But then at this point, so was Ranger 6 except for the mystery of the television turning on. JPL officials, cautiously optimistic, predicted a fifty-fifty chance for success.

Early on the morning of July 31, Ranger 7 entered the moon's gravity and quickened its descent to the surface. On cue at 9:07 A.M., the two wide-angle television cameras warmed up as did the four telephoto cameras at 9:10 A.M. Ninety seconds later, years of frustration and heartache in trying to reach the moon were forgotten in one ecstatic moment when clear video signals were received at JPL's Goldstone tracking station.

The initial photos sent 15 min before impact equaled the best telescopic views from earth. Now as Ranger continued to drill home toward the Sea of Clouds, each minute revealed greater lunar detail than ever seen before. Closer and closer. Then—IMPACT! Ranger was a smashing success, punching into the moon at 2615 m (8578 ft) per sec. Years of disappointment, technical setbacks, political browbeating, and public humiliation were swept aside. America had at last successfully reached the moon. Technicians, project managers, politicians and newsmen gathered to view the event at JPL in Pasadena and in Washington, D.C. People reacted in a thousand different ways. Some cheered and leaped for joy; others openly wept. Spacecraft controllers abandoned their consoles, throwing papers in the air in a miniature ticker-tape parade of backslapping and handshaking.

Ranger 7 not only impacted the moon, it impacted the public and lifted American spirits during a troubled time in our space program. Some believed Ranger's success was a greater achievement than sending men into orbit. Ranger 7 had redeemed America's cold-war humiliation from a time when the Russian Sputniks danced in space while American rockets floundered.

After the joy of the success subsided, scientists looked at what they had achieved. Ranger had struck the moon at 10.7 degrees south and 20.7 degrees west, only 16 km (10 mi) from its target point and had sent back a flood of 4308 photographs of the lunar surface. The last photo had been taken at an altitude of only 460 m (1500 ft) and showed craters as small as one m (3 ft) in diameter. Astronomer Gerard Kuiper ecstatically proclaimed that Ranger had surpassed the resolution of earth-based telescopes not by a factor of ten as was hoped, but by a factor of hundreds. Kuiper concluded from the photos that the lunar surface was indeed strong enough to support the Apollo LM and that astronauts could walk on the moon.[10] Good news indeed for the builders of Apollo, who were now locked into their present design that assumed a hard surface on which to land.

In recognition of Ranger 7's achievement and to honor the thousands of people who struggled so long to reach the moon, the area of the Sea of Clouds near the crater Guericke where the craft impacted was renamed "Mare Cognitum," or the "Sea That Is Known."

RANGERS 8 AND 9 UNDERSCORE AMERICAN TRIUMPH

As Ranger 8 was prepared to again reconnoiter the smooth lunar mare for Apollo, it seemed almost anticlimactic. The long uphill struggle to reach the moon was over. The thrill of chasing the elusive target was gone. Now that the *how* of getting to the moon was solved, the scientific investigation of the moon could at last proceed.

Departing earth at 6:05 A.M., February 17, 1965, Ranger 8 flew another picture-perfect mission. Smacking the moon only 24 km (15 mi) from its target point, the craft's impact left a man-made crater at 2.6 degrees north and 24.8 degrees east. Returning 7137 photos of the Sea of Tranquility, Ranger once again brought cheering engineers and congressmen alike to their feet. Perhaps now America's lunar curse really was over.

The new views were similar to those returned the previous July. But, to some, they still did not completely answer the question of whether the lunar surface could support the Apollo LM. As Thomas Gold, now with Cornell University, lamented, the Ranger pictures were like mirrors: every scientist saw his own theories reflected in them.[11] Only the next step in lunar exploration, an actual robotic landing, would answer the question of whether Apollo could safely land on the moon.

An equally vexing question was who would achieve that landing first. America's unmanned Surveyor lander was nearly two years behind schedule and millions of dollars over budget. The Soviets were relentlessly driving to achieve their own landing at the earliest opportunity. Would America's new-found lunar luck hold out long enough for Surveyor to make it to the moon, or would a Russian lander greet the surface first? Time would tell.

Concluding that Ranger could do no more for Apollo, the final television flight was directed toward a more scientifically interesting location than a flat target for manned landers. Ranger 9 streaked off toward the lunar highlands on March 21, 1965. Lifting of at 4:37 P.M., Ranger 9 followed a course so accurate that it would hit the moon even without a correction. A day later, a brief rocket burn assured an impact within the the 112-km (70-mile)-wide crater Alphonsus.

The mission took on an added urgency when just three days before, Russian cosmonaut Alexie Leonov left his Voskhod 2 spacecraft to take the world's first space walk, an important step before sending men to the moon.

At the same time, JPL engineers also devised a marvelous public relations trick of their own. They had rushed completion of a device built for the Surveyor missions called an electronic scan converter. This device would allow Ranger's live photographs to be converted to the broadcast television signal standard. With this device, everyone could ride with Ranger to the lunar surface via a live nationwide television broadcast from the moon.

At 8:48 A.M., March 24, Ranger 9's cameras began their warm up. Then, the American television audience experienced a lunar scene never before encountered—from an altitude of 2100 km (1300 mi), the ringed crater Alphonsus slowly loomed ever closer as the entire nation experienced the thrill of live lunar exploration. At 9:08 A.M., Ranger crashed at 13.3 degrees south and 3.0 degrees west, near the 1050-m (3500-ft) central mountain peak within Alphonsus. The lunar picture show was over. In all, 5814 increasingly detailed photos had been returned. Most of the public who watched the drama unfold really did not understand the scientific implications of what they saw, but just being in a front-row seat was worth the ride.

Seven years later, a camera aboard Apollo 16 would locate the 14-m (46-ft) diameter crater blasted by Ranger 9 as it struck the moon only 6.5 km (4 mi) from its target point.

As the data from the 9th Ranger were analyzed, the Apollo project continued to swallow larger portions of NASA's budget. As a result, the remaining Block V landers were canceled. After spending $267 million (uninflated 1965 dollars) to get Ranger to the moon, the $72 million earmarked for the scientifically promising Block V craft was canceled and channeled, instead, into the thrust to get Americans to the moon before Russian footprints appeared on its surface.

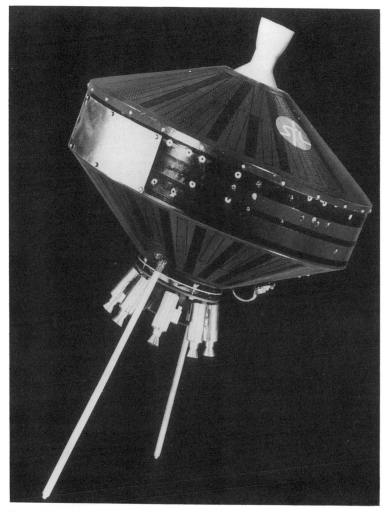

Figure 1. The 38-kg (84-lb) Pioneer 1, America's first lunar probe, was intended to orbit the moon and transmit a crude image of its far side. Protruding from the bottom of the craft were twin radio antennae and eight small solid-fuel rockets to adjust its velocity. A retrorocket protruding from the top was to slow the craft, allowing it to enter lunar orbit. (NASA photo)

Figure 2. Pioneer 1 sits atop its 27-m (90-ft) tall Thor-Able booster. Launched on October 11, 1958, the craft only reached one-third of the way to the moon, but still returned valuable radiation data. (NASA photo)

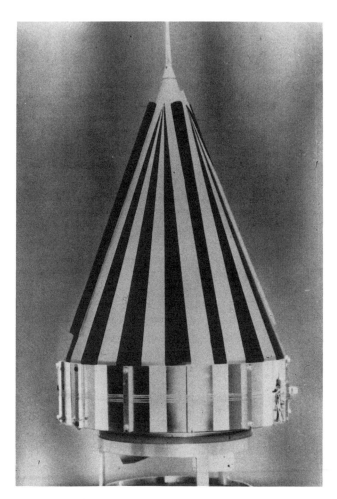

Figure 3. The first American probe to escape earth's gravity was the 6.1-kg (13.4-lb) Pioneer 4. After its launch on March 3, 1959, the tiny spacecraft passed the moon at a distance of about 60,000 km (37,000 mi) and entered solar orbit. (NASA photo courtesy of the Jet Propulsion Laboratory.)

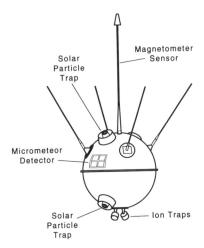

Solar
Particle
Trap

Magnetometer
Sensor

Micrometeor
Detector

Solar
Particle
Trap

Ion Traps

LUNA 1 & 2

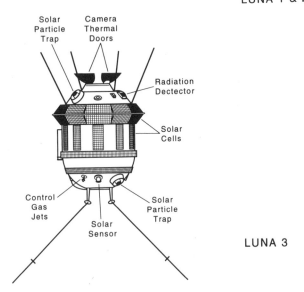

Solar
Particle
Trap

Camera
Thermal
Doors

Radiation
Dectector

Solar
Cells

Control
Gas
Jets

Solar
Sensor

Solar
Particle
Trap

LUNA 3

Figure 4. The first generation Soviet lunar probes were lunar impact and farside photography missions. The spherical Luna 1 missed the moon on January 3, 1959, and became the first artificial planet of the sun. Luna 2 impacted the moon on September 13, 1959, while the cylindrical Luna 3 photographed the far side on October 7, 1959. (Artwork by Ron Dawes.)

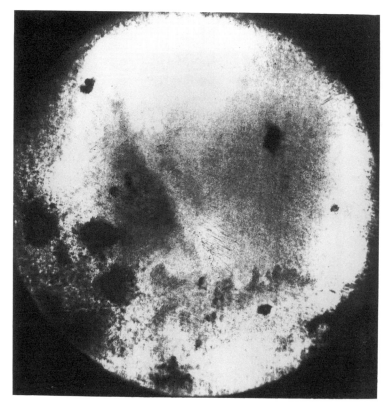

Figure 5. A composite of three of Luna 3's historic first photos of the moon's far side. While technically crude by today's standards, the photos were a sensation in 1959, revealing for the first time the rough features of the never-before-seen hidden side of the moon.

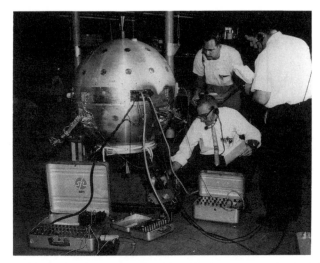

Figure 6. NASA tried four times to launch the Atlas-Able Pioneer moon probes, but failed each time. The 1-m (3.3-ft) diameter spacecraft were amazingly advanced for their time, featuring solar panels (not attached in the photo) for power and an on-board propulsion system for velocity adjustment. (Photo courtesy of TRW.)

Figure 7. The Ranger series of lunar landers launched in 1962 was NASA's first effort to land instruments on the moon. The spacecraft was the first lunar probe to fully stabilize itself, correct its own course to the moon and use a directional antenna for high-speed data transmission. (NASA photo)

Figure 8. After the failure of the Ranger lunar landers, the Ranger Block III television reconnaissance probe, shown here with its protective covers removed, became the most tested NASA space probe to date. The craft's only cargo was six downward-looking television cameras. (NASA photo)

Figure 9. America's first successful lunar probe, Ranger 7, departs earth aboard an Atlas-Agena D booster on July 28, 1964. Three days later, the spacecraft returned thousands of closeup television images of the Sea of Clouds and scored the first American triumph on the moon. (NASA photo)

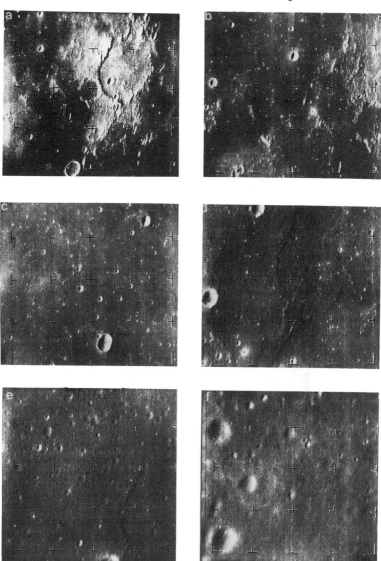

Figure 10. Ranger 7 transmitted these first close-up views of the lunar surface on July 31, 1964. Impacting near the horseshoe-shaped crater Guericke, the probe mapped a part of the Sea of Clouds later renamed the "Sea That Is Known" in honor of Ranger 7's achievement. (NASA photos courtesy of the Lunar and Planetary Institute.)

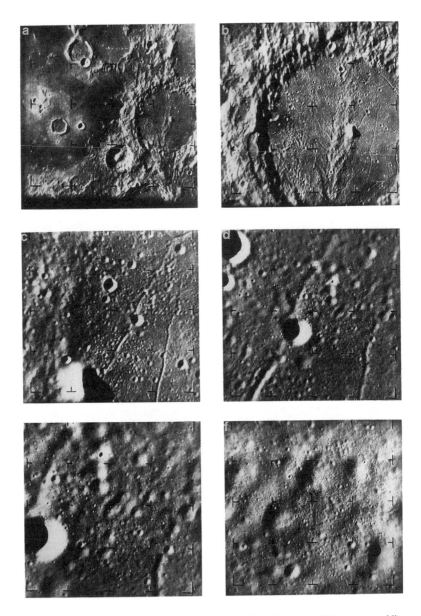

Figure 11. On March 24, 1965, Ranger 9 plunged into the crater Alphonsus, providing increasingly detailed views until the spacecraft was destroyed on impact. (NASA photos courtesy the Lunar and Planetary Institute)

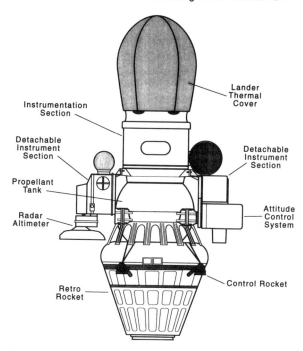

LUNA 9 & 13

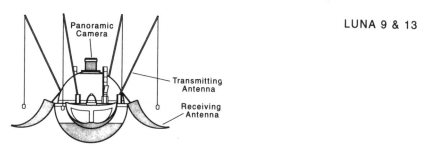

LANDING CAPSULE

Figure 12. While appearing complex, the second generation Soviet Luna probe was actually simple in design and purpose. The lower section of the spacecraft contained a retrorocket to slow the craft so the shock-resistant landing capsule housed under the thermal cover could be ejected just above the lunar surface for a rough landing on the moon. (Artwork by Ron Dawes.)

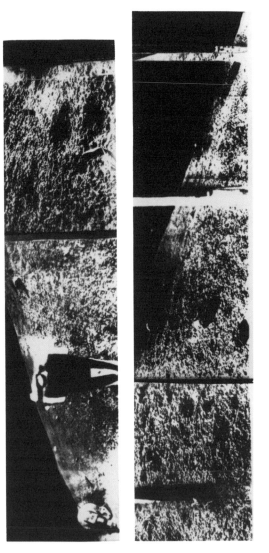

Figure 13. The Soviet Luna 9 lander returned this historic first panorama from the moon's surface on February 3, 1966. The imaging system was tilted to allow the panorama to view the surface nearby out to the horizon. The vertical objects are spacecraft antennae and mirrors for stereoscopic imaging. (Novosti—London)

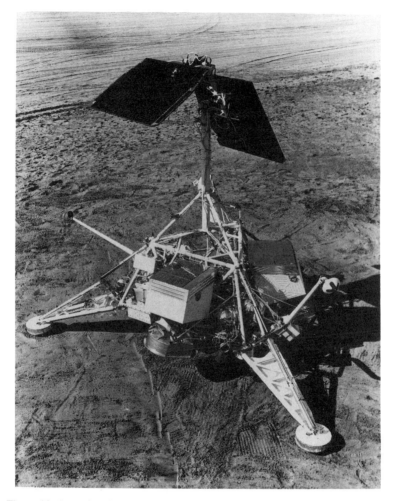

Figure 14. An engineering mock-up of the Surveyor lander. The spacecraft made the first automatic soft landing on the moon on June 2, 1966. The success proved the rocket-powered landing concept for the Apollo manned lander. (NASA photo)

Figure 15. After a solitary 944 days on the moon, Surveyor 3 is visited by the crew of Apollo 12 which landed a mere 200 m (660 ft) away on November 19, 1969. Small components from Surveyor 3 which were returned to earth by Apollo 12 showed that earth microbes had survived the two-and-a-half-year stay on the moon. (Photo courtesy of Hughes Aircraft Corporation.)

Figure 16. The single most important piece of information relayed by Surveyor 3 was images of the imprints of its own footpads in the lunar soil. These demonstrated that the lunar surface was capable of supporting a manned lander. This photograph was taken by the crew of Apollo 12 which visited thirty-one months after Surveyor 3 arrived on the moon. (NASA photo)

Figure 17. Surveyor 7 returned this mosaic view of the terrain at its landing site near the crater Tycho. The hills are 13 km (8 mi) distant while the nearby crater next to the boulder casting a prominent shadow is 3 m (10 ft) in diameter. (Photo courtesy of Hughes Aircraft Company.)

Figure 18. A photomosaic of trenches dug into the lunar surface by Surveyor 7's mechanical arms and scoop (which extends outward in the middle). To the left is the mirror-finish box containing the Alpha-scattering experiment for determining the composition of the lunar soil. (NASA photo courtesy of the Lunar and Planetary Institute.)

Figure 19. An artists conception of the Lunar Orbiter photographic reconnaissance spacecraft above the moon. The Lunar Orbiter program was NASA's first completely successful lunar probe series with all five missions achieving outstanding results. (NASA photo)

Figure 20. The first view of our world from the moon was this view snapped by Lunar Orbiter 1 during its 16th orbit on August 23, 1966. A cloud-covered, crescent earth shows the sunset terminator from eastern Europe to Antarctica. (NASA photo)

Figure 21. From an altitude of 46 km (29 mi), Lunar Orbiter 2 snapped what was called the "picture of the century." The 100-km (60-mile)-wide crater Copernicus, as seen from an oblique angle, showed the three-dimentional depth of the crater. The central mountains rise 400 m (1200 ft) while the far rim is 900 m (3000 ft) high. (NASA photo courtesy of the Lunar and Planetary Institute.)

Figure 22. Lunar Orbiter 4 provided this unique view of a lunar "bullseye," the 900-km (560-mile)-wide multirimmed impact basin seen from earth as the Eastern Sea. Only foreshortened portions of this massive feature along the rim of the moon can be seen from earth. (NASA photo courtesy of the Lunar and Planetary Institute.)

Figure 23. As seen from earth, the 85-km (530-mile)-diameter crater Tycho, distinguished by its distinctive ray system, is one of the few lunar features which can be seen with the unaided eye. Lunar Orbiter 5 revealed Tycho's geology to be amazingly rugged. (NASA photo courtesy of the Lunar and Planetary Institute.)

Figure 24. Lunar Orbiter 5 imaged the 120-km (75-mile)-long Alpine Valley which juts through the Lunar Alps between the Sea of Rains and the Sea of Cold. (NASA photo courtesy of the Lunar and Planetary Institute.)

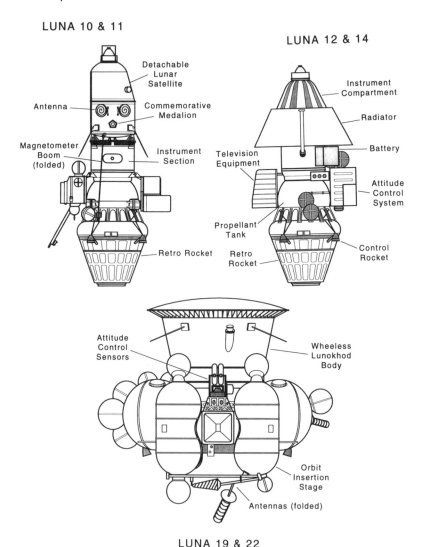

LUNA 10 & 11

Detachable
Lunar
Satellite

Antenna

Commemorative
Medalion

Magnetometer
Boom
(folded)

Instrument
Section

Retro Rocket

LUNA 12 & 14

Instrument
Compartment

Radiator

Television
Equipment

Battery

Attitude
Control
System

Propellant
Tank

Retro
Rocket

Control
Rocket

Attitude
Control
Sensors

Wheeless
Lunokhod
Body

Orbit
Insertion
Stage

Antennas (folded)

LUNA 19 & 22
HEAVY ORBITER

Figure 25. The Soviet lunar satellites were adaptations of the second- and third-generation landers. The craft used their propulsion systems to enter lunar orbit instead of descending to the surface. Luna 10 and 11 were scientific satellites while Luna 12 and 14 were photographic probes. The heavier Luna 19 and 22 carried out both scientific and photographic studies. (Artwork by Ron Dawes.)

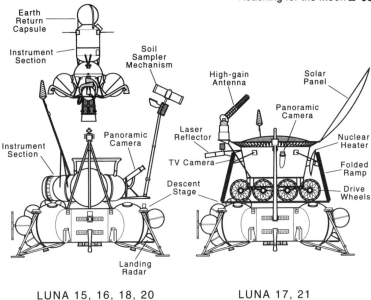

LUNA 15, 16, 18, 20   LUNA 17, 21

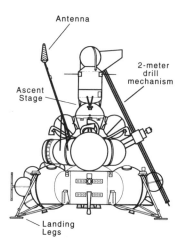

LUNA 23, 24

Figure 26. The third-generation Luna landers evolved into three versions. The early lunar sample return missions, Luna 15, 16, 18, and 20 carried a pivoting drill capable of reaching a depth of 0.3 m (1 ft). Luna 17 and 21 carried the Lunokhod rovers. Luna 23 and 24 carried an advanced drill capable of reaching a depth of 2 m (6.6 ft). (Artwork by Ron Dawes.)

A HIT AND A MISS

The first Russian attempt to land instruments on the moon during 1965 came just days before the success of Ranger 9, but the March 12 launch failed to leave earth orbit. Designated Cosmos 60, the probe entered an initial 195 × 248-km (121 × 154-mi) orbit inclined 64.7 degrees, then fell back to earth five days later.

Launched May 9, 1965, the 1476-kg (3254-lb) Luna 5 was also to attempt a soft landing. This latest moon explorer was launched on the 20th anniversary of the World War II defeat of Nazi Germany in what the Russians call The Great Patriotic War. For several days prior to the launch, rumors had been circulating in Moscow that a moon launch would be timed to coincide with the huge ceremonies marking the Red Army's conquest of the eastern front. Indeed, the launch announcement came just after a giant Victory in Europe Day military parade in Red Square.

On May 10, Luna 5 performed a mid-course correction burn which assured a lunar impact, but the craft was still off course. Instead of targeting the western edge of the moon, Luna 5 was headed for the southern portion. Perhaps the on-board rocket malfunctioned because, after 75 hr of flight, Luna 5's retrorocket failed to fire and Luna 5 crashed into the Sea of Clouds.

Only 30 days later, Soviet technicians tried again with the launch of the 1442-kg (3179-lb) Luna 6 on June 8, 1965. The planned landing was thwarted, however, by an engine controller which jammed and failed to shut off the mid-course correction rocket burn on June 9, 1965. By accidentally expending all of its fuel, Luna 6 literally leaped off course like a jack rabbit and missed the moon by a record 160,000 km (99,000 mi).

At this point, the Soviets still released no information about their Luna spacecraft or its booster. NASA deputy administrator Hugh Dryden commented that the Russians classified their space hardware at the same level that America classified the hydrogen bomb.[12]

ZOND 3 PHOTOGRAPHS HIDDEN SIDE OF THE MOON

After the Luna 3 reconnaissance of 10,000,000 square km of the moon's far side in 1959, there still remained twenty percent of the entire lunar surface which had not yet been seen by human eyes. This gap was filled July 20, 1965, when the Russian Zond 3 Mars probe photographed the rest of the lunar far side while passing the moon on the way to the Red Planet's orbit.

Launched from an earth parking orbit on July 18, 1965, Zond 3 arrived near the moon 33 hr later. Photography of the hidden side began at 4:24 A.M. on July 20 while the craft was 11,570 km (7190 mi) from the moon. It continued as the craft approached within 9220 km (5729 mi) of the moon, then ended at 5:32 A.M. when the craft had receded to 9960 km (6169 mi). A smaller portion of the moon was photographed than on the previous Luna 3 mission, but lighting conditions were more favorable and surface relief was well defined by long shadows. As the probe approached the western edge of the moon, the far-side sunrise terminator nearly coincided with the limit of the Luna 3 photography. Thus, Luna 3 and Zond 3 together completed charting all but 1.5 million square km of the 19 million square km of lunar surface invisible from earth.

The photographic sequence was fully automatic and was activated by a command from earth. Upon initiation, a moon-seeking sensor pointed the photo apparatus toward the brightest area. During the 68 min period of photography, 25 photographs were taken spaced at intervals of 2 min, 15 sec. The probe used a camera with a 106.4-mm focal length, f/8 lens to image the moon on 25-mm film. Because photography was in progress for over an hour, the probe's angle from the center of the moon changed by 60 degrees during the fly-by. This allowed stereoscopic and spectroscopic study from differing sun illumination angles.

The photographic system was an improved version of the one used by Luna 3. Each photo was scanned at a resolution of 1100 lines with 860 pixels per line. A rapid quick-look scan allowed a coarse resolution image to be transmitted in 135 sec, the same interval as between the original exposures. High resolution images required 34 min to complete.

Nine days after fly-by, from a distance of 2.2 million km (1.36 million mi) from earth, the far-side photographs were transmitted. Transmission was delayed until the probe had receded far enough from earth to allow the directional high-gain, centimeter-band antenna to be properly focused on earth. The Soviet photo system was flexible enough that specific images could be transmitted first after being selected from the quick scan images.

The Soviets valued the propaganda gains as a matter of equal importance with the science gained on the flight and emphasized the size of the area photographed on the lunar far side. The Soviets were pursuing the spectacular lunar far-side vistas at a time when the U.S. was concentrating on achieving high resolution close-ups of the near side in support of manned landings.

In September 1965, Soviet astronomer Alla Massevitch revealed some preliminary studies of the Zond 3 photos where she noted more than one thousand previously uncharted craters. A size breakdown showed six hundred craters between 5 and 20 km (3 and 12 mi), 200 between 20 and 50 km (12 and 31 mi), about 40 between 50 and 100 km (31 and 62 mi), and about a dozen over 100 km (62 mi) in diameter. The limiting resolution of the Zond photos was 3 km (1.8 mi). An interesting item seen on the far side, but rarely on the near side, is chains of craters, some reaching up to 1500 km (932 mi) in length.

Massevitch also revealed that, as was found on the Luna 3 views, the moon's far side was largely devoid of broad dark plains like the near side mare areas, is lighter in color, and is more mountainous. However, there existed mare-like depressions called "thalassoids" (from the Greek word "thalassa," or "sea"). Some extended up to 500 km (310 mi). These thalassoids were different than near-side mare in that they lacked the familiar dark color.

LANDING STILL PROVES ELUSIVE

Three months later, Soviet technicians completed modifications to the Luna design hoping to eliminate the troubles which plagued the spacecraft. On October 4, 1965, the eighth anniversary of the launch of Sputnik 1, the 1506-kg (3320-lb) Luna 7 was propelled into a translunar trajectory. Luna 7's braking rocket ignited at 12:58 A.M. on October 8. This was apparently several minutes too soon, stopping the spacecraft too high above the moon. Desperately searching for the surface, the spacecraft exhausted its fuel, then again fell toward the moon. Luna 7 crashed onto the Ocean of Storms near the crater Kepler.

Launched on December 3, 1965, Luna 8 weighed a record 1552 kgs 3422 lb), 46 kgs (101 lb) heavier than its predecessor. Part of this weight increase was possible because the craft used a lower inclination parking orbit. Beginning with Luna 8, the Soviets shifted from a 65-degree inclination parking orbit to one inclined 52 degrees. The shallower inclination made more effective use of the earth's rotational speed to assist in attaining earth orbit.

Two days after launch, Luna 8 performed a successful course correction which targeted it on the Ocean of Storms. All went well until the craft was very near the moon at which point its retrorocket fired several seconds late. Firing the engine at full thrust, Luna 8 could not overcome its own inertia and it crashed on the Ocean of Storms southeast of the crater Galilaei.

At the time, Jodrell Bank indicated that Luna 8 was a near success.

Bernard Lovell explained that the craft did not actually crash on the moon. Though the craft did not survive, it had decelerated significantly and hit the moon hard. For a time, there were fears that Luna 8 had successfully landed, but had been swallowed up by soft lunar dust. If this had been the case, it would have serious implications for the feasibility of a manned landing.

Luna 8 would be the last mission that Chief Designer Korolyov would oversee. He entered a hospital for medical tests in mid-December. In mid-January, he underwent surgery, but died on the operating table from massive hemorrhaging. He did not live to see his spacecraft design finally reach the moon intact on its next mission two weeks later.

With five lunar launches in 1965 alone, the Luna program was the most ambitious flight schedule yet attempted by Soviet space scientists. It was also clear that the program was facing the same technical crisis that haunted the early American attempts to reach our airless natural satellite. The Soviets now held the lead not only in space firsts, but space failures as well. It was clear that Moscow was committing enormous resources to a furious attempt to land on the moon before an American craft could do so. It was just a matter of time before Soviet science teamed with a bit of luck and actually landed on the surface of the moon.

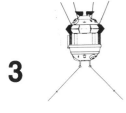

3   # Exploring the Moon

NEW YEAR, NEW HOPES

By the arrival of 1966 both the Americans and the Soviets had hit the moon. The dazzling close-up photographs returned by Ranger had given the public something more tangible than Luna 3's blurry and indistinct far-side photos, and America was riding tall in the saddle again. But the critical goal was still up for grabs. A probe had to soft-land on the moon to determine if a manned craft could survive.

After the Ranger project concluded, America's unmanned lunar efforts shifted toward the Surveyor lander and Lunar Orbiter photo reconnaissance projects. However, both craft were still far from completion. In the meantime at Tyuratam, another Luna was readied.

Liftoff came at 2:42 P.M., Moscow time, January 31, 1966, and Luna 9 was on its way. Curiously, while the moon probe remained in its temporary earth parking orbit, it pushed the number of space hardware objects known to be in low orbit up to exactly 1000. Near the end of the first revolution, the escape stage fired to propel the 1583-kg (3490-lb) Luna 9 into a 79-hr moon-bound trajectory.

With the craft sailing toward the moon, Russian technicians could only wait and hope. Their lunar landing effort had suffered a terrible blow when its founder, Sergei Korolyov, died two weeks before. Now perhaps the new year would bring Luna 9 fresh luck and overdue success.

The spacecraft's initial path would have resulted in a 9600-km (6000-mi) lunar miss, so, on February 1, while still 233,000 km (144,786 mi) from its target, Luna 9 performed a 71.2-m (234-ft)-per-sec course correction to ensure accurate lunar impact. By 4:00 P.M. on Febraury 3, tracking information was transmitted to Luna 9's computer sequencer and verified in preparation for landing.

Almost five hours later, the craft approached within 8300 km (5157 mi) of the moon where it assumed a vertical attitude for landing. At this point, lunar gravity was accelerating the spacecraft at 1.3 m (4.3 ft) per sec.

As the craft dropped past 75 km (47 mi), a radio altimeter fired the retrorocket. Jodrell Bank monitored Luna 9's signals as it approached the moon. Director Bernard Lovell reported that the craft fired its braking rocket at 9:44:10 P.M. The engine burned for 46 seconds while slowing the lander to a speed of 25 km (15.5 mi) per hr. Touchdown occurred at 9:44:56 P.M.

Luna 9 arrived at the surface just after local sunrise at 7.8 degrees north, 64.2 degrees west in the western area of the moon's Ocean of Storms. Luna's rocket descent stage was not designed to survive the landing and its radio signals ceased when it crashed. The television-carrying landing capsule was thrown clear one second before impact. It bounced to the surface and rolled upright like a child's bottom-heavy toy, coming to rest halfway up the inner slope of a small 25-m (80-ft)-diameter crater.

ON THE SURFACE AT LAST

Back on earth, mission controllers had no way of knowing if success had been achieved. Scientists nervously passed the 4 min and 10 seconds it took for the capsule's stabilization petals to open and the antennae to deploy. Then success! A signal at 183.538 MHz established radio contact with the first craft to report from another world.

The Russians had finally done it. They had reached the lunar surface first and beaten the Americans again. But, strangely, the magnitude of the achievement overpowered the propaganda and expected cold war rhetoric. One question was on everyone's mind: What was the moon really like? Could a cosmonaut walk on the moon? Had Luna submerged in loose dust or was it sitting firmly on solid ground? The answers would have to wait another seven long hours until the sun was high enough for photography to begin.

The historic initial photos were sent between 4:50 A.M. and 6:37 A.M., February 4. A second panorama was transmitted later that day between 5:00 P.M. and 8:54 P.M. The next day, a third was received between 7:00 P.M. and 8:41 P.M. The sun elevation angles increased from 7 to 14, then to 27 degrees, causing the shadow relief to change. The descent stage apparently crashed over the edge of a crater and was not visible.

To conserve its batteries, the craft was shut down when it was not in range of the Soviet Deep Space Communication Center's antenna at Yevpatoria. When Luna 9 was active, live signals from the lander were played over Moscow radio and television. The signals sounded like the slow ticking of a grandfather clock through the hiss of radio static.

Professor A. I. Lebidinsky reported that between the first and second panoramas, the lander shifted slightly as it settled into the lunar soil, then shifted further between the second and third panorama. As Luna 9 rested upon the moon, its weight in the weak lunar gravity was only 16 kg (35.3 lb). The lander probably shifted because the slowly diminishing water supply in the thermal control system changed the weight distribution. This tilted the imaging system from 16.5 to 22.5 degrees and moved it several degrees in azimuth. The camera's perspective was thus moved approximately 100 mm (4 in), or about the distance between two human eyes. This fortuitous accident allowed for stereoscopic study of nearby areas.

On February 7, 1966, the Soviets announced that contact with Luna 9 had concluded at 8:41 A.M. after a total of eight hours and five min of communication over three days. However, Luna 9 surprised observers by transmitting three more poor quality photos beginning at 11:37 P.M., February 7, when the solar elevation was 41 degrees. Higher than expected battery reserves had allowed the lander to function one more time.

A LOOK AT THE REAL MOON

Several days after the landing, the Luna 9 panoramas were released by Moscow. Academician Mstislav Keldish said: "We can see the lunar surface consists of adequately durable rocks of the pumice or slag type. It turned out to be hard enough for the station not to sink."[1] Academician Alexander Vinogradov announced that Luna 9 found no loose dust on the landing site. The views showed the lunar surface to be a rough textured surface of volcanic origin, covered with rocks and boulders of various sizes, but smooth enough to be easily traversed by a visiting astronaut.

There were none of the postulated loose fairy castle structures, no billowy dust, and no clumping of low density dust by vacuum fusion. What the photos did show were many, many overlapping depressions a few centimeters across, each of which cast a small shadow. The nearby rocks were sharply outlined monolithic structures which depressed the ground below them very little, indicating they were likely ejecta from a meteor impact. The lack of fine, low-mass lunar dust was also shown when the craft did not electrostatically attract dust as expected and when there was no dust build-up on the camera lens and the photography remained sharp.

Luna revealed an undulating, porous surface in which the scale from near to far contained so few references that the horizon seemed very close. The craft was tipped to the east, so no land mass was seen to the west, only projections from the lander against the black sky. Small depressions 2 to 3 m (6.5 to 10 ft) in diameter were visible as well as 10-to-20-cm (4 to 8-in) diameter rocks several meters from the lander.

In his interpretation of the photographs, Soviet lunar expert Nikolai P. Barabashov reported that: "The upper layer of lunar soil is a sponge-like rough textured mass, scattered with individual sharp-edged fragments of various sizes... This layer is clearly strong enough to support heavier objects."[2] The Luna 9 photos destroyed the myth that the lunar surface was a thick layer of soft powdery dust which would swallow up a spacecraft.

Scientifically, Luna 9's single most important discovery was the fact that it rested firmly on a solid surface. This was welcome news to planners in the American Apollo manned moon-landing project. The photos returned by Luna 9 reduced our lunar perspective from Ranger's 1/2-km (1500 ft) altitude to only one m (3 ft), and reduced many of the theories postulated from the Ranger photos to historical footnotes.

Luna 9's only other instrument, the SBM-10 radiation detector, showed the average radiation dosage on the lunar surface was 30 millirads per day, a level safe for human exploration of the moon. It was deduced that this radiation came primarily from cosmic rays.

THE POLITICS OF LUNA 9

The successful first landing of a spacecraft on the moon was a vital step toward the eventual goal of landing human beings on the moon. However, the importance of the first soft landing by a spacecraft on another world must be examined not only from a scientific standpoint, but from its place in political history as well. In the 1960s, the moon race was very much a matter of national pride and prestige for the United States and a continuous source of communist propaganda for the Soviets.

Any mention of Soviet attempts to reach the moon in the 1960s brings images of Soviet Premier Nikita Khrushchev gloating about the success of Soviet space accomplishments while the early American space efforts floundered. Although Khrushchev had been removed from power sixteen months before the Luna 9 landing, the momentum from his space legacy was still a driving force in the competition between the U.S. and the U.S.S.R. to reach the moon first. Indeed, when Luna 9 made its historic landing, Soviet newspapers blared the headline: "The Moon Speaks Russian."

Soviet media commentators said much to praise the landing of Luna 9, but used few words to describe the event itself. Few technical details were revealed, but a stream of well known astronomers and cosmonauts appeared on Soviet broadcasts to praise the mission's achievement.

PIRACY

The historic first photos from the surface of another world also became embroiled in international intrigue when the Russians did not immediately release the lunar photos. During the Soviet delay, scientists at the Jodrell Bank radio telescope in England intercepted the signals from Luna 9. Listeners at Jodrell Bank realized that they were not being transmitted in code. On a hunch, they sent a car to the *Daily Press* in Manchester to pick up a Creed-type wire service facsimile machine used to transmit photographs.

Initially, there were problems in adjusting the scan rate. The first effort showed a series of dark lines about 6 mm (0.25 in) apart. Another showed just light lines. Then the correct combination was hit and, incredibly, when the Luna video signals were fed into the machine, it began to produce a photograph of the lunar surface. By a stroke of insight and resourcefulness, the Jodrell Bank staff and assembled reporters were the first people outside the Luna control center to view the stark landscape of the moon. When Lovell saw the photograph, he could only utter, "Amazing!"[3]

Within minutes the photos were relayed around the world. The Soviets were outraged by what they called "piracy" by the British for having scooped them to the first release of the lunar images. In a TASS news report, academician Anatoly Blagonravov verbally blasted Lovell for releasing the photos without obtaining "the information necessary for correct reproduction of the image." Blagonravov further said "apparently some motives of sensational nature played a role in this case."[4] Lovell defended his release of the Luna images, saying he made no scientific analysis or mention of scale. A Jodrell Bank spokesman said that the photographs were of such international importance their immediate release was justified.

Not knowing the true scale of the lunar views as transmitted by Luna 9's photo apparatus, the British versions were distorted vertically by a factor of 2.5. This had the effect of making all lunar features appear taller and more jagged than they really were. This distortion misled some experts into declaring that snowshoe-like devices would be needed to walk on the moon and that American equipment would have to be modified prior to a manned landing. Gerard Kuiper of the Lunar and Planetary Laboratory speculated that the view was from low angles with a wide angle camera and that the horizon was very close. Bernard Lovell believed the view was from three m (10 ft) above the surface, that the rocks shown were 3 to 6 m (10 to 20 ft) tall and that the horizon was several kilometers away.[5]

While the unauthorized release of the distorted Luna photos by the British annoyed the Soviets, it did give world-wide credibility to the Soviet achievement at a time when many doubted that the Soviets had really succeeded in landing on the moon. It was several days later when Moscow finally released their own version of the images. In the meantime, while the rest of the world was awed by the British versions of Luna's photographs, Soviet citizens could only contemplate simulated lunar scenery devised by a planetarium.

U.S. ALSO INTERCEPTS SOVIET SIGNALS

The radio frequency used by Luna 9 was too low for reception by the NASA-JPL Deep Space Tracking Network. The signals were instead intercepted by U.S. Army monitors at Ft. Monmouth, New Jersey, and the National Security Agency at Ft. Meade, Maryland. The executive secretary of the National Aeronautics and Space Council, Dr. Edward Welsh, did admit that the U.S. had intercepted information from Luna 9, but did not elaborate. One unofficial explanation for the Government's vagueness was that it was anxious to show the world that it could identify and track Soviet space activity, but was reluctant to reveal its specific capabilities.

American agencies also processed good-quality images at the same time as Jodrell Bank, but the British photos, followed by sharper images released in Russia, led to a U.S. decision not to release its own versions. In Welsh's opinion, the U.S. world image would have been tarnished if it had tried to steal the Russian show by releasing them after the Soviets published their photos.[6] American space officials were ready to release them only if the Soviets had refused to publish anything or altered the results.

Meanwhile, in Washington, a House subcommittee chaired by John E. Moss (D., Calif.) investigated why NASA did not release its intercepted photos. The subcommittee accused NASA of excessive secrecy regarding some facets of the Soviet space program. NASA countered that not releasing the Luna 9 photos was due to secrecy imposed by the Defense Department. Another NASA spokesman, however, stated there was no legal reason for the secrecy.

LUNA 10 ENTERS MOON ORBIT

Another Russian lunar shot was attempted on March 1, 1966, but remained stranded in its earth parking orbit. The failure, designated Cosmos 111, was thought to be an attempt to place the first satellite into lunar orbit.

Luna 10 followed on March 31, lifting off from Tyuratam at 1:47 P.M. This time, official Soviet announcements left no doubt. The new Luna was "to test a system ensuring the setting up of an artificial moon satellite with the object of exploring near-lunar outer space."[7] The flight, if successful, would also upstage the American moon effort by orbiting a lunar satellite several months before NASA's Lunar Orbiter arrived.

During transit, Luna 10 had a mass of 1582 kg (2987 lb) and relied on the same spacecraft bus and propulsion system used on Lunas 4 through 9. A course correction on April 1 moved the target point from a wide miss to a point 1000 km (620 mi) above the moon.

While still about 8000 km (5000 mi) from the moon, Luna 10 was oriented with its engine facing the direction of travel. After an 80-hr flight, Luna 10 made its closest approach to the moon and, on command from earth, fired its retrorocket at 9:44 P.M. April 3. The burn slowed the craft by 850 m (2789 ft) per sec, allowing the moon's gravity to capture Luna 10. As with landing missions, two no-longer-needed equipment modules were jettisoned at retrorocket ignition. Twenty minutes later, the rocket body separated on command from earth, leaving the 245-kg (540-lb) Luna 10 satellite alone in a 349 × 1017-km (235 × 610-mile) orbit inclined 71.9 degrees with a 178.25 min period.

Luna 10 preceded the American Lunar Orbiter by 4 months, but the purpose of each craft was totally different. Lunar Orbiter was to be a high-resolution photographic mission while Luna 10 had no cameras and was to gather strictly scientific data. Indeed, one of its goals was to study the moon's gravitational field by studying its effect on the probe's orbit.

The satellite was an airtight, tapered cylinder 75 cm (2.5 ft) in diameter and 1.5 m (5 ft) long with an extended 1.5-m (5-ft) magnetometer boom. The probe slowly tumbled at two revolutions per minute. Pressurized to 1.3 atm, Luna 10 used a fan to transfer internal heat to the satellite's skin, maintaining an internal temperature of 25°C (77°F). Instruments included micrometeor detectors; a gamma ray spectrometer; infrared detector; cosmic ray, X-ray, and solar wind detectors; and a three-axis magnetometer. The new magnetometer was 15 times as sensitive as that carried by Luna 2. Luna 10 was battery-powered and thus had a limited lifetime. It was tracked for 56 days through 460 orbits before its signal faded on May 30, 1966.

Some analysts believe that Luna 10 may have been a quick adaptation of a Cosmos earth satellite employed to beat the American Lunar Orbiter as the first satellite of the moon. It is interesting that just nine years into the space age, the first lunar satellite, Luna 10, weighed three times as much as the first earth satellite, Sputnik.

MUSIC FROM THE MOON

Luna 10 arrived at the moon during the 23rd Communist Party Congress meeting in Moscow. Jodrell Bank announced Luna 10's success on Sunday, April 3, but the Russians withheld the news for twelve hours until the Party Congress reconvened after a weekend recess. Not missing a major propaganda opportunity, the designers of the craft included with the scientific equipment a series of solid state oscillators programmed to replay the musical notes of "The Internationale," the international communist anthem. Once in lunar orbit, one of Luna 10's first jobs was to bring the 6000 party congress delegates to their feet by broadcasting the political anthem from the moon.

The lunar satellite studied gamma and X-irradiation emitted from topographically different areas. As the moon is bombarded by solar and cosmic radiation, elements in the soil are raised to a higher atomic energy state. When these elements decay back to their original state, they emit low-level gamma or X-rays. Luna 10's instruments measured this induced radiation. Most of the X-irradiation was caused by solar X-rays while the gamma radiation was induced by cosmic rays. The data implied that the lunar surface rocks were roughly the same as basalt rocks on the earth. There was no significant difference in radiation from mare lowlands and the mountainous highlands.

The magnetometer detected a weak magnetic field registering 24 to 38 gammas, or units of magnetic field intensity; only 0.05 to 0.1 percent of that of earth's field. The magnetic intensity did not change with increasing distance from the moon, leading researchers to believe that the moon's magnetic field was merely the result of the interplanetary magnetic field as it deformed around the mass of the moon. They also concluded that the moon has no magnetic poles. Luna's magnetometer also detected the earth's magnetic tail, that portion of earth's magnetic field which is stretched out by the solar wind and which extends all the way to the moon's orbit.

Radiation studies determined that the number of energetic particles trapped by the moon's weak magnetic field were approximately 0.1 percent of those trapped near earth. Cosmic ray intensity in lunar orbit was established at 5 particles per cm^3 per sec. This reading was slightly elevated over normal background cosmic ray levels because solar activity was at a minimum during the Luna 10 mission. High solar activity tends to shield the inner solar system from galactic cosmic rays while low activity allows more to reach the area of the earth.

Between April 3 and May 12, 1966, the meteoroid detector detected 198 impacts. This rate is 100 times that which occurs in open space but still posed no threat to spacecraft. The matter detected was thought to be grain-like material blasted into orbit by meteor impacts on the moon.

Orbital tracking of Luna 10 provided information on the strength and variation of the lunar gravitational field. The implications of these findings refuted previous theories that the moon was a 3473-km (2158-mi)-diameter sphere with a slight bulge toward earth. Instead, the moon proved to be pear-shaped with an elongation facing away from earth. Repeated radio occultation experiments in which the spacecraft's signal was occulted by the lunar limb as it passed behind the moon failed to detect any tenuous lunar atmosphere. If present, an atmosphere would have had a detectable muting effect on the radio signal.

However, the next Soviet step toward the moon was a stumble. A launch on April 30, 1966 was intended to loft another lunar satellite, but the booster failed and the craft never reached orbit.

SURVEYOR TO ANSWER LUNA'S CHALLENGE

In the early 1960s, the JPL-managed Surveyor program had been envisioned as a $58 million project which was scheduled to reach the moon's surface in 1963. After a tortured six-year evolution, its cost had ballooned to eight times the original estimate, to $469 million (1967 dollars). The project had been delayed for years not only by the complexities of developing the spacecraft itself, but also by the equally vexing difficulty of perfecting the hydrogen-powered Centaur upper stage needed to launch Surveyor.

Unlike the Ranger hard landers which were to splatter on the moon like the watermelons dropped by David Letterman on his late-night TV show, Surveyor had to alight gently. And unlike orbiters, Surveyor needed a lot of brute force to slow its approach to a touchdown bump that would satisfy even Otis Elevator. To do this required rocket power, and such power required weight. The great weight of Surveyor dictated the use of the Centaur, the only American booster then capable of lofting the heavy Surveyors to the moon.

But in the early 1960s, American planetary exploration was stalled by problems in developing the hydrogen-powered vehicle. Liquid hydrogen was attractive as a rocket fuel because it had far greater power pound-for-pound than did other rocket fuels. However, liquid hydrogen has to be maintained at the incredibly low temperature of −253 degrees Centigrade (−423°F) in the Centaur's fuel tank. Plumbing to pipe the super-cold fluid to the engines also has to be capable of withstanding temperatures low enough to cause ordinary steel to shatter. This problem proved to be far more complex than anticipated.

Like the technical challenges which preceded Ranger's success at the moon, Surveyor also dashed many careers and garnered congressional scrutiny when the spacecraft failed to live up to overly optimistic early goals. Both NASA and Hughes Aircraft later admitted to vastly underestimating the job of building Surveyor and getting it to the moon. The "hurry-up-and-go" attitude to catch up with the Russian space program also contributed to the project's woes by encouraging NASA to leap into the complex Surveyor program before researching just how difficult a soft landing on the moon was.

Two other aspects of development that complicated Surveyor's evolution were NASA's use of "cost-plus-fixed-fee" contracting and the inability of Hughes Aircraft to initially manage the rapidly expanding program. Surveyor had been contracted to Hughes under an agreement which virtually guaranteed the company a profit no matter how high the eventual cost. This type of arrangement came under increasing NASA disfavor and caused much management friction within the project. JPL had chosen Hughes to build Surveyor because of the company's understanding of spacecraft design, but Surveyor was also Hughes' first large space project. Initially, the company was poorly equipped managerially and technically to deal with a program of such magnitude. But, to their credit, once the true scope of the project unfolded, Hughes officials responded and the complex Surveyor evolved brilliantly.

In early 1966, NASA, JPL, and Hughes Aircraft finally succeeded in getting the spacecraft and the Centaur booster ready. Surveyor now represented the highest hopes of American robotic space exploration.

COMPLEX ROBOTIC EXPLORER

The lunar lander used a combination of solid-fueled and liquid-fueled engines to autonomously approach the moon and slow down to a feather-light touchdown. Designed as a 1040-kg (2293-lb)-class spacecraft, Surveyor stood 3 m (10 ft) high and measured 4.27 m (14 ft) across its three shock-absorbing landing legs. The frame of the tripod-shaped explorer was a 27-kg (60-lb) triangular aluminum tube structure with a landing leg at each corner. Electronics were housed in two thermally stable boxes attached to the spacecraft frame as were propellant tanks for the liquid-fueled engines. The craft was topped with a mast which supported a flat planar array high-gain directional antenna and a 76 × 112-cm (30 × 40-in) solar panel containing 3960 solar cells supplying 85 watts of power. Twin 10-watt radios would relay television images to earth. Two omnidirectional antennas were mounted on folding booms.

Surveyor was designed to carry a high-resolution panoramic television system, mechanical tools to dig into the lunar surface, and instruments to determine the chemical composition of the lunar soil. Additional spacecraft engineering sensors would return data about lunar conditions by analysis of the spacecraft's reaction to the heat, the cold, and the radiation environment.

The bulk of Surveyor's mass was a 3630- to 4536-kg (8000- to 10,000-lb)-thrust, solid-fueled retrorocket which was to be fired by a radar altimeter at 76 km (47 mi) altitude. At 10 km (6 mi) altitude, the burned-out motor would be jettisoned and the descent would continue using three liquid-fueled, throttle-controlled 13.6- to 47.2-kg (30- to 104-lb)-thrust vernier engines. A radar altimeter Doppler velocity-sensing (RADVS) system determined the descent velocity and would automatically control the thrust of the verniers to slow the spacecraft to 1.5 m (5.2 ft) per sec about 4 m (13 ft) above the surface. Surveyor's radar control system was important for proving a similar control system for the Apollo lunar lander.

FIRST MISSION CARRIES NO SCIENCE INSTRUMENTS

The fluctuating estimations of Centaur's cargo capacity played havoc with Surveyor's science payload. Over the years, the spacecraft's allowable weight had dropped from 1134 kg (2500 lb) to 953 kg (2100 lb), then climbed back up to 1111 kg (2450 lb) for the final missions. As a result, the scientific payloads of the first four missions were scaled back to lighten the crafts, and the flights were considered engineering tests. Thus, Surveyor 1, the first of these missions, carried no scientific instruments. Once considered "very ambitious," Surveyor was scientifically a mere shell of what was originally expected. Surveyor 1 had a mass of 995 kg (2194 lb), but carried only 9 kg (20 lb) of television cameras. Of the seven missions firmly scheduled, only the last three would carry a full 52-kg (114-lb) complement of experiments.

Of two television systems installed on Surveyor 1 and 2, one was not even used. The downward-looking television system adjacent to landing leg #2 was to return a Ranger-like sequence of approach photos to provide lunar surface data for Apollo. Before Surveyor's first launch, NASA decided this capability was no longer needed so that system was not used on either mission. The panoramic television system however, proved to be of immense value on the moon. The vertically mounted, 7.3-kg (16-lb) vidicon camera used a rotating and tilting mirror and 25- to 100-mm, f/4- to f/22-zoom lens to make highly detailed 360-degree panoramic mosaic images of the local terrain. Controlled from earth, the camera could focus from 1.2 m (4 ft) to infinity and scanned 600 lines per image. Red, green, and blue filters could be used to reconstruct color images. The camera also had the ability to transmit 200-line, low-resolution images through the low-gain antennas.

Strain gauges installed on the landing legs would provide data about landing a legged vehicle on the moon. These engineering data, being directly applicable to Apollo, were considered a primary goal of the mission while lunar science studies were considered a secondary goal. Data about the moon's radar reflectivity would be gathered during landing while temperature sensors and accelerometers would report engineering data about the condition of the spacecraft during landing and its active period on the moon. In all, two hundred engineering measurements examined the status of the spacecraft.

SURVEYOR 1 OFF TO A GOOD START

On May 30, the same day that contact with Luna 10 was lost, America's lunar soft lander at last took flight. Surveyor 1 lifted off from Cape Canaveral at 10:41 A.M. on the maiden planetary exploration flight of the Atlas-Centaur rocket. The booster flawlessly propelled Surveyor into a direct-ascent trajectory toward the smooth plains of the moon's Ocean of Storms. The path was so accurate that it would miss its target by only 400 km (250 mi). Sixteen hours after launch, the vernier engines burned for 21 seconds to place Surveyor 1 within 14 km (6 mi) of its desired target point. The only flaw was the failure of an omnidirectional antenna boom to deploy. The antenna was to be used for slow transmission of data at low power and its loss was not considered critical.

As Surveyor 1 approached the moon late on June 1, 1966, the real question on everyone's mind was not about the lunar surface, but about the spacecraft itself. Four months before, Luna 9 answered the critical question of whether the moon would support a lander. Now everyone silently questioned if Surveyor would touchdown gently or if it would become the first of a long string of technical horrors as with the first Pioneers and Rangers.

The answer came with decisive swiftness after 63.6 hr of flight. Dropping closer and closer to the moon, Surveyor oriented itself to point the big retrorocket downward. At an altitude of 75.2 km (46.7 mi), the engine fired and Surveyor braked its screaming dive like a race car entering the pits. Soon, the vernier engines took over and brought the craft to a near hover just above the moon. Then they cut off and Surveyor 1 plopped onto the surface, all three footpads touching down simultaneously at 2:17 A.M., June 2. The craft bounced 6 cm (2.5 inch) then touched down for good. The landing jar shook loose the stuck omnidirectional antenna, and it fell into place, adding to Surveyor 1's astounding accomplishment.

AMERICA ON THE MOON

Back on earth, JPL and Hughes engineers stood in slack-jawed amazement. They could not believe it—it worked! Surveyor 1 had landed.

On the first try with an unproven spacecraft, American engineers had soft-landed one of their products on the moon. Ranger had taken seven attempts to succeed and Pioneer had never made it to the moon. Now Surveyor had made it on the first try. It was a sensational achievement which marked a turning point in the unmanned exploration of the moon. Surveyor's success had consequences far beyond the first American soft landing on the moon. The very act of successfully slowing under radar-guided rocket power to a controlled vertical landing using landing legs was also proof that the Apollo concept of manned lunar landing would work.

Surveyor 1 had landed inside a 100-km (62-mile)-diameter ghost crater, a crater which had been filled almost to its brim with lava and smoothly "paved over." The craft came to rest at 2.5 degrees south and 43.2 degrees west near the crater Flamsteed. Thirty-six minutes after touchdown, a ghostly 200-line image was returned showing footpad #2 pushed 2.5 cm (one inch) into the soil. During the first lunar day, hundreds of overlapping, individual, 600-line high-resolution images were returned. These were assembled to create wide-field mosaics showing surface details as small as one mm (0.04 inch) in size. The panoramas showed Surveyor had landed on a dark, level area with craters up to several hundred meters in diameter. In the distance were piles of rounded boulders which bordered a large crater. In all, the spacecraft responded to 100,000 commands and 10,732 images were returned before the sun set for the two-week lunar night.

While the television camera was the only instrument carried, Surveyor 1 was also stuffed with engineering test instruments. These measured the shock of the touchdown and the deflection of the landing legs. These data, coupled with television views of how far the footpads sank into the dust, showed the mass-bearing strength of the lunar soil to be about 350 grams per square cm. Surveyor thus showed that the local lunar soil had the same mass bearing strength as plowed soil on earth. This was welcome news for those who were still worrying about Thomas Gold's fairy castles.

The spacecraft survived the −160°C (−256°F) nighttime cold. Efforts to revive the spacecraft at sunrise failed, although on July 6 it did respond and return 618 more low-resolution images from the surface. Surveyor's primary mission was declared completed on July 14, but the spacecraft remained in contact until January 7, 1967.

LUNAR ORBITER SUPPLEMENTS MOON STUDIES

During the time when Ranger matured into a viable exploration program and Surveyor was suffering its growing pains, the Lunar Orbiter project progressed with little difficulty. The photo reconnaissance satellite evolved into a 387-kg (853-lb) spacecraft consisting of various modules attached to a main equipment mounting deck topped by a circular open framework standing 2 m (6.5 ft) high. Four solar panels extended 3.8 m (12.5 ft) and carried 10,856 solar cells providing 375 watts of power. Nickle-cadmium batteries powered the craft when it was in the moon's shadow. A 92-cm (3-ft) diameter steerable, high-gain, dish antenna and a low-gain antenna on the opposite side of the spacecraft both spanned 5.2 m (17 ft).

After launch from Cape Canaveral by an Atlas-Agena booster, Lunar Orbiter was to use a propulsion system based on a 45-kg (100-lb)-thrust control rocket adapted from the Apollo Command Module attitude control system. The rocket assembly was attached above the main spacecraft body and was to be fueled by four tanks carrying nitrogen tetroxide and hydrazine. The thruster would act as a mid-course correction motor, as a retro-rocket to decelerate the craft into lunar orbit and, after completion of the mission, it would crash the craft deliberately into the moon to prevent it from becoming a navigational hazard to the manned Apollo craft.

The spacecraft was stabilized in space using star and sun sensors and an inertial reference unit to control the craft using eight nitrogen gas-powered jets. During each photographic pass, the control system was to point the craft within 0.2 degrees of local lunar vertical. A 10-watt transmitter would relay data back to earth while a 128-word memory computer would store commands allowing 16 hr of photography. Twenty small pressurized containers acting as meteoroid detectors and a series of radiation dosimeters were the craft's only nonphotographic experiments.

The heart of the to Lunar Orbiter was a 68-kg (150-lb) photographic system. The orbiter was the only nonrecoverable American spacecraft to use photographic film to image its target. A television vidicon system would have been much simpler, but the need to image objects as small as one m (3.3 ft) dictated a higher resolution system. Housed in a pressurized ellipsoidal aluminum shell, the camera system was based on a previous military application. It was designed to peer through a quartz window to image the moon on 70-mm Kodak SO-243 aerial film. Seventy-nine meters (259 ft) of film would allow 212 image pairs to be taken. An image motion detector would move the film during exposure to compensate for the orbiter's motion across the surface of the moon. The exposed film was to be stored in a looping mechanism which could hold up to 21 exposures. The film would then pass through a device which would press the emulsion against a Bimat monochemical layer for 3.5 min. This would develop and fix the film in a manner similar to a Polaroid camera.

Lunar orbiter used a facsimile scanning system similar in principle to that used on Luna 3 and Zond 3 to transmit the photographic images to earth. However, the orbiter advanced the concept to a remarkable degree. The film would be scanned by a 0.005-mm (0.0002-in) diameter light beam at 287 lines per mm (7290 lines per in) on the original negative. The variation in the transmitted light intensity resulting from different densities on the negative would to be measured by a photomultiplier (a device which produced a signal proportional to the incident light intensity) and the signal beamed to earth for reconstruction. Each negative would take 43 minutes to scan.

FIRST ORBITER SIGNALS SUCCESS

Lunar Orbiter 1 roared up from Cape Canaveral at 3:26 P.M., August 10, 1966. After its Atlas-Agena placed it into a brief earth parking orbit, the Agena upper stage propelled the craft toward the moon. One day after launch, a 32-sec course correction rocket burn targeted the reconnaissance craft to within 80 km (50 mi) of the desired point above the moon. The only annoying problem was that sunlight, reflecting off of a bright portion of the spacecraft, blinded the Canopus sensor and complicated the operation of the orientation system. By the time the orbiter arrived at the moon, an alternative method of navigation had been devised.

After a journey of 92 hr, Lunar Orbiter 1 arrived and fired its engine for 578.7 sec. This slowed the craft by 790 m (2592 ft) per sec, dropping it into a 191 × 1854-km (119 × 1152-mi) orbit, inclined 12.2 degrees. The orbiter thus became the first American spacecraft to orbit the moon, doing so every 3 hr and 37 min.

Initial test images were taken between August 18 and 20, then the spacecraft was readied for its prime mission to photograph nine primary and seven secondary potential Apollo landing sites spread across 4830 km (3000 mi) of the moon's face just below the equator. The craft would also try to pinpoint Surveyor 1 on the surface and return close-up images of the far side. On August 21, the orbiter's perilune was lowered to 58 km (36 mi), then further reduced to 50 km (31 mi) on the 25th by firings of its on-board rocket motor. The medium-resolution images of the landing sites were outstanding but the motion compensation device failed, smearing the high-resolution images and disappointing scientists. The first picture from the moon showing the earth from afar was received on August 23. By August 30, all 211 frames were exposed and the photographic mission was complete.

Precise tracking of the spacecraft's path around the moon revealed irregularities in the orbit. Something was making Lunar Orbiter dip slightly, then sail back up again as it circled the moon. This was the initial clue to the moon's irregular gravitational field. Such information was crucial for Apollo since gravitational anomalies would tug the manned craft off its planned landing course. The perturbations were eventually traced to mass concentrations, now known as "mascons," under the moon's lava-filled Mare. This discovery was a major contribution to lunar science.

On October 29, its mission over, Lunar Orbiter 1 fired its engine for 97 seconds and deliberately crashed on the far side of the moon at 8:30 A.M. so as to not interfere with the upcoming Lunar Orbiter 2 mission. The craft became the first NASA probe intentionally destroyed. Curiously, the spacecraft had not received a single meteoroid hit during its eight-week lifetime. A similar detector in earth orbit would have expected an impact every two weeks. In all, the craft mapped 5 million square km (2 million square mi) of the moon and accomplished seventy-five percent of its goals.

Preliminary photo results showed large rocks on the surface, suggesting that it was strong enough to support a manned spacecraft. This proved that the landing of Luna 9 and Surveyor 1 on a hard surface was not a fluke. The photos also showed that the Ocean of Storms had 20 percent fewer craters than other smooth areas of the moon and would be a good candidate for a manned landing site.

ANOTHER RUSSIAN MOON SATELLITE

Now that Soviet probes had American company both on the surface and in orbit, continued robotic exploration of the moon started to take on an almost routine nature. The road to the moon had been paved and the highway was open for traffic. The next two years would see an unmatched flurry of spacecraft scuttling off to the moon.

Next up to our celestial neighbor was Luna 11, launched at 11:03 A.M., August 24, 1966. Initially, there was some mystery about the fate of Luna 11. Jodrell Bank reported that the craft's signals stopped 4 minutes after retrofire. Continued Soviet silence about the outcome of the mission fueled speculation that it had crashed or overshot the moon. The next night, as the moon rose above the English horizon, Jodrell Bank received a new burst of signals from the craft and there was no doubt that it was in lunar orbit.

Generally, little was said in the Soviet media about Luna 11, leading to speculation that it had partially failed. It is thought that Luna 11 carried a television system which did not operate properly. Jodrell Bank reported receiving signals similar to Luna 9's photo transmissions, but they were scrambled and the British could not construct images from them. In 1972, an illustration of Luna 11 was published in *Pokorenie Kosmosa* (Conquest of Space) and showed the craft was externally similar to Luna 10.

One month after Luna 11 departed earth, it was Surveyor's turn. The second craft in the American series lifted off at 8:32 A.M., September 20, 1966, and again carried only a television payload. About 16.5 hr after launch, a course correction burn was planned to aim the probe toward a lunar region called the Central Bay. However, when the engines were fired, only two of the three ignited, pushing Surveyor 2 into a one-revolution-per-second tumble from which the spacecraft never recovered. Surveyor 2 crashed in the area southeast of the crater Copernicus.

A THIRD RUSSIAN ORBITER

The Soviets finally mounted their own lunar photo reconnaissance when Luna 12 was launched from Tyuratam by the usual SL-6 Molniya booster at 11:42 A.M., October 22, 1966. The new orbiter left earth 21 days after transmissions ceased from Luna 11. The 1625-kg (3582-lb) battery-powered spacecraft rode atop the standard second generation Luna bus and propulsion system. The conical instrument section was referred to simply as the "apparatus compartment" and was surrounded by a cone-shaped radiator skirt. In addition to carrying scientific instruments similar to previous Russian orbiters, a surface photo-mapping system was housed in one of the strap-on modules attached to the bus. The main payload also remained on the spacecraft bus in order to use the stabilization system.

On October 25 the Jodrell Bank radio observatory confirmed that Luna 12 had entered lunar orbit at 11:47 P.M. Settling into a 133 × 1200-km

(82.6 × 745.7-mi) orbit inclined 10 degrees, the probe began lunar photography. Luna 12 thus became the ninth spacecraft to return lunar images. As was the usual Soviet practice, the imaging system used photographic film which was developed on board. The film was then scanned by a dual-mode facsimile machine. A low resolution quick-look mode allowed the entire image to be scanned at 67 lines per frame in 135 sec. The more interesting frames could then be selected for high-resolution 1100-line, 860-pixel-per-line transmission requiring 34 min. On October 29, 1966, Moscow television showed two photographs of the Sea of Rains and the crater Aristachus. Taken from between 100 and 340 km (62 and 211 mi), they were not as sharp as those returned by NASA's Lunar Orbiter, but still showed objects as small as 15 m (50 ft).

After the photo mission was complete, Luna 12 was spin-stabilized with a slow roll every 255 sec. The craft then repeated the micrometeor, gamma radiation, and gravity field observations performed by previous orbiters. It also tested the electric drive motors to be used in future lunar rovers.

SECOND U.S. ORBITER EVEN MORE SUCCESSFUL

America's Lunar Orbiter 2 rode its Atlas-Agena into the Florida sky at 6:21 P.M., November 6, 1966, and followed its predecessor on a flawless flight to the moon. The new orbiter was to investigate 13 primary and 17 secondary Apollo landing sites located just north of the moon's equator. Two days out, the craft's own engine was fired to give it a 22.8-m (74.8-ft)-per-sec correction to ensure a proper approach to the moon.

At 3:56 P.M., November 10, the orbiter approached within 2027 km (1260 mi) of the moon and fired its braking engine. Entering an initial 196 × 1871-km (122 × 1163-mi) orbit inclined 12.2 degrees, Lunar Orbiter 2 circled the moon every 3 hr and 38 min. On the fifteenth, the perilune was lowered to 50.5 km (31 mi) to ready the craft for its photographic mission due to begin on November 18.

A week later, on November 25, 208 of the planned 211 photographs had been taken, including large portions of the far side. Transmission of the photographs continued until December 6 when the high-gain antenna's transmitter failed. Three medium and two high-resolution images of Apollo landing site 1 yet remained to be transmitted. The loss of the five images was offset by adequate previous coverage.

The mission is best remembered for the "picture of the century," an oblique view looking across the crater Copernicus from an altitude of 45 km (28 mi). The image was a sensation in the newspapers and showed the three-dimensional character of the moon's surface as the crater's central peak rose 400 m (1300 ft). The orbiter also pinpointed Ranger 8's 13 × 14-m (43 × 46-ft) impact crater and even resolved its raised central peak. The craft also provided additional evidences of past lunar volcanic activity.

As the second American Lunar Orbiter looped around our satellite six and a half times a day, the robotic exploration of the moon seemed to lapse into an unexciting routine. However, the purpose of the missions, pathfinders for Apollo, still lent them an air of urgency. Only three years remained to fulfill President Kennedy's mandate to land men on the moon in the 1960s.

On December 9, the orbiter's engine was fired for 62 seconds to change the orbital plane to 17.5 degrees. The first ever change in plane of a lunar orbit was accomplished to provide greater tracking data of the moon's gravitational anomalies. Still in contact in 1967, Lunar Orbiter 2's micrometeor detectors received three hits before the craft was deliberately crashed into the far side of the moon on October 11.

Because of the success of Surveyor 1 and the two Lunar Orbiters, the heavier 1111-kg (2450-lb) science-oriented Surveyors 8, 9, and 10 were canceled in December 1966. NASA continued its policy of directing all its lunar efforts into engineering support of the Apollo manned landings. Science was no longer considered a goal even though the Surveyor had proven its ability to land on the moon.

AN IMPROVED RUSSIAN LANDER

The Soviet Union enjoyed its final 1966 lunar success when the second automatic lunar station (ALS), Luna 13, rose up from Tyuratam at 1:17 P.M., December 21. The 1620-kg (3571-lb) spacecraft was nearly identical to Luna 9 except that the 58-cm diameter lander now weighed 112 kg (250 lb) and carried several new soil analysis experiments.

Luna 13 followed the same flight sequence as the previous lander and a December 22 course correction aimed it toward the Ocean of Storms. After 79.7 hr of flight, the engine was fired at an altitude of 69.2 km (43 mi) to decelerate the craft for a landing. Less than a second before the spacecraft bus crashed at 30 km (18 mi) per hr, the Luna 13 lander was ejected with touchdown occurring at 9:01 P.M., December 24.

The landing occurred just before local sunrise about 400 km (250 mi) north of the Luna 9 site. Coming to rest in a slight depression at 18.9 degrees north, 62 degrees west, Luna 13 lay between the craters Seleucus and Sciaparelli in an area the Soviets called the "the lunar cosmodrome."

The mission objective was to study lunar soil composition as well as return more panoramic images. To do this, Luna 13 had two 1.5-m (5-ft) spring-loaded mechanical arms which extended two different instruments. Five minutes after landing, an arm-mounted "gunpowder jet device," or explosively driven impact probe, pushed a 5-cm (2-in) rod with a 3.5-cm (1.5-in) wide conical titanium tip into the lunar soil with a force of 7.9 kg (15.5 lb) for one second. This determined that the local lunar soil, up to a depth of 4.5 cm (2 in), had the consistency and load-bearing characteristics of average terrestrial soil.

The other arm had a soil density meter which probed the surface with gamma rays. This instrument consisted of a cesium-137 gamma radiation source, three gas-discharge detectors, and a shield to protect the detectors from the gamma-ray source. As the instrument lay on the surface, it irradiated the lunar soil. By measuring the proportion of gamma rays scattered back by Compton Effect radiation, or the change in wavelength of radiation scattered within a chemical element, it determined that the surface density to a depth of 15 cm (6 in) was approximately 0.8 g per cm^3. This indicated a loose surface soil layer much less dense than the moon's average density of 3.34 g cm^3.

Another check of the surface conditions was performed by a dynamograph, a device which converts mechanical energy into electrical energy at a rate proportional to the increase in the mechanical energy to be measured. This instrument was housed inside the lander's body and used piezoelectric transducers, or crystals which produce electricity when compressed or struck, to record the size and duration of the deceleration pulse when the lander thumped down at landing. Comparison of the Luna 13 dynamograph results with those obtained from laboratory comparison drop tests showed that the surface was solid and free from dust.

CHRISTMAS ON THE MOON

At 3:30 A.M. Christmas Day, the sun rose at the landing site and increased in elevation by 0.5 degrees per hr. Twenty hours after touchdown, a solar sensor activated the camera. The first photographs were made with the sun at an elevation of only 6 to 7 degrees and the camera automatically compensating for changing light conditions. The terrain was similar to that seen by Luna 9 although the previous craft landed in a hilly area. Luna 13 showed a flatter area with the horizon farther away.

On December 27, 1966, a large portion of a 360 degree panorama taken the previous day was shown in Moscow. It clearly showed the spacecraft's shadow, the deployed arms lying on the surface and two spring coils which were thrown out by the spacecraft when it landed. The photographs showed broken-up soil with grains up to several millimeters in size. Also visible were stones which apparently fell at slow speed and were ejecta from meteorite impacts, showing that the moon's surface was relatively firm.

The Luna 13 images were also received by Jodrell Bank. Bernard Lovell said the pictures were clear and showed the shadow of the lander on the surface. However, following the Russian protests after Jodrell Bank released the intercepted Luna 9 photos, Lovell declined to show them.

Infrared radiation from the surface was recorded by four radiometers mounted around the lander's circumference. They indicated the noontime temperature at the landing site would reach $117 \pm 3°C$ ($243 \pm 5°F$). Luna 13 also carried radiation measurement devices which were sensitive to cosmic rays. These reported that the normal level of radiation on the moon would not be immediately hazardous to human visitors.

Four more panoramas were transmitted with the sun reaching 32 degrees above the horizon before the craft's batteries gave out. It was hoped Luna 13 would last long enough to broadcast a New Year's message from the moon. However, the mission ended on December 30 when power was depleted.

Luna 13 was the last of the second-generation landers. As impressive as its achievements were, its limited capabilities paled compared to the American Surveyor lander. These shortcomings were to be addressed in the next generation of Lunas. Even as Luna 13 operated on the moon, new heavy landers were being developed by the Babakin Bureau to perform more complex analysis of the moon, including returning soil samples to earth and delivering roving explorers to travel over the surface.

Luna 13 was also the final Russian lunar exploration before the moon became an exclusively American playground. After a laborious development period, the American unmanned lunar exploration program was about to explode into a furious period of activity. The Russian efforts would seem minor in comparison. Indeed, the entire Lunar Orbiter and Surveyor programs would run their course before another Soviet craft would approach the moon.

APOLLO RECONNAISSANCE SUCCESSFUL

The first moon launch of 1967 saw Lunar Orbiter 3 take off at 8:17 P.M. on February 4. During its lunar scouting mission, the orbiter also located Surveyor 1 on a photo taken February 21 and showed the lander's elongated shadow in a field of shallow craters. The Apollo reconnaissance was very successful and, by April 1967, eight potential sites were selected for manned landings. Site 2 would receive the Lunar Module "Eagle" carrying Neil Armstrong and Buzz Aldrin just two years later. Additionally, the first three orbiters mapped 15.5 million square km (6 million square mi) of the moon's near side and 650,000 square km (250,000 square mi) of the far side for scientific purposes. The consecutive successes of the first three orbiters were surprises and allowed the remaining two to be dedicated for purely scientific purposes.

A BOUNCY LANDING

Following a perfect launch at 3:05 A.M. on April 17, 1967, Surveyor 3 sailed toward the moon. A course correction one day after launch aimed Surveyor 3 at the Ocean of Storms about 370 km (230 mi) south of the crater Copernicus. This time a new scientific instrument was added, a Soil Mechanics Surface Sampler (SMSS). This consisted of a 5 × 13-cm (2 × 5-in) scoop attached to a pantograph mechanical arm. This device was able to reach 1.5 m (5 ft) from the lander over an arc of 112 degrees and dig a trench up to half a meter (20 in) deep. Two additional mirrors allowed the camera to see underneath the spacecraft.

The spacecraft executed a perfect approach to the moon on April 20 and slowed to a near hover close to the surface. Then, just seconds before the vernier engines were to cut off to allow the craft to settle, the landing radar lost its lock on the ground. The guidance system automatically switched to inertial control, a system similar to an autopilot, and continued firing the engines. Surveyor 3 thus had the lowest landing speed of all the landers, but what followed bordered on the bizarre. The craft touched down at 8:04 P.M., then slowly rebounded 10.7 m (35 ft) back into space, its engines still firing. A slow 0.3-m (1-ft)-per-sec horizontal velocity carried it 6 m (20 ft) to the side where it again rebounded 3.4 m (11 ft) back into space and shuffled 2.4 m (8 ft) further to the side. A third rebound took it back up one more meter (3.3 ft) before a command from earth cut the engines and Surveyor 3 landed for the last time, sliding another 30 cm (1 ft). The three-bounce episode continued for 34 seconds before the craft came to rest on a 14-degree slope.

The multiple touchdowns clouded the mirrors used to view under the craft, but a study of the footprints provided extra data about the area's surface properties. During its operations, the lander returned 6326 television pictures and performed a series of tests with the soil scoop. A total of 5879 commands were sent over a total of 18.3 hr to dig four trenches, perform seven load-bearing tests and 13 impact tests of the lunar soil. The surface material acted like coarse damp beach sand, being cohesive and clumpy, but presented no difficulty to the soil scoop.

Although it did not survive the lunar night, Surveyor 3 made its mark as the first craft to send back images of both Venus and the earth. A total lunar eclipse on April 24 provided Surveyor with the unusual perspective, photographing the earth appearing as a ring, with the sun's illumination shining around the atmosphere. Coming only three months after the tragic Apollo 1 fire which killed three American astronauts during a ground test of the Apollo spacecraft, Surveyor 3's soft landing did much to bolster the sagging image of the American space program.

SUCCESS IN ORBIT, FAILURE ON THE SURFACE

The next Lunar Orbiter was dedicated to targets of scientific interest. After lifting off at 6:25 P.M. on May 4, 1967, the photographic probe joined the ranks of the orbiter predecessors by successfully going into lunar orbit on May 8. Lunar Orbiter 4 became the first polar orbiter, traveling in a high 2705 × 6034-km (1681 × 3750-mi) path inclined 85.5 degrees. This allowed for the 60-m resolution needed to study 99 percent of the moon's near side as well as part of the far side. Taking the first images of the moon's south pole was the highlight of the mission.

Surveyor 4 took off at 7:53 A.M., July 14, 1967, and was again targeted toward the moon's Central Bay. The spacecraft was a twin of Surveyor 3 and was to dig into the lunar soil once more. On July 16, the lander's retrorocket fired and began to slow the spacecraft. Then disaster struck. Two seconds before the motor was to burn out, contact was lost with Surveyor 4. Efforts to reestablish contact were abandoned the next day.

The sudden failure was a shock to JPL and NASA. The previous craft sent toward the Central Bay had also crashed and the destination seemed haunted. But Surveyor 4 would be NASA's last failure on the moon. Indeed, it was the last probe JPL would lose in space for the next twenty-six years.

SUCCESSES BUOY APOLLO EFFORT

The next launch, Lunar Orbiter 5, was the last of the phenomenally successful series of mapping spacecraft. Launched 6:33 P.M., August 1, 1967, the craft entered lunar orbit on August 5. After the orbit was trimmed to 100 × 6050-km (61 × 3759-mi), inclined 84.6 degrees, mapping began on August 6. By the twenty-seventh, all 212 frames had been transmitted to earth.

The final orbiter covered 36 sites of scientific interest on the near side, five more potential Apollo sites, several Surveyor sites, and completed mapping most of the far side. After the mapping mission was complete, the spacecraft was used as a practice target by the Apollo tracking network. Precision tracking allowed further investigation of the newly discovered mascons, showing their increased gravitational attraction could indeed pull the Apollo manned landers off course.

The Lunar Orbiter series was NASA's first completely successful spacecraft series. Performing beyond their creator's wildest dreams, the mappers marked a turning point in NASA deep-space exploration. In 800 days of lunar operations between the five orbiters, none suffered major failures and all accomplished their design goal. The craft received a total of 25,000 commands and executed 2000 maneuvers without an error. Additionally, only 18 meteoroid impacts were registered, proving the moon safe for an exposed astronaut. But beyond the needs of Apollo for which the craft were designed, the Lunar Orbiters also provided detailed images of never-before-seen areas on the moon. Their photographic results will be studied for many more years.

A CLIFFHANGER FLIGHT

Surveyor 5 got off to a good start toward the Sea of Tranquility after its 3:57 A.M. launch on September 8, 1967. This mission was the first American landing to carry an alpha-scattering experiment which would bombard the lunar surface with radiation, then analyze the reflected radiation to determine the chemical composition of the soil. However, the flight quickly turned into a cliffhanger when a leak developed in the fuel system's helium pressurization system after the mid-course correction. If the pressure fell too low, the helium would be unable to force the fuel into the engines as they fired to lower the craft to the moon and disaster would quickly follow.

To save the mission, a desperate plan was quickly devised which would use less helium. Instead of firing the main retrorocket at 83.5 km (52 mi), it would be fired at 45.7 km (28 mi). Upon burnout, Surveyor 5 would be a mere 1.34 km (0.8 mi) above the surface instead of the usual 10.7 km (6.6 mi). This would eliminate several minutes of vernier rocket firing time usually needed to lower the craft the additional 9.3 km (5.8 mi), but there would also be no margin for error. When the retrorocket burned out, the craft would still be falling at 96 km (60 mi) per hr and Surveyor's control system would have just seconds to further slow the craft to a safe landing speed. This would be a risky but necessary gamble to shorten the vernier burn time to within that allowed by the remaining helium supply.

Several vernier test firings to check out the crippled propulsion system had first pushed the craft off course toward one side of the moon, then back across to the other side. Surveyor 5 thus zigzagged toward the moon, its new target ending up some 29 km (18 mi) from its original target. By now, the overriding task was simply to save the spacecraft. When it approached the surface at 8:46 P.M., September 10, its descent speed was still 15 km (9 mi) per hr, the highest landing speed of all successful Surveyors. As if nothing were amiss, the lander slapped down on the 20 degree slope of a 9 ×12-m (30 × 39-ft) rimless crater on the Sea of Tranquility. The site, at 1.5 degrees north and 23.3 degrees east, was only 25 km (15.5 mi) from the future Apollo 11 landing area.

SURFACE CHEMISTRY STUDIED

Surveyor 5 went to work quickly. For the first time, in situ analysis of lunar material was done when the alpha-scattering experiment was dropped to the surface. A curium-252 radioactive source bombarded the soil with alpha particles and protons, then measured the backscatter of these particles. From this, the elemental makeup of lunar soil could be determined. The experiment showed that the composition of the soil was 15.5 to 21.5 percent silicon, 10 to 16 percent sulphur, 4.5 to 8.5 percent aluminum, with iron, cobalt, and nickel detected as well as small quantities of magnesium, carbon, and sodium. The experiment also detected 53 to 63 percent oxygen, indicating that the minerals present were in the form of oxides. This analysis was similar to terrestrial basalt and provided the first evidence that the composition of the moon was like volcanic rocks on earth.

A half-second burst from the vernier engines 53 hr after touchdown produced no craters and did little to disturb the soil. In all, Surveyor 5 returned 18,006 television images during its first lunar day. Reviving after the long night, it returned 1048 more on the second day. No imagery was done on the third day, but 64 more low-resolution images were returned on the fourth day of operations.

ANOTHER PERFECT MISSION

Following a flawless launch at 7:31 A.M., September 7, 1967, Surveyor 6 landed within 6.4 km (4 mi) of its target. The third attempt to soft land on the moon's Central Bay succeeded when Surveyor 6 came to rest at 0.5 degrees North and 1.4 degrees West on November 9, and performed a textbook-perfect mission. The spacecraft was identical to Surveyor 5 with the exception of a box-like hood covering the TV camera.

The new craft's alpha-scattering experiment showed that the soil was similar in makeup to that at the Surveyor 5 site. A total of 29,952 television pictures were returned before the craft was shut down for the night. Surveyor 5 was still active on the moon when the new craft arrived, but weak signals from Surveyor 5 prevented joint operations with both explorers.

The highlight of the mission came on November 17 when the vernier engines were fired for 2.5 sec. With that Surveyor 6 became the first spacecraft to liftoff from another world. The craft was thrust upwards 3 m (10 ft) and traveled 2.5 m (8 ft) to the west before thumping down again. The movement allowed stereoscopic analysis of the area and study of the original landing imprints to determine the mechanical properties of the surface. Unfortunately, the alpha-scattering experiment landed upside down.

A FINAL SURVEYOR FOR SCIENCE

The final Surveyor left earth at 1:30 A.M., January 7, 1968. The previous four landings had fulfilled the technical needs of Apollo and Surveyor 7 was released to scout a scientifically interesting site. Landing on the ejecta blanket thrown over the lunar highlands from the crater Tycho, the lander came to rest 29 km (18 mi) north of the crater at 40.9 degrees South and 11.5 degrees West. This was the farthest south of any area ever investigated on the moon. The first views from a highland area showed a surface scattered with rocks but with fewer small craters than mare areas.

This time, the craft was equipped with both a sample arm and an alpha-scattering experiment. This was fortuitous as, a day after landing, the soil analyzer refused to drop to the surface on command. A few well directed taps from the sample arm convinced the device to perform its duties. Later, the sample arm moved the analyzer to examine a rock, then the subsurface soil, in a 1-cm (0.4-in) trench dug by the arm. The analyzer determined that the local soil was lower in iron than the soils of the flat mare areas.

The sample arm was put through its paces when it performed 16 surface bearing-strength tests and dug seven trenches, one up to 15 cm (6 in) deep. The end scoop was also used to turn over a rock and "weigh" another by measuring the current needed to operate the arm motor. A figure of 2.4 to 3.1 g per cm^3 was obtained.

A total of 20,993 television images were returned on the first day. These included observations 15 hr after sundown which showed the sun's corona, or bright outer atmosphere, extending 34.8 million km (21.6 million mi) from its surface. Images taken of earth showed our home planet waxing and waning as the sun's phase angle changed while the moon moved around its orbit. The camera also detected two 1-watt lasers fired at the moon from California and Arizona. Nighttime temperatures reaching −107°C (−250°F) damaged the spacecraft's battery and only limited contact was possible on the second lunar day with 45 low-resolution pictures being returned.

Overall, the program had returned a scientific treasure of 87,700 television pictures showing the lunar surface, earth, the sun, the bright planets, and stars to the sixth magnitude. But, more important to Apollo,

Surveyor had proved the moon was safe for a manned landing. Apollo could confidently alight on a surface made up of earth-like basaltic material which behaved like wet beach sand. However, while the robotic landings gave the blessing for men to follow, their scientific return, although great, did little to resolve the truth between the three rival lunar formation theories—double planet (two bodies which evolved separately); splitting off from earth, where the moon was once part of earth; or capture, where the moon evolved elsewhere in the solar system and was gravitationally captured by the earth. Even today, 25 years later, this issue is not yet fully resolved.

A SOLITARY RUSSIAN MOON FLIGHT

The only Soviet lunar mission in 1968 was a bit of a mystery. When Luna 14 was launched from the usual earth parking orbit on April 7, 1968, the officially announced mission objectives sounded superficial. Mstislav Keldysh, the President of the Soviet Academy of Sciences, stated that the flight would have great significance for future ambitious flights to the moon. No photographs of this spacecraft have ever been released but it is believed to have been configured like Luna 12.

As Luna 14 approached the moon on April 10, it became the fourth Soviet lunar satellite. The stated objectives were to study the relationships between the masses of the earth and moon and study the propagation and stability of radio signals sent to and from the craft in lunar orbit. Solar radiation and the lunar gravitational field were measured and further tests of geared electric drive motors for future lunar rovers were performed.

Luna 14 was the last of the second generation Lunas. In light of the 15-month delay since the previous Luna mission, it is likely this was simply a stopgap mission to provide continuity in lunar exploration before the delayed introduction of the third generation Lunas.

Throughout the 9-year history of the Luna program, the series represented an enormous technical undertaking which enjoyed the full support of the Soviet government. While military personnel were involved in launching the Lunas, the lunar exploration program was basically a civilian operation under the guidance of the Soviet Academy of Sciences.

Over the course of the Luna program, only two of the thirteen landers launched, Lunas 9 and 13, succeeded in reaching the surface. This contrasts with 5 out of 7 touchdowns for the American Surveyor landers. The Luna 10 and 11 radiation and meteoric environment missions, as well as the Luna

12 and 14 photographic missions, supplemented the rudimentary Soviet landers to provide broad general knowledge about the moon. These simple missions, while achieving scientific and propaganda firsts, merely acted as pathfinders for more advanced future craft which would study the moon in greater detail.

4  Russian Robots on the Moon

AMERICA ABANDONS THE MOON

After Surveyor 7 completed its mission, U.S. unmanned lunar exploration ended for the next quarter-century. An American presence on the moon did continue for the next five years, but only under the manned Apollo program. The goal of the unmanned explorations had focused increasingly on support of the politically motivated Apollo manned landings. When the manned lunar landing goal was achieved in 1969, further unmanned scientific explorations were canceled by the cost-conscious Nixon administration which was trying to finance the Vietnam War.

The initial American manned landings were to concentrate on the mechanical and engineering aspects of landing men on the moon. Their primary mission was simply to get Americans on the moon and return them safely. Actual science on the moon was still a secondary objective. Without the specter of Russian competition to drive Apollo after the first manned landing in 1969, a fickle Congress and unsupportive White House canceled the final three of the planned Apollo landings. Expensive rocket hardware built to send the science-oriented Apollos 18, 19, and 20 to the moon were never launched and became massive museum pieces for amazed tourists and mourned by those who dreamed of reaping American scientific glory with these great metallic beasts. When Apollo 17 lifted off from the moon in 1972, America totally abandoned further lunar exploration. For the rest of the 1970s, only robotic machines designed by the Babakin Bureau and carrying the symbol of the Red Star approached the moon.

But in early 1969, the moon race did not have a sure outcome or victor. NASA gained more confidence with each success, but not knowing what the Russians were up to worried many American officials. Perhaps the Russians had a trick or two up their sleeve? It was still very much a race.

A CHANGE OF DIRECTION

The soft-landing success of Luna 9 in 1966 was the culmination of a half-decade effort begun in the early 1960s by Korolyov and Babakin. After the first historic landing, an often spirited scientific debate was waged between Soviet scientists as to how best to continue the exploration of the moon. Some saw robotic spacecraft as the most practical method while others favored either manned exploration or a combination of the two. By mid-1966, the debate seemed to be settled in favor of continuing robotic exploration while the separate Russian manned lunar program pressed ahead on its own.

On July 11, 1966, cosmonaut Vladimir Komarov revealed that the robotic course had been chosen. Komarov told the Japanese newspaper *Asahi Evening News* that the Soviets would surely beat the Americans to the moon, but before men landed there, robotic craft would first land and pick up rock samples for return to earth.[1] Komarov was speaking of craft already on the drawing board at the Babakin Bureau which would be revealed to the world as Luna 16.

By the end of 1968, Babakin had completed development of the massive third generation Luna lander. The five-ton craft was built to land two different types of payloads on the moon: either a small spacecraft capable of returning samples of lunar material to earth, or a remote control-led rover called Lunokhod which would scout wide areas of the lunar surface. In the 1960s, the United States had considered putting heavy emphasis on automation, but rejected this route in favor of manned exploration of the moon. Now such robotic explorations were to be almost exclusively a Russian domain.

In December 1968, Apollo 8 carried Americans into lunar orbit while the manned flight of a Russian Zond spacecraft around the moon was delayed. The Soviets hoped the embarrassment of losing the race to send men to the moon would be eased by obtaining lunar soil samples with a robotic spacecraft.

NEW LUNA A TECHNICAL MARVEL

The third generation Luna was the first created exclusively by Babakin. Having previously assumed responsibility for preparing lunar and planetary spacecraft, Babakin gained more autonomy after the untimely death of his former mentor, Korolyov. He now put his own ideas to work with a vengeance.

Babakin's new lunar creation was a weird conglomeration of eleven fuel tanks, connecting struts, protruding antennae and landing legs. Perched like a monument above this structure was the cylindrical instrument compartment of the ascent stage topped by a small spherical return capsule. Like the Apollo manned lunar craft which started its moon journey as a 2.6-million-kg (6-million-lb) machine only to return to earth as a cramped 6.5-ton capsule, Luna also shed 99 percent of its mass, returning only the 40-kg (88-lb) sphere to earth. To the untrained eye, the machine looked like pure Rube Goldberg, but it was, in fact, extremely functional and state-of-the-Soviet-art.

Although Babakin answered to no one, he did carry over one key trait from Korolyov's design philosophy: simplicity of design and the pure functionality of the hardware. Compared to NASA space probes which were pieced together like fine jewelry, Luna looked as if it had been built in a foundry. But, though the craft looked stange, it was actually a simple machine. In this simplicity lay the key to its eventual success.

The craft consisted of three sections: a lunar orbit insertion stage which was jettisoned prior to descent, a lunar landing stage with a soil-sampling mechanism, and an ascent stage with the earth-return capsule. Early versions of the new lander had a total mass of 5800 kg (12,787 lb). Most of this was propellant as the craft had not only to enter lunar orbit and land, but it had to take off again. As the spacecraft would appear on the moon resting on its four short landing legs, it stood 3.96 m (13 ft) high and an equal span between the landing legs. The craft was powered only by batteries.

The lunar orbit insertion stage, which decelerated the craft into lunar orbit, consisted of four strap-on tanks which piped nitric acid and hydrazine fuel to the same engine used for lunar descent. Nestled in a box between one pair of tanks were the astro-orientation sensors while the nitrogen gas-powered attitude stabilization thrusters were between the other pair.

The core structure of the new Luna spacecraft was the descent stage which was topped by a toroidal instrument section. Four shock-absorbing landing legs and the lunar drilling apparatus were attached to the fuel tank structure. The single-chamber throttle-controlled KTDU-417 engine, rated at a maximum thrust of 1850 kg (4079 lb), was used for both lunar orbit insertion and descent. The basic structure of the insertion and descent stages was used for all future Lunas, including orbiter missions.

On a platform atop the descent-stage instrument section was the ascent stage carrying a 0.45-m (18-in) diameter sample return capsule. The upper part of the stage consisted of a $\frac{1}{2}$-m (20-in) diameter cylindrical command and control section with four protruding rod antennae. Below this were three fuel tanks feeding nitrogen tetroxide and hydrazine to a single-chamber 1250-kg (2756-lb)-thrust KRD-61 engine. This stage used the lander as a launch platform.

THIRD GENERATION MISSION PROFILE

The third generation Luna missions all originated from Tyuratam. Although essentially still in development, the SL-12 Proton booster was to be used to loft the heavy Lunas and their escape stage into an earth parking orbit. Near the end of the first revolution around the earth, the escape stage would propel the Luna into a trajectory toward the moon.

After separating from the booster, Luna would stabilize itself for a 4.5 day flight to the moon. All of the third generation landers would enter a precise lunar orbit before landing. Orbit insertion was to be accomplished by a 705-m (2220-ft)-per-sec retro burn at an altitude of 110 km (68 mi) above the lunar far side.

Unlike the second generation landers which were restricted by a direct trajectory to the "magic spot" 62 to 64 degrees along the western equator, the new Lunas could theoretically land anywhere by descending from lunar orbit. This was useful for landing rovers at diverse locations, but earth-return navigational constraints similar to those which limited second generation landers to one area of the moon also limited the soil-sample return missions to an area around 56 degrees east along the equator.

Several days of tracking would establish the craft's orbit, and refinements were to be made to align the orbital path with the potential landing site. Shortly before landing, a 20-m (66-ft)-per-sec engine burn would lower the orbit to 20 × 110 km (12 × 68 mi) and adjust the inclination. Luna's insertion tankage was then to be jettisoned and fuel flow drawn from the descent-stage tanks.

Unlike the manned Apollo which used a lengthy shallow descent trajectory in case the landing needed to be aborted, Luna could use brute force to quickly drop out of orbit. The entire orbital velocity could be canceled in one 265-sec engine firing over the landing site. Luna would then drop straight to the surface with no horizontal velocity. Within 2 minutes Luna would drop from its 20-km (12-mi) orbital altitude to a 600-m (1969-ft) altitude. A radar altimeter would then fire the descent-stage engine again to slow the craft to 2.5 m (8 ft) per sec at an altitude of 20 m (66 ft). With no provision to preview the landing site, Luna would then commit to a go-for-broke landing no matter what lay on the terrain below. The main engine would be cut off and the final descent would use lower-thrust secondary engines to minimize disturbance of the surface.

SAMPLING ANOTHER WORLD

Upon landing, twin facsimile cameras would return a stereo image of the surface within range of the soil-sampling mechanism. The cameras were mounted on a forked boom tilted 50 degrees from vertical and extending from the lander's tank assembly. This allowed them to scan the sample area between two landing foot pads and later to view the insertion of the soil-sample package into the return capsule. The cameras' protruding appearance on their mounting booms were reminiscent of lobster eyes.

The Soil Sample Assembly (SSA) was to be berthed and locked in position next to the sample-return capsule during flight. An hour after landing, the core-sample drill mechanism was to be lowered to the ground by a boom pivoting at the base of the lander. The sampling mechanism reached 0.8 m (2.95 ft) beyond the lander and could sweep a 100-degree arc.

Inside the SSA was the drill motor, transmission screw, rotator and percussion mechanism, and the core-sampling drill stem. The drill stem consisted of a hollow tube with teeth cut into the leading edge. The drill could reach a maximum depth of 35 cm (13.8 in) and cut into solid rock if necessary. A clean-cut pillar of undisturbed rock would enter the hollow drill. A spiral pattern inside the tube helped hold the lunar material. Readings of the drill-motor current, drill depth and temperature would allow comparison with test drilling of terrestrial samples to determine lunar soil properties.

After the drilling was complete, the SSA was to be raised and the drill head rotated 180 degrees. The pivoting arm engaged a socket on the return stage for stability. The core sample was then to be transferred into a hermetic container and sealed inside the return capsule. The capsule door was to be hermetically sealed when a mousetrap-like spring mechanism snapped it shut..

LUNAR LIFTOFF

The manner in which Luna returned its precious cargo to earth dictated stringent navigational requirements on the lunar landing site. Just as the second generation Luna landers used a simple ballistic trajectory which intercepted the moon at 63 degrees west, the new Lunas used a direct three-day ballistic trajectory to return to earth. To accomplish this, the craft had to lift off from the moon at 56 degrees east along the equator. From this position, a vertical liftoff and acceleration to 2700 m (8858 ft) per sec would assure a ballistic trajectory which would automatically intercept earth's atmosphere.

Complicating this simple navigation was the effect of lunar libration. As the moon revolves around earth each month, its rhythmical nodding and rocking must be taken into account. The exact liftoff point to assure a proper aim toward earth slowly describes a circle at the 56-degree-east location. Luna had to land in a spot which would have moved to the proper liftoff point a day after landing.

Luna had to lift off from the moon at the exact instant the projected three day trajectory, constantly altered by libration, swept across the 80 × 100 km (50 × 61 mi) recovery area in Kazakhstan. To determine this moment, the lander's exact location and attitude on the moon had to be known. Ground controllers would then calculate the deviation from vertical and update the ascent-stage guidance equipment. A signal from earth would then fire the ascent stage at the proper moment.

GETTING BACK HOME

Shortly before entering the atmosphere, the spherical capsule was to be released. Heavy batteries and transmitting equipment were placed at the bottom of the capsule to shift the center of gravity and stabilize the capsule during the brutal but short entry into the atmosphere. This automatically placed the thickest portion of the heat shield against the area from which the heat of atmospheric friction would come. Instead of using a skipping reentry like Apollo which reduced deceleration loads to 10 *g*s, Luna would slam into the atmosphere like a bullet plunging into water, producing a deceleration of 350 *g*s.

Once in the lower atmosphere, the capsule's upper cover was to be ejected. Upon deployment of the bright orange parachute, flexible recovery beacon antennas would uncoil and a cloud of metallic needles would be released to mark the location on search radars. The capsule was buoyant in case it landed in water, and two sausage-shaped balloon floats would keep the antennae above water. An oscillator circuit would broadcast a recovery beacon signal which sounded somewhat like a tired cricket.

The Luna sample-return capsule was among the most tested pieces of Russian space hardware developed up to that time. Considering the torture awaiting it on entry into earth's atmosphere, the device had to be tested in ways never done before. Several versions of the capsule were built. They were dropped from airplanes over the sea, mountains, deserts, and forests. They were shaken on vibration stands, placed in vacuum chambers, and seared in plasma to simulate the conditions of atmospheric entry.

This author once spoke to Alexie Milovanov, who in the 1960s and 1970s was the chief engineer of the Lavochkin Association, which built the capsule. He related that early in the testing of the capsule, it was placed in a special centrifuge which simulated the crushing 350-g entry into the atmosphere. On the first trials, the interior of the capsule was smashed. To give an idea of the effect of such forces, the Russian word Milovanov used to describe the capsule's interior after being crushed, translates into English as "garbage."[2] Such tests revealed the weaknesses of the design and they were effectively corrected.

MYSTERY MISSIONS

In December 1968, America achieved an important space goal with the Apollo program: orbiting three men around the moon. The Apollo 8's ten lunar orbits were a crucial test prior to committing Apollo to an actual manned landing. Its success enormously boosted American prestige and showed that the U.S. was close to claiming the manned lunar prize.

Three weeks after Apollo 8's lunar-orbiting astronauts returned to a hero's welcome on earth, the first Luna soil-sample return mission was launched. On January 19, 1969, the Soviet's scientific reputation and political pride were put to the test as the first Proton booster used in the Luna program rose from Tyuratam. As the booster failed in flight, any hope of recouping Soviet prestige in the race for the moon was dashed. The mission was relegated to official obscurity. A similar fate awaited another sample-return mission launched the following June 4. As the booster rose into space in an effort to beat Apollo 11 to the moon, disaster again struck it down.

One month later, another Proton booster worked perfectly and Luna 15 finally succeeded in leaving the earth just days before Apollo 11. Details of the Luna 15 mission, its objective, and ultimate fate remained a mystery for many years. American space officials worried that the Soviets would attempt a space propaganda coup that would upstage the Apollo 11 landing. It had been just over a year since the last Luna probe had flown to the moon and even activity with the Zond moon probes, a series of unmanned tests of manned lunar spacecraft, remained strangely quiet. NASA feared that an unmanned Luna craft would land just ahead of Apollo, grab a sample of lunar material, and return it to earth before Apollo attempted the same goal. Such a feat would be a tremendous Soviet propaganda victory in the moon race.

LUNA 15 TARGETED TOWARD LUNAR SURFACE

Luna 15 departed from the earth at 5:55 A.M., Moscow time, July 13. The craft traveled the usual single revolution in an earth parking orbit before being dispatched to the moon. The timing of Luna's launch would place the craft at the moon just as the Apollo 11 astronauts were preparing to leave earth for their journey to the moon. As British and American tracking stations watched the mission unfold, it became apparent that Luna 15 was indeed racing with Apollo. However, Soviet silence frustrated western efforts to fully understand what was happening.

After a 102-hr flight from earth, Luna 15 looped behind the moon. Firing its engine on the far side of the moon, the probe entered lunar orbit at 1:00 P.M., July 17. Luna 15's initial orbit ranged 55×203 km (34×126 mi), inclined 120.5 degrees. By now, Apollo 11 was also en route to the moon. Maneuvering on July 19 and 20 trimmed Luna 15's orbit to 16×110 km (10×68 mi), inclined 127 degrees with a period of 114 min. It was clear to observers that Luna 15 was preparing for a significant maneuver. Veteran Luna tracker Bernard Lovell stated that he expected that this stage of the Soviet mission was the beginning of something, not the end.[3]

At the very culmination of the U.S./U.S.S.R. space race, the secrecy surrounding the mission of Luna 15 delighted the news media. The fantastic story of the first manned landing on the moon was exciting, but the race with the Russian mystery ship made the adventure even more thrilling.

Then, on July 20, 1969, Neil Armstrong and Buzz Aldrin achieved mankind's ultimate exploratory goal: they landed on the moon. After twelve years of cosmic competition, American astronauts walked on the moon and claimed the political and scientific lunar prize as a Soviet mystery ship circled overhead. The drama was played on a world-wide stage.

On its 52nd orbit, two hours before Apollo 11 was due to lift off from the moon, Luna 15 began its descent to the Sea of Crises at 6:47 P.M., July 21. A short time later, an official announcement stated that while the Apollo 11 astronauts were still on the moon, Luna 15 had reached the surface in a preset area. The statement fell short of admitting that Luna 15 had failed. Only after Apollo 11 had departed from the moon and was bound for earth did it become clear that the Luna 15 mission had ended disastrously.

Luna 15 apparently fired its braking engine for 4 min and began its drop toward the lunar surface, but then the mission ran into trouble. As Luna 15 descended, the engine did not refire to make the final deceleration before landing and the 1770-kg (3902-lb) lander crashed. Jodrell Bank, measuring the Doppler shift of Luna's signals, estimated the craft impacted at a speed of 480 km (298 mi) per hr at 17 degrees North and 60 degrees East on the Sea of Crises, approximately 800 km (500 mi) from Apollo 11 on the Sea of Tranquility.

History cannot record what might have happened if Luna 15 had succeeded. Nor can it record what might have happened if Apollo had failed catastrophically, causing the deaths of the astronauts, while Luna succeeded. If Luna 15 had beaten Apollo back to earth with its cargo of lunar samples, it would have been both a Soviet scientific triumph and a political embarrassment for the United States. After the U.S. marshaled the greatest government and industrial alliance since World War II for the purpose of beating the Russians to the moon, losing the moon race to a robot by a margin of hours would have been a bitter blow. If Apollo 11 had crashed, a public outcry against risking lives in space might have ended a glorious period in American science.

ROBOTS AND MEN TO THE MOON

The next Soviet lunar attempt using the Proton booster came on September 23. Shortly after ignition, the escape stage malfunctioned and stranded what was called Cosmos 300 in low earth orbit. Another Soviet lunar attempt, Cosmos 305, resulted one month later. Launched on October 22, it also remained stranded in low earth orbit.

In November, 1969, Apollo 12 landed two American astronauts on the Ocean of Storms. The second U.S. manned landing was highlighted by a precision landing only 200 m (660 ft) from the Surveyor 3 robot craft which had arrived three years before. As astronauts Pete Conrad and Alan Bean made two moon walks, one visiting the derelict Surveyor 3, the Soviets had yet to mount a successful soft landing with their unmanned third generation Lunas.

In February 1970, yet another Russian lunar launch failed when the Proton booster malfunctioned. After this string of Proton failures, the Luna flights ceased for half a year while improvements were made to the booster.

Two months later, Apollo 13 was scheduled to land the third American crew on the moon. Fate, however, reserved Apollo 13's destiny for something far different. While more than 322,000 km (200,000 mi) from earth, an oxygen tank in the Apollo service module exploded. For the next four days, people all over the world sat on the edge of their seat as the moon landing was aborted and Apollo 13 bravely limped home to earth from what could have been a fatal space disaster.

SOVIET SUCCESS AT LAST

Seven months after the previous Soviet lunar effort, Luna 16 was launched at 4:26 P.M., September 12, 1970. This time, everything worked perfectly and the Proton's escape stage boosted Luna 16 toward the moon. On September 17 Luna 16 entered a circular 111-km (69-mi), 119-min lunar orbit with a 70-degree inclination. Refinements made on September 18 and 19 altered Luna's orbit to 15 × 106 km (9 × 66 mi), inclined 71 degrees.

At 6:06 A.M., September 20, the Computing and Coordinating Center radioed the landing instructions to Luna's computer. Luna's retrorocket fired at 8:12 A.M. and the descent to the surface began. At a 600-m (1969-ft) altitude, the retrorocket fired again for the final approach. At 2 m (6 ft), the last of the rockets were cut off. Luna 16 dropped to the surface at 8:18:20 A.M. on the the Sea of Fertility at 0 degrees, 41 seconds South and 56 degrees, 18 seconds East. The site was in one of the oldest ringed basins on the moon, but the material which fills the basin is underlain by younger ejecta material from other basins. As seen from earth, the landing area was on the "Man-in-the-Moon's" left cheek.

Similar to the famous "We-came-in-peace-for-all-mankind" plaque attached to the Apollo 11 Lunar Module "Eagle," Luna 16 also had a plaque attached to its landing gear. The inscription read "Union of Soviet Socialist Republics, Luna 16, September 1970." Bracketing the inscription was the Soviet hammer and sickle and an engraving of Luna on the moon with the earth in the background on which the Soviet Union was clearly outlined.

An hour after landing Luna 16 drilled for 7 min and reached a depth of 35 cm (13.8 in). Here, the drill mechanism either struck bedrock or a buried stone and drilling was stopped to prevent possible damage to the sample collector. A 101-g (3.5-oz) soil sample was gathered in a core sample 18 by 330 mm (0.7 by 13 in) in size.

A RETURN TO EARTH

After a 26-hr and 25-min stay on the moon, the spherical sample-return capsule was launched by a command from earth. Using the descent stage as a launch platform, the ascent stage lifted off at 10:43 A.M., September 21. Accelerating to a velocity of 2708 m (8885 ft) per sec, it entered a direct ascent, earth-return trajectory. The lunar descent stage continued to transmit temperature, radiation, and engineering data. The return capsule struck the atmosphere at 8:10 A.M., September 24. Entry was at a speed of 11 km (6.8 mi) per sec at an angle of 60 degrees above the horizon. This produced a temperature of 10,000°C (18,032°F) in the shock wave ahead of the capsule.

At a height of 14.5 km (9 mi), the craft had slowed to 300 m (984 ft) per sec. An accelerometer then signaled the release of the drogue chute. At 11 km (6.8 mi) altitude, a barometer signaled the opening of the larger recovery parachute and started the radar transponder, a device which amplified signals from search radars, greatly enhancing the ability of search teams to locate the moon craft. While still at 2 km (1.2 mi) altitude, the capsule was spotted by a recovery helicopter. The landing occurred at 8:26 A.M. about 80 km (50 mi) southeast of the town of Dzhezkazgan, Kazakhstan. This was just several hundred kilometers northeast of the Tyuratam launch site. It was then returned to a special lunar receiving laboratory at the Soviet Academy of Sciences in Moscow. Total mission time was 11 days, 16 hr.

MORE POLITICS

After six attempts over a 20-month period the Russians had managed to return a lunar sample to earth. The Soviet triumph received little publicity, however, as the world's attention focused on a crisis in the Middle East. The success of two Apollo manned landing followed by the drama of the Apollo 13 abort had also dulled the public's appetite for lunar spectaculars.

The success of the completely automatic soil-sample-return mission was a major engineering and scientific achievement. However, while the mission was a technical marvel, the scientific achievements of Luna 16 were small compared to Apollo. The primary contribution of the Soviet mission may actually have been the competition it fostered for Apollo which caused that program to continue in the face of cutbacks in NASA's budget.

Academician Boris N. Petrov claimed the unmanned Luna sample-return missions were carried out at one-twentieth to one-fiftieth the cost of the American manned flights to the moon.[4] U.S. experts countered that there was no reliable measure of Soviet costs available for comparison and that Luna was extremely limited in its scope compared to the activities of American lunar astronauts. Once they landed on the moon, Apollo astronauts performed a much broader scientific investigation. They were able not only to set up additional science experiments which were left on the moon but to select as well specific and more interesting geological samples instead of "random grabs." Comparing the Apollo and Luna missions on a cost per unit of soil sample, Apollo was cheaper. Luna returned 101 g (3.5 oz) of lunar material versus the tens of kilograms from Apollo 11 alone.

The Luna 16 success also rekindled blunt attacks on the United States by the Soviet propaganda machine. Using the lunar achievement to "prove" the superiority of communism over western democracies, the harshness of articles appearing in *Pravda* rivaled those from the beginning of the space age a decade before. *Pravda* reported that the American Apollo program with its risk of human life was fitting "in a country where...with unusual ease they murder presidents, candidates for the presidency and public figures, where armed clashes on racial grounds take a daily toll..." The Party newspaper went on to say that Soviet science "has chosen its own route."[5]

The decades since the flight of Luna 16 have placed the mission in a better perspective, away from the heat of the race to the moon and the abrasive politics of the cold war. The craft, designed by Babakin's team and built in the shops of the Lavochkin Association, showed great ingenuity and the flight's success was a marvelous achievement in space exploration.

LUNA 16 RESULTS

Preliminary Luna 16 sample results were reported by academician Alexander Vinogradov to the second annual Lunar Science Conference held in Houston, Texas, in January 1971. Clearly, the Soviets were happy to have lunar samples of their own about which to report. Vinogradov announced the conclusion that the Luna 16 material was very similar to that returned by Apollo 11 from the Sea of Tranquility and by Apollo 12 from the Ocean of Storms. Vinogradov added that the low content of the rare-earth elements titanium and zirconium oxide in the Luna sample was the greatest difference from Apollo. The Luna samples did have a greater ferric oxide content. He also noted that the rocks from the Luna and two Apollo landing sites were largely basaltic rock fragments and impact produced glassy fragments of basaltic composition. Spherical glazed particles, which looked like droplets similar to tektites found on earth, were called "cosmic globules" by Soviet scientists. They probably originated in impact craters.

Early analysis of the Luna sample identified 70 chemical elements as well as short-lived radionuclides formed by the action of the solar wind. No unknown elements were found in the sample. The basalts were composed mainly of pyroxene, plagioclase, olivine, and ilmenite—the main elements of rock on earth—as well as mesostasis minerals. Tests showed that the lunar soil was a better insulator against heat transfer than the best insulating materials on earth. Another interesting property is that the sample easily retained static electricity and clung to organic glass and polyfluoroethylene resin surfaces. In spite of easily passing through sieves, the material also tended to clump together like wet beach sand.

NEW EXPLORER PERFECTED

While Luna 16 was restricted to investigating its immediate vicinity, the next Russian lander carried an amazing machine which would expand Soviet lunar explorations. Luna 17 deposited a wheeled robotic mobile laboratory called "Lunokhod" which would explore extended areas by remote control.

The genesis of the Lunokhod rover (pronounced "Luna-hod") dates to the birth of the space age. Shortly after the first satellite, Sputnik, was launched in 1957, Soviet authorities released a film showing plans conceived by Yuri Khlebtsevich in 1955 for a remote-controlled, television-equipped "tankette" to robotically explore large areas of the moon. If the film had been released before Sputnik, it would have been dismissed as Disney-like science fiction. The success of Sputnik, however, showed the world that Soviet science had the potential of accomplishing such a mission. But as the political, technical, and personal fortunes of Russian space exploration played out, it would be 13 years before Khlebtsevich's pre-Sputnik prophecies were realized.

The Lunokhod which reached the moon in 1970 was similar to lunar rover concepts proposed by U.S. aerospace companies in the early 1960s. Indeed, Lunokhod's wire mesh wheels closely resembled an American design. However, the American Prospector lunar rover had been canceled years before, partly because it clashed with the politically mandated Apollo program for the human exploration of the moon.

WHEELS ON THE MOON

Luna 17 was launched at 5:44 P.M., November 10, 1970. The craft was similar to Lunas 15 and 16 in that it used the same descent stage to land on the moon. However, in place of the lunar ascent stage and earth return capsule, a new robotic rover was bolted to a flat platform above the lander. After a five-day flight, it entered an initial circular 84-km (52-mi) retro-grade orbit inclined 141 degrees with a period of 116 min. The next day, the perilune was lowered to 19 km (12 mi). At 6:41 A.M. on the seventeenth, the braking engine was fired and descent to the surface began. The craft then approached the moon in a manner similar to Luna 16.

Touchdown occurred at 6:47 A.M. in the northwestern part of the Sea of Rains. The site at 38.3 degrees North and 35 degrees West was on the inner slope of a shallow crater 150 m (492 ft) in width. Two pairs of ramps, one forward and one aft, were included in case one was blocked by an obstacle. The rover's high gain antenna was deployed and radio links with earth were established at 7:20 A.M. The first television images were returned at 8:31 A.M. and showed that the lander was on a level surface. Explosive bolts then released the rover. Three hours after landing, Lunokhod rolled down the forward ramp and became the first self-propelled, wheeled vehicle on the moon. The propulsion undercarriage had a mass of 105 kg (230 lb on earth). Each wheel had an independent two-speed electric-drive motor and a small explosive drive-shaft cutter to disengage the wheel if the motor or wheel froze up in lunar dust. Lunokhod was capable of traveling 0.8 to 2 km per hr (0.5 to 1.2 mi per hr). Automatic sensors applied disc brakes if, while traveling, the slope angle became too steep. These brakes also held the vehicle at night. The rover turned by stopping one set of wheels and powering the other. Titanium blades on the wheels acted as cleats to help propel the vehicle through lunar dust.

The tub-shaped instrument compartment was covered by a convex lid with solar cells on the inside. The lid was opened during the day to charge the rover's batteries and closed at night to retain warmth. Lunokhod was the first Soviet lunar explorer since Luna 3 to use solar cells for power.

Lunokhod sprouted numerous antennae and television cameras, giving it the appearance of a big silver bug. The rover was not a true autonomous robot, but was controlled by a team of drivers at Zv'zdnyy Gorodok, the Soviet manned space center near Moscow. The Lunokhod was basically controlled like today's radio-controlled toy cars, and some critics of unmanned robotic lunar exploration called the rover just that, citing the limited scope of investigations possible without on-site human intervention.

The Lavochkin Association oversaw the entire design of Lunokhod, but the propulsion chassis was designed by a team led by Chief Designer Dr. Alexander Kermurjian of the Industrial Transport Institute of the Ministry of Defense Industries. The Institute for Space Research provided the instruments.

ROVING SCIENCE ON THE MOON

The rover's instruments for lunar-surface studies included two television and four high-resolution facsimile cameras, the RIFMA X-ray spectrometer for soil analysis, an odometer-speedometer assembly, and a surface penetrometer which would test the load-bearing strength of the soil. Other instruments were an X-ray telescope for astronomical studies, cosmic ray instruments, and a French-supplied retroreflector which would bounce laser beams back to earth.

The most successful instrument beside the television cameras was the roentgen isotopic fluorescence method of analysis (RIFMA), which used an X-ray emission to scan lunar rocks. The instrument worked by focusing a beam of electrons on the sample to be analyzed. The electron beam rearranged the electron shells of the atoms in the sample, inducing the sample to emit X-rays whose spectrum was measured to determine concentrations of aluminum, silicon, magnesium, potassium, calcium, iron, and titanium.

Lunokhod also carried a zenith-looking X-ray telescope. This was used for studying celestial X-irradiation from a more stable location than free-flying rockets or satellites. X-ray exposures of up to six hours in length were taken when the rover was parked. This is 1000 times that possible by an instrument carrying sub-orbital sounding rockets launched from earth, and it resulted in a ten fold increase in sensitivity.

At the time of Lunokhod 1's mission, little was known about celestial X-rays, but it was theorized that they originated from diffuse superheated gas in intergalactic space. It was further theorized that this hot gas might be the matter holding the Universe together gravitationally and preventing its expansion forever following the "Big Bang" 15 to 20 billion years ago. Data from Lunokhod's X-ray telescope would play an important part in understanding this celestial puzzle.

The rover carried a 3.7-kg (8.2-lb) French laser retroreflector consisting of 14 10-cm (4-in) tetrahedral corner cube prisms mounted above the forward cameras. The reflectors were uncovered at night while the rover was parked. Laser shots were fired from the 262-cm (103-in) Shajn telescope at the Crimean Astrophysical Observatory in the Russian Crimea and the 102-cm (40-in) telescope located at Pic du Midi, France. By precisely measuring the time interval between the laser shot and its reflected return, the exact distance to the moon could be calculated to within centimeters.

During the first lunar night on December 5, Russian scientists were successful in receiving laser "echoes" off Lunokhod's reflectors, while the French were not. Speculation was that the French were given erroneous position data so that the Soviets would find the rover first and be able to claim that honor.[6]

Attached to the rear of the rover's undercarriage was a spiked free-wheeling "ninth wheel" which measured the true speed of the rover compared to the drive wheels which often slipped in loose dust. This free wheel was part of an instrument called "PROP," a Russian acronym for surface evaluation instrument, which also contained the penetrometer. Also called the "passability assessment instrument," the penetrometer was a conical tool with a flat cruciform face which was forced into the lunar soil, then turned 180 degrees. The force needed to penetrate the surface and rotate the tool was measured and its depth recorded by television.

The two vidicon cameras were mounted on the front center and front right of the rover to provide stereo views with a 50-degree field of view. A forward-looking television frame was transmitted every 20 seconds enabling the earth operators to monitor and steer the vehicle.

A second television system used four high-resolution panoramic cameras to view the local terrain and the sun and earth for navigation purposes. The cameras were like those used previously on Lunas 9 and 13 and produced 500 × 6000 pixel images. Fore and aft cameras had a range of 30 degrees horizontally and 360 degrees vertically, while the side cameras had a range of 180 degrees horizontally and 30 degrees vertically. Because of the slow transmission rate, the panoramic cameras could only be used when Lunokhod was parked.

The rover used two antennas to communicate with earth, a conical low-gain, omnidirectional antenna, and a high-gain helix that was gimbal-mounted so it could point toward earth no matter which way the rover was oriented. In addition, a 4-rod antenna received a constant stream of commands to drive the vehicle, point its antenna, and operate its experiments.

Lunokhod was remotely "driven" by a five-man team which included a commander, driver, navigator, systems engineer, and radio operator. The radio operator was responsible for keeping the high-gain antenna aimed toward earth. Control of the moving robot was complicated by the delay in communication between earth and moon and the fact that Lunokhod would already be several meters ahead of what the slow-scan television pictures were showing the driver. The stress of operating the remote vehicle was said to be so great that it exhausted many experienced drivers and pilots, mainly because of the television-scan delay. The frustration of driving Lunokhod can be appreciated by anyone who has experienced the exasperation of driving one of today's popular radio-controlled toy cars. Complicating the driving was glare from the sun, black shadows, and lack of depth perception.

During the day, the rover's interior was kept cool by a water evaporation heat exchanger which radiated excess heat from the top of the instrument section. Adjustable louvers regulated the temperature between 15 and 20°C (59 and 68°F). Temperature was controlled at night by a combination of thermo-vacuum insulation and fan-circulated gas warmed by an internal radioisotopic heat source powered by polonium-210.

SLOW TRAVELS ON THE MOON

Over the next ten months, Lunokhod slowly zig-zagged its way across the crater-pocked surface. As controllers got accustomed to driving the vehicle, its pace picked up as it travelled in a southeasterly direction from the landing stage. Often, an interesting feature was examined closely or the vehicle was parked while soil analysis or celestial X-ray observations were performed. The RIFMA experiment determined that there was iron, chromium, titanium, magnesium, and potassium in the lunar soil. At the end of the third lunar day (each lasting 14 earth days), Lunokhod was brought back to its landing stage after having traveled a total of 3.5 km (2.2 mi).

In February 1971, Lunokhod was joined on the moon by Apollo 14 carrying the crew of Alan Shepard and Edgar Mitchell. The American astronauts stayed on the moon for two days and performed two moon walks, including the first long-distance exploratory venture away from the Lunar Module. Meanwhile, Lunokhod continued its slow robotic crawl across boulder fields, shallow craters, and loose dust. This was the first time that American and Soviet lunar explorations were simultaneously performed on the surface. After Apollo 14 departed, the Russian robot continued its travels, climbing slopes, investigating craters, returning hundreds of soil tests and many photographs.

Lunokhod was still operating when yet another two Americans visited the moon. Apollo 15 touched down on July 30 and David Scott and Jim Irwin prepared for a three-day stay on the moon. This time the astronauts brought with them an electrically driven car to extend their explorations. During three trips, they traveled 27.8 km (17.3 mi) over the moon, many times the distance covered by Lunokhod in its eight months on the moon.

In September 1971, telemetry indicated that the Russian rover was failing. In anticipation of failure, it was parked on a level surface with the French laser reflector aimed toward earth in case Lunokhod did not survive the next lunar night. As feared, it did not revive on October 1 after the 11th lunar night because the radioisotopic heater was spent. The announcement of Lunokhod's end was made October 4 on the anniversary of Sputnik 1.

The rover was designed for a 90-day life but actually operated 332 days, returning 200 panoramas and 20,000 separate photos and performing analyses which covered an area of 80,000 m^2 (861,000 ft^2). It also traveled over 10.5 km (6.5 mi) and performed 500 mechanical soil analyses. The RIFMA experiment required lengthy stops to acquire data, thus only 25 chemical soil analyses were performed. However, its results supported the hypothesis that the lunar surface was comprised primarily of basalt.

POLITICS CONTINUE

Soviet propagandists got carried away and called Lunokhod's success a "cause for rejoicing all over the world,"[7] but it was indeed one of the Russian's greater technical achievements in space exploration.

A toy battery-operated model Lunokhod was produced in Minsk by the Soviet Ministry of Light Industry. It was billed as being highly maneuverable and capable of overcoming any sandbox crater.[8]

Soviet scientists claimed that Lunokhod was capable of performing all exploration tasks that a human could, without the risk of human life, and could do it much more cheaply. The Lunokhod mission came seven months after the near fatal Apollo 13 mission. Russian propagandists used the Apollo mishap as part of the justification for unmanned exploration. The fact that the Apollo 14 crew nearly reached the point of exhaustion on the moon and were advised by medical personnel to abandon their attempt to walk to Cone Crater was cited by the Soviets as another example of why robotic exploration was superior to manned exploration.[9] In reality, the Soviet's own desperate attempt to land men on the moon had been delayed indefinitely.

The Lunokhod proved the Soviets were still in the lunar exploration business, however, the slow crawling robot was a crude substitute for human exploration. In ten months, Lunokhod 1 covered only 10 km (6.2 mi) while manned Apollo rovers traveled more than that distance in several days.

The Soviet claim that robotic exploration of the moon was cheaper than manned exploration was challenged by Charles Sheldon, a Soviet space analyst with the Library of Congress. He established that while the Apollo landings cost $20 billion in 1960s dollars, the Soviet lunar effort, based on their economy and gross national product, cost the equivalent of $49 billion.[10]

NEXT LANDER FAILS

Lunokhod 1 was entering its 11th lunar day of operations as Luna 18 was launched at 4:41 P.M., September 2, 1971. After a launch hiatus of nearly a year, the new mission was to land another spacecraft designed to return a surface sample. This time the landing was aimed toward an area in the Sea of Fertility chosen based on scientific interest. At about midnight on September 7, the craft entered a 100-km (62-mi) lunar orbit inclined 35 degrees with a period of 119 min. After 54 orbits, Soviet controllers attempted a landing in a highland region at 3.5 degrees North and 56.5 degrees East.

Communication with the lander was lost shortly before touchdown at a site approximately 120 km (75 mi) north of the Luna 16 landing area. As the landing was obviously a failure, the Soviets were forced to admit the mission was not a success. The *Novosti* news agency reported the failure in unusually stiff language stating: "In connection with this, as measurements indicated, the lunar landing in such difficult topographic conditions turned out unpropitious."[11] In other words, the mission had crashed in mountainous terrain at 10:48 A.M., September 11. This report was one of the few times that Russia actually admitted a space failure.

HUGE ORBITER STUDIES MOON

After a decade of space glory, the Soviets experienced a particularly dismal period in their space program during 1971. The manned Soyuz 10 mission experienced a mystery-shrouded emergency return to earth; the Soyuz 11 mission suffered a horrifying and fatal depressurization at the end of an apparently brilliant three-week manned mission. Then Luna 18 crashed on the moon.

Following these major space setbacks, the Russians were understandably reluctant to reveal the exact nature of Luna 19's mission after its launch on September 28, 1971. Only after entering lunar orbit on October 3 was it announced that Luna 19 was the fifth Soviet lunar satellite. Three days later, its orbit was adjusted to 127 × 135 km (79 × 84 mi) with a period of 121 min.

This first orbiter in the third generation series consisted of the third generation Luna orbit insertion and descent stages with a drum-shaped wheel-less Lunokhod body attached. This was a major advance over the limited second generation orbiters, allowing nineteen experiments to be housed in the pressurized Lunokhod-style body. A Lunokhod solar panel provided power. The lunar-orbit insertion stage was not jettisoned since its attitude sensors and gas jets were needed for control in orbit. Extra nitrogen tanks were carried for prolonged attitude control. The Soviets did not have the luxury of placing extensive instrument packages aboard orbiting manned lunar spacecraft as did the American Apollo program. The heavy Luna orbiter thus became the primary craft for a wide range of Soviet exploration from Lunar orbit.

Instruments carried by Luna 19 included a photographic-film-facsimile-scan imaging system, meteoroid detectors, cosmic ray detectors, magnetometer, radiation detectors, radar altimeter, and gamma-ray spectrometer. TASS reported that by October 19, Luna 19 was performing general photographic surface mapping. Images were still being returned the following February.

During the first four months of lunar operations, the orbiter completed 1258 revolutions while performing its primary mission: a systematic survey of the moon's gravitational field and the effects of mascons under the near-side maria. Precise tracking of Luna's orbital motions defined the moon's asymmetrical gravitational field between the northern and southern hemispheres. It was established that the near-side surface was 2 km (1.3 mi) higher than the 1737.54 km (1079.7 mi) mean radius of the moon. During May and June 1972, Luna 19's radio occultation experiment indicated that a plasma of charged particles from the sun with a density of 1000 particles per cm^3 exists above the day side of the moon at an altitude of 10 km (6 mi).

Luna 19 also studied the solar magnetic field carried by the solar wind to see if the moon disturbs the interplanetary magnetic field. Magnetic observations made during full moon, when the moon was immersed in earth's magnetic tail, were compared with observations taken at first and last quarter-moon. These established that the interplanetary magnetic field on the day side of the moon is several times stronger than on the night side and that the moon does indeed have an effect on the interplanetary magnetic field.

At least ten powerful solar flares (violent outbursts from the sun) were observed by Luna 19. Radiation measurements of these events were compared with readings from Mars 2 and 3 in Mars orbit, Venera 8 en route to Venus, and Prognoz 1 and 2 in earth orbit. During one solar chromospheric flare in December 1971, Luna 19 recorded a millionfold increase in energetic particles from the sun, resulting in lethal levels of radiation.

HIGHLAND SAMPLE RETURNED

The next sample-return mission, Luna 20, was aimed at a continental highland area in contrast to the mare lowland visited by Luna 16. The goal was to retrieve a core sample containing both loose rock and hard basalt samples from a region thought to be one of the oldest on the moon.

Luna 20 lifted off at 6:28 A.M., February 14, 1972, and followed an unusual trajectory because the flight was carried out during New Moon—when the gravitational fields of the sun and moon are aligned and the flight can be accomplished with a minimum of fuel consumption. One day after the probe's arrival on February 18, its orbit was adjusted to 12 × 100 km (7.5 × 62 mi), inclined 65 degrees.

Seven and a half days after departing earth, Luna's retrorocket fired at 10:13 P.M., February 21, and the landing followed at 10:19 P.M. Touchdown was 120 km (75 mi) north of the Luna 16 site. The area was on a highland peninsula south of the Sea of Crisis and on the extreme northeast end of the Sea of Fertility near the crater Alphonsus C, 2 km (1.2 mi) from where Luna 18 had crashed.

The descent stage carried a metal plaque showing Luna 20 on the moon with the ascent stage just lifting off. A line depicted the course back to earth with the Eurasian land mass prominently outlined and the landing spot depicted with a star. The plaque carried the words, "Luna 20 February 1972."

Photos of the surface were returned to a receiving station near Moscow for selection of a sample site. After guiding the drill mechanism to a "gray cloddy structure" near one of the lander's foot pads, the rotary percussion drill quickly sank 100 to 150 mm (4 to 6 in) into soft soil. It then hit rock so hard that the drill began to bind. The drilling was halted three times during the 7-min operation so the drill would not overheat. The small sample brought back to earth, only half the size of the Luna 16 sample, led to speculation that the operation had not been completed as planned.

After remaining on the moon for 27 hr, 39 min, the ascent stage was fired at 1:58 A.M., February 23. The capsule reentered the earth's atmosphere at a shallower angle than did Luna 16, encountering the atmosphere at an angle of 30 degrees. The forward side of the heat shield was eroded only 5 mm (0.2 in) while the lee side was unaffected. In spite of returning at the height of a nighttime blizzard, the capsule's beacon was spotted by a recovery aircraft. Landing occurred at 10:12 P.M., February 25. The next morning, after the blizzard passed, a helicopter found the capsule and its orange parachute in deep snow on an island in the River Karakingir, 40 km (25 mi) northwest of Dzhezkazgan, Kazakhstan.

A LOOK AT THE HIGHLANDS

Luna 20 brought back about 50 g (1.8 oz) of soil. The samples were light gray whereas the Luna 16 material was dark slate color with a metallic glitter. It also had larger grains, average size 70 to 80 microns. When the lunar material was emptied into the receiving tray, its appearance was likened to the ash of a big cigar or a roll of gray cement powder with grains slightly larger than poppy seeds. The deeper end of the core sample contained particles the size of a pea. Using mass spectroscopy, traces of 70 chemical elements were found. The sample had a density of 1.7 to 1.8 g per cm^3. The samples were thought to be a billion years older than those from the Luna 16 site.

No samples of lunar material with such a high concentration of aluminum and calcium oxides had been brought back before Luna 20. Mare samples from Luna 16 only had 1 to 2 percent anorthosite, while Luna 20's highland samples contained 50 to 60 percent anorthosite rocks consisting mainly of feldspar. Of the iron-containing minerals, 36 percent were olivene, while 57 percent were pyroxene. The new sample was only 1 percent ilmenite while Luna 16's was 10 percent and the Apollo 11 rocks more than 25 percent.

Over 80 research organizations examined the Luna 20 sample. Some of the analysis was done at facilities in the United States, France, Czechoslovakia, and Hungary. The Luna 20 results, when taken with Apollo 16 and 17 results, indicate that old crustal rocks in the highlands are primarily anorthositic gabbros and related-type rocks, while the mare areas sampled by Luna 16 and Apollo 11 contain mainly basaltic rocks. Luna 20 also found a larger quantity of metallic iron than did Luna 16. This iron was unusual in that it did not rust in the air. Experiments showed that this type of iron is sublimated out of basalt rocks at high temperature in a vacuum.

The following chart summarizes the percentage of components in the Luna 20 highland sample as compared to the Luna 16 mare sample.

	Luna 16		Luna 20	
	Basalt rock	Regolith rock	Anorthosite rock	Regolith rock
Silicon oxide	42.95	41.90	42.40	44.40
Alumina	13.88	15.33	20.20	22.90
Iron oxide	20.17	16.66	6.40	7.03
Calcium oxide	10.80	12.53	18.60	15.20
Magnesia	6.05	8.78	12.00	9.70
Titanium oxide	5.50	3.36	0.38	0.56
Sodium oxide	0.23	0.34	0.40	0.55
Potassium oxide	0.16	0.10	0.52	0.10

RUSSIANS HAVE THE MOON TO THEMSELVES

After Luna 20 returned to earth, two more Apollo missions carried Americans to the moon in 1972. Apollos 16 and 17 each spent three days on the moon with the astronauts exploring wide areas of the surface by using an electric car. The last of these Apollo manned explorations ended just a month before the Luna 21 mission, and no follow-on program for continued American lunar flights had been approved. The Russian Luna explorations took on added significance because they were the only means available for surface exploration on the moon until the 21st century. Now having a lunar monopoly, Soviet propagandists continued to drum home their point that manned expeditions to the moon were too expensive and future Lunas would explore our natural satellite cheaply and without risking lives.

The Luna 21 spacecraft carrying the Lunokhod 2 rover was launched at 9:55 A.M., January 8, 1973. The mission was almost aborted when engineers at the Zv'dnyy Gorodok manned spaceflight center where the mission was controlled received a false indication that one of Luna 21's landing legs had failed to deploy. A day after launch, an unexplained problem developed with Lunokhod's power supply. To maintain power in the craft's batteries, the rover's solar panel was opened and exposed to the sun during the trip to the moon.

Lunokhod 2 was similar in appearance and operation to its predecessor, but had a mass of 840 kg (1848 lb on earth), 84 kg (185 lb) heavier than Lunokhod 1. An extra, higher-resolution navigation television camera was mounted at eye level and returned an image every 3 seconds. The new camera gave a more realistic view of the surface so the driver could see farther ahead and drive with more confidence. The protruding television cameras contributed to the rover's bug-like appearance. The slow-scan, wide-angle facsimile cameras were also improved but still required 30 min to transmit a complete panorama. Improvements made to Lunokhod 2's propulsion system now allowed changes in direction without first stopping.

A new instrument aboard Lunokhod 2 was a magnetometer mounted ahead of the vehicle on a 1.5-m (4-ft) boom. The magnetometer, nicknamed "The Cobra," was used to measure the magnetic properties of individual rocks and material masses. Another new device was an astrophotometer which measured the sky glow over the moon during the day and studied the zodiacal light and light level of the Milky Way at night. The new rover also carried the improved RIFMA-M X-ray spectrometer to analyze soil chemistry. Additional instruments included a radiometer to measure cosmic rays and the Rubin 1 photo receiver for detecting laser bursts from earth.

Both Lunokhod 2 and its landing stage carried the Soviet flag as well as commemorative pennants. A bas-relief of Vladimir Lenin was attached to a Luna 21 landing-leg strut while the other medallion showed the national emblem of the U.S.S.R. with the inscription "50 Years of the U.S.S.R."

ARRIVAL AT THE MOON

Lunar orbit was achieved on January 12. Over the next two days, the orbit was trimmed to 16×100 km (10×62 mi). Descent to the lunar surface was begun on January 16 during the 41st orbit and followed the standard third generation Luna landing profile.

Touchdown occurred at 1:35 A.M. on the eastern edge of the Sea of Serenity in the crater Le Monnier. This area, at coordinates 25 degrees North and 30 degrees East, was only 180 km (112 mi) from the Apollo 17 landing site where the last human beings on the moon had departed the month before. The site was selected because of its proximity to both mare and highland terrain.

The first television images from the surface showed the lander had come to rest on a level plain between two small craters. The foothills of the Taurus Mountains were visible 6 km (4 mi) away. At 4:14 A.M., the rover rolled down two ramps onto the surface. Ahead of the rover was a 15-m (49-ft)-diameter crater. Using the experience gained driving Lunokhod 1, controllers quickly negotiated the obstacle and maneuvered to a spot 30 m

(98 ft) away. After turning the vehicle to face the sun, it remained parked for the next two days while it recharged its batteries.

In spite of the experience gained with Lunokhod 1, the high solar elevation made maneuvering difficult because there were few shadows to show surface features. On the first lunar day, there was a near collision between Lunokhod 2 and the Luna 21 landing stage. The vehicle made an emergency stop only 4 m (13 ft) from the lander.

MORE LUNAR TRAVELS

Lunokhod 2 was then commanded to begin travels toward the Taurus Mountains. The new rover traveled twice as fast as its predecessor and experience gained with Lunokhod 1 allowed the higher speed to be utilized. According to a local Russian joke, the Lunokhod "driver" was a former Moscow cabbie.[12]

Chemical tests by the RIFMA-M experiment showed that the local lunar soil was similar in composition to that at the Sea of Rains, but generally there were more boulders and rocks. During the first lunar night, the temperature measured by a thermometer on the magnetometer boom fell to a record −183°C (−297°F) while the wheel temperature only fell to −128°C (−198°F). While not acknowledged by Soviet authorities, there were apparently more problems with Lunokhod's electrical system during the first day's operations.

On the second day Lunokhod moved steadily toward the Taurus Mountains, taking magnetic measurements along the way. The moon has no significant magnetic field, but lunar mountains and seas have local magnetic fields. At one point the rover climbed an 18-degree slope and entered a 100-m (328-ft)-wide crater, only to sink to its axles in dust. Lunokhod was safely backed out and given a more sure-footed route. As the rover zigzaged up slopes, wheel slippage often approached eighty percent as the wheels churned in loose lunar soil. From atop a 400-m (1312-ft) peak, Lunokhod transmitted views of the opposite shore of Le Monnier Bay and the main peaks of the Taurus Mountains 55 to 60 km (34 to 37 mi) away. The television cameras also showed a thin crescent earth in the lunar sky.

On the third and fourth day, the rover worked along a tectonic abyss known as Direct Furrow. The chasm was 40 to 80 m (131 to 262 ft) deep and 300 to 400 m (984 to 1312 ft) wide. The lack of weathering on the moon preserved the structure of Direct Furrow and allowed the study of a cross section of the subsurface layer exposed by the fault. Traveling along the western edge, then along the eastern side, Lunokhod established that it was on solid basalt rock which had been split by movement of the moon's crust. As the edge of the fracture was approached, the depth of surface soil declined until there was just a stone rim. Navigation was difficult because of meter-sized boulders along the edge.

The X-ray spectrometer revealed that the lunar soil near the landing site contained 24 percent silicon, 9 percent aluminum, 8 percent calcium and 6 percent iron. As Lunokhod 2 climbed higher into the hills near the Taurus Mountains, it was found that the amount of elemental iron in the soil declined. Eight kilometers (five mi) from the landing site, it had dropped to 5 percent while the aluminum content rose to 11 percent. A month later, while farther away, the iron reading was only 4 percent, the lowest ever found.

A discovery of high scientific consequence was detecting the presence of residual magnetism in lunar rocks. This implies that in the past the moon possessed a strong magnetic field, perhaps caused by a faster rotation rate and a molten iron core. The instrument also measured changes in the minute lunar magnetic field while the rover was stationary. This provided data about the moon's interior and established that the moon does indeed possess a weak magnetic field. This discovery was in agreement with Apollo findings.

Laserology with Lunokhod 2 established precisely the earth-moon distance to within 40 cm (16 in). The accuracy of laser measurements also revealed that the position of the earth's poles had shifted 10 cm (4 in) during the several months of laser experiments. Lunokhod's laser reflectors also confirmed the theory that the moon, like earth, experiences continental drift. Another part of the laser experiment was the Rubin 1 photodetector which optically detected each laser shot fired from earth and responded with a radio signal to earth. This time laser shots from the 2.7 m (107-in) telescope at McDonald Observatory in Texas also spotted the rover. Lunokhod's laser reflection had about the same strength as that from the Apollo 15 laser reflector array, the largest placed on the moon.

The Rover's fifth lunar day began on May 9. Controllers reported that Lunokhod 2's movement had begun in a northeasterly direction away from Direct Furrow while the RIFMA-M experiment was detecting solar X-rays. Then contact was abruptly lost for unknown reasons. It is possible the craft's balky electrical system suffered a fatal breakdown or that the rover's interior was depressurized by a meteorite puncture. However, the terrain was treacherous so that it is equally likely that Lunokhod 2 simply fell over and crashed down a slope.

Though Lunokhod 2 only operated until the beginning of its fifth lunar day, it was much more active than the first rover. It traveled a total of 37 km (23 mi)—or three and a half times as far as Lunokhod 1. During its four months, Lunokhod 2 performed 50 percent more soil tests while producing 86 panoramas and 80,000 television pictures. Additionally, 4000 laser contacts were made by the Rubin 1 photodetector, 1500 photographs were made from earth of laser reflections off Lunokhod, and 740 mechanical soil tests were performed by Lunokhod's penetrometer.

THE LAST LUNAR SATELLITE

The sixth Soviet lunar satellite, Luna 22, rose up from Tyuratam at 11:57 A.M., May 29, 1974. It was similar to the Luna 19 satellite and was based on the heavy Luna descent stage carrying a wheelless Lunokhod body as an instrument carrier. On June 2, it entered a circular 220-km (137-mi) lunar orbit inclined 19.35 degrees with a period of 130 min. It then began a one-year research program extending Luna 19's photography, radar altimetery, magnetic field, cosmic ray, micrometeor, gravitational, and gamma-ray spectrographic studies of lunar composition.

On June 9, its orbit was lowered to 25 × 224 km (15.5 × 139 mi) for panoramic photography and gamma ray studies of rock chemical composition. While not specifying exact numbers, Soviet announcements said that many high resolution photographs had been obtained although few were ever released. Four days later, Luna 22 was returned to a 181 × 299-km (112.5 × 186-mi), 131-min period orbit to continue study of the lunar gravitational field and cosmic rays. To conserve attitude control fuel, the craft was switched to spin stabilization. For the next five months, Luna 22 made no adjustments to its orbit in order to study the perturbations of lunar gravity. Between June and August it recorded 23 micrometeor impacts.

On November 2, Luna 22 was raised to a 171 × 1437-km (106 × 893-mi) orbit with a period of 191 min. Five months later, Luna's path was trimmed slightly on April 2, 1975 to 200 × 1409 km (124 × 875.5 mi), inclined 21 degrees. Then, after a year in orbit, Soviet scientists announced that the primary mission was complete.

After 4000 revolutions in 14 months, Luna continued an extended flight plan. The orbit was lowered on the August 24 to 30 km (18.6 mi) for more photography. Following the photo session, Luna 22 had nearly exhausted its reserve of attitude control gas. The craft was then reboosted into a 100 × 1286-km (62 × 799-mi) orbit. On September 2, 1975, the attitude control gas ran out but the mission continued until November.

The long duration of the Luna 22 mission exhibited a new maturity in Soviet deep-space operations. Over the course of the mission, a total of 1500 trajectory measurements were made and 2400 communication sessions were held during which 30,000 commands were sent. To this day, Luna 22 remains the last dedicated Russian lunar orbiter.

HARD LANDING SPOILS AMBITIOUS PLANS

Luna 23 was the second Soviet moon flight in 1974. Intended to be another surface-sample return mission, the craft was launched at 5:30 P.M., October 28. The planned landing site was at the southeast region of the Sea of Crises at 13 degrees North and 62 degrees East, the same area at which Luna 15 had aimed five years before. At about 12:50 A.M., November 2, Luna 23 entered a 94 × 104-km (58 × 64.5-mi) lunar orbit inclined 130 degrees with a period of 117 min. Three days later, this orbit was lowered to 17 × 105-km (10.5 × 65-mi) in preparation for landing.

After the Luna 20 success, a new drilling mechanism was introduced. This modified soil sampler was capable of drilling 2 m (6.6 ft) below the surface. Instead of being mounted on a pivoting arm, the improved drill was rigidly mounted to the side of the descent stage on an inclined framework which extended up to the return capsule. With the solid mount and increased bracing, the new drill was capable of penetrating deeper into the surface.

The new sampler would use a percussion drill, or hammering device, to penetrate soft material. When resistance was encountered, such as a rock, an increase in drill-motor current would signal the mechanism to switch to a rotary drilling mode and bore through the obstacle. Maximum depth would be reached after several minutes of operation. The new hollow saw-tooth drill had a flexible inner liner, which, during the process of drilling into the surface, would be stuffed with soil and rock chips like a sausage casing. When the drilling was complete, the drill mechanism would be hoisted up its mounting framework to the return capsule and the 8 × 1600-mm (.3 × 63-in) drill liner containing the core sample would be coiled like a rope on a winch. The sample would then be transferred and sealed into the return capsule and the drill swung away to clear the ascent stage for liftoff.

On November 6 Luna 23 touched down on the Sea of Crises at 8:37 A.M. The landing was made in rough terrain and the craft's drilling device was damaged beyond use. The rough nature of the terrain may have confused the radar altimeter, causing the craft to descend at too high a velocity. Damage from the accident must have been severe. Not only was the drill inoperative, the empty ascent stage was not launched to earth as an engineering exercise. The descent stage was still functional, however, and a reduced research program was conducted for the next three days.

A replacement mission to complete the task which eluded Luna 23 was launched on October 16, 1975. However, Russian lunar investigators were again frustrated when the Proton booster failed and the new moonship never reached space. The final successful Luna sample return mission was thus delayed two years following the Luna 23 failure. This mission hiatus was the longest in the program since the early 1960s.

The cause of the delay was not explained by Soviet space officials, but there are likely several interlocking reasons for the long gap between the two final Luna landings. The Apollo manned explorations had been terminated in 1972 and no other American lunar exploration program took their place. Without the competition from Apollo, there was no political pressure to achieve lunar results for the sake of national prestige. The landing operations conducted by Lunas 20, 21, and 23 were the result of inertia from the Luna program when it was competing with American moon flights and not a result of program expansion. Even though the Luna 24 spacecraft existed, launch operations and manpower to conduct all phases of the mission required funding. Without the political expediency of answering yet another American moon flight, the Academy of Sciences was hard pressed to secure funds from the Soviet government to repeat a Luna 23 mission. Only one flight per year was authorized under a reduced lunar exploration program.

A LAST TRIP TO THE MOON

Luna 24, Russia's last flight to the moon, was launched at 6:04 P.M., August 9, 1976. The spacecraft was again designed to sample 2 m (6.6 ft) below the lunar surface. Arriving in lunar orbit at 2:11 A.M., August 14, the lander entered an initial 115-km (71.5-mi) circular orbit inclined 120 degrees. Over the next four days, the orbit was lowered to 12 × 120 km (7.5 × 74.5 mi). Descent to the surface began after the 53rd orbit at 9:30 A.M. on August 18 with touchdown at 9:36 A.M.. The landing was at 12.8 degrees North, 62.2 degrees East, in the southeast area of the Sea of Crises where Luna 23 had tried to land.

This site was chosen because of its low elevation, relatively flat topography, and comparative youth. The site was also of interest because it was close to a 10-km (6.2-mi)-wide, 2 km (1.2-mi)-deep crater, and it was hoped that the drill might obtain ejecta samples, or material from deeper within the moon which was thrown out when the crater was formed. Shortly after landing, drilling began. A total of twelve cake-like samples were collected, each about 10-cm (4-in) long and 2.5-cm (1-in) thick, from depths up to two meters.

After a 23-hr stay on the moon, the return capsule lifted off at 8:25 A.M., August 19. The Luna 24 descent stage continued to transmit data and operate the lunar drill. Three days later, the capsule entered the earth's atmosphere and was recovered in a manner similar to previous sample return missions. The capsule landed at 8:55 P.M., August 22, after parachuting into a forest 200 km (124 mi) southeast of Surgut in the U.S.S.R.

Early reports from the Vernadsky Institute indicated that the drilling mechanism encountered several distinct layers of deposits with differing densities, possibly due to the ejecta blankets from meteoric impacts occurring up to 3 billion years before. Both fine dust and small particles were collected by the automated drill. Yuri Zolotov, deputy director of the Vernadsky Institute, said the color of the soil was silver or gray with a brownish tint similar to the Luna 16 samples but that the Luna 24 soil was lighter and had larger grains. A total of 150 g (5.3 oz) were recovered. The sample was broken up into 30-cm (12-in) segments for analysis. X-ray and microanalysis revealed 60 different chemical elements.

Fourteen years after the craft returned to earth, this author was privileged to view and actually touch the Luna 24 return capsule. The simplicity of the beachball-sized capsule belied its significance, for it had been on another world. The capsule was brownish in color, its surface seared by the intense heat of atmospheric entry which gave it a glassy feel. There was seemingly no entry into the sphere as the partially melted heat shield had fuzed the original door shut. To retrieve the core sample container, a round opening had been precision-cut with a lathe.

Many of us have seen the Apollo Command Module which carried men to the moon. However, this craft never landed on the surface. It just ferried them between earth and lunar orbit. The actual Lunar Module which landed never returned to earth. Luna 24 is therefore unique, being among only three craft, all Russian, to have actually landed on the moon and returned to earth. To touch this mechanical emissary to another world was electrifying. Handling Luna 24 was as close as I will ever come to reaching another celestial body. I will remember the thrill of that experience forever.

POLITICS STILL DRIVE LUNA

The Soviet government reduced public emphasis on the Luna 24 mission. Official announcements of the landing did not carry the "Urgent" designation that TASS assigns to manned spaceflight dispatches. Also there was uncharacteristic silence following the launch of the return capsule to earth. This led to premature speculation that the mission had failed.

Three grams (0.1 oz) of Luna 24 material were shared with American scientists who were eager to compare them to samples collected by Apollo 15 and 17 from a 1.6- and 2.6-m (5.2- and 8.5-ft) depth, respectively. U.S. scientists were able to study these with superior age dating and chemical analysis equipment. In exchange, the Soviets received 6 g (0.2 oz) of Apollo samples. A year later, U.S. scientists received another Luna 24 sample. This was of particular interest to lunar scientists because it came from an area of the moon not visited by Apollo.

The Soviets, while justifiably proud of their lunar achievements, felt nonetheless compelled to stress that the automated sample-return flights represented great strides in economy and safety over the American manned Apollo flights. However, analysis of the Luna surface sample return missions by Soviet space program analyst Charles Sheldon revealed that the cost of the unmanned missions was approximately twenty to twenty-five percent that of manned missions, but a dozen automated missions would have to be undertaken to equal the scientific return collected by a single manned flight.[13]

The total combined weight of the samples returned from the moon by the three successful Luna sample return missions was 400 g (0.9 lb). This compares with the 380,000 g (838 lb) collected by all six of the manned Apollo landings. All Luna return missions landed in the cratered uplands that separate the Sea of Crises and the Sea of Fertility while the Apollo landings took place over a wide equatorial area of the moon.

Luna 24 marked the end of the initial phase of lunar exploration for both America and Russia. To this day, there are no firm plans by either the Americans or the Russians to return to the lunar surface. As the American Apollo manned lunar missions were canceled by the Government just when they achieved an operational maturity, the Soviet Luna missions were also stopped just as they began to return large amounts of scientific data.

Looking back at the brief period when lunar exploration was a priority, so much was done in so little time. With cold-war politics pushing both nations, Russia and America reached the moon less than a decade after the space age began. Then after a hard, expensive struggle by thousands of dedicated scientists and engineers from both nations to pave the road to the moon in the 1960s, the lunar goal was completely abandoned in the 1970s.

Billions of dollars were spent by both countries in the race to the moon. While science was the stated goal, what the vast expenditures really purchased was national prestige at a time when propaganda and national image outweighed everything. Both participants canceled their research just as it reached the maturity needed to perform the science that was the alleged goal because the moon race was no longer a political race. If there is any such thing as a scientific crime, the abandonment of the moon—after two decades of national sweat, heartbreak, and enormous expense—certainly qualifies as one.

AMERICAN LUNAR REVIVAL

Twenty-two years would pass before an American space probe again soared toward the moon. The two-decade hiatus was broken on January 25, 1994 when Clementine 1, the first lunar probe launched from Vandenberg Air Force Base, California, lifted off at 11:34 A.M. The box-shaped 230-kg (508-lb) spacecraft was unusual in that it was to both survey the moon, then later proceed to an encounter with the asteroid Geographos.

Clementine was a true sword-to-plowshare story. The spacecraft was initially developed to test military missile-detection sensors for the now abandoned Strategic Defense Initiative Organization (SDIO) "Star Wars" program. The successor to SDIO, the Ballistic Missile Defense Organization (BMDO), continued the program. However, it was decided to allow Clementine, named after the prospector's daughter in the folk song of the same name, to perform meaningful science with the special sensors developed for defense technology. Thus the flight to the moon was proposed, then expanded to include an asteroid fly-by. Clementine's booster, a converted Titan 2G ICBM, had spent 25 years in a missile silo in Arkansas with an H-bomb in its nose while on war alert. Now it would be used for science, not destruction.

The first of a new generation of smaller, cheaper, yet highly capable lunar and planetary explorers, Clementine 1 is also unusual in that it was developed and launched for only $80 million. This is remarkable in NASA's era of billion-dollar space programs.

Clementine took a curious route to the moon. After several days in low earth orbit, it was boosted into a 170,000-km (105,600-mi) apogee orbit. From halfway to the moon, Clementine looked back at our planet and relayed detailed photographs of the night side of earth which showed the sparkling city lights. Although the spacecraft performed flawlessly, there were anxious moments. A ground station sent a faulty command which accidentally discharged the probe's nickle-hydrogen battery. If the craft had been powered by a conventional nickle-cadmium rechargeable battery, such an incident would have resulted in the loss of the spacecraft.

After Clementine looped high above the earth, it used two return passes by earth to gravitationally slingshot itself toward the moon. On February 20, it entered a 395 × 2959-km (245 × 1837-mi) lunar orbit. Here Clementine settled into a mapping routine scheduled to last two months.

Clementine delighted researchers with perfect performance and a constant flow of high-resolution photographs. The spacecraft returned between 4000 and 5000 digital images of the moon on each of its five daily orbits. One researcher gushed, "It was wonderful. They're absolutely stunning."[14] The object of this scientific awe was the images returned by ultraviolet, visible light, and infrared charge-coupled-device (CCD) cameras which viewed the moon in eleven different, narrow spectral regions. The minerals in the rocks of the moon can be identified over a wide field by their respective "colors" as seen in these narrow spectral regions. At perilune, the cameras can resolve surface features as small as 100 m (328 ft) in visible light.

One area of research for which Clementine is uniquely suited is the search for ice in the moon's "Cassini regions," the polar areas of the moon which receive little or no sunlight. Ground-based searches in the past have detected ice-like returns from radar scans. From its polar orbit around the moon, Clementine could provide better data than that available from earth radars. By aiming the narrow beam from its 1-m (3.3 ft) telemetry antenna at the polar regions of the moon, Clementine performed bistatic radar searches for lunar polar ice. With this technique, the radio signal emitted by Clementine was received by JPL's Deep Space Network antennae.

By late April 1994, the results of the ice search were not conclusive, but Clementine deputy science team leader Paul Spudis explained, "The moon is bambarded by comets that are mostly water, and the theory is that the water molecules could become trapped in the very cold shadowed areas. If we do confirm the presence of ice, it will be a very interesting—if not major—discovery."[15]

By early May, Clementine completed its astoundingly successful moon mission, but not without further bureaucratic flack. Although it performed beautifully in lunar orbit, the mission was nearly cancelled while in progress because of Defense Department budget cutting.

On May 3, 1994, Clementine fired its propulsion system for 270 seconds to push the craft out of lunar orbit. Using the gravity of earth to slingshot the spacecraft into deep space, Clementine was placed on a course toward the 1.5 × 4-km (1 × 2.5-mi) asteroid Geographos. It was hoped that the spacecraft would pass within 100 km (61 mi) of the asteroid on August 31 and snap 2000 images of the tiny asteroid.

This bold plan was dashed four days after leaving the moon when either a computer or software malfunction accidentally exhausted all of Clementine's attitude control fuel, leaving the craft in a 30 rpm spin. Without any means of stabilizing the craft, mission controllers were forced to leave the otherwise healthy Clementine rooted in a highly elliptical earth orbit with no hope of reaching the asteroid.

Although the loss of the secondary asteroid mission was a disappointment, Clementine was, nonetheless, a fantastic success as a lunar mission. Clementine was developed from a concept on paper to a flying, data-gathering machine in only 22 months by the Naval Research Laboratory. This pace has not been matched since NASA's "can-do" era in the 1960s. Clementine program manager for the BMDO, Lt. Col. Pedro Rustan declared, "The spacecraft has been designed, built, tested, and controlled in space by a team of about 55 people. We don't need a lot of fancy scientist Ph.D.s to build a spacecraft."[16] An example of the straightforward simplicity used in perfecting the spacecraft is illustrated by the method used to test Clementine's star sensors. The craft was pushed outside the assembly building at night and the sensors tested under the real stars instead of in a multimillion-dollar space simulation chamber.

On the heels of Clementine's fabulous success, a scientific mandate is already growing for the development of Clementine 2. Bipartisan congressional support is even calling for funding of a follow-on Clementine mission in fiscal year 1995. However, the Clementine concept faces an uphill political battle with President Clinton's Democrat administration which regards the science program as a carryover from the "Star Wars" program endorsed by previous Republican administrations.

A lot is riding on the success of Clementine, for it holds the key to the way future deep-space explorations will be carried out in modern, cost-conscious times. The concept of smaller, lighter, yet highly capable space probes launched by modest boosters promises to reinvigorate the exploration of the moon and inner planets.

5 Probing the Unsolved Planet

In early 1961, Venus hung like a brilliant inviting beacon in the twilight. As the "Evening Star" approached within 42 million km (26 million mi) of earth, rocket travel time to Venus was only four months, nearly half that required to reach Mars, making it a tempting target. Both America and Russia desperately wanted to reach Venus first to claim a space-race political prize. NASA's lack of powerful booster rockets allowed Russia the first attempt to reach the planet, but America eventually succeeded in actually reaching Venus first.

Russian scientists regarded Venus as "the unsolved planet" because its surface was permanently hidden from view behind total cloud cover. Their early flights to the planet were thus blind probes into the unknown. Later, as American interest in Venus waned in favor of Mars explorations, Russian persistence paid off as their Venera probes solved many of the Venusian riddles. In time, these explorations became the pride of Russian science and much of what we know about Venus was discovered by the Veneras.

PRELUDE TO VENUS

Before the first Sputnik and the birth of deep space exploration, Soviet scientists openly speculated about interplanetary flight. Among them was Sergei Korolyov who, on September 17, 1957, published an article in *Pravda* marking the 100th anniversary of the birth of Russian space-travel theorist Konstantin Tsiolkovsky who was the first to envision rocket-powered, deep space travel. Korolyov praised Tsiolkovsky's idea to use "permanent space stations...to facilitate the flight of cosmic rockets to distant destinations."[1] Also in 1957, Yuri Khlebtsevich published ideas about sending rocket probes to Venus in the 1960s in order to relay television pictures of the planet for the final 24 hr before impacting the planet.

About the same time, writing in *Krasnaya Zvezda* (*Red Star*, the Soviet army newspaper), Professor Gavril A. Tikhov, director of the Alma-Ata Observatory, speculated about the conditions a space probe may find on Venus. His thinking showed the overly optimistic views, common in the late 1950s, about the perpetually cloudy planet. Tikhov wrote: "There may be little crystals of ice in the clouds enveloping Venus. Perhaps there are also water vapors and even oxygen in the lower strata of the planet's atmosphere inaccessible to our observation. And perhaps the great amount of carbon dioxide in the upper atmosphere stems from the rich vegetation on Venus. In any case, to form carbon dioxide, there must be oxygen and carbon, the chief ingredients of plants and the prerequisites for emergence of animal life. Thus even though Venus is still an 'unsolved' planet, we have reasons to suppose that life does exist there."[2]

On January 10, 1959, Academician Anatoly A. Blagonravov, a leading Soviet space scientist, made the first comment regarding plans to send a Soviet probe to Venus. He said, "Perhaps we shall try as early as June this year to send a payload with a mass of 270 to 370 kg (595 to 816 lb) on a journey to Venus."[3] In retrospect, we now know that no planetary flights were attempted by the Soviets in 1959. The timing of Blagonravov's statement must then be taken in the context of the Russian euphoria surrounding the flight of Luna 1 past the moon the week before.

WHAT WOULD BE FOUND?

Since the Russian astronomer Mikhail Lomonosov detected evidence of a thick atmosphere surrounding Venus in 1761, it had been generally accepted that the clouds in this atmosphere were made up of water vapor. However, later studies through the mid-20th century showed that the clouds likely had a high content of carbonic acid and little oxygen. Beyond this meager conclusion, little was known for Venus had proved to be a secretive planet, not yielding her mysteries easily. Earth-bound observers pressed in vain for clues about the silvery sphere and for glimpses of the guarded surface. Yet, while little could be learned, there was much room for conjecture.

Leading specialists ran the gamut theorizing about a surface they could not see. Speculation ranged from ideas that the planet was a hot, dusty place lashed by high winds, to the concept of a lush jungle-covered planet. Some believed Venus was covered with one huge ocean, perhaps composed of petroleum. Others envisioned a searing planet so hot that any lakes and seas would be composed of molten metal.

Soviet space engineers wasted no time in preparing to fill the void in the knowledge of Venus. After completing the initial Soviet moon flights in 1959, Korolyov expanded his attention to the planets. In the early planning for the exploration of Venus, it became evident that returning rock samples to earth would require huge, prohibitively expensive spacecraft capable of landing on Venus, then returning to earth. Academician Mstislav Keldyish, then a leading theoretician in the Soviet space program, suggested that the surface of the planet should be analyzed by landing instruments and transmitting the results to earth. In order to do this Korolyov and Babakin began preparing spacecraft to land on Venus.

As the time for the first Venus launches neared, the prospect of investigating Venus first-hand was greeted with high anticipation by the astronomical community—any new shred of information about the virtually unknown planet would be invaluable. With Venus hiding herself so well, it was anyone's guess what the first probe would find.

Clues to the truth of what really awaited robotic visitors from earth had already been uncovered by telescopic observations, but lay hidden in speculation and theory. Planetary expert Gerard de Vaucouleurs, then with Harvard College Observatory, concluded from observations of an occultation of the star Regulus by Venus that the atmospheric pressure was several times that of earth.[4]

Other clues also lay unrecognized. When radio astronomy observations in the late 1950s revealed evidence that the surface was extremely hot, possibly hundreds of degrees, many authorities remained unconvinced. However, a young doctoral student at the University of Chicago, Carl Sagan, based his graduate thesis on the radiation and heat balance of Venus. He proposed that the implied high temperatures on Venus were real, not an artifact of radio observations. Sagan further proposed that the blanket of carbon dioxide around Venus trapped solar heat with a greenhouse effect, raising the planet's temperature to levels incompatible with human life.[5] While at the time Sagan's theory sounded like science fiction, in retrospect, he was one of the few theorists who understood the sizzling hell that lay below the clouds of Venus.

At the beginning of the space age, Carl Sagan also had revolutionary ideas about the surface pressure on Venus. He was so sure that the pressure was an incredible 100 times that of earth that he had a $100 wager with Harvard's de Vaucouleurs on the true figure. Time would eventually show Sagan to be richer when future explorations forced de Vaucouleurs to accept the higher figure. Taking his $100 loss in good stride, de Vaucouleurs defended himself by declaring that he was, after all, a Mars not a Venus expert.[6]

Soviet engineers however, chose to ignore Sagan's theories. Based on their own estimates of the Venusian environment, they designed the initial Venera probes assuming they would encounter surface temperatures of 60 to 80°C (140 to 176°F) with surface pressures no more than five times that of earth.

PLANETARY SPACE RACE

The Russians were not the only ones thinking about Venus. NASA initiated plans in November 1958 to construct two spherical 1-m (3-ft) diameter 169-kg (373-lb) Pioneer spacecraft to orbit Venus the following year. Plans called for the twin probes to be launched by Atlas-Able boosters during the June 1959 Venusian launch opportunity. When the Soviets launched their Luna 1 probe past the moon in early 1959, space-race politics and American embarrassment quickly changed these plans. The Venus orbiters were downgraded to lunar probes in an effort to quickly match the Soviet space achievement.

Other American Venus plans called for the June 1959 launch of lighter spacecraft on a fly-by mission to the planet. When the mission of the 43-kg (98-lb) spacecraft was delayed for 9 months, the Venus mission was downgraded to the Pioneer 5 solar-orbit mission.

In summer 1960, NASA looked for another way to get to Venus. With the heavy Pioneers politically diverted toward the moon, it was time to initiate new plans. A fitting name was chosen for a new spacecraft series which was to sail the ocean of space: "Mariner." Three versions of the new craft were sketched with launches planned for 1962, 1964, and 1965. Mariner A was to be a fly-by probe to investigate the Venusian environment while sailing past the planet. Mariner B was more ambitious. It would eject a planetary lander to study Venus before impacting the surface. Each version would weigh one ton and be launched by the Atlas-Centaur, a rocket which in 1960 existed only on paper. The third probe, known as Mariner R, was the runt of the litter and was thus assigned a low priority. It was a much lighter, scaled-back probe based on the Ranger lunar spacecraft (thus the "R" designation). It had the advantage of being small enough to reach Venus using the existing Atlas-Agena rocket. However, NASA had grander visions for the planets and banked on the larger probes. But when the space agency's 1961 budget was prepared, only Mariner A was funded at a modest $11 million.

A FAILED VENUS ATTEMPT

Regardless of what truth lay behind Soviet Venus efforts in 1959, they definitely prepared planetary payloads for the next launch opportunity toward the veiled planet. With NASA's Venus plans aimed at the mid-1960s, the only hardware readied for flight in 1961 was stamped "Made in the U.S.S.R." As the year drew to a close, two Venus probes developed by Korolyov and Babakin lay in a hangar at Tyuratam. While snow fell on the steppes of Kazakhstan, the machines awaited their turn on the launch pad.

At a time when large U.S. satellites weighed only a ton, the world was amazed by the launch of the 6.5-ton Sputnik 7 on February 4, 1961. The monster 6482-kg (14,290-lb) satellite, called "Tyazh'yy (Heavy) Sputnik 4" by the Soviets, was a record mass to enter orbit. (Tyazh'yy Sputnik 1 through 3 were the initial three Luna probes.) Mysteriously, after a single orbit, the spacecraft broke up into several pieces.

Regarding the huge satellite, official announcements said it was for "perfecting spaceships of increased weight" and that the craft performed normally, accomplishing its tasks. Beyond these statements, little official news was released. In light of the past Soviet practice of flooding the news media with propaganda and rhetoric about space launches, the uncharacteristic silence surrounding Sputnik 7 was both very mysterious and very noticeable.

In reality, the statement was a fabrication to hide the fact that the mission was a failure. While the gigantic satellite was billed as an engineering test to study the dynamics of large satellites, it was actually, as many in the west suspected, a failed launch toward Venus.

The launch had been scheduled for late January, but in their haste to prepare the mission, technicians overlooked several problems and the flight was delayed. The craft eventually became trapped in earth orbit as a result of two flaws. The final stage separation mechanism failed to work because it was not pressurized, and the fourth stage had an inherent flaw which meant that startup of its rocket engine in the weightlessness of earth orbit would not be reliable.

Because of the Sputnik's record mass, some western observers hinted that the craft's mission may have been a failed manned flight. Seeking to avert suspicion that the mysterious Sputnik 7 was related to the upcoming manned launch of the first Soviet cosmonaut two months hence, academician Leonid Sedov downplayed rumors circulating in Europe that the craft carried animals or human beings. Sedov stated such rumors "do not accord with reality."[7]

With little information about the giant satellite's mission, western observers were able to do little except perform observational exercises of Sputnik 7's orbit. Years after the attempted mission, when the east-west political climate thawed, Soviet space officials admitted that Sputnik 7 was indeed a failed Venus mission. Cold war politics and iron-curtain paranoia thus deprived history and humanity from savoring the moment when interplanetary flights to Venus were inaugurated.

THE BIRTH OF PLANETARY SPACE EXPLORATION

Eight days after the Sputnik 7 failure, the Soviets again tried to reach Venus. When the massive 6474-kg (14,273-lb) Sputnik 8 satellite was launched on February 12, some western analysts suspected it was another planetary attempt. Called "Tyazh'yy Sputnik 5," or "Heavy Sputnik 5," it was the backup for Sputnik 7.

Sputnik 8 entered an initial 227 × 285 km (141 × 177 mi) earth orbit, inclined 65 degrees. Near the end of its first orbit, the final-stage booster successfully ignited over Africa and accelerated to 661 m (2170 ft) per sec faster than escape velocity. It then released a probe into a trajectory designed to intercept the planet Venus.

Dubbed "Mezhplanetnaya Automaticheskaya Stantsiya 2" (MAS 2), or "Automatic Interplanetary Station 2," by the Soviets, the craft was the first interplanetary probe to be launched from an earth parking orbit. (MAS 1 was the Luna 1 moon probe which entered solar orbit two years before.) Although the Venus probe was called MAS 2, in keeping with the convention of naming later Venus probes "Venera," the craft's accepted name is now Venera 1.

The launch of Venera 1 was not announced until the probe was more than 100,000 km (62,100 mi) from earth. The initial TASS news agency announcement said: "A heavy artificial satellite of the earth was orbited... by an improved multistage rocket. On the same day, a guided space rocket, launched from the Sputnik, sent an automatic interplanetary space station on a flight to the planet Venus." Later, the phrasing "to Venus" in the announcement was changed to say that the probe was aimed to "reach the areas of the planet Venus in the second half of May 1961."[8]

Over the next two days, Venera 1's trajectory was still influenced by the gravitational pull of earth. Then, on February 14, at 11 P.M. Moscow time, Venera 1 was free of earth's gravity. As the probe receded at 4 km (2.5 mi) per sec, it was traveling in relation to the sun at 27.7 km (17.2 mi) per sec.

The mission's unstated objective was to impact Venus, but the craft had no mid-course correction capability. Actually striking the planet was only a remote possibility. Still, the booster apparently performed its job with admirable accuracy since the Soviets said the craft would pass only 100,000 km (62,100 mi) from Venus.

Soviet engineers stated that inaccuracies in aiming at Venus resulted not only from minute guidance errors at launch, but also from lack of a precise measurement of the astronomical unit (AU), or the distance from earth to the sun. This measurement is essential for calculating interplanetary trajectories. Indeed, one of the objectives of the Venera 1 mission was to refine the measurement of the astronomical unit to increase future accuracy. The final solar orbit calculated for Venera 1 was approximately 107×152 million km (66.5×94.5 million mi) with a period of 300 days.

THE VENERA 1 SPACECRAFT

The Venera 1 probe was the most elaborate scientific spacecraft yet developed by the Soviets. The ambitious craft was shaped basically like a blunt-nosed artillery projectile, being just over a meter (3.3 ft) in diameter, slightly more than two m (6.6 ft) in length, with a mass of 643.5 kg (1419 lb) on earth.

The interplanetary probe consisted of two sealed compartments. The first of these, termed the orbital compartment, carried the "housekeeping" equipment necessary for the probe to function as it sped toward Venus. Scientific instruments for the study of interplanetary space were also carried in this compartment. These included a cosmic ray detector, a magnetometer to study the interplanetary and Venusian magnetic fields, charged particle traps and solar radiation detectors to study the sun, and micrometeor detectors. Data were relayed to earth using a four-channel telemetering system. The second planetary compartment carried the instruments designed specifically for studying Venus. Presumably, this was a rudimentary atmospheric entry capsule.

As soon as the spacecraft separated from its booster, the solar panels and low-gain antenna were deployed. The twin 1.5-m (4.9-ft) solar panels charged the probe's chemical batteries. Short-range communications were done through a 2.4-m (7.9-ft) omnidirectional rod antenna that pivoted outward from the spacecraft. Long-range communications were to have been done through a two-meter (6.6-ft) diameter wire mesh high-gain directional dish antenna which was to unfurl as the spacecraft approached Venus. To orient the solar panels and aim the main antenna toward earth, Venera 1 was stabilized in all three axes and did not spin as most spacecraft did at the time. An earth-seeking sensor was attached to a solar panel. Other sensors to locate the sun and a bright navigation star were attached to the craft's main body.

Temperature regulation inside the spacecraft was controlled by movable metal louvers that were dark on one side and reflective on the other. Temperature sensors in the spacecraft directed the louvers to orient as necessary to cool or warm the instruments. As the probe approached the orbit of Venus, solar radiation would increase by a factor of two, making the thermal-control system a vital part of the spacecraft.

NAIVE SCIENTIFIC EXPECTATIONS

Oleg Melnikov, in charge of the Leningrad Astronomical Observatory's stellar physics section, optimistically stated the probe would pass through Venus' atmosphere and return data. However, a more realistic expectation was expressed by A.A. Severny, director of the Crimean Astrophysical Observatory. Noting that Venera would be exposed to meteoroids, solar particles, and cosmic rays, he said problems of lengthy exposure to these phenomena are of great scientific and practical importance.[9]

The skimpy information available about the Venusian surface in the late 1950s led some Soviet engineers to believe there were large amounts of water on Venus and in the atmosphere. This led to planetary lander design considerations which seem laughable in light of modern knowledge about Venus.

Thirty years after the Venera 1 flight, Valery Timofeev, a Soviet aerospace engineer who worked on later Venera spacecraft, related to this author: "In 1960, engineers did not know about the true conditions on Venus and they thought there was water on the planet. In some cases on Venera 1, they suggested that antennae and other equipment could be kept closed with the application of sugar! They figured when the equipment landed in water, the sugar would dissolve, allowing the equipment to open. They actually tested this equipment on earth before the flight."[10]

The probe's radio transmitters operated at 922.8 MHz, but did not broadcast continuously to earth as did U.S. deep-space probes. To conserve the spacecraft's battery for the powerful radio transmitter, the probe transmitted infrequent bursts. After daily communications sessions shortly after launch, contact with Venera 1 was to be maintained at five-day intervals when the transmitter was switched on by a signal from earth.

Venus, at the time of Venera 1's encounter, would be 70 million km (43.5 million mi) away, or 175 times farther than the moon. The signal strength from Venera's transmitter at these distances would be minuscule. To receive signals from spacecraft at interplanetary distances, a massive 1500-ton antenna assembly consisting of eight separate 15-m (49-ft) diameter dishes was constructed on the State Farm at Yevpatoria in the Crimea. The Soviets referred to this tracking station as the "Distant Space Radio Center." Signals received by the complex were relayed to processing computers at the "Coordinating Computer Center." Communications with Venera 1 were carried out only when it was in sight of Yevpatoria.

MEMENTOS FROM EARTH

Since Venera 1 was to be the first interplanetary spacecraft to arrive at another planet, it continued Luna's tradition of carrying mementos from earth to other celestial bodies. The craft carried a hollow 70-mm (3-in) diameter earth globe made of titanium alloy. The globe was engraved with the outline of the continents, which were inlaid with gilt while the oceans were light blue. Inside the globe was a commemorative medal with the Coat of Arms of the U.S.S.R. on one side. On the opposite side was a diagram of the inner solar system with earth and Venus in their relative locations at the time of the craft's planetary encounter. Along the edge of the diagram was the inscription "Union of Soviet Socialist Republics—1961." The earth globe was placed in a container made of stainless steel pentagonal segments. The container was also inscribed with the coat of arms of the U.S.S.R. and the inscription "Earth-Venus 1961."

After five days of flight, Venera 1 was 1.9 million km (1.2 million mi) from earth and receding at 3.9 km (2.4 mi) per sec. Telemetry reported that the spacecraft's internal temperature was 28 to 30 degrees Centigrade (82 to 86°F) and internal pressure was steady at 900 mm (35 in) of mercury.

Initial scientific results from the Venera 1 observations taken shortly after launch showed the solar wind was light. Dr. E.R. Mustel of the Astronomical Council of the Soviet Union reported that on February 17 the probe detected one billion charged particles per cubic cm of space. These readings coincided with a magnetic disturbance occurring on earth which was created by huge energy outbursts from the sun called solar flares. At the same time, the probe reported no magnetic variations at its position in space.

PREMATURE END TO THE MISSION

While there were high hopes for the first mission to another planet, there was no scientific return from Venus. The planned communication session with Venera 1 scheduled for February 27 never materialized. On March 2 Radio Moscow announced that contact with Venera 1 had been lost fifteen days after launch. The broadcast stated: "Radio contact with the interplanetary station is lost. Sabotage during assembly is therefore possible."[11] More recent revelations about Venera 1 have shown that in reality, the probe was lost before it reached 2 million km (1.2 million mi) from earth.

Western speculation did not try to shift the blame for the spacecraft's failure to others as did Radio Moscow, but instead considered a possible failure of the power supply or stabilization system. From an engineering standpoint, the most likely cause of the failure was a malfunction of the craft's attitude control system. If the probe were slowly tumbling, the solar panels could no longer point toward the sun, leading to battery failure.

The British also were tracking the progress of Venera 1 with the giant 76-m (250-ft) Jodrell Bank radio telescope using coordinates supplied by the Soviets. They last received signals on February 17, and following the five-day cycle of planned transmissions from Venera 1, unsuccessfully searched for signals for three hours on March 4, 1961, and for seven hours the next day.

The now silent Venera 1 traveled 269 million km (167.2 million mi) around the sun during its trip to Venus. As viewed from the earth, the celestial paths of Venus and Venera 1 converged between the constellations of Pisces and Cetus as the craft approached the planet. As the mute spacecraft passed Venus on May 19 there was hope that the probe was still functioning and that contact could be re-established when the high-gain antenna was to unfurl upon approach to the planet. The Soviets requested that the Jodrell Bank radio telescope monitor the area where the craft was expected to be during its rendezvous with the veiled planet. Unfortunately, the observatory announced that no signal had been received.

On June 9, 1961, the Jodrell Bank radio telescope was made available to Soviet technicians for another attempt to re-establish contact with Venera 1. The importance the Soviets placed on this recovery attempt was reflected in the caliber of the specialists they sent for the effort. Professor Alla Masevich, a Soviet female astronomer who held the prestigious post of Vice President of the Astronomical Council of the U.S.S.R. Academy of Sciences, and academician Jouli Khodarev were present. The two Soviet scientists spent several weeks using the facility trying to recover the lost spacecraft. According to Masevich, when Venera automatically transmitted every five days, it would initially send out an unmodulated signal for seventeen min, then transmit coded scientific data. On June 11 and 12, Masevich and Khodarev succeeded, with Bernard Lovell's help, in picking up very weak signals from the area of space where Venera 1 should have been. However, at the time Venera 1 was almost 100 million km (61 million mi) from earth and signals were so weak that nothing of their nature could be determined.

AMERICAN PLANS ALTERED

While Venera 1 was in flight toward its destination, Russian scientists accomplished the ultimate triumph in the politically charged race into space; they orbited Yuri Gagarin. A Russian name thus became imprinted in the history books as the first human to orbit the earth. America's only immediate answer was two suborbital space hops by astronauts Alan Shepard and Gus Grissom. The second U.S. flight on July 21 resulted in more embarrassment for NASA when the spacecraft sank in the ocean after landing, nearly drowning Grissom. Two weeks later, the Russians compounded their own triumph by lofting Gherman Titov into orbit for an entire day.

The American space image was rapidly dimming relative to that of the Soviets. Our attempt to orbit a man was still months in the future. NASA desperately wanted to beat the Russians to the planets to even up the "race." NASA and JPL looked at their planetary options and came to a decision on August 30. It was clear that the Centaur booster would not be ready in 1962. NASA decided to cancel Mariner A and prepare a Mariner B for either Venus or Mars in 1964 under the assumption that Centaur would be ready by then. In the meantime, plans for the smaller Mariner R were dusted off for twin shots toward Venus in 1962. NASA was going to do whatever it took to get to Venus quickly, even if it meant using the smaller probe aboard an Atlas-Agena.

From the time the project was approved, only one year remained before the launch window to Venus opened on July 18, 1962. In the fall of 1961, JPL furiously prepared the little planetary explorers. Mariner R's weight was shaved to the bone while some existing Mariner A electronics and experiments were integrated into the design. Even the Agena booster was placed on a crash diet to sweat off unneeded pounds which would impede its escape from earth. As JPL's Mariner team dug into the fine details of the mission, they were aware that the first two Rangers, Mariner's parent craft, had failed. In light of this they redoubled their efforts. While similar to Ranger in design, Mariner came under the jurisdiction of a different team within JPL and the probe's development accelerated.

BUILDING THE INTERPLANETARY TRAVELER

Mariner's assignment seemed deceptively simple: pass near Venus, perform a meaningful planetary experiment and communicate the results back to earth. In other words, its only goal was to survive the trip so that the United States could claim it got to Venus first. However, sending a probe to another planet presented special challenges to American spacecraft designers. The sheer distance to even the closest planet presented awesome dependability and communications problems. The Mariners would have to travel three months to reach Venus. Results would be communicated back to earth over record distances. Additionally, all of the craft's components had to operate in a vacuum. Unlike heavy Soviet space probes which had the luxury of enclosing their instruments in a cozy pressurized container, instruments aboard the lighter Mariners had to learn to work in the harsh nothingness of space. If these obstacles were not formidable enough, JPL had only eleven months to design, build, test, and launch both of the new spacecraft.

The new Venus probe took the same hexagonal shape as the Rangers, their body being built around a 1.5-m (4.9-ft)-wide magnesium and aluminum frame. Topped by a derrick-like superstructure, the probe stood 3.6 m (11.8 ft) high. Twin solar panels unfolded to a span of 5 m (16.4 ft) and contained 5810 solar cells providing 222 watts of power to a 1-kilowatt/hr silver-zinc battery. At the base of the spacecraft, a 22.7-kg (50-lb)-thrust course correction rocket had the capability of changing Mariner's velocity by up to 61 m (200 ft) per sec. The hydrazine-fueled motor could be fired once for up to 57 seconds duration.

The first Mariners had no imaging capability because Venus was totally cloud covered. Seven experiments, weighing a total of 18.6 kg (41 lb), were chosen to provide the first basic data about space between earth and Venus and the environment near Venus. All except one was mounted on the superstructure. Five would operate continuously on the way to Venus while two were exclusively used at the planet. The solar plasma analyzer used to study the solar wind was mounted on the craft's hexagonal body while the magnetometer was tucked under the omni-directional antenna atop the superstructure. A particle flux detector studied cosmic rays, an ion chamber analyzed electrically charged solar particles, and a cosmic dust detector looked for micrometeor impacts. Looking like a miniature radio telescope, a 48.8-cm (19.3-in)-diameter dish-shaped device called a scanning radiometer would measure microwave emissions from the surface of Venus to deduce the planet's temperature. An infra-red radiometer, mounted piggy-back on the microwave dish, measured the temperature higher in the atmosphere.

To successfully accomplish its mission, Mariner would have to remain in continuous contact with earth for 2500 hr, carefully maintaining the aim of its hinged 1.5-m (4.9-ft)-diameter directional antenna within one degree of its home planet. Data would be trickled back to earth at 8.3 bits per sec over a 3-watt radio link (the same power as a common citizens band radio.)

Mariner was to be stabilized in space by ten gas jets drawing from a 1.95-kg (4.3-lb) nitrogen supply. This was enough to last an estimated two hundred days. Its control system would keep the solar panels aimed at the sun while aiming the directional antenna toward earth. The craft could drift up to one degree before firing a control jet for 0.02 seconds to nudge the craft back into alignment. Mariner would then take an hour to reach the opposite one degree limit before another gas jet fired. The craft would thus gently rock back and forth during its entire 4-month trip to Venus.

As the Mariners would be approaching the sun during their flight, their heat load would double near Venus. The various parts of the spacecraft were painted white, covered with gold foil or polished to reflect solar heat. In all, the new planetary explorers comprised 54,000 components packed into a machine weighing only 203.6 kg (449 lb).

A NONHYPHENATED FLIGHT

By May 1962 three spacecraft, Mariners 1 and 2, plus a backup, had been shipped to Cape Canaveral. Amazingly, only 324 days after the program was approved, the first Mariner was poised atop its Atlas-Agena. After a two-day launch delay, Mariner was set to lift off on the morning of July 22.

Mariner's moment of truth came at 4:21 A.M. as the Atlas-Agena rose into the night from Launch Pad 12 and arced over the Atlantic. For two minutes all seemed well, then the Atlas wobbled, slipped off course and started to drift toward populated areas. The vehicle pushed progressively further off course until the Range Safety Officer had no choice—293 seconds into the flight he blew up the rocket. But the spacecraft did not die easily. Torn from its launcher at the edge of space, Mariner 1 desperately tried to radio data for 64 sec, then fell silently into the ocean.

As pieces of the shattered Mariner lay with the fishes, an exasperated Congress grew impatient with JPL. Ranger probes to the moon using similar hardware had also been failing in space with unnerving regularity. One Congressman lamented Mariner 1's $14 million loss when he angrily declared that America should be beyond this stage of space exploration.[12] But then, these were NASA's "shoot 'n learn" days. An earlier analysis had pegged the mission's chances of complete success at only forty-two percent. Regrettably, this was one NASA prediction that came true.

A desperate investigation searched for the cause of the booster's deviation. Only fifty-two more days remained to get Mariner 2 away from earth before Venus traveled out of range of the Atlas-Agena booster. A twofold problem was quickly uncovered. The Atlas booster's radio guidance antenna was defective. After two minutes of flight, it ceased functioning four separate times. Unable to hear the guidance signal, the Atlas' own guidance system was then supposed to search for another signal from the ground and restore the rocket's proper trajectory. But a computer programming error had left out a command in the form of a single hyphen and the Atlas was unable to execute the search—with disastrous results. The lack of a single keystroke had caused NASA considerable anxiety and expense.

FLIGHT TO VENUS

Thirty-six days later, Mariner 2 was ready to leave earth after heroic efforts by the launch crew to overcome a vexing series of technical problems. At 1:53 A.M., August 27, the Atlas-Agena flared into life and rose into space. This time it followed the desired trajectory, but not without causing anxiety among the flight controllers. One of the Atlas' small steering rockets jammed in a fully deflected position causing the Atlas to roll at one revolution per min. After nearly overwhelming the Agena's guidance system, the roll was corrected just before the Agena stage separated. Liberated from the cranky Atlas, the Agena stage then performed flawlessly, first entering an earth parking orbit, then dutifully blasting Mariner into deep space.

Rushing away from earth, Mariner 2 obediently unfolded its antenna and solar panels, then stabilized itself. As the craft began to report on interplanetary space, tracking data determined Mariner 2 would miss Venus by 375,900 km (233,584 mi) instead of the desired 29,000 km (18,020 mi). On September 4 a 28.3-sec firing of the course correction motor gave Mariner 2 a 112 km (70 mile) per hr push. The craft would now pass just under 35,000 km (22,000 mi) from Venus on December 14, well within mission tolerances. Care had to be taken not to hit Venus accidentally and contaminate the planet with stowaway earth microbes.

As Mariner fell toward the sun, it confirmed theories that solar plasma, or the solar wind, flowed outward from the sun throughout the solar system. It also noted that, unlike craft near the earth which register many micrometeor impacts, Mariner only detected two during its entire voyage.

On October 30, mission controllers received another scare when the spacecraft's power suddenly decreased by half, probably because of a solar panel short circuit. The experiments were turned off to conserve remaining power. Then, nine days later, the power mysteriously restored itself and all was well again until November 15 when the panel went dead for good. Fortunately, Mariner 2 was now close enough to the sun that its increased intensity allowed the remaining panel to deliver the needed power.

By November 25, Mariner had broken Pioneer 5's long-distance communication record of 36.2 million km (22.5 million mi). However, as the craft approached the sun it began to heat up, causing worry among the mission controllers.

On December 7, the Venusian gravity began to have a noticeable effect on Mariner's trajectory. As Venus loomed closer, the temperature sensors also reached their upper limits. The overheating raised fears that the spacecraft's sequencer would fail to activate the radiometer experiments at planetary encounter. As a hedge, controllers radioed a command to Mariner 2 just twelve hours before its closest approach. Then 57.6 million km (35.8 million mi) from earth, the radiometers responded. The instruments began to search for Venus by scanning back and forth through a 120-degree arc at one degree per sec.

Approaching Venus from the night side, Mariner passed 34,827 km (21,641 mi) from the planet. The probe's radiometers found their target, then slowed their scan rate to 0.1 degrees per sec. They first scanned the dark side, then across the day-night terminator, then the day side during a 35-min close encounter. Slipping into uncharted territory inside the orbit of Venus, Mariner 2 was almost anticlimactic as it claimed the Venusian planetary prize for the United States. To the public, the flight to Venus seemed routine, but NASA now had its desperately needed planetary victory.

During the close pass, the dust detector found no impacts and the magnetometer and particle detectors found no evidence of magnetic fields or radiation belts like those which surround earth. As the radiometer data were analyzed, it revealed that the Venusian surface was an even more shocking hell than most had dared to anticipate. The instrument reported a surface temperature of 425°C (800°F) with little difference between day and night temperatures. Infrared data showed that the clouds were between 50 and 70 km (31 and 43 mi) above the surface. Additionally, the gravity of Venus had deflected Mariner's path by 40 degrees as the spacecraft passed the planet. This allowed the first determination of the overall density of the planet, showing an average of just over five grams per cubic cm, a close match to earth.

Mariner 2 remained in contact and reported on interplanetary space out to a distance of 86.7 million km (53.9 million mi). By the new year it was overheating badly. Then, after 129 days of continuous operation, the historic first planetary probe gasped its last message before succumbing to the heat. On January 3, 1963, Mariner 2 expired after having done an outstanding job, relaying 90 million bits of pioneering data.

Although JPL director William Pickering was under congressional fire because of continuing problems with Mariner's parent spacecraft, the lunar Rangers, a grateful America paid him homage for guiding the successful Mariner program. Pickering even rode a Mariner float leading the 1963 Rose Bowl parade in Pasadena, California.

BOOSTER PROBLEMS IMPERIL VENERA PROGRAM

As the initial U.S. attempts to reach Venus with two Mariner spacecraft progressed in summer 1962, space officials expected the Soviets to try again for the veiled planet. The western news media played up the expected Venus flights as a "race." The Soviets were expected to launch their next Venera probe shortly after Mariners 1 and 2 had already departed from earth. Although the Soviet spacecraft would leave earth later than the Mariners, celestial mechanics would allow the Russian planetary upstarts to arrive at Venus before the Mariners, supplying the Soviets with another of their familiar space exploration propaganda triumphs.

During the interval following the last Venus launch window, Korolyov had redesigned the initial Soviet planetary probes as a unified spacecraft to carry out missions to both Venus and Mars. The resulting spacecraft, the heaviest interplanetary probes to date, were known as "Object MV" (Object Mars-Venera) and came in four versions. MV-1 and MV-3 were for dispatching Venus and Mars landers while MV-2 and MV-4 were Venus and Mars photographic fly-by probes.

The 1962 Venus launch window saw three Soviet attempts lift off from Tyuratam using the same type SL-6 Molniya rocket used for the Venera 1 flight the year before. However, the history of the new triple Venus attempt would be less glorious than previous Soviet space triumphs.

The first was launched August 25, just 48 hr before the Mariner 2 spacecraft successfully departed. This was to be an MV-1 lander which would leapfrog Mariner's simple fly-by. But as with Sputnik 7 the year before, the new probe was stranded in earth orbit when the persistent defect in the escape stage again caused ignition failure. The Soviets never admitted the malfunction and remained silent about the rocket debris left in low orbit. The U.S. Air Force's North American Air Defense Command space surveillance radars based in Alaska, Greenland, and Britain detected the failed shot as it silently circled the globe. While U.S. intelligence-gathering capabilities unmasked the now-secret rocket flight, governmental policy was to not disclose its existence, preventing the Soviets from deducing the extent of U.S. missile-detecting capabilities.

Satellites are recorded in NASA's bimonthly Goddard Satellite Situation Report using a sequential number listing. When debris from the failed Soviet launch was detected, its existence was not recorded on the Goddard report, but the numbers identifying the debris were omitted from the report. The Soviet representative at the United Nations, not knowing when to let a sleeping dog lie, raised a controversy when he accused the United States of launching secret military satellites and omitting these numbers on the Goddard report. U.S. representatives at the United Nations, rather than revealing the failed Soviet launch, simply stated that this story was not completely accurate.[13]

POLITICS AS USUAL

The problem of what to do about reporting the Soviet planetary launch attempt was solved when a television network broke the story. The source that accidentally made the disclosure asked not to be identified. NASA chief administrator James E. Webb also shied away from comment on the validity of the failure report. NASA even withheld all information about the trajectory of the fragments left in orbit.

The Soviet Union declined to confirm that a Venus attempt had been made, and no mention of U.S. allegations was made in the Soviet press. On August 30, 1962, after the failure was detected by the U.S., academician Leonid Sedov, attending the fourth International Symposium on Space Technology and Science in Tokyo, was caught in a bare-faced lie when he stated the Soviet Union was not planning a launch toward Venus. He further stated that no Soviet space shots had ever failed and claimed that the Soviet Union "makes an announcement" as soon as a rocket is launched.[14] Up to this time, the Soviets had always claimed complete success with their space exploration endeavors and carefully kept failures from the public eye. With orbital debris being tracked, Sedov's statements were exposed as nonsense.

After the news leak about the August 25 Venus launch, as well as another failed attempt to launch an MV-1 lander on September 1, Congress called for action. The chairmen of the Senate and House space committees, Senator Robert S. Kerr (D-Okla.) and Representative George P. Miller (D-Calif.), wrote a letter to James Webb stating that any information U.S. officials have about Soviet space failures should be made available to the American people. Kerr and Miller's letter to Webb was simply a political smoke screen occasioned by cold-war tensions between the United States and the Soviet Union. They were, in fact, trying to hide the fact that the American government already knew about the failures as congressional committees had been told the full details of Soviet space operations for some time.

After it became clear that the security lid was off, Webb agreed to the chairmen's requests. In a reply to the committees on September 5, 1962, Webb stated that NASA does not have the tracking ability to assess such failures, but instead receives that data from other government agencies, such as the Air Force and covert intelligence agencies.[15] On this point, Webb was correct. NASA was only capable of tracking active, transmitting space probes and possessed no radar surveillance equipment. He further disclosed that, thus far, two Soviet Mars attempts had been made (Webb was in error, only one Mars launch occurred) as well as four attempts to send a spacecraft to Venus.[16]

SOVIET SUCCESS IMAGE TARNISHED

Now that the rumors of Soviet space failures had been substantiated by Webb, the State Department and the U.S. Information Agency (USIA) disclosed that they had long argued that the world should be told about Soviet space failures as well as their successes. Their efforts had been thwarted by the military on the grounds that intelligence confidentiality and security needs outweighed any propaganda benefits. After the story broke in the U.S. news media, the National Security Council decided to allow disclosure of the Russian failures which were discovered by means outside the Soviet Union and, thus, would not endanger western espionage operatives. The U.S. Information Agency began broadcasting the news of the Soviet failures over its world-wide press network and the Voice of America Radio Network.

NASA agreed with the new policy of making Soviet space weaknesses public because its own space exploration program had endured humiliation over repeated failures in the late 1950s and early 1960s. The public image of NASA's hit-or-miss successes suffered in comparison to the apparent perfection of the Soviet program. Now that the truth was known, NASA would not have to bear as much fingerpointing by a scornful press.

Adding insult to injury, a third Soviet Venus probe also became trapped in a useless earth orbit following its launch September 12. The same booster design deficiency deprived an MV-2 Venus fly-by craft of its chance for glory.

Faced with the backfire of their propaganda efforts, the Soviets clammed up. When asked for comment after the world-wide revelation of their failed planetary attempts, the Soviet Foreign Ministry in Moscow proclaimed they had nothing to say and could not understand why anyone was interested.[17]

A TIME FOR ENGINEERING AND REANALYSIS

Following the 1962 triple failure, Korolyov and his assistant Semyin Kosberg realized that there was a generic fault in the SL-6 escape-stage propulsion system. The problem appeared to be in the engine fuel feed. This system had to supply fuel to the rocket engine while the propellant was floating in the tanks during the weightlessness of orbital freefall. To correct the recurring misfire, a way had to be found to keep the propellant around the tank's propellant feed ports.

After corrections were designed, a diagnostic flight was flown November 11, 1963, to test the new Molniya booster upper stage configuration. The payload was a different class of fly-by spacecraft, an MV-1A which was to pass the moon and photograph the remaining unseen part of the far side. Unfortunately, in an all-too-familiar scenario, this craft also remained rooted in a low earth orbit after the command was given to accelerate away from earth's gravity. The Soviets hid this new escape stage failure by designating the craft Cosmos 21, supposedly a scientific earth satellite.

VENUS REMAINS AN ENIGMA

By 1963, radio astronomy experiments performed by both Russian and American radio astronomers detected astonishingly high temperatures on Venus, but conflicting data caused some confusion. Studies in the millimeter-wave range indicated that the temperature on the surface of Venus was only 100°C (212°F), while centimeter-wave studies indicated a temperature of 300°C (572°F). Other infrared observations had shown the temperature at the cloud tops to be −40°C (−40°F).

Several theories were advanced to explain the discrepancy between the radio astronomy readings. One theory reasoned that the surface of Venus was indeed 300°C (572°F) while the atmosphere was cooler and that the atmosphere absorbed the centimeter wave emissions from the surface and re-emitted them as millimeter waves. A second theory assumed that the surface was emitting the millimeter-wave radiation and was only 100°C (212°F), while the ionosphere was the source of the high-temperature, centimeter-wave radiation.

Though these radio studies could be interpreted as confirming the Mariner 2 findings, many Soviet scientists did not accept these readings. They chose instead to retain the theories that the surface was cool, that the high temperatures were in the ionosphere. Therefore, the design for future Venus landing capsules did not allow for extremely high atmospheric temperatures.

One Russian researcher, Professor Dmitry Martynov, director of the State Astrophysical Institute in Kiev, put forward theories postulating that if the surface temperature was 300°C (572°F) while the cloud tops were −40°C (−40°F), then the Venusian atmosphere must be very dense. He stated that, for the observed temperature ratio, the lower atmosphere must be at least 50 km (31 mi) thick, with a surface pressure of up to 50 atmospheres.[18] No one realized just how prophetic Martynov's words were to be.

FOUR PROBES TO BLITZ VENUS

In 1964, Korolyov's attention became more focused on the burgeoning manned space program. Concentrating his efforts on the space spectaculars demanded by Khrushchev, he delegated more responsibility for lunar and planetary exploration programs to his assistant, Georgi Babakin. From here on, the Korolyov bureau would concentrate on manned spaceflight while the Babakin bureau, in cooperation with the experimental laboratories of the Lavochkin Association, would build unmanned lunar and planetary spacecraft.

After making additional engineering changes to the SL-6 Molniya booster, Korolyov and Kosberg felt sufficiently confident to commit the rocket to planetary flight once more. The Soviets lacked a world-wide tracking network like JPL's Deep Space Network. To make up for this shortcoming, they mounted huge tracking antennae on ocean-going ships to monitor the initial phases of the flight. Their deployment around the world usually signaled that something important was about to happen in their space program. When Soviet space tracking ships left port in February 1964, it was clear to western observers that Venus launches were imminent.

The 1964 Venus launch window provided time for no less than four attempts to loft the hybrid engineering test spacecraft known as the MV-1A. The objective was to secure close-up photographs of Venus during a fly-by.

The series got off to a bad start when the first two, flown on February 19 and March 1, failed to achieve earth parking orbit and crashed. The third Venus launch on March 27 reached orbit, but continuing problems with the escape stage left another Venus probe stranded. The latter was designated Cosmos 27.

On April 2, the original Sputnik launch pad at Tyuratam was the site of the fourth launch. Liftoff occurred at 5:30 A.M. and, this time, the escape stage ignited and propelled the planetary payload out of earth orbit. Western analysts estimated the craft's mass to be 825 kg (1819 lb).

ZOND 1 OBJECTIVE CLOAKED IN SECRECY

This was the Soviet's eighth Venus attempt to reach low-earth orbit, but only the second to successfully escape earth's gravity. Having been embarrassed seven consecutive times on Venus launch attempts, the Soviets engaged in deception to hide the objective of the mission and save face in case of failure. Initial Soviet announcements after the craft entered a low-earth parking orbit stated the payload was a small weather-testing laboratory. No mention was made of the Venus objective and details of the payload were not disclosed. After successfully leaving earth, the craft was given the generic name of Zond 1, or "Probe 1."

A day after launch, at 9:18 P.M., while at a distance of 563,270 km (350,016 mi) from earth, Zond performed a mid-course correction using an on-board rocket engine to refine its aim at Venus. At this point, the Soviets still refused to admit the true nature of Zond's mission. The TASS news agency said the probe was launched for the purpose of "further development of a space system for distant interplanetary flights."[19] Soviet announcements simply gave the probe's celestial coordinates and omitted all mention of Venus. When these coordinates were compared with values given in the NASA Planetary Flight Handbook, an examination of options available for reaching the planets prepared by NASA's Dr. Stanley Ross, it became apparent that Zond was indeed bound for Venus.

Zond would have passed 100,000 km (62,100 mi) from the sunlit side of Venus; therefore, another mid-course correction was attempted on May 14 at a distance of 14 million km (8.7 million mi) from earth. To align its course-correction engine, Zond had to roll its directional antenna away from earth. After that, the craft never reaimed its antenna toward earth. Either the craft suffered a control failure which prevented it from realigning its antenna, or the propulsion system experienced a catastrophic failure. Two months later, the probe silently arrived at the planet on July 24, 1964 after a 114 day flight. By late July, continuing Soviet silence indicated another Soviet Venus failure.

Some American planetary investigators were actually disappointed by the failure of Zond 1. At the time the U.S. planetary exploration program was in the shadow of the more glamorous Apollo manned lunar program. As one anonymous NASA official put it, the interplanetary program "has been shoved out in left field" by the manned program.[20] Had Zond 1 been successful, officials thought it would have spurred more NASA interest in interplanetary flight by fostering competition.

NEW CRAFT SPEARHEAD SOVIET PLANETARY ASSAULT

The successful launch of Zond 2 toward Mars in November 1964, followed by the lunar fly-by of Zond 3 in July 1965, showed that the flaws in the SL-6 booster's upper stage had apparently been eliminated. In late 1965, two MV-1 fly-by craft and two MV-2 landers were readied for ambitious flights to Venus.

The first probe was launched on November 12, 1965. After the usual one-orbit coast in an earth-parking orbit, Venera 2's escape stage ignited and propelled the 963-kg (2123-lb) probe away from earth. Soviet announcements stated that the craft was not designed to land on Venus, but instead carried "highly sophisticated and diverse" equipment to study the planet's atmosphere and its water content.

Three days later, when Venera 2 was 1,250,000 km (776,750 mi) from earth, a second Venus probe was launched. Using the same launch pad as its predecessor, the 960-kg (2116-lb) Venera 3 also successfully left the earth. This was the first time the Soviets had succeeded in flying two planetary spacecraft at the same time. An article in the newspaper *Izvestia* stated that the two craft would help develop "the technique of controlling the flight of a group of spaceships."[21]

Shortly after the second launch, the TASS news agency stated that Venera 3's "scientific equipment is somewhat different from Venera 2 as it is to solve a number of new scientific tasks."[22] Academician Leonid Sedov was quoted in *Izvestia* as saying that Veneras 2 and 3 were to pass on opposite sides of the planet and provide complementary data.[23]

Two more 1965 Venus flights carrying an MV-1 lander and MV-2 fly-by probe were attempted on November 23 and 26, however, the first, designated Cosmos 96, exploded in earth orbit while the second failed to reach orbit.

VENERA DESIGN REVEALED

The design of Veneras 2 and 3 was similar to previous MV spacecraft, being cylindrical in shape, roughly 1 m (3.3 ft) in diameter and 3.6 m (11 ft) long. Two solar panels spanning 4 m (13 ft) charged chemical batteries. Attached to the side of the spacecraft was a high-gain 2.25-m (7.3-ft) parabolic wire-mesh antenna. The spacecraft's orientation system used optical-electronic sensors and gyroscopes to stabilize it. Its prime task during the interplanetary cruise was to keep the solar panels facing the sun. A sun-seeker kept the solar panels aimed at the sun while an earth-seeker in the center of the parabolic antenna pointed toward earth during communications.

A major improvement over the earlier Venera 1 design was the inclusion of a mid-course correction rocket motor. Another improvement was replacing the old system of movable metal louvers with a new forced-gas cooling system which regulated the spacecraft's internal temperature. Coolant was circulated through hemispherical radiators mounted on the ends of the solar panels.

WIDE RANGE OF INSTRUMENTS CARRIED

In addition to conducting studies of interplanetary space the craft carried payload modules which Soviet announcements called "special compartments." After the completion of the dual Venus missions, it was revealed that on Venera 2 this module was a photographic payload while on Venera 3 it was a planetary lander.

Venera 2's camera was similar to the film and facsimile photo payload tested by Zond 3, which extended photographic coverage of the far side of the moon. In addition to visible light images, the system was also to gather ultraviolet and infrared spectra. On Venera 3, the special compartment consisted of a parachute-equipped 337-kg (743-lb) atmospheric entry capsule containing atmospheric measurement instruments which was to be ejected from the spacecraft just prior to entering the atmosphere.

To protect the capsule from the intense heat encountered during the meteor-like entry into the Venusian atmosphere, the TASS news agency said it had "heat-resisting substances applied to its surface."[24] This heat shield would face a severe test when Venera 3 slammed into the planet's atmosphere at the highest entry velocity yet for any spacecraft.

After the flight, the Soviets said that Venera 3's lander had been sterilized to protect the Venusian environment from contamination by earth microbes. No mention was made about sterilization of the spacecraft bus, but it was presumed that it would not survive atmospheric entry.

The Soviets called the entry capsule "the descending apparatus." The 90-cm (35-in)-diameter spherical descent capsule had its center of gravity positioned so that it would be self-righting on atmospheric entry, thus exposing the heaviest portion of the capsule's ablative coating to atmospheric heating. After decelerating into the lower atmosphere, the capsule's back plate was to be ejected and the parachutes deployed. Instruments would then switch on to measure atmospheric temperature and density. Due to uncertainty about the surface composition of Venus, the Venera 3 lander carried sensors to determine if the capsule landed on a solid surface or in a liquid ocean.

The capsule also contained Soviet emblems to commemorate the first landing on another planet. The lander carried a 70-mm (3-in) sphere with the outline of earth's continents. The sphere contained a medal similar to that carried by Venera 1. It had the U.S.S.R. coat of arms on one side and the inner planets on the other, with earth and Venus in the correct position for the time of launching. An inscription read "Union of Soviet Socialist Republics, 1965."

INTERPLANETARY CRUISE

Following separation from its booster rocket, Venera 2's flight path was so accurate that no mid-course correction was needed. Venera 3, targeted for planetary impact, required more accurate aim; a slight course correction was necessary. Both Veneras carried a transponder, a device to retransmit radio signals beamed to the spacecraft, to measure the craft's speed and distance using Doppler measurements of the craft's radio signal. This method listened for a frequency shift in the retransmitted radio signals which is analogous to the change in pitch of a passing train whistle. Minute changes in the velocity of the spacecraft would measurably change the pitch of the signal, allowing its precise velocity to be determined. Venera 3's initial miss distance without any correction would have been 60,550 km (37,626 mi). Forty days after launch and 10 million km (6.2 million mi) from earth, the craft executed its course correction at 7:04 P.M., December 26.

When changing the aim of the spacecraft, another factor had to be considered: Venera 3's arrival time at Venus. Before the correction, the craft would have arrived at Venus at about midnight Moscow time, when the planet was not in the line of sight of the tracking facility. It was necessary to change the probe's arrival by almost ten hours to put it in the field of view of receiving antennas at Yevpatoria.

The total velocity change imparted on Venera 3 was 21.7 m (71 ft) per sec. Most of this was in the form of a lateral push perpendicular to the spacecraft's trajectory, a maneuver known as an orbital plane change, to place the probe on an impact trajectory. The actual forward velocity of the spacecraft was changed by only a few centimeters per sec, but this was enough to alter the time of planetary rendezvous by the necessary 10 hr.

FIRST SOVIET ENCOUNTER WITH ANOTHER PLANET

After 108 days in space, Venera 2 approached its target on February 27, 1966. Communications were lost just as the final command was given to begin the planetary encounter photo sequence, i.e., at the critical moment of planetary encounter. It is not known if Venera 2 actually photographed Venus after contact was lost. There were plans to attempt contact with the spacecraft later in the year when it made a close approach to earth, but the lack of published results indicates that this attempt was probably not successful.

Just before arrival at Venus, telemetry from the spacecraft showed an unexplained increase in internal temperature prior to communications failure. Apparently the cooling system failed, causing the electronics to overheat at a crucial time; or the increased solar radiation at Venus overwhelmed the craft's cooling system. The now-silent Venera 2 flew past Venus at an altitude of 24,140 km (15,000 mi), making its closest approach at 5:52 A.M.

Two days later, Venera 3 approached Venus. Following in Venera 2's footsteps, Soviet announcements recounted that communications were lost just before the lander was to separate. After a 106-day flight from earth, the silent Venera 3 entered the Venusian atmosphere on the night side of the planet and struck the surface at an estimated 9:56:26 A.M. on March 1, 1966. At the time, Venus was 61 million km (37.9 million mi) from earth. Soviet officials claimed that their aim was incredibly accurate, declaring that the craft impacted only 450 km (280 mi) from the center of the visible disk of the planet.

Modern revelations about the mission of Venera 3 tell a different story. Communications with the probe were actually lost during the first half of its flight. The stated trajectory was therefore one calculated after launch. In light of this, the phenomenal aim of Venera 3 would seem to be merely propaganda embellishment. If the craft indeed struck Venus, the landing capsule likely survived the entry into the atmosphere, but the true nature of Venus was not known at that time and the capsule was not designed to withstand the planet's high atmospheric pressure. It probably was crushed as it sank into the lower reaches of the atmosphere.

While planetary data were lost, Veneras 2 and 3 did report on magnetic fields, cosmic radiation, the charged particles and plasma from the sun, micrometeor strikes, and cosmic long-wave radio emissions. In spite of not receiving any planetary data, the arrival of Venera 3 on Venus was regarded as a momentous display of space navigation.

Up to this point, the Soviet planetary program had a total of eighteen launches, including Mars shots. Although there were some engineering successes and new photos of the far side of the moon, the Soviets had not received one bit of planetary information. U.S. planetary efforts fared better with NASA batting 0.500. Mariners 2 and 4 had succeeded far beyond their designers' wildest dreams and returned stunning data from Venus and Mars.

WAS THE PLANETARY STRIKE AN ACCIDENT?

As the historic Venera 3 impact on Venus faded into aerospace history, some observers seriously questioned whether the planetary strike was intentional or just an accident. Although it would seem that a planetary hit would be a natural goal of the Venera program, the possibility does exist that this was not the mission's objective. Prior to Venera 3's historic encounter with Venus, both academician Leonid Sedov and Professor V. Ivanchenko stated that the objectives of the Veneras 2 and 3 missions were to investigate Venus by passing on opposite sides of the planet. They said that complementary data could be obtained by opposite fly-by missions.

How do these announcements square with the end result of the Venera 3 mission? One scenario presented in the prestigious British magazine, *Spaceflight*, is that the Soviets were not aware that the craft was on a collision course until it was too late to correct the trajectory.[25] Some observers speculated that the Soviets had taken advantage of the communications failure of Venera 3 to change the description of the mission for propaganda purposes. With no radio contact with the craft, no western observers could say that Venera 3 did not have a lander. Subsequent descriptions of the descending apparatus could have referred to actual equipment designed for the next planetary attempt. In rebuttal to these speculations, Ivanchenko wrote in *Izvestia* that a direct hit on Venus was the flight assignment of Venera 3.[26]

Regardless of what future examination of historical archives reveals about the purpose of the Venera 3 mission, for now history records the flight as delivering the first object from earth to the surface of another planet. Even though the Venera 3 craft failed to return any data, it restored the Soviet honor demeaned by losing the race with Mariner 2 to Venus.

6 Mysteries Slowly Revealed

VENERA 4 TO PROBE THE ATMOSPHERE

In the mid-1960s, most Soviet planetary scientists still did not accept theories that the Venusian surface was very hot. They maintained this position in spite of radio astronomy observations of the planet and the Mariner 2 results which indicated that the visible disk of the planet was hot while the limb was cool, implying that the heat was from the surface, not the upper atmosphere and ionosphere. The scientists who designed the Venera lander chose to interpret this evidence differently, as indicating a high-temperature ionosphere, rather than a hot surface. The specifications for the Venera landing capsules thus anticipated a low-temperature, low-pressure atmosphere.

Although Babakin made engineering changes to improve the Venera spacecraft's reliability, the next Venus probe was still outwardly similar to the previous craft. The overall mass at launch was 1086 kg (2394 lb), the heaviest probe yet. As a result of the Venera 2 and 3 overheating problems, a new temperature-control system was incorporated. External equipment used insulation and reflective coatings for thermal protection. Heat-producing equipment in the pressurized compartment was cooled by forced-gas circulation through flat radiators on the back side of the solar panels.

The spacecraft's trajectory could be altered using an onboard KDU-414 engine. This 202-kg (445.5-lb) thrust engine carried 35 kg (77 lb) of unsymmetrical dymethyl hydrazine and nitric acid propellants, and could be fired twice. Its engine design proved so satisfactory that it was used on all future first-generation Veneras through 1972.

For monitoring interplanetary space between earth and Venus, the spacecraft bus carried a magnetometer, cosmic-ray counters, and solar charged particle detectors. Hydrogen and oxygen ion detectors and an ultraviolet photometer were to study the upper reaches of the Venusian atmosphere.

ATMOSPHERIC PROBE CARRIED

The new probe was designed to deliver an entry capsule into the atmosphere of Venus to measure its temperature, pressure, bulk composition, and density. It was designed as well to attempt a landing on the surface. The 1-m (3.3-ft) diameter, 383-kg (844-lb) capsule carried a heat-resistant parachute, radio telemetric equipment, two temperature sensors, an aneroid barometer, a radio altimeter, an ionization densitometer (atmospheric density detector), eleven gas analyzers and an accelerometer.

The temperature sensors operated between 0 and 400°C (32 and 752°F), and determined the temperature by measuring the changes in the conductivity of a platinum wire across an electrical bridge circuit. The atmospheric-density detector operated by measuring the current between the inner surface of a strontium-90-coated cylinder and a central electrical filament. The lander's gas analyzers were capable of detecting molecules of oxygen, nitrogen, carbon dioxide, and water vapor. Each analyzer consisted of two chambers, one of which contained a material which absorbed the particular gas to be detected. After the chambers were filled with atmospheric gas and sealed, the pressure difference between the twin chambers caused by the absorption of a particular gas molecule determined the amount of that gas present in the sample.

The entry capsule was designed to withstand a 350-g atmospheric deceleration. The heavy battery was at the bottom, lowering the center of gravity to stabilize the capsule. The thickest portion of the heat shield was also at the bottom of the capsule. As the outer layers of the shield were eroded by friction with the atmosphere, it protected the capsule by carrying away heat through the evaporation of its surface. The parachute was at the cooler top of the capsule. Even the possibility that Venus was covered with an ocean of petroleum was anticipated as the lander was designed to float.

Academician Mstislav Keldish related that special high-strength, heat-resisting materials with high melting points had been used in the construction of the capsule. When asked for particulars at a post-flight press conference, he added with a smile, "Those are the secrets of the firm."[1]

The capsule contained two hermetically sealed compartments, one for the parachute, the other for the instruments which were spring-suspended for shock protection. The instrument compartment contained batteries, the radio transmitters, telemetry system, control system, temperature-control system, radio altimeter and scientific instruments. Like Venera 3, the new craft also carried a pennant with the U.S.S.R. coat of arms to commemorate the planned landing. The descent capsule's batteries were connected to a section of the main spacecraft's solar panels so they could be constantly charged during interplanetary cruise. The parachute compartment contained a drogue chute and a 50-m² (538-ft²) main parachute capable of withstanding temperatures of 450°C (842°F). Also in the parachute compartment were three radio antennae, one to broadcast a narrow conical beam toward earth and two for the radio altimeter. The parachute was to be ejected only seconds before landing to prevent the capsule being pulled over by winds and breaking radio contact with earth.

To test their designs, Lavochkin engineers conducted a simulated mission to the vicinity of Venus prior to the actual flight. Simulations also tested the descent capsule using vacuum and pressure chambers. The capsule was placed in a vacuum chamber above a high-temperature, high-pressure chamber so the craft could be quickly dropped from one environment to the other.

FLIGHT TOWARD THE INNER PLANET

Venera 4 was launched June 12, 1967. A twin spacecraft was also launched June 17, but after achieving an earth parking orbit, the second probe's escape stage failed to ignite, stranding the craft in orbit. To cover the failure, the launch was designated "Cosmos 167."

By July 14, Venera 4 had reached a distance of eight million km (five million mi) from earth. The probe reported that the intensity of solar flares and cosmic radiation had increased hundreds of times over that measured in 1964 and 1965 by previous interplanetary probes.

Calculations performed after launch showed the spacecraft would miss its target by 160,000 km (99,424 mi). Venera 4 therefore performed a mid-course correction on July 29 while at a distance of 12 million km (7.5 million mi) from earth.

Engineers revealed that an exact replica of Venera 4 was kept in a thermobarometric simulation chamber. The space environment as reported from deep space was duplicated in the chamber to serve as a systems check. This underscored continuing Soviet concern about the reliability of their planetary spacecraft. The duplicate spacecraft was exercised in this environment to check its reactions to various commands before they were sent to the Venera 4 in space. Several changes were made in the procedures to control the temperature of the spacecraft as a result of these simulations.

After a flight of 128.4 days, covering a distance in solar orbit of 338 million km (210 million mi), Venera 4 reached its destination on October 18. Communication was begun 117 min before the spacecraft entered the planet's atmosphere. The atmospheric entry capsule detached from the Venera 4 bus while still approximately 45,000 km (28,000 mi) from the planet. The "radio capsule," as the Soviets called it, encountered the planet's atmosphere at 7:34 A.M., October 18. Entry velocity was 10.7 km (6.65 mi) per sec on the night side of the planet at latitude 19 degrees North and longitude 38 degrees.

A heat shield made of glass fiber and polymer materials protected the capsule from temperatures reaching 11,000°C (19,832°F) in the surrounding shock wave. After aerodynamic deceleration to 300 m (984 ft) per sec, a pressure sensor triggered the ejection of the capsule's upper cap. A braking parachute was deployed to further slow the capsule before the main parachute canopy was deployed. The antenna system was deployed simultaneously and transmissions to earth began. After reaching a preset pressure at 7:39 A.M., the capsule's scientific instruments were switched on and the craft provided the first direct measurements from within the Venusian atmosphere. Initially, the parachute descent rate was 10 m (32 ft) per sec. In the denser lower portions of the atmosphere, the rate of descent slowed to only 3 m (9.8 ft) per sec.

BRITISH HELP TRACK PROBE

Because of communications problems with previous planetary probes, the Soviets asked Bernard Lovell to use the 76-m (250-ft) radio telescope at Jodrell Bank to monitor Venera 4's signals when it encountered Venus. A Soviet communiqué asked Lovell to do so because of the "extraordinary importance and significance" of the event.[2] They did not, however, say the craft was to enter the atmosphere of Venus.

Jodrell Bank received signals starting at 6 A.M. As Venera 4 made its final approach to Venus, a command was sent from earth to orient the main parabolic antenna toward earth. Signal strength then increased 300-fold. At 7:38 A.M., the signal ceased. After fifteen seconds, new signals with only twenty percent of the previous strength and different in tone were picked up. Atmospheric data were radioed across the 80-million-km (50-million-mi) void between earth and Venus for 96 min, continuing until 9:14 A.M. when transmission suddenly stopped. Not having the key to decode the Venera 4 signals, Lovell sent the recorded tapes directly to Moscow for analysis.

Jubilant Soviet technicians thought they had reached the surface of Venus at last. After fourteen attempts to probe the veiled planet, they proclaimed their spacecraft had touched down on another planet a mere ten years after the dawn of the space age.

Few initial details were released about the historic encounter. The lack of official information from the Soviet Government prompted the newspaper *Pravda* to actually telephone Jodrell Bank in England for details of what happened to the Venera 4 probe.

But why had the signals ceased at touchdown? Had the parachute failed? Was the lander blown over by high winds with its antenna now pointing away from earth? Had it crashed on a mountain side? The answer lay in a Venusian atmosphere even more bizarre than the Soviets had dared anticipate. Later analysis showed the first signal ended when the spacecraft bus was destroyed by atmospheric entry. For the next 15 seconds, the lander was decelerating through the atmosphere. The second set of weaker signals were from the descent capsule parachuting through the Venusian atmosphere. The signal loss at 9:14 A.M. did not occur on reaching the surface, but instead came when the capsule was crushed by Venus' high atmospheric pressure.

Although the mission was a stunning success, Venera 4 nearly ended prematurely. Babakin, writing anonymously in the newspaper *Krasnaya Zvezda*, reported that Venera 4 was overheating when it approached Venus and that controllers did not always have firm communications with it.

SAMPLING AN ALIEN ATMOSPHERE

At an altitude of 200 km (124 mi), just moments before plunging into the atmosphere, the probe's magnetometer determined that the planet's maximum magnetic field was only 10 gammas. This is 5000 times less than earth's magnetic field. Observations of the solar wind bow shock, or the zone where the solar wind is repelled by a planet's magnetic field, showed the bow shock is much closer to Venus than it is above earth. While the shock wave above earth is at 20,000 km (12,500 mi) altitude, the corresponding phenomenon on Venus is only 500 km (310 mi) above the planet because of the weak magnetic field. Without a strong planetary magnetic field to contain solar energetic particles, it was not surprising that no radiation belt was detected around Venus.

As the capsule drifted downward, the atmospheric pressure rose to 18.5 kg per square cm (263 lb per square in). The temperature also rose from 39 to 270°C (102 to 518°F). Data transmission began at an altitude of 55 km (34 mi) and stopped at 27 km (16.7 mi). Venera project scientists were surprised that the probe fell more slowly than anticipated and that the probe was crushed by the atmosphere. The longer than expected drop to the surface almost exhausted the lander's 100-min battery life.

During atmospheric descent, the probe's gas analyzers were used twice. The first sampling took place immediately after the parachute was deployed. Here, the atmospheric pressure was equal to 520 mm of mercury, or half of the earth's surface pressure, and the temperature was 40°C (104°F). The second sampling was carried out 347 seconds later when the pressure was 1500 mm of mercury and the temperature had risen to 80°C (176°F).

In November 1967, published results showed that the atmosphere consisted of 98.5 percent carbon dioxide, 0.4 to 0.8 percent oxygen and less than 2.5 percent nitrogen. The Venusian climate was described as cloudy, but without precipitation. A water vapor reading of 1.5 percent was in error because the early Venera humidity sensors were contaminated by sulphuric acid, a chemical which at the time was not known to be present in the Venusian atmosphere.

Noting the high concentration of carbon dioxide, researchers speculated that Venus' early water supply evaporated when Venus' proximity to the sun caused greenhouse-like heating. When the temperature reached about 250°C (482°F), calcium and magnesium carbonates disintegrated from the heat, releasing vast amounts of carbon dioxide into the atmosphere. Curiously, earth and Venus contain about equal amounts of carbon dioxide, but on earth it is locked in the crustal rocks while on Venus it is in the atmosphere.

The high concentration of carbon dioxide in Venus' atmosphere creates an unusual optical effect called "super refraction"—where the curvature of light rays is greater than the curvature of the horizon. Theorists speculated that an observer on the surface would see the illusion of a raised horizon.

After fully comprehending the superheated, high-pressure nature of the Venusian atmosphere, it was realized that the planet could not contain the same amount of water as does earth. The extreme temperature on the planet obviously precluded the presence of liquid water. Further, if a volume of water vapor equal to earth's water supply were present in Venus' atmosphere, it would create a surface pressure of 300 atmospheres. Not even the most far-fetched Venusian atmospheric theories postulated such a pressure.

Since that huge amount of water vapor and pressure was not found on Venus, scientists speculated over the rate at which Venus loses its water. Assuming the density of the observed hydrogen corona (the halo of rarified hydrogen high above the planet) remains constant, it was calculated that photodissociation, the splitting of water vapor into atomic oxygen and hydrogen by solar ultraviolet radiation, produces an annual loss of one-third of a cubic kilometer of water.

The Venera 4 findings did not deter the ongoing debate about the possibility of life on Venus. Some noted that certain earth microbes can withstand temperatures of 130°C (266°F) and others could withstand pressures of 100 atmospheres. It was thought similar organisms might survive in the upper Venusian atmosphere.

POLITICS REMAINS A FACTOR

Venera 4 was a major space exploration milestone, being the first successful Soviet planetary mission as well as the first successful penetration of the Venusian atmosphere. Their space program had suffered a loss of international prestige following the death of cosmonaut Vladimir Komarov earlier in the year when his Soyuz 1 spacecraft crashed. The Venera 4 success did much to bolster the sagging image of Soviet space science. Strangely enough, and in spite of mounting evidence showing the Venusian atmosphere was a high-pressure furnace, some Soviet scientists stubbornly clung to the belief that Venera 4 had reached the surface before it ceased transmitting. Nationalistic pride pushed the Soviet Academy of Sciences into maintaining this scientific facade in spite of evidence showing the probe had failed while still high in the atmosphere.

For several years after the Venera 4 encounter, the Soviets continued this pretense. When they used the altitude at which Venera 4's signal ceased as the elevation of the surface of the planet, Soviet scientists were forced to extrapolate calculated figures which showed the planet's actual surface was below the crust of the planet. It was not until later missions scored a genuine Soviet landing triumph that such scientific cover-ups disappeared.

While the Soviets were commended for their Venus achievement, it should also be seen in context with U.S. planetary successes in the modest Mariner spacecraft program. Russian scientists achieved their goal basically with brute force while American scientists were forced to approach Venus with more finesse. The mercurial fortunes of the U.S. space research budget made the unwavering Soviet assault on Venus the envy of western government-sponsored science. The success of U.S. efforts can be traced to the dedication of a small group of engineers who used innovation and wit to wring planetary success from chronic congressional underfunding. The Soviets, on the other hand, using the great power of their booster rockets, were able to build heavier spacecraft and use the "shotgun" approach, shooting at Venus again and again. While American scientists were forced to use bargain basement methods to reach Venus, the sheer magnitude of the decade-long Russian Venus effort eventually gave them their just planetary rewards.

A RECYCLED SPACECRAFT

The Russians were not the only ones knocking at Venus' door in 1967. The American Mariner 5 probe arrived at the cloud-shrouded planet a mere 37 hr after Venera 4 dropped in. The two missions would end up complementing each other with each spacecraft confirming the basic discoveries of the other. However, this happy circumstance was not according to a master plan. In fact, American scientists were in the dark about the true objectives of the Venera 4 flight until after the mission's success.

NASA's decision to return to Venus was not made until December 1965. This left only eighteen months to ready Mariner 5 for its solo flight to Venus in 1967. While the planning of the mission was complex, JPL had an ace up its sleeve. The 245-kg (540-lb) Mariner 5 could be fashioned from the backup Mars spacecraft built along with Mariners 3 and 4. After the successful Mariner 4 fly-by of Mars the previous summer, NASA decided to use the remaining spacecraft for a low-cost, single launch to Venus. In fact, the Mariner 5 mission was the most frugal of all NASA planetary missions.

Mariner 5 was to penetrate ten times closer to Venus than Mariner 2, increasing the chances of detecting any magnetic field or radiation belt. Scientists were especially interested in using the probe to carry a specialized radio system to answer a crucial question about the planet's environment: what was the surface pressure? This could be accomplished by a radio occultation experiment which measured the fading of the spacecraft's radio signals as they passed through progressively thicker layers of the Venusian atmosphere when Mariner 5 would fly behind the planet.

To accomplish the occultation experiment, a radio signal would be transmitted to Mariner from JPL's Deep Space Network antennas. This signal would be amplified and rebroadcast by Mariner in a continuous two-way radio loop. In addition to exploring the atmosphere, this would also allow the craft's position to be precisely determined to within 6 m (19.7 ft) at an 85-million-km (52.8 million mile) range by Doppler measurements of the signal's frequency. Determining Mariner's precise location was an important factor during the occultation experiment to define the atmosphere's altitude above Venus. A second dual frequency radio propagation experiment aboard Mariner was to probe the atmosphere down to the surface.

Mariner 5 retained the original craft's 46-cm (18-in)-high, 138-cm (54-in)-diameter octagonal body. Many subsystems such as the course correction rocket capable of 92 m (302 ft) per second velocity change and the attitude control system fueled with 2.35 kg (5.18 lb) of nitrogen gas were also the same. However, because Mariner 5 would be headed toward the sun instead of away as was Mariner 4, the spacecraft was modified to adapt to the increased heat. Stronger solar radiation closer to the sun allowed the luxury of reducing each of the four solar panels to 90 by 122 cm (35.5 by 44 in) since the 17,640 solar cells in that environment would still provide 550 watts of power at Venus. Also, because the craft was to travel between earth and the sun, the panels were mounted facing the opposite direction as before. To protect the spacecraft from the sun's heat, the solar panels were spaced half a meter (20 in) away from the spacecraft body. As the panels opened, attached lanyards also unfolded a 1.23-square-m (13.24-ft^2) aluminized teflon sun shield.

A major change from the original craft's payload was the deletion of the television camera and its tape recorder. This decision was made with regret, but the spacecraft's data handling capability could not support both the crucial radio occultation experiment and television imaging. Mariner 5 was NASA's last planetary mission which did not have an imaging capability. As a result, the new probe's tape recorder had only a one-megabit capacity using 15 m (49 ft) of continuous loop tape. During the encounter with Venus, 648,000 bits of data would be recorded for later playback at 8.3 bits per sec.

Three instruments were retained from the original Mariner 4-style design; a magnetometer, a solar plasma probe, and a radiation detector. A fourth instrument, an ultra-violet photometer, flown for the first time, would search for atomic hydrogen and atomic oxygen in the upper atmosphere.

Mariner 5's elliptical 53 × 117-cm (21 × 46-in) directional high-gain antenna was modified to operate in two different positions. During the spacecraft's close approach to Venus, the planet's gravity would quickly bend its trajectory. Thus, when Mariner popped out from behind the planet after its occultation, it would be traveling in a considerably altered trajectory. To assure that the directional antenna would be aimed at earth to provide the important atmospheric density measurements, the antenna would heel over to a different orientation relative to the spacecraft.

MARINER 5 CHASES VENERA 4

An Atlas-Agena lofted Mariner 5 from Cape Canaveral's Pad 12 at 2:01 A.M., June 14, 1967. The probe's initial path was deliberately aimed to miss Venus by 75,000 km (46,600 mi) to prevent the unsterilized Agena rocket from accidentally impacting Venus. Five days later, Mariner 5 performed a 15.4-m (50.5-ft)-per-sec velocity change to close the miss distance to 4094 km (2544 mi) across the leading side of Venus. This would allow the trajectory to pass directly behind Venus as seen from earth. As Mariner 5 chased the Russian Venera 4 across deep space, it enjoyed an uneventful flight to Venus, sampling interplanetary space with its nonradio experiments along the way.

On October 18, about 15 hr before passing Venus, the close encounter sequence was started by a command from earth. While still an hour away from Venus, the ultraviolet photometer located the planet and began scanning its upper atmosphere. Radio sounding of the atmosphere began shortly thereafter. Just five minutes before the 1:34 P.M., October 19, closest approach, the spacecraft slipped behind the limb of Venus and disappeared from earth view. Midway behind the planet, the directional antenna was shifted 18 degrees to ensure that it would be aimed at earth when the 26-min occultation ended. As the spacecraft swung around the planet, Venusian gravity deflected its path by 101.5 degrees and hurled it toward the sun at 30,650 km (19,046 mi) per hr.

The next day, Mariner 5 began the three-day process of transmitting recorded data. Some of the early results confirmed the Venera 4 findings and showed that Venus differed significantly from earth. No trapped radiation like earth's Van Allen radiation belts were found and the planet's magnetic field was no greater than one percent that of earth's. Additionally, the solar wind was found to press within several hundred kilometers of Venus compared to the tens of thousands of kilometers above earth. The ultraviolet photometer detected a high atomic hydrogen corona around Venus, but no oxygen. The same instrument detected a faint ultraviolet glow over the night side of the planet, this possibly being the origin of the mysterious "ashen light," or the faint glow on the night side of Venus, sometimes seen from earth. By analyzing the effect of Venus' gravity on Mariner's trajectory, the planet's mass was determined to be 81.5 percent that of earth.

The most important data from the flawless mission were yet to come. Extensive computer analysis of the occultation experiment eventually confirmed what American scientists had suspected after Mariner 2's encounter with Venus five years before. The surface of the planet was indeed extremely hot, at least 430°C (806°F) with a surface pressure between 75 and 100 atm. This pressure was equal to the pressure 780 m (2560 ft) below the surface of earth's oceans.

Mariner's radio occultation data about the depth and temperature of the lower atmosphere disagreed with Venera 4's readings. However, after factoring in the Mariner data, the Soviets finally revised their own temperature and pressure calculations to show that the planet's surface was closer to 500°C (932°F) with a pressure of 75 atm. The American data was so compelling that Russian scientists later admitted their probe did fail high in the atmosphere and had never reached the surface.

The Mariner 5 mission had been a complete success and valuable new data about the veiled planet revealed that it was far from "earth's twin" as previously imagined. Venera 4 and Mariner 5 together had proven that Venus was in fact a high-pressure hothouse surrounded by a thick cocoon of deadly carbon dioxide gas.

By November 21, Mariner 5 had traveled 117 million km (72.7 million mi) from earth where its faint signal was lost. After passing Venus, the probe entered into a solar orbit approaching within 86 million km (53.4 million mi) of the sun, closer than any deep space probe to date. Attempts to re-establish contact for an extended scientific mission began the following April. These efforts were not successful until October 1968, but even then only the unmodulated carrier signal was detected. No telemetry was received and the spacecraft did not respond to commands. On the November 5, 1968, Mariner 5 was given up as lost.

BASIC RUSSIAN SPACECRAFT DESIGN RETAINED

After Venera 4 vividly demonstrated the crushing atmospheric pressure on Venus, there was insufficient time before the 1969 launch opportunity to develop a Russian lander capable of surviving the pressure at the surface. Instead, quick improvements were made to the existing design. Scientists knew the craft would not reach the surface, but valuable information about the Venusian atmosphere would be gained. At the same time, a program was started to build reinforced landers capable of reaching the surface in 1970.

Externally, Veneras 5 and 6 were near duplicates of Venera 4, retaining the design which had proved capable of reaching Venus. The primary goals of the new flights were to repeat the Venera 4 experiment and consolidate information already obtained about Venus. At the time of launch, the twin Veneras 5 and 6 each weighed 1139 kg (2511 lb) and both carried a 405-kg (893-lb) descent capsule.

The Venera 4 experience had educated Soviet planetary scientists about the nature of the dense, superheated Venusian atmosphere. It was clear that, in order to make significant new discoveries, future probes would have to traverse the atmosphere more quickly to avoid prolonged exposure to the rapidly rising temperature. The descent through Venus' atmosphere was a race against time. Slowly drifting through the atmosphere under a large parachute guaranteed instrument failure by the electronic equivalent of heat stroke.

The parachutes were reduced to 15 square m (161 square ft) and upgraded to withstand 500°C (932°F). While Venera 4 had a pressure rating of 20 atm, Veneras 5 and 6 were to withstand 27. Further improvements included a special liquid, shock-absorbing mechanism to help the instruments survive an anticipated 450-*g* deceleration. These higher stresses would be caused by the different alignment between earth with Venus at the time of launch, forcing the probe to arrive at a higher velocity and enter at a steeper angle.

Scientific instrumentation was similar to that on Venera 4. Additions included a new atmospheric density meter which performed measurements based on the changes in the oscillation of a tuning fork in response to the surrounding atmosphere, and a brightness meter with a threshold of the approximate brightness of dusk on earth. Radar altimeters were to register the altitude of the probes as they descended between the altitudes of 50 and 10 km (31 and 6.2 mi). To commemorate the flight, both Veneras carried a pentagon-shaped medal with the coat of arms of the Soviet Union and a bas-relief of Lenin.

A SUCCESSFUL TWIN LAUNCH

January 1969 was a busy time at Tyuratam. As soon as the twin Venera launches were complete, the same launch pad had to be readied quickly for the dual flights of Soyuzes 4 and 5 scheduled less than a week later. These politically important manned missions were undoubtedly a force driving the decision to launch Venera 6 during a snowstorm. While the SL-6 Molniya rocket showed remarkable flexibility by operating in such climatic extremes, the launch likely would have been delayed for more benign weather had it not been for the manned mission to follow.

Venera 5 was launched at 9:28 A.M., Moscow time, on January 5, 1969. The probe entered an initial parking orbit, then the escape stage was fired over Africa at 10:47 A.M. Its path was so precise that it would pass within 25,000 km (15,535 mi) of Venus without a course correction.

The snowy liftoff of Venera 6 followed at 8:52 A.M., January 10. However, Venera 6's trajectory was not as accurate and the craft would miss the planet by 150,000 km (93,210 mi) without a course correction. The twin Venus craft were separated in space by 1,125,000 km (700,000 mi).

Venera 5 performed a 9.2-m (30.2-ft)-per-sec trajectory correction on March 14 while 15.5 million km (9.6 million mi) from earth. This aimed it at a point 2700 km (1678 mi) into the night side of Venus at about 20 degrees longitude along the equator. While at a similar distance from earth, Venera 6 performed a 37.4-m (122.7-ft)-per-sec course correction on March 16. The trajectory of Venera 6 was also altered slightly so both probes would arrive at Venus a day apart. The course corrections were so accurate that they placed the twin Veneras within 200 km (124 mi) of their desired approach paths.

During the cruise to Venus, about 1500 commands were sent to both spacecraft during 73 communications sessions with Venera 5 and 63 sessions with Venera 6. Most of the commands were for orienting the craft so tape-recorded data could be transmitted via the high-gain antenna. As with previous Soviet planetary probes, the narrow-beam antenna was not independently steerable so that the orientation system had to move the entire spacecraft to aim the antenna at earth. Transmissions from the parabolic antenna were 64 times faster than those from the omnidirectional antennas.

Increased periods of solar activity occurred during the dual flights and the craft were able to monitor changes in the solar wind due to large chromospheric flares on the sun. Twelve instances of increased solar proton flux were observed where the probe was showered with increased amounts of radiation from the sun. Four of these events lasted seven or more days.

The final communications session began two hours before each Venus encounter. For eight minutes, radio tracking provided data on the effect of the Venusian gravity on the probes; then details showing how Venus interacts with the solar wind were transmitted. Both craft confirmed that Venus has no appreciable magnetic field of its own, but instead interacted with the sun's magnetic field which in turn induced a weak magnetic field at the planet.

TWO ENCOUNTERS A DAY APART

After a 130-day flight and still 50,000 km (31,000 mi) from Venus, Venera 5's atmospheric entry sequence was activated by a signal from earth at 7:08 A.M., May 16. An hour before entry, at 37,000 km (23,000 mi) altitude, the descent capsule separated. At 9:01 A.M., the capsule plowed into the atmosphere at an angle of 62 to 64 degrees. The carrier spacecraft was not designed to survive and was quickly incinerated.

In a matter of seconds, the dense atmosphere slowed the capsule from 11.17 km (6.94 mi) per sec to 210 m (690 ft) per sec. At 60 km (37.3 mi) altitude, the drogue and main parachutes were deployed along with the antennae. The scientific instruments were then switched on and contact with earth established.

Data were returned for 53 min as the probe parachuted through 36 km (22.4 mi) of increasingly dense and hot atmosphere. As expected, when atmospheric pressure reached the capsule's design limit of 27 atm, contact was lost. The probe's upper cover caved in and smashed the radio apparatus. The probe was still 24 km (15 mi) above the surface and the atmospheric temperature had increased to 320°C (608°F). During its drop, Venera 5's internal temperature had risen to only 28° (82°F).

After a flight of 127 days, Venera 6 arrived at the planet one day later. The descent capsule separated 25,000 km (15,500 mi) from Venus and entered the atmosphere at 9:02 A.M., May 17, only 300 km (186.4 mi) from where Venera 5 arrived. The capsule transmitted for 51 min while parachuting 37.8 km (23.5 mi) through the atmosphere. Contact was lost when the probe was crushed by the same atmospheric pressure as Venera 5.

Veneras 5 and 6 both entered the Venusian atmosphere just south of the equator at latitudes −3 and −5, and at longitudes 18 and 23 respectively, with the sun 27 degrees and 25 degrees below the horizon.

While the dual Russian planetary success was a great technical and scientific achievement, the launch the next day of the U.S. Apollo 10 manned mission to the moon captured the world's attention. The dual missions proved that the Soviets had attained the technology necessary to reach the planet, but compared to the excitement surrounding the manned lunar mission, the Venus success was merely a curiosity.

A NEW PICTURE OF VENUS

Atmospheric sampling elevations were staggered between the probes to allow analysis at four altitudes. The first measurement by Venera 5 occurred at a pressure of 0.5 earth atmospheres and a temperature of 25°C (77°F), while the second occurred at 5 atm and a temperature of 150° (302°F). Venera 6 complemented these readings by sampling at one atmosphere pressure and 60° (140°F), then again at 10 atm and 225°C (437°F). Temperature and pressure measurements were made every 40 to 50 seconds during the descent. More than 70 pressure and 50 temperature measurements were accumulated. Gas sampling again showed that the atmosphere was 93 to 97 percent carbon dioxide, 2 to 5 percent nitrogen and other inert gases, and a maximum of 0.4 percent oxygen.

The photometer carried by Venera 5 detected a possible lightning flash with an intensity of 25 watts per square m 4 min before the probe ceased transmitting. A similar instrument aboard Venera 6 detected no flashes and the Soviets dismissed the reading as a telemetry failure.

After Venera 5 and 6 corroborated the surprising Venera 4 measurements, Soviet planetary scientists finally accepted theories postulating high Venus surface temperatures and pressures. It became apparent that the earlier expectations of an ocean or jungle-covered planet were fantasy. Even the hope of a semihospitable desert planet was swept aside. It became clear that the evolution of the planets had in fact left our inner neighbor with the harsh reality of a deadly atmosphere and a surface hot enough to melt lead.

VENUS RESEARCH RELATES TO EARTH

At the same time the Venera investigations ruled out the possibility of human existence on Venus, they also raised disturbing questions about human habitation of earth in the future. Studying the alien world of Venus lends valuable insights to understanding the ecological events happening on earth. Greenhouse effects, in which carbon dioxide gas and water vapor trap solar heat within the atmosphere, naturally raise earth's overall temperature by 30°C (54°F). Without this natural effect, earth's climate would be harsher. Venus vividly demonstrates the results of a runaway greenhouse effect and may foretell a hellish fate for future earth.

Our new-found understanding of Venus is very timely since it relates to changes in our atmosphere. During the past one hundred years, industrialization and the burning of fossil fuels have raised earth's atmospheric carbon dioxide level by fifteen percent while simultaneously consuming fifteen percent of all the biologically produced oxygen. Over the next fifty years, heavy dependence on fossil fuels is expected to double the amount of carbon dioxide in earth's atmosphere, with a corresponding global temperature increase of 4° (6°F). If unchecked, this heating will facilitate polar melting which could raise the sea level by 2 m (6.6 ft). Accompanying this, altered rainfall patterns may have disastrous effects on food-producing areas. The only way to study the long-term future of earth's atmosphere is to compare it to the atmospheres of other planets. The Venusian environment provides a planet-wide laboratory for investigating the possible consequences of unwise exploitation of earth's resources and the accumulation of pollutants in our atmosphere.

A REACH FOR THE SURFACE

After three Veneras had succumbed to Venus' harsh environment, engineers at Lavochkin made an all-out effort to ensure that the next landers would make it to the surface intact. This goal was emphasized in an announcement by the TASS news agency which stated: "The main purpose of the launching of the automatic station Venera 7 was to effect a landing on the planet, to explore the atmosphere in the process of descent down to the very 'bottom,' and to take measurements directly from the surface."[3] This announcement left no doubt that the Soviets felt their goal of reaching the Venusian surface was at last within their grasp.

While retaining the proven MV-style spacecraft bus, modifications to Venera 7 increased the spacecraft mass to 1180 kg (2601 lb) at launch. The spacecraft bus carried the usual instruments to study interplanetary space and data were transmitted at 928.429 MHz. The main changes were in the redesigned and strengthened landing capsule, which gained 100 kg (220 lb) in the process. The new 495-kg (1091-lb) lander was built to withstand 180 atm pressure and a 540-°C (1000-°F) temperature for 90 min.

The capsule was similar in size to previous landers, about 1 m (3.3 ft) in diameter. Inside the egg-shaped outer shell, which provided thermal and physical protection, was a smaller pressure vessel in the shape of a sphere for strength. No holes were drilled through the pressure vessel. Only when the cover was blown off to deploy the parachute and antennas were the instruments exposed. Soviet engineers likened the capsule's pressure hull to bathyscaphes used for undersea exploration on earth.

It was expected that heat instead of pressure would limit the lifetime of the lander on the surface. To increase the lander's survival time, it was internally chilled to −8°C (18°F) by cold gas injection before separation from the spacecraft bus.

Instruments included an aneroid barometer to measure pressure, resistance thermometers to measure temperature, and an apparatus to perform atmospheric analysis. As with previous Soviet planetary landers, Venera 7 carried the usual assortment of commemorative pennants.

Venera 7's parachute canopy, capable of withstanding 530°C (986°F), retained its strength even though charred and volatilized by high temperatures. The parachute design was modified to allow it to remain reefed, or only partially inflated, after deployment. This was done for two purposes: to limit the initial opening shock to 25 gs, and to allow the craft to descend rapidly through the hot atmosphere. At lower altitudes, the increased heat would melt the nylon reefing cord, allowing the parachute to fully deploy and to slow the descent. This rapid initial descent allowed more of the probe's 90-min lifetime to be spent on the surface.

Developing the Venera parachute presented special challenges for its designers. The unique atmosphere of Venus made it impossible to fully test the parachute system all at once. High-speed tests were conducted by dropping a mockup of the descent capsule from supersonic aircraft at 12 km (7.5 mi) altitude. To test the parachute material's resistance to burning and erosion, samples were "seasoned" in cylinders filled with carbon dioxide and heated to 600°C (1100°F) and pressurized to 120 atm for several hours.

TWIN LAUNCHES BAT .500

Venera 7 was the seventeenth Soviet attempt to reach Venus. Liftoff from Tyuratam occurred at 8:38 A.M., August 17, 1970. Eighty-one minutes later while over Africa, a 244-sec burn of the SL-6 escape stage put Venera 7 on its way to Venus.

A twin Venus probe was launched five days later on August 22. The spacecraft entered a parking orbit, but the subsequent firing of the escape stage malfunctioned and the engine shut down after twenty-five seconds. The probe, now designated Cosmos 359, was stranded in an elliptical earth orbit.

To refine Venera 7's aim, two corrections were made on October 2 and November 17 using the probe's on-board KDU-414 rocket engine at distances of 27 and 50 million km (16.8 and 31 million mi) from earth.

During the interplanetary cruise, Venera 7 monitored a powerful chromospheric flare on December 10. Solar data were compared with data received simultaneously from earth satellites and the Lunokhod 1 probe, which was active on the moon. There was a high degree of correlation between Venera and Lunokhod cosmic-ray data.

A SUSPECTED FAILURE AT ENCOUNTER

Landing preparations began on December 12 when the lander's interior was cooled and power was switched on from the solar panels to charge the lander's batteries. Then, after a 120-day flight from earth,

Venera 7, with the landing capsule still attached, entered the atmosphere of Venus at 7:58 A.M., December 15. Entry was at 5 degrees south and 351 degrees longitude on the night side of the planet, about 2000 km from the sunrise terminator.

Previous landers were ejected from their carrier spacecraft about an hour before atmospheric entry. This time, the craft's designers wanted the landing capsule to remain hooked up to the cooling system aboard the spacecraft bus as long as possible. When the resistance of the atmosphere disturbed the spacecraft's directional antenna lock on earth, the lander was automatically ejected. Even if all four redundant separation systems had failed, the straps securing the lander to the spacecraft bus were designed to quickly burn through, releasing the lander.

Atmospheric friction slowed the capsule to 720 km (447 mi) per hr by the time it reached an altitude of 60 km. Here, the parachutes were deployed and data transmission was begun. The first signals were received at 8:03 A.M. The frequency of the lander's radio transmitter was precisely controlled by a crystal oscillator so the signal's Doppler shift could be determined as the probe fell through the atmosphere. Speed measurements deduced from the Doppler shift were so accurate that they registered the velocity reduction from 27 to 19 m (89 to 62 ft) per sec when the parachute canopy unreefed, or fully opened, 10 min after deployment.

Two samplings of the atmosphere were made during descent, once when the main chute opened and then again several minutes later. The readings confirmed earlier Venera findings showing 97 percent carbon dioxide.

For sixteen minutes, the descent went as planned, then disaster nearly ended the mission. The capsule suddenly accelerated and reached the planet's surface in 35 min instead of an hour as planned. Apparently, the parachute had failed and the lander descended much faster than expected. Had winds collapsed the parachute canopy, or had the probe been struck by lightning? No one knew what really happened. The lander crashed to the surface at 8:37:32 A.M., striking the ground at 16.5 m (54 ft) per sec. Then transmissions apparently ceased.

AFTER NINE YEARS, TOUCHDOWN AT LAST!

Initially, Soviet designers believed the mission had come to an end. But miraculously, the lander survived the impact, bounced, and fell back on its side. The craft's antenna was now tipped over, and nothing but silence was heard on earth. But Soviet scientists did not give up. They kept listening.

On January 26, 1971, the Soviet Academy of Sciences announced that they had indeed received additional data and, for the first time, scientific information was relayed from the surface of another planet. The faint signal, about 100 times weaker than before, was recovered by computer enhancement from what was thought to be radio noise recorded after Venera 7's signal seemed to quit. After the landing, temperature data were received until 8:57 A.M. when the signal grew fainter. Finally at 9:00:30 A.M., it went silent.

Analysis of the signal's Doppler shift showed that the point where the lander's radio signal strength had dropped radically occurred when the lander actually struck the surface. Also, after the signal strength dropped, the temperature reading held steady, indicating that the craft was no longer descending. The lander had indeed made it to the surface, but lay wounded from its hard fall, and whispered its precious information to earth in muted tones, reporting an astounding temperature of 475°C (887°F).

Project scientists later admitted that the lander's telemetry system had become stuck on the temperature signal channel and no pressure data were returned from the surface. Extrapolating from the limited pressure data received, as well as reports from previous probes, scientists deduced the planet's surface pressure was 90 ± 15 atm.

Venera investigators also reported that the hot Venusian atmosphere stored an enormous amount of heat. This heat trapped within the Venusian atmosphere was hundreds of times greater than the heat lost during the Venusian night. Because of this, it was calculated that the day-to-night temperature fluctuation on the planet was probably less than a degree.

As the new data from Venus were examined, planetary scientists were delighted to find close agreement with previous explorations. The new Venera 7 data agreed in overlapping areas with Veneras 4 through 6, and Mariner 5 data also matched. All spacecraft data concurred that Venus had a diameter of 12,100 km (7519 mi).

In spite of the success, the composition of the Venusian clouds was still not known. The prime objective of the Venera 7 flight had been to reach the surface as fast as possible before the planet's environment disabled the lander. For that reason, detailed sampling of the clouds would have to wait until more advanced landers could concentrate on the upper atmosphere.

SOVIET PRIDE RIGHTFULLY PLACED

The road to Venus had been a torturous nine-year path for Russian scientists. Some American experts were incredulous when Soviet announcements proclaimed the success of Venera 4. They did not think it was possible to reach the surface of Venus.[4] When Venera 7 landed, Soviet space exploration reached its finest hour. After losing the politically motivated manned race to the moon, the Russians could point to their unmanned successes as a non-life-threatening alternative to hazardous human space exploration. The Soviets claimed, with a great deal of deserved pride, that they were simultaneously receiving data from two celestial bodies: from Venus and the Lunokhod 1 robot rover on the moon.

Valery Timofeev, an engineer who helped design the Venera craft, recalled the Venus landing with both personal and nationalist pride. He declared: "It is very important to me that the Lavochkin Association is received as a well-known company throughout the world from the success of the Venus program. It is also very important to me that I worked with this program and made some of the devices. It was an honor to work for this company and contribute to science and the prestige of my country."[5]

After a decade of intense technical effort, the Venera explorations had shown conclusively that human survival on Venus was out of the question. As if an unbreathable carbon dioxide atmosphere were not bad enough, the crushing 90-atmosphere surface pressure on Venus would smash the senses out of an unprotected human visitor within seconds. These brutal conditions are compounded by the fact that the furnace-like surface temperature would boil the flesh from the bones of the unfortunate visitor within a minute. While beckoning mankind for ages, Venus, the goddess of love, in reality harbours fiery death. A fine welcome indeed—to be burned into a lump of charcoal.

AMERICAN GOALS LESS DEFINED

American planetary goals in 1970 were less defined than the Soviet Venus objective. The only planned mission that had been approved was a low-budget fly-by of Venus by Mariner 10 while on its way to the planet Mercury. This modest mission, initiated in 1969, was seen by U.S. scientists as the only real chance of getting scientific instruments near Venus for the next decade. In spite of this low-key approach to exploring the inner solar system, U.S. space leaders had the audacity to claim leadership in planetary exploration. Even in the face of the Soviet Venera 7 success, acting NASA administrator George Low claimed that America was still the leader in the exploration of space.[6] Low's remarks reflected Apollo's brilliant manned lunar landings, but not the political reality of the cancelled Apollo 18, 19 and 20 landings and repeated funding delays in U.S. planetary exploration.

After the 1962 Mariner 2 mission had shown that Venus was probably a lifeless hothouse, NASA's interest in the inner planet had waned in favor of manned lunar exploration and the investigation of the planet Mars. The U.S. goal was the detection of life on another planet. Mars still held hope for life, but Venus was clearly a lifeless world surrounded by hot, poisonous gas. The Soviet's dogged compulsion to reach Venus puzzled some U.S. planetary investigators.

Though the average Soviet citizen may have been less concerned about space exploration, the Soviet scientific elite took to heart the thoughts of rocketry pioneer Konstantin Tsiolkovsky who wrote: "Man will not stay on the earth forever, but... will... advance until he has conquered the whole of circumsolar space."[7] Tsiolkovsky's prophesy was adapted to Soviet visions of Venus exploration. After the U.S. virtually abandoned Venus in favor of Mars, the Soviet Union chose to pursue the hard road to the inner solar system. The agressive Soviet push toward the veiled planet had garnered its share of failure, but the massive technical effort also insured eventual success. After tasting failure for nine years, Venera investigators could now savor the sweet taste of victory.

REDESIGNED LANDER PREPARED

Ten years of intense effort by the Academy of Sciences and the Lavochkin Association had paved the road to Venus. Venera 7 had established the true atmospheric pressure on Venus and Russian planetary scientists finally held the key to reaching the surface. Now real planetary science could begin.

The overall appearance of the 1184-kg (2610-lb) Venera 8 was much like that of Venera 7. However, the lander was redesigned, essentially from scratch. Structurally, the lander was scaled back to safely accommodate the actual pressure on Venus and was built to withstand only 105 atm. With the weight saved, the new design incorporated more instrumentation, a stronger parachute and more insulation. Now that the lander could withstand the atmospheric pressure, the only problem was the nearly 500-°C (932-°F) surface temperature. The redesigned landing capsule therefore included a refrigeration unit to cool its interior to below 0°C (32°F) during the initial atmospheric descent. The capsule also had an internal fan and a heat sink to dissipate internal temperatures from the heat sensitive instruments. The current mission would concentrate on scientific exploration rather than on engineering questions. Research instrumentation aboard the 495-kg (1091-lb) Venera 8 lander included atmospheric temperature and pressure sensors, a wind anemometer, photo resistors to measure sunlight intensity, a gamma-ray spectrometer to analyze soil composition, and atmospheric gas analyzers. The capsule also carried the usual commemorative images of Lenin and the official emblem of the U.S.S.R.

To speed the lander's descent, the parachute was further reduced to one-third the size used by Venera 7. While barely large enough to stabilize the lander in an earthly atmosphere, the 2.5-m (8.2-ft) diameter parachute was more than adequate in the ultra-dense Venusian atmosphere. By comparison, the same parachute used in earth's thinner atmosphere would drop the capsule at 50 to 60 m (164 to 197 ft) per sec, resulting in a crash.

After the near loss of the Venera 7 lander's radio signal, a dual-antenna design was incorporated. Soviet engineers tested the new landing capsule and parachutes in a wind tunnel using 500-°C (932°F) carbon dioxide to simulate Venus' atmospheric conditions. To ensure that the lander could function on the surface of Venus, the probe's design was repeatedly tested in a heated pressure chamber at more than 100 atm and 500°C (932°F).

Venera 8 was launched from Tyuratam at 7:15 A.M., March 27, 1972. One orbit later, while over Africa at 8:42 A.M., the escape stage accelerated the probe into a 117-day, 312-million km (194-million mi) voyage toward Venus. A course correction on April 6 ensured a planetary strike.

Four days later, a second Venera was launched. Its mission was to land on the opposite side of Venus and gather data in order to compare the night and day sides. This plan was spoiled when the launch failed to leave earth orbit. The escape stage prematurely shut down after 125 sec, trapping the probe in a 205 × 9805 km (127 × 6093 mi) orbit.

During its interplanetary cruise, Venera 8 communicated on a frequency of 928.4 MHz. Four strong solar flares were recorded which increased radiation levels in space to a potentially lethal level for a human space traveler. Simultaneously, Venera 8 recorded a decrease in galactic cosmic rays, or radiation originating from outside the solar system. This implied that the increased solar activity shielded the inner planets and diverted radiation originating outside the solar system. The ultraviolet spectrometer also measured the ultraviolet radiation produced by the traces of neutral atomic hydrogen which exists throughout the open reaches of the solar system. The instrument showed that the hydrogen was not uniform between earth and Venus, but was instead clumpy, sometimes registering a two-to-three-fold increase in some areas. The background ultraviolet radiation entering the solar system which is produced by young hot stars was also measured.

A PRECISION PLANETARY ENCOUNTER

An unusually small surface area, only 500 km (311 mi) wide, was targeted for landing. This size was dictated by the need to land on the daylight side of the planet while maintaining line-of-sight communications with earth. Venus was near its closest approach to earth at the time of landing, when the dark side of the planet faced earth. This reduced the available landing area to a thin sunlit crescent where earth could still be seen very low on the Venusian horizon.

Several days before atmospheric entry, the batteries aboard the landing capsule were charged and its interior cooled to −15°C (5°F) by cold gas injection. At 10:40 A.M., an hour before encountering Venus on July 22, the straps retaining the landing capsule were released. Hydrogen and deuterium levels in the planet's upper atmosphere were recorded as the spacecraft bus approached Venus. At the time, the craft's distance from earth was 107.8 million km (77 million mi).

At 11:37 A.M., the landing capsule dove into the atmosphere at an angle of 77 degrees. The fierce deceleration reached a maximum of 335 gs at 67 km (41.6 mi) altitude, slowing the capsule's velocity to 250 m (820 ft) per sec within eighteen seconds of entry. Soon after, the parachute deployed and the lander began transmitting data at 11:38 A.M.

During descent, data transmission was interrupted for 6 min at 11:52 A.M. while instruments were being calibrated. After calibration, continuous temperature and pressure measurements were transmitted to earth from 55 km (34 mi) altitude down to the surface. The data showed no differences from the night side atmospheric profile obtained by Venera 7.

Touchdown occurred at 12:29 P.M., about 500 km (311 mi) into the sunlit side of the planet. The landing site was at 335 degrees longitude and

10 degrees south latitude—about 2896 km (1800 mi) from the Venera 7 touchdown area. Upon landing, the second omnidirectional antenna was ejected several meters (6 ft) from the lander to prevent a loss of signal strength in case the capsule tipped over. The flat disk-shaped antenna was attached to the lander by a heavy electrical cable and had spring loaded stabilizers to ensure that it would lie flat on the surface. The antenna could function even if it landed upside down. The initial 13.3 min of data transmission, reporting the surface temperature, pressure and light level, came from the primary antenna. The auxiliary antenna was used for the next twenty minutes to relay data about surface composition at the landing site. The final 30-min data stream came again from the primary antenna.

SOLID SCIENTIFIC RESULTS

The successful descent and landing of Venera 8 represented a new phase in Russian Venus exploration where precise measurements of the environment were the mission's primary goal. During the lander's parachute descent, gas analysis was consistent with previous Venera atmospheric readings. Ammonia was an important chemical needed to explain theoretical models of the Venusian atmosphere. An instrument aboard Venera 8 looked for ammonia by passing atmospheric gases through tetrabromophenol-sulphaphthalein (bromophenol-blue), a substance known to turn blue in the presence of ammonia. A photosensor measured the color change in the reagent. This instrument did two samplings, first at 46 km (28.6 mi) altitude with a pressure of 2 atmospheres and again at 33 km (20.5 mi) with a pressure of 8 atmospheres. Between 0.01 and 0.1 percent ammonia was detected, confirming earlier earth-based observations.

The lander made three readings of naturally occurring background gamma radiation during descent. No change between the readings showed a lack of short-lived isotopes formed by the interaction of cosmic rays with the upper atmosphere, indicating that the upper atmosphere effectively shielded the planet from energetic cosmic particles.

Atmospheric wind speeds were obtained by measuring the transmitter's Doppler shift and also by an on-board anemometer, or wind speed indicator. Above 48 km (30 mi) altitude, velocities of 100 m (328 ft) per sec were recorded with the prevailing winds in the direction of the planet's rotation. These decreased to between 40 and 70 m (131 and 230 ft) per sec between 42 and 48 km (26 and 30 mi) altitude, and diminished to 1 m (3.3 ft) per sec below 10 km (6.2 mi) altitude. This lack of wind indicated that surface heating was very uniform.

A simple cadmium-sulfide cell light meter was used to measure sunlight intensity during the decent. A sharp drop in sunlight intensity ocurred at 30 to 35 km (18.6 to 21.7 mi) altitude where the clouds reduce incoming sunlight by 50 percent. The thick atmosphere below the clouds further reduced the intensity of sunlight. Only 1.5 percent of the sun's illumination reached the surface at Venera 8's landing site. However, at the time the sun was only 5 degrees above the local horizon.

Two measurements of natural gamma radiation occurring in the soil were made by the gamma-ray spectrometer. The instrument was housed in a hermetically sealed container within the lander and used sodium iodide crystals doped with titanium to detect radiation. The thick atmosphere prevented cosmic gamma radiation from reaching the surface, thus, the instrument would register radiation that emanated from the soil exclusively. Readings indicated the presence of 4 percent potassium, 0.0002 percent uranium, and 0.00065 percent thorium. Laboratory comparisons indicated a similarity to terrestrial granite, a type of rock with volcanic origin.

This evidence of volcanic rocks showed that Venus was similar to earth and the moon in that it was "differentiated," meaning the planet was once hot enough for its material to melt and flow. This process allowed the heavier elements to sink toward the planet's core, while the lighter elements rose to the surface, carrying radioactive elements with them.

Venera 8 revealed a surface temperature of 530°C (986°F) with a pressure of 90 atm. These were identical to previous night side measurements and showed the existence of powerful atmospheric mixing between the day and night sides of Venus.

FUNDAMENTAL ANSWERS ALLOW NEW QUESTIONS

Venera 8 was the most successful Soviet planetary probe to date. Russian scientists felt a great deal of pride when the probe completed all its design tasks. Venera 8's success even altered U.S. Venus exploration plans. NASA proposals had called for a 1980 Venus landing to determine if the planet was differentiated like the earth and moon. The Venera 8 findings answered that question and opened the door for other American Venus explorations.

After eleven years of effort, Soviet planetary scientists achieved their ultimate triumph with Venera 8. The stunning success gave Soviet space efforts a needed boost in prestige following the tragic death in space of the crew of Soyuz 11 the previous year. In spite of losing the manned race to the moon, the Venera success showed the world that Russian space efforts were not taking a back seat to anyone.

Veneras 1 through 8 were all considered first-generation Venera probes. They provided the initial rudimentary data about the atmospheric and surface conditions which were essential to the design of more precise instruments aboard future landers. The first phase of the Russian exploration of Venus was now ended. The limited capability of the 1-ton MV-style Veneras had been taxed to their limits and had answered all the Venus questions they could ask. More complex investigations would commence with the second-generation Veneras which were already on the drawing board. Indeed, the Venera redesign was so extensive that the next Venus launch window in November 1973 was passed up to allow completion of the next generation of Russian Venus explorers.

FLYING ECONOMY CLASS

Having already reached Venus and Mars in the 1960s, NASA wanted to complete its sweep of the inner solar system with a visit to the innermost planet, Mercury. Being the closest planet to the sun, tiny Mercury races around the sun four times every earth year. Its proximity to the sun and distance from earth also makes it an exceptionally difficult planet to study. The only way to discover the true nature of swiftly moving Mercury was to send a spacecraft for a close inspection.

A mission to Mercury had been approved in 1969. This timing was fortuitous because of an upcoming alignment of Venus and Mercury which offered a great opportunity for those bold enough to seize it. Between 1970 and 1973, it was possible to reach Mercury using the gravity of Venus to "slingshot" a probe toward the yet-unknown Mercury. In this way, two planets could be explored for the price of one. A 1,312,000-kg (2,892,000-lb) thrust Titan 3 booster could reach Mercury directly, but at a much greater cost than using a smaller Atlas-Centaur with the assistance of Venus' gravity.

In February 1970 it was discovered that, if launched at the proper time in 1973, the craft now called Mariner Venus/Mercury 73 (MVM73) could reach Mercury once via Venus, then achieve a second "free return" to Mercury six months after its first encounter. Three planetary fly-bys for the price of one clinched the deal and what was to become Mariner 10 quickly took shape. While Russian scientists skipped the 1973 Venus opportunity, American scientists indirectly aimed for Venus by shooting for Mercury. Because NASA's planetary exploration budget was mostly dedicated to Mars, they realized the swing past the veiled planet was their last opportunity for closeup Venus investigations for another decade, making the mission even more attractive.

Budget crunches in the late 1960s had forced NASA to place a spending cap on the last of the Mariners. JPL began the Mariner 10 project agreeing that it would be a one-shot deal: one spacecraft, one launch to the inner planets, no backups and spending no more than $98 million to accomplish the entire mission. NASA had never before imposed such a restriction. If a cost overrun was encountered, spacecraft performance was sacrificed because no additional money was available. Born in such tight constraints, Mariner 10 was an unprecedented planetary challenge. Not only would an untried celestial "billiards shot" have to be successful, but enormous amounts of television data would have to be transmitted across great distances. If anything, these barriers did not impede the mission, but instead enhanced it by challenging JPL engineers to produce a spacecraft with even greater potential than designers had initially envisioned.

Mariner 10's rich heritage from previous Venus and Mars explorers was invaluable in creating a cheap, yet versatile new probe. About 50 percent of the craft's development cost was saved by using hardware created for previous missions. While retaining the basic Mariner 46 × 138-cm (18 × 54-in) hexagonal body, MVM73's 58 million-km (36 million-mi) approach to the sun dictated major modifications because of the unprecedented heat. Many of the instruments were mounted on the shadow side of the 503-kg (1109-lb) spacecraft while the main body was shielded by a reflective teflon-coated beta cloth sunshield. Insulation blankets and reflective coatings covered the rest of the probe. The dual 98 × 269-cm (3.2 × 8.8-ft) solar panels could also be tilted partly away from the sun to keep their temperatures less than 115°C (239°F). Intensified solar radiation near the sun increased the panel's output from 200 watts at earth to 505 watts at Mercury.

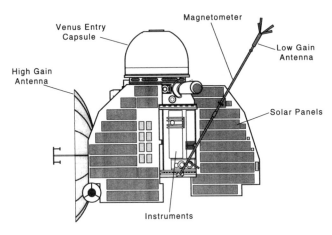

VENERA 1

Figure 27. The Soviet Venera 1 Venus probe was the first interplanetary probe to depart earth successfully and travel toward another planet. Venera 1's objective was to enter the Venusian atmosphere, but contact with the probe was lost shortly after launch. (Artwork by Ron Dawes.)

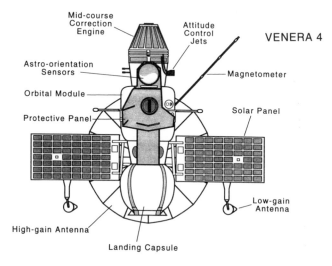

Figure 28. After 14 previous Soviet Venus probe efforts had failed, Venera 4 successfully reached the planet on October 18 and ejected its landing capsule into the atmosphere. The probe made the first measurements from within the atmosphere of another planet. (Artwork by Ron Dawes.)

Figure 29. Mariner 2, America's first successful planetary probe, visited Venus on December 14, 1962, and showed that the veiled planet was surprisingly hot. Mariner 2 shows its distinctive heritage derived from the Ranger lunar probes. (NASA photo courtesy of the Jet Propulsion Laboratory.)

Figure 30. Built for JPL by Boeing Aircraft Company, the Mariner 10 Venus and Mercury explorer had a distinctive bug-like appearance which resulted from hiding its twin television cameras on the shadow side of the spacecraft. The cameras were located there to protect them from the fierce solar radiation resulting from Mercury's proximity to the sun. (NASA photo)

Figure 31. As Mariner 10 receded to 760,000 km (472,000 mi) from Venus a day after its fly-by on February 5, 1974, it recorded this view of the Venusian atmospheric circulation by using an ultraviolet filter to see features not visible from earth. (NASA photo)

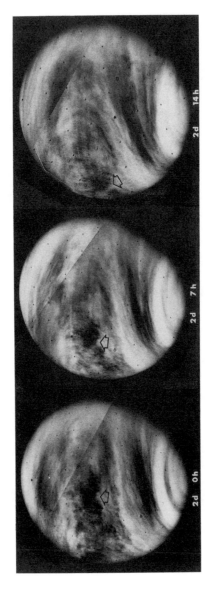

Figure 32. Two days after passing Venus, Mariner 10 recorded this series of photo mosaics showing the movement of the Venusian atmosphere. The shots were taken at 7-hr intervals. The arrow points to a moving 1000-km (620-mile)-diameter feature. (NASA photo)

Figure 33. This photomosaic of Mercury was assembled from 18 photos taken at 42-sec intervals 6 hr after Mariner 10 flew past the planet on March 29, 1974. Taken from a distance of 210,000 km (130,000 mi) the images show the north pole at the top and many overlapping ray structures extending from craters. (NASA photo courtesy of the Lunar and Planetary Institute.)

Figure 34. During its second fly-by of Mercury on September 21, 1974, Mariner 10 imaged this 100-km (62-mile)-wide crater field near the south pole from a distance of 48,000 km (30,000 mi). While distinctly lunar-like in appearance, Mercurian craters are shallower because the planet's gravity is greater than our moon's. (NASA photo courtesy of the Lunar and Planetary Institute.)

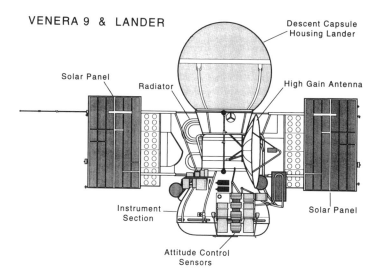

VENERA 9 & LANDER

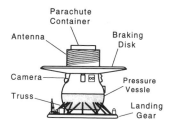

Figure 35. The second-generation Soviet Venera probe utilized the powerful Proton rocket to make possible a launch weight four times as great as earlier probes. The new Venera carried a redesigned lander which carried out extensive atmospheric analysis, surface photography, and soil analysis. (Artwork by Ron Dawes.)

Figure 36. The Pioneer Venus Orbiter (PVO) (front) and the Pioneer Venus Multiprobe (rear) were built by Hughes Aircraft Corporation. Both spacecraft used a common carrier bus, but PVO remained in Venus orbit while the Multiprobe and its four atmospheric probes all entered the atmosphere of Venus. (Photo courtesy of Hughes Aircraft Company.)

Figure 37. The Pioneer Venus Orbiter (PVO) lifts off from Cape Canaveral's Launch Complex 36 at 10:13 A.M., May 20, 1978 aboard an Atlas-Centaur booster. (NASA photo)

VENERA 15

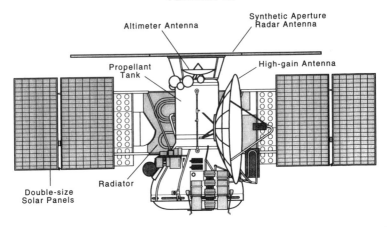

Figure 38. The Soviet Venera 15 and 16 radar-mapping missions both used a lengthened second-generation Venera spacecraft bus to transport a synthetic aperture radar system and its 6-m (19.7-ft)-wide antenna into Venus orbit. The solar panels were doubled in size to provide power for the radar. (Artwork by Ron Dawes.)

VEGA 1 & 2

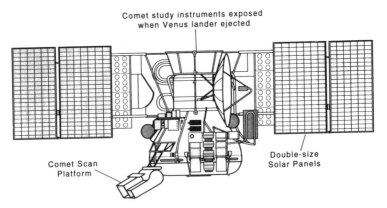

Figure 39. The Vega spacecraft, also based on the second generation Venera, became the first probe to investigate Halley's Comet. After ejecting a Venus lander, both Vega 1 and 2 traveled eight months to reach Halley and act as a pathfinder for the European Giotto probe which followed a week later. (Artwork by Ron Dawes.)

Figure 40. After a flawless 14-year mission in Venus orbit, the Pioneer Venus Orbiter finally lost its struggle with Venusian gravity and fell from orbit on October 8, 1992. The spacecraft transmitted valuable data up to the time it burned in the Venusian atmosphere. (Artwork courtesy of Hughes Aircraft Company.)

Figure 41. Venera 9 and 10 each returned a single image of the Venusian surface following their touchdown on October 22 and 25, 1975. The Venera 9 image (top) shows a young surface with sharp rocks while Venera 10 (bottom) shows an older, more worn surface. (Photo courtesy of the Lunar and Planetary Institute.)

Figure 42. Venera 13 and 14 carried improved, higher resolution cameras. The Venera 13 image (top) shows the crescent-shaped camera cover lying next to the surface penetrometer arm. In an unfortunate break, Venera 14's (bottom) penetrometer landed on the camera cover and ruined the experiment. The horizon is visible in the upper left of each image. (Photo courtesy of the Lunar and Planetary Institute.)

Figure 43. Venera 15 and 16 radar data provided this two-km (1.2-mile) resolution photomosaic of the Venusian north pole. The concentric markings are at two-degree intervals. (Photo courtesy of the Lunar and Planetary Institute.)

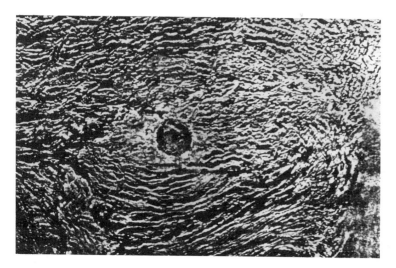

Figure 44. Venera 15 and 16 radar imagery revealed a large crater, later named "Cleopatra," in rugged territory near the Venusian north pole. The field of view covers approximately 700 km (430 mi). (Photo courtesy of the Lunar and Planetary Institute.)

Figure 45. Assembled essentially from spare parts, the Magellan Venus radar mapper displays a unique profile because of the dual-purpose radar-communications antenna salvaged from the Voyager spacecraft. (Artwork courtesy of Hughes Aircraft Company.)

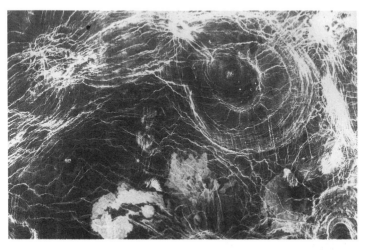

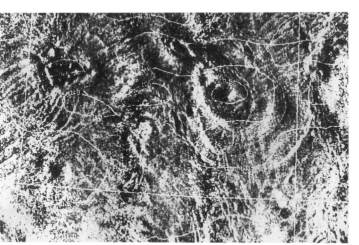

Figure 46. A comparison of the Fortuna region of Venus as imaged by Venera 15–16 on the left and Magellan on the right. Magellan's 120-m (400-ft) resolution readily distinguishes the lower coronae feature as well as the spider-like "arachnoid" feature at the top while Venera's 1.5-km (0.9-mile) resolution is far less discriminatory. (NASA photo courtesy of the Lunar and Planetary Institute.)

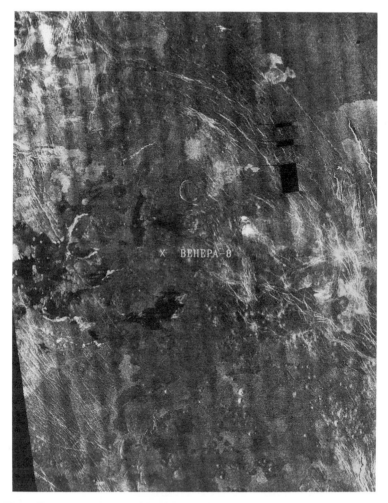

Figure 47. Radar data from 24 orbits of Magellan formed this 400-km (240-mile)-wide view of the Navka region of Venus. At the center is the landing site of the Soviet Venera 8 (BEHEPA 8), whose data indicated that the area was composed of granite-like rocks. (NASA photo courtesy of the Lunar and Planetary Institute.)

Figure 48. Magellan imaged these three "pancake" volcanoes in the Guinevere Planitia lowlands. The center feature is 50-km (31-mi)-wide and overlaps a 45-km (28-mile)-wide volcano to the southwest. The smaller 25-km (15-mile)-wide volcano to the southeast is the highest of the three. (NASA photo courtesy of the Lunar and Planetary Institute.)

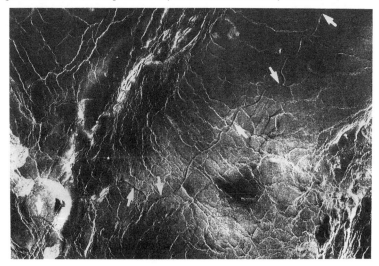

Figure 49. The arrows point out a 600-km (360-mile) segment of a 7000-km (4200-mile)-long lava channel on Venus. Originally found by Venera 15 and 16, the full length of the feature was determined from Magellan data. The channel is several hundred kilometers longer than earth's longest river, the Nile. (NASA photo courtesy of the Lunar and Planetary Institute.)

Figure 50. This Magellan image spotlights the 48-km (30-mile)-wide crater Danilova and reveals a complex ejecta blanket surrounding the radar-dark, flat crater floor and central peak. (NASA photo courtesy of the Lunar and Planetary Institute.)

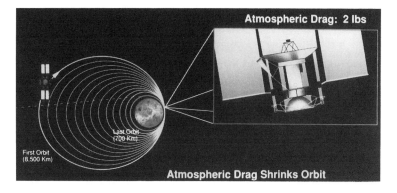

Figure 51. This diagram demonstrates how Magellan used the atmosphere of Venus to lower its 8470-km (5263-mi) apoapsis to 540 km (335 mi) in order to perform precision mapping of the gravitational field during the spacecraft's fifth Venusian year. (NASA photo courtesy of the Lunar and Planetary Institute.)

VENUS TO BE IMAGED

The most important of the 78 kg (172 lb) of scientific instruments aboard were twin television cameras and an ultraviolet spectrometer mounted on a shadow-side scan platform. These had the appearance of bug eyes peering over the edge of the spacecraft and gave Mariner 10 the most alien look of all interplanetary probes. The cameras produced 700-line images and viewed through a 1500-mm focal length telephoto and a 62-mm focal length, wide-angle f/8.5 lens. After arriving at Mercury, these cameras would magnify our earth-bound view of the planet 5000 times. An eight-position filter wheel allowed imaging in various parts of the spectrum from the infrared to the ultraviolet. Investigators who were dismayed when the imaging capability was deleted from Mariner 5 were anxious to see what Mariner 10 would reveal of Venus in wavelengths unseen from earth. Data transmission capability jumped dramatically from Mariner 5's 8.3 bits per sec to 117,600 bits per sec in order to transmit thousands of television images in real time, as quickly as they were created. A 119-cm (3.9-ft) steerable dish antenna would send the image torrent to earth.

Other instruments mounted on the body of the craft were an infrared radiometer, another ultraviolet spectrometer, charged particle and plasma detectors, and twin magnetometers mounted on a 6-m (19.7-ft) boom.

To reach Mercury via Venus, then loop back to Mercury again six months later required astoundingly accurate celestial navigation. But ahead of this planetary triple play, mission controllers wanted to squeeze one final bit of science out of the spacecraft. If launched at precisely 12:45 A.M., November 3, 1973, Mariner 10 would also fly over the northern areas of the moon. This area had not been completely investigated by spacecraft in the 1960s and Mariner's contributions would be valuable. Normally, a planetary launch is targeted at the beginning of the launch window to allow for possible technical delays. However, Mariner 10's extraordinary trajectory called for the flight to begin three weeks after the launch window opened. For complete success, NASA would have to gamble on a precise, on-time liftoff.

To gravitationally steer Mariner 10 toward Mercury, exact targeting to pass Venus within a 400-km (250-mi) "window" was required. To accomplish this navigation, Mariner 10 carried a 22.7-kg (50-lb) thrust mid-course correction rocket fueled with 29 kg (64 lb) of hydrazine. Capable of multiple restarts, the rocket could alter the craft's velocity by 122 m (400 ft) per sec.

In spite of the $98 million spending cap, the Mariner 10 mission was not such a do-or-die situation. Although MVM73 was billed as a single spacecraft mission, JPL had been extremely resourceful with their meager allocation of NASA funds and had assembled and tested a complete back-up spacecraft. Additionally, mission managers had tactfully arranged to "borrow" the next Atlas-Centaur available in case Mariner 10 dove into the Atlantic instead of toward the sun. JPL was determined to get to Mercury, no matter what.

COSMIC CLIFFHANGER CHALLENGES CONTROLLERS

Mariner 10 lifted off within a few thousandths of a second of the optimal time set years before, a remarkable achievement. As the Atlas-Centaur rose perfectly into the humid Florida night, one observer was moved to comment that the sight was like a modern technical cathedral flying toward heaven.[8]

The launch was accurate, but to perform the delicate interplanetary ballet to intercept Mercury, three course corrections were required over the three-month trip to Venus. The net result of these rocket nudges was a course within 27 km (16.8 mi) of the perfect target point.

While Mariner 10 was on a flawless path, the performance of the spacecraft was less than sterling. It continuously vexed its controllers with a long series of heart-stopping malfunctions. Mariner 10 had not even cleared the moon's orbit when the first potentially fatal flaw manifested itself. The heaters on the television imaging system had failed and the camera system was rapidly cooling off. If it fell too low, the cameras would cease to function. The only remedy was to turn the cameras on so their own electronics would keep them warm. This stabilized their temperature at about −20 degrees Centigrade (−4°F). Test photos of the moon's northern areas and the receding earth showed that the chilly imaging system still worked, but there was another problem. The cameras were qualified to work for weeks during their encounters with Venus and Mercury, but not for months during their transit between the planets. There was no choice however—to avoid certain failure, the cameras were left on.

As Mariner sailed toward Venus, other problems kept controllers on their toes. Eighteen days after launch, the spacecraft's computer experienced the first of many unscheduled "resets," nearly causing the loss of the computer memory. On Christmas Day 1973, the radio signal fell to one-fourth power, then mysteriously returned to normal four days later. Even more serious problems developed on January 8, 1974. Mariner automatically, and irreversibly, switched to its backup power supply. It was also found that interaction between the gyroscopically controlled stabilization system and the spacecraft's flexible body set up oscillations which wasted sixteen percent of the attitude control gas. Fortunately, JPL found a way to stabilize Mariner 10 using the pressure of the solar wind on the craft's movable solar panels. Finally, in early February, as Mariner approached Venus, controllers discovered that the movable camera scan platform was sticking. Mercury still lay two months ahead and exasperated controllers wondered if the craft would survive.

VENUS UNVEILED

At 11:50 A.M. February 5, the first images of Venus showing the lighted cusp of the north pole were received. Twelve minutes later, the craft swung within 5768 km (3584 mi) of the planet and picked up an additional kilometer (0.6 mile) per sec in velocity from Venusian gravity. As Mariner 10 departed from Venus and continued to fall toward the sun, it sent back its best views, showing a fully illuminated planet. In all, 4165 Venus photos were returned through February 13. Through these photos, Venusian weather patterns were analyzed. This was not only useful in understanding our neighboring planet, but eventually proved useful for improving weather forecasts on earth.

Ultraviolet imaging quickly showed what an error it was to delete Mariner 5's camera six years before. In the unseen ultraviolet, Venus came alive. The upper atmosphere whirled around Venus every four days at 300 km (186 mi) per hr, carrying with it swirling cloud patterns which streamed around the planet. Simultaneously, winds blowing north and south to the poles stretched the clouds into chevron-shaped patterns which spread across the face of Venus. The veiled planet was far from a featureless ball, it was beautiful. The rapid movement of the Venusian clouds is unique in the solar system in that Venus' upper atmosphere not only rotates faster than the surface of the planet, but does so eighty times faster than the surface.

MOON-LIKE OUTSIDE, EARTH-LIKE INSIDE

Imaging Venus had filled many gaps in our understanding of that celestial hellhole, but Mariner 10's arrival at Mercury was a true voyage of discovery. Virtually nothing was known about the planet beyond its orbit and a rough estimate of its size. A course correction on March 16 aimed the trajectory to within 200 km (124 mi) of that desired. Then for the eleven days spanning Mariner's March rendezvous with the little planet, Mercury slowly became a familiar and understood body.

Initial imaging from 5.3 million km (3.3 million mi) showed unresolved bright spots on the surface. As Mariner closed in, these spots resolved into hundreds and hundreds of craters. Mercury appeared to have undergone the same intense period of meteoric bombardment that earth's moon had suffered between 4 and 3.3 billion years ago. Mercury, with a distinctive lunar appearance complete with mare-like lava plains devoid of craters, was almost indistinguishable from our moon in side-by-side photo comparisons. The only observable difference was that Mercury's craters were shallower because the planet's higher gravity limited the travel distance of the ejecta.

Mariner 10 approached within 703 km (437 mi) of Mercury then passed behind the planet. Radio occultation measurements showed that the planet had a diameter of 4878 km (3031 mi). Its density turned out to be 5.5 g per cubic cm, making the tiny planet one of the densest bodies in the solar system. A complete surprise to scientists was Mercury's magnetic field measuring one-sixtieth that of earth, complete with an accompanying Van Allen-like radiation belt. This led to speculation that Mercury possessed a metallic core containing 80% of the planet's mass. Mercury, though it looked like the moon on the outside, was very similar to the earth on the inside.

Mercury also turned out to be a planet of vicious extremes. Mercury's slow rotation coupled with its short year gave the planet a day nearly twice as long as its year, 176 earth days long. During that slow rotation, the noon temperature climbs to 430°C (806°F), hot enough to melt lead, tin, and zinc. Just before dawn, the other extreme is reached at −173°C (−279°F). No other planet in the solar system has such a strange day or a 600°C (1100°F) temperature range.

Shortly after the first Mercurian encounter, more problems plagued Mariner 10. A major electrical short developed and the data tape recorder failed. Now, mission controllers had no choice but to transmit all television pictures and other data in real time because there would be no playback at a more leisurely data rate after the next Mercury encounter. Mariner 10 was a very sick spacecraft, but controllers nursed it around the sun once again. Three more course corrections ensured a second Mercury intercept.

After looping around the sun once while Mercury raced through two orbits, Mariner 10 became the first spacecraft to revisit a celestial body. Passing within 48,069 km (29,870 mi) on September 21, the probe took a more southerly route allowing geologists to study another terrain.

In spite of the continuous struggle to control the spacecraft, engineers had aimed Mariner so precisely that now a third Mercury encounter was possible. In fact, the probe's aim was so phenomenal that care had to be taken during the three following course corrections to guide Mariner 10 *away* from a direct planetary strike. Then, one final malfunction nearly terminated the mission. Mariner had rolled into an attitude which prevented the craft from receiving signals from earth. The problem was corrected just 36 hr before approaching Mercury for the third encounter. On March 16, 1975, the craft zipped by a mere 327 km (203 mi) above Mercury. This closest of all approaches confirmed the first estimate of the planet's magnetic field and allowed Mariner to image features with a 140-m (459-ft) resolution. Just eight days later, the balky spacecraft finally expired, its attitude control gas exhausted.

In all, Mariner 10's 4000 pictures of Venus and 8000 pictures of Mercury opened the first real door to understanding the inner planets. But just as important, Mariner 10 had pioneered the use of multiple planet, gravity-assisted trajectories to reach distant worlds. Built as an economy-class spacecraft, Mariner 10 had performed four planetary encounters within thirteen months while staying within its straightjacket budget. The intrepid explorer proved to be the most prolific and productive deep space experiment yet flown.

7 Routine Science on Venus

A NEW GENERATION OF VENUS EXPLORERS

The Venera 7 and 8 landings had demonstrated that the Venusian heat portends a brutally short life for any craft that descends to the surface. Despite its beauty in the sky, Venus was now known to be a cruel, scorching, and punishing place upon which a probe would function for only about an hour. In spite of these formidable obstacles, Soviet space officials and scientists were eager to land complex analytical laboratories to perform extensive chemical and geological studies on this challenging planet. To do this, Babakin scrapped the MV-style Venera and struck out toward Venus with a completely new spacecraft which would send back torrents of revealing data.

During the 1975 launch window, the orbits of Venus and earth allowed a probe to maintain a slower than usual encounter speed, making it easier to brake into Venusian orbit. Taking advantage of this, the spacecraft bus was redesigned to be a planetary orbiter that would circle Venus for long-term studies. Designers also took advantage of the SL-12 Proton booster which could loft a payload four times heavier than that of the previous Venus rocket. The SL-6 Molniya was now retired as a planetary launcher.

The new Venera spacecraft was adapted from the second generation Mars probe already in use. The spacecraft bus was topped by a 2.4-m (7.9-ft)-diameter aeroshell, or hollow spherical heat shield, which surrounded a 1560-kg (3439-lb) atmospheric-descent capsule housing a 660-kg (1455-lb) surface lander. The spacecraft's mass jumped from 1184 kg (2610 lb) on Venera 8 to 4936 kg (10,882 lb) for Venera 9 and 5033 kg (11,096 lb) for Venera 10.

The orbiters housed complex laboratories packed with a vast array of instruments to study Venus. However, their first duty was to relay the lander's radio signal from the surface. Their orbits were arranged so that they would be in line of sight of the landers when they descended on the day side of Venus, which, at the time, was on the side opposite earth.

Once their relay duties were accomplished, the orbiters would concentrate on planetary studies. A magnetometer, a plasma spectrometer and charged-particle traps were to be used to investigate the solar wind. Extensive Venusian cloud-layer research was to be performed by a panoramic camera to study the dynamics of atmospheric circulation, an infrared spectrometer which would study the atmospheric gases, and an infrared radiometer which would measure cloud temperatures. A French-supplied photometer would measure ultraviolet brightness and the temperature of the cloud tops, while a photopolarimeter would measure brightness and polarization of solar radiation reflected by the cloud layers to determine the size of cloud particles. A spectrometer was also to be used to study the atmospheric layer above the clouds. Upper atmosphere research would use a photometer to measure solar radiation scattered by hydrogen atoms in the outer layers of the atmosphere and a spectrometer to measure the atmospheric glow.

INNOVATIVE LANDING SYSTEM USED

The new Veneras retained a 1-m (3.3-ft)-diameter pressure-resistant spherical design for their landers. However, instead entering the atmosphere "naked," the second generation landers would be protected from heating and aerodynamic forces by the aeroshell. To prevent the aeroshell from somersaulting through the atmosphere, it was bottom-weighted with a massive inertia damper to reduce any tendency to tumble.

The lander would use six parachutes containing a total of 180 m^2 (1937 ft^2) of material. After slowing to 250 m (820 ft) per sec at 65 km (40.4 mi) altitude, a series of three parachutes further reduced the lander's velocity to 50 m (164 ft) per sec, at which time the three 4.3-m (14.1-ft) main chutes were to be deployed. Upon reaching an altitude of 50 km (31 mi), the parachutes were to be cut loose.

At this point, the lander would use a novel system to retard its fall. Mounted above the lander's spherical body was a 2.1-m (6.9-ft)-diameter aerobraking disk that looked much like the brim of a broad hat. This disk would utilize the extreme thickness of the atmosphere to function as a parachute. At the planet's surface, the density of the Venusian atmosphere is approximately one-tenth that of water. If calculations were correct, the aerobraking disk would allow the lander to traverse quickly the thinner upper atmosphere, yet be effectively retarded by the lower atmosphere for a gentle touchdown. Attached by struts below the main spherical, pressure-resistant body of the lander was a ring-like apparatus made of crushable metal. This functioned as a shock absorber to cushion the 7-to-8 m (23-to-26 ft) per sec touchdown.

MINIATURE LABORATORY CARRIED

With the parachute compartment above and the landing ring below, the new lander stood 2 m (6.6 ft) high. The spherical body was covered with a thick layer of insulation. Two coolant pipes extended from the lander's hull up through the aerobraking disk. During transit to Venus, these would be attached to a refrigeration unit aboard the orbiter which precooled the lander's interior to −10°C (14°F).

The Venera 9 and 10 landers housed the most extensive complex of instruments yet carried to the Venusian surface. An accelerometer would chart the upper atmosphere by measuring the rate of deceleration during entry while other instruments measured temperature and pressure from 63 km (39 mi) to the surface. During the descent through the atmosphere, other optical instruments would measure the atmospheric brightness and wave-lengths in the green, yellow, red, and near-infrared spectrum. These would help determine the chemical composition of the atmosphere. Other optical instrumentation would measure solar radiation intensity in the atmosphere and in the clouds between 63 and 18 km (39 and 11 mi) altitude. A mass spectrometer would determine the chemical composition of the atmosphere between 63 and 34 km (39 and 21 mi). Once on the surface, a camera would return a panoramic photograph of the surface while two anemometers, which were basically four-vaned, whirlygig-like devices, measured surface wind velocity. A gamma-ray spectrometer would analyze surface rocks while a radiation densitometer measured soil density.

To image the previously unseen surface, Russian scientists designed a remarkable camera which would work in the horrid Venusian environment. The 5.8-kg (12.8-lb) camera used a mere five watts of power and was housed in an insulated container within the body of the lander. The surface was imaged via a scanning mirror which nodded and swiveled to view the surface through a periscope-like quartz window. The scene was relayed through a lens and diaphragm to a detector which converted the light intensity into a video signal containing 64 shades of gray. The complete exposure took 30 min and the field of view of the 517-scan-line frame was 40 by 180 degrees. Each lander was equipped with two cameras, one on each side, although only one would be used. In case the thick atmosphere made sunlight too dim, the landers were equipped with four 10,000-lux floodlights.

Valery Timofeev, an engineer with the Lavochkin Association, explained some of the special measures needed to test the design of the new Venera spacecraft: "In order to solve the special problems encountered with the Venusian environment, we tested more than twenty variations of the spacecraft design. We also had to create unique test equipment; 400-G centrifuges and pressure chambers with 100-atm pressures and temperatures of 500°C (932°F).

"A special problem was the different atmospheric pressures and the sealing of scientific equipment. The pressure on the surface was nearly 100 atm. To seal flanges at these pressures, the engineers sometimes used the application of pure gold."

"Another technical problem to deal with was the special glasses to take pictures of the Venus landscape. They must resist vibration and high temperature. The engineers made a special quartz glass which they tested in a heated pressure chamber. Inside the chamber, these glasses resisted high temperature and pressure, but they broke once outside the chamber. For a long time they could not understand why. It turned out that they broke because of the 480°C temperature drop outside the chamber."[1]

SUCCESSFUL DUAL LAUNCH

The inaugural Proton launch to Venus took place at Tyuratam at 5:37 A.M. June 8, 1975. Venera 10 followed six days later at 5:20 A.M., June 14. At the time, the Proton's design was still a state secret and no photos of the launch had ever been revealed. The uneventful flight to Venus was punctuated by twin course corrections by each spacecraft.

After the final course correction, the refrigeration system aboard Venera 9 cooled the lander and on October 20 it was ejected toward the daylight side of Venus. The spacecraft bus then performed a 247.3-m

(811-ft)-per-sec engine burn to miss Venus by 1600 km (1000 mi) and position itself for entry into Venusian orbit.

After a 136-day journey, the Venera 9 lander encountered Venus at 6:58 A.M. on October 22 and slammed into the atmosphere at an altitude of 125 km (77.7 mi). Deceleration produced 300 tons of pressure on the ball-shaped vehicle as it descended at an angle of 20.5 degrees.

At the same time, the Venera 9 spacecraft bus performed a 922.7-m (3027-ft)-per-sec braking burn and became the first artificial satellite of Venus. As the orbiter looped outward on its first orbit, it approached the lander from the opposite side of the planet and acted as a radio relay for the lander's signals. Venera 9's orbit was trimmed to 1510 × 112,200 km (938 × 69,721 mi), inclined 34.2 degrees with a period of 48 hr.

First signals from the Venera 9 lander were heard at 7:03 A.M., 5 min after atmospheric entry. Descent through the atmosphere took 75 min. At 8:13 A.M., the lander struck the surface at 33 degrees north latitude and 293 degrees longitude. It came to rest on a slope of 15 to 25 degrees about 2500 m (8200 ft) above the mean Venusian surface level. Today, this area to the east of the Beta Regio region is known to be the eastern slope of Rhea Mons, a shield volcano, a volcano which erupts with little explosive force and produces expansive lava flows. The sun was 54 degrees above the local horizon and photometers aboard the lander detected a brief darkening caused by the dust cloud kicked up by the 24-km (15 mile)-per-hr impact. The lander transmitted until the orbiter dropped below the horizon 53 min later.

On October 23, the Venera 10 lander was also released, and the bus made a 242.2-m (795-ft)-per-sec engine burn to align itself for entry into orbit. Two days later, as its lander descended, Venera 10 also placed itself into an orbit which was later adjusted to 1620 × 113,900 km (1007 × 70,777 mi) inclined 29.5 degrees, with a 49 hr and 23 min period.

The second lander entered the atmosphere 7:02 A.M., October 25. After a 168-g atmospheric deceleration, it floated down to the surface for 75 min and thumped down at 16 degrees north latitude and 291 degrees longitude.

Touchdown occurred at 8:17 A.M. on the southeast foot of the shield volcano Theia Mons, located east of Beta Regio about 2200 km (1367 mi) from Venera 9. The Venera 10 lander came to rest on a 3-m slab of rock and listed several degrees backward and to the left. Data were received for 65 min until the Venera 10 orbiter dropped below the horizon.

SCIENCE DURING DESCENT

Extensive atmospheric analysis showed that the clouds surrounding Venus were more like relatively transparent mists and that visibility within them is 1 to 1.5 km (0.6 to 0.9 mi). Their appearance of opacity from earth was therefore due to their depth. The clouds were generally arranged in three deep layers. The upper layer was 13 km (8 mi) deep and centered at 63.5 km (39.5 mi) altitude. The middle layer was 5 km (3 mi) deep, centered at 54.5 km (33.9 mi), while the lower layer was 3 km (1.9 mi) deep, centered at 50.5 km (31.4 mi).

Large cloud particles about 7 micrometers in diameter made up ninety percent of the cloud mass, while medium particles 2 to 2.5 micrometers in size and small particles 0.4 micrometers in size made up the remainder. Large particles were present in all cloud layers while medium and small particles were present only in the upper two layers.

Below the clouds, the atmospheric temperature climbed steadily until touchdown where Venera 9 recorded a surface temperature of 460°C (860°F) at 90 atm pressure. The surface conditions at the Venera 10 site were similar, being 465°C (869°F), with a pressure of 92 atm.

Wind velocity measurements showed there were high winds in the clouds, followed by a large wind shear, a change in wind velocity, at the base of the clouds. Wind speed then slowly diminished, dropping to about 1 m (3.3 ft) per sec at the surface. While these winds may not seem like much, their velocity combines with the high density of the Venusian atmosphere to produce a force comparable to an ocean wave on earth driven by 80-km (50-mile)-per-hr winds. The prevailing winds were blowing from the east.

During their descent, the landers detected a mysterious radio noise initially interpreted to be lightning. It was speculated that lightning there might be caused by localized volcanic heating of the atmosphere, but the lack of a reliable explanation led Russian researchers to call the effect "the electrical dragon on Venus."[2]

Radioactive elements in the surface rocks were examined by a gamma-ray spectrometer to determine their chemical composition. Venera 9 detected 0.00006 percent uranium, 0.00036 percent thorium, and 0.47 percent potassium. Venera 10 showed 0.00005 percent uranium, 0.00007 percent thorium, and 0.3 potassium. This analysis was similar to laboratory readings of slowly cooled volcanic basalt of low porosity which released very little gas. Rock density was 2.7 to 2.9 g per cm^3.

FIRST PLANETARY SURFACE PHOTOGRAPHS

Veneras 9 and 10 each transmitted one black-and-white surface image. Unlike NASA's planetary encounters where images from spacecraft were played over dozens of control room monitors, the historic first photo from the surface of Venus slowly ticked off line by line from a single thermoprint machine at the control center in the Crimea. These first photos were considered to be a scientific sensation, and while scientifically fascinating, they actually raised more questions than they answered.

The head of the Venera science team, Dr. Mikhail Marov, said he was surprised how sharp the photos were. He expected the pictures to be dark due to the thick clouds.[3] Instead, the views showed the sky and surface clearly separated. Shadows were easily visible and proved that the natural light level at the surface was relatively strong. The lander's floodlights were on during photographic scans, but their effect was not evident. A spacecraft designer who helped build the lander's telemetry system, Dr. Arnold Selivanov, remarked that it was as bright on Venus as it is on a cloudy June day in Moscow.[4] Selivanov's remarks imply that either Venus was brighter than expected or that it is terribly gloomy in Moscow on cloudy June days.

The photos destroyed contemporary theories that Venus' surface was a sandy desert created by wind and heat erosion. The Venera 9 photo revealed a surface littered with sharp-cornered rocks up to 40 cm (16 in) in diameter. Detail was good out to a distance of 50 to 100 m (164 to 328 ft), but little dust or sand was observed. One Venera investigator, K. P. Florensky, said the landing site appeared to be at the base of a hill in the midst of a rock slide.[5] The sharp-edged rocks, lacking eroded edges, showed that the local surface was created recently by some sort of tectonic activity, earthquake, or volcanism, implying that Venus is internally active.

The Venera 10 photo revealed slab-like rocks with dark markings which could have been different minerals within the rock. These rocks were eroded, indicating that the surface could be radically different from spot to spot. Large areas of debris and rubble, requiring long-term erosion to be created, were seen between larger stones, indicating an older site.

The basic appearance of the surface was similar to a terrestrial sea bottom with all organic material removed. Venus' extremely dense atmosphere apparently acts like an ocean in shaping the landscape with currents instead of winds. The atmosphere appears even capable of rolling boulders across the surface. Venera 10's site seemed to be older than Venera 9's, and gamma-ray analysis established that both areas were younger than the Venera 8 site.

Some confusion exists about the distance to the horizon in the photographs. Some investigators determined that it was up to 300 m (985 ft) away. Others, assuming the surface rocks were all the same size, determined that the horizon was less than 100 m (328 ft) away, a distance possible considering that the craft landed on a steep slope. The fact that the horizon was visible was proof that it was less than 1 km (0.6 mi) away because the thick atmosphere would obscure it at greater distances. The horizon was, however, not far enough away to enable a determination of whether the super refractive effects of the high atmospheric pressure would cause the horizon to appear concave.

One major finding was the discovery that Venus was covered with rocks and not with regolith, or granular material above the bedrock, as on earth's moon. At the Venera 9 and 10 sites, the surface seemed to resemble the crust of earth. Russian investigators likened the observed rocks to the shallow bedrock of the central Kazakhstan steppes.[6] Overall, they showed that the surface of Venus could be considered young and evolving.

THE VIEW FROM VENUS ORBIT

On October 26, both orbiters began relaying cloud-cover pictures and other observations. In the month following the landings, the Venera 9 and 10 orbiters, respectively, made 15 and 13 revolutions around the planet. The orbiters were not tracked continuously and were only stabilized when they were near periapsis, the low point of the orbit.

The twin orbiters also marked the beginning of French cooperation in the Venera program. Using a French-made ultraviolet spectrometer, the orbiters noted that the brightness of Venus' cloud cover varied by 20 percent across the planet. Repeated 1200-km (746-mi)-wide scans with the instrument led to a large-scale composite picture of the cloud cover.

Using spectrometers and radiometers, as well as photopolarimeters, devices which studied various characteristics of reflected light from the planet, the orbiters studied the structure, temperature, and radiation signature of the clouds. One of the earliest discoveries was that cloud particles were positively not water drops, yet were some sort of liquid. Spectroscopic and polarimeteric studies showed the clouds could not be more than 5 parts per 10,000 water vapor. Temperature measurements showed that the tops of the clouds were −40°C (−40°F), precluding the presence of large water drops.

Orbital studies confirmed the occasional presence of the mysterious "ashen light" seen on the dark side of the planet from earth. By averaging the readings from 50 separate spectra, a constant night-side airglow caused by molecular oxygen was detected by the orbiter's spectrometer. In contradiction, infrared studies indicated that the cloud layers on the night side were several degrees warmer than on the day side.

On October 26, Venera 9 used a spectrometer to search optically for lightning. In a 450-km (280-mi) area on the night side around 7 P.M., local Venus time, many strong flashes were detected over a 70-sec period. Assuming the flashes were lightning, analysis showed they were about 15 times more intense than lightning on earth.

The Venera 10 orbiter also surveyed the surface with a small radar. This determined that the surface elevation under the orbital path varied by only a few kilometers, implying that the planet surface, overall, is smoother than that of earth.

Studies from orbit proved that Venus' weak magnetic field did not originate from a magnetic core within the planet but instead arose from currents flowing in the ionosphere which are induced by the solar magnetic field. As visualized looking at the planet from space, the solar magnetic field lines drape around Venus like a hairpin, with the planet at the apex. Because of the tenuous magnetic field, the solar wind presses to within one-third of the planetary radius above Venus as opposed to the same phenomenon being tens of thousands of kilometers above earth.

The density of ions and electrons in the ionosphere were measured using radiosounding. At higher orbital altitudes, their energy spectra were measured directly using ion traps. Measurements showed that electron concentrations fell by a factor of 50 at night, confirming previous spacecraft data implying that the nighttime ionosphere was very irregular.

Observations from orbit continued until March 22, 1976, when the research program was ended. A year after arriving, both orbiters were still functioning but were scientifically dormant.

Veneras 9 and 10 can be considered true "breakthrough" missions. Russian scientists became the undisputed masters of Venus exploration when they advanced planetary studies into complex analyses performed directly on the surface. The success of the latest missions represented a maturing of Russian space technology which opened the door to future explorations to pursue very specific questions about the Venusian environment.

AMERICAN VENUS RETURN LONG IN COMING

America's fourth return to Venus took more than a decade to accomplish, during which time the Russians were racking up stunning successes there. The seeds of what would evolve into the Pioneer Venus program were planted shortly after NASA visited Venus in 1967 by flying a "used" spacecraft as Mariner 5. In the late 1960s orbiters, descent probes, and balloon probes were all evaluated for the next investigation of the veiled planet. By 1969 these ideas were merged into the spin-stabilized Planetary Explorer spacecraft concept which used a "universal bus," an orbiter-probe combination which would both drop instruments onto the planet and scout from orbit.

In the early 1970s, the Vietnam war sapped the national treasury while an upsurge in social programs further drained government funds. Congress was therefore reluctant to fund new space exploration ventures. The Venus mission was transferred to NASA's Ames Research Center which then considered less expensive options. By 1972, Ames came up with a financially modest plan to send two multiprobe missions in 1977, two orbiters in 1978 and a lander in 1980. Even this stretched-out exploration plan came under congressional fire, so the plan was shortened to one multiprobe in 1977 and an orbiter in 1978. With the understanding that the combined missions would not exceed $250 million, the plan was finally approved by NASA in 1974, and Pioneer Venus was born.

Hughes Aircraft was selected to build the new Venus craft and NASA chose the instruments to be flown. In spite of successful Russian probes, very little was known about the composition of the Venusian ionosphere, atmosphere, and surface. Pioneer Venus was dedicated to investigating these areas. However, Congress continued to withhold funding even though the program had been approved. After much debate with Congress, NASA decided to delay the multiprobe mission until 1978, flying both spacecraft during the same launch window. Finally Pioneer Venus seemed to be on track.

By 1975 $50 million had been invested in the mission. But then Congress again showed its penchant for killing scientific programs before completion, even after spending huge amounts of money on them. Reversing its earlier commitment, Congress cut $48 million from Pioneer's 1976 budget, which rang the death knell for the project. The scientific community, tired of being fiscally abused, rallied an intense lobbying effort. Eventually funding was restored and the dual mission proceeded.

The missions of Pioneer Venuses 1 and 2 were twofold. An orbiter was to perform long-term observations of Venusian phenomena, mapping the surface by radar and observing the clouds for one Venusian year (243 earth days). The multiprobe was to drop four separate probes into the atmosphere and perform the first American studies from within the Venusian environment.

To accomplish these missions, the Pioneers evolved into what seemed to be two entirely different spacecraft, but appearance were deceiving. Hughes Aircraft Company engineers drew on experience gained with the Surveyor lunar probes and various military space programs to develop a drum-shaped common spacecraft bus used by both Venus explorers. To control costs, existing earth satellite designs and hardware were used, such as the communications and radar systems. Where possible, duplicate systems were used for both craft. In fact, the multiprobe bus and orbiter bus had a 76 percent commonality which significantly reduced development costs.

It had taken years of struggle to mount an intensive American scientific mission to Venus. In their final form, both Pioneers became extraordinarily sophisticated machines which promised to fulfill at last the scientific hopes of American planetary scientists. Russian scientists had repeatedly sent spacecraft after spacecraft to Venus and now American scientists were going to make the most of their opportunity at the mysterious planet.

ORBITER TO SEE THROUGH CLOUDS

The Pioneer Venus Orbiter, known as PVO, housed 12 scientific instruments totaling 45 kg (99 lb) on an equipment deck atop the bus. A majority of the instruments would study the interaction between Venus and the solar wind, measure the temperatures of the clouds, and use radio waves to probe the atmosphere. All would scan Venus as the craft slowly rotated.

At launch, PVO had a mass of 553 kg (1219 lb). This included the internally mounted 179-kg (395-lb) solid-fueled retrorocket and 32 kg (70.5 lb) of hydrazine propellant for the control thrusters. A 2.99-m (9.8-ft) central boom extended above the bus. On this was mounted a 1.1-m (3.6-ft) diameter despun, an earth-pointing, directional antenna which focused a 7.6-degree beam toward earth. Another 4.72-m (15.5-ft) boom carried the magnetometer.

Upon arrival, the 1815-kg (4000-lb)-thrust retrorocket would slow the craft by 3780 km (2359 mi) per hr, allowing it to enter a 24-hr orbit. This path would be maintained during the radar mapping mission by the hydrazine thrusters.

Because the spacecraft would enter the shadow of Venus for up to 26 min each day, two 7.5-amp-hr, nickel-cadmium batteries powered the experiments while in darkness. A 750-milliwatt transmitter would probe the atmosphere by beaming a signal through it to earth when the orbiter was occulted by Venus each day. Two recorders with a combined one-megabit capacity stored data while the craft was in eclipse with respect to earth.

By far the most exciting part of Pioneer Venus was the radar experiment. Because Venus is shrouded permanently by an all-encompassing cloud cover, overhead views of the planet's surface are hidden from human eyes. Our only peek at the mysterious place was Venera 9 and 10's glimpse of a local area near the landers. It was thus anticipated that the orbiter's radar would open a never-before-seen world.

Earth-based radar scans are most effective when Venus and earth are in close proximity. However, a celestial problem complicates terrestrial radar-imaging of Venus. The slow retrograde rotation of the planet, coupled with the timing of its orbital period, results in the same side of Venus facing earth whenever the two planets pass near each other. This celestial dance limits our view from earth to a small portion of Venus.

The Pioneer Venus orbiter was equipped to fill the huge blank on the Venusian map. A radar mapper would peer through the clouds to produce a crude continental map of Venus. The radar used only 30 watts of power, about one-third that of a light bulb. It was a technical marvel in that it packed 1000 microcircuits into a package with a mass of 11 kg (24 lb).

As the orbiter arced high above Venus on its daily orbit, it would image the planet's clouds by using a device adapted from the Pioneer spacecraft previously sent to Jupiter and Saturn. The rotation of the spacecraft allowed a photopolarimeter with a 0.03-degree field of view to slowly scan the face of Venus line by line and complete an image every four hours.

ONE PROBE IS REALLY FIVE

The 875-kg (1929-lb) multiprobe was unique in that it was designed to split into five independent probes carrying a total of 18 experiments. The carrier bus housed four ejectable atmospheric probes, none of which were supposed to survive impact on the surface. One large probe was supplemented by three small probes, called North Probe, Day Probe, and Night Probe according to their destinations on the planet. All were designed to study the structure of the atmosphere from 200 km (120 mi) to the surface. The bus itself also housed two spectrometers to investigate the ionosphere and upper statosphere during its suicide plunge into the atmosphere. These areas were inaccessible to the probes because they were hermetically sealed prior to atmospheric entry.

The 316-kg (695-lb) large probe consisted of two parts: the deceleration module (the heat shield) and a pressure vessel. The 1.42-m (4.7-ft)-diameter conical aluminum heat shield was covered with carbon phenolic material to protect the pressure vessel from the atmospheric entry temperatures which would briefly equal that on the surface of the sun. It would have to endure 280 gs while decelerating from 42,000 km (26,000 mi) per hr to subsonic speed in just 38 sec. The shield would then fall away while the 73-cm (29-inch) pressure vessel descended from 64 to 45 km (39.8 to 28 mi) under a dacron parachute. At this point the parachute would be cast off and the probe would fall freely, taking another 39 min to sink to the surface.

Eight instruments totaling 28 kg (62 lb) would scan during descent. A mass spectrometer and gas chromatograph would measure the composition and density of the atmosphere. The cloud structure and composition would be studied by a spectrometer and a nephelometer (cloud particle detector). Two radiometers would sample the temperatures within the clouds to determine how solar radiation interacted with the atmosphere. Other instruments would study the temperature, density, and winds in the atmosphere.

The three identical 90-kg (200-lb) small probes were simpler in design and used no parachute. Their pressure vessels would remain nested inside their 80-cm (31.5-inch)-diameter heat shields after a fierce 565-g deceleration. The small probes carried 3.5 kg (7.7 lb) of instruments including a nephelometer to study cloud structure, a radiometer to study the atmospheric heat balance and instruments to measure temperature, pressure, and wind speed in the atmosphere all the way to the surface.

UNIQUE PROBLEMS OVERCOME

To endure the high-temperature environment and the bone-crushing 90-atm pressure, the probes were constructed in the shape of spheres made of titanium, a strong but lightweight metal with a high melting point. Casting and machining the two hemispheres was an exacting nine-month process. One project engineer described the manufacturing process as more like sculpting in titanium than performing engineering work.[7]

The radiometer viewing windows on the probes presented special problems because of the harsh environment. Sapphire was chosen to pass visible light through the two windows on the small probes. Diamond was required for the large probe because it was transparent to the infrared radiation to be studied by the infrared radiometer. After a two-year search, a 200-carat natural diamond was chosen and cut into a window about the size of two stacked pennies. Oddly, the gemstone-derived windows required special legal handling. Because of government gem-export regulations, a special waiver was issued for the Pioneer Venus windows because they were to be shipped outside the United States, indeed, shipped to another planet!

Only the large probe used a parachute to slow its initial descent. The small probes fell free to the surface after atmospheric entry. However, developing the parachute proved particularly vexing because it had to deploy at near supersonic speeds high in the Venusian atmosphere. Test drops from jet aircraft repeatedly failed. When a crucial test drop from a balloon 30,000 m (100,000 ft) above New Mexico smashed into the desert floor, the Venus project appeared to be in jeopardy. But, eventually, these and many other roadblocks were overcome and by mid-1978 the two Pioneers were ready.

OFF TO VENUS AT LAST

On May 20, 1978, an Atlas-Centaur rumbled to life at Cape Canaveral and rose into the bright morning sky at 10:13 A.M. The launch of Pioneer Venus 1, the PVO, came almost three months before its counterpart, the multiprobe, departed earth. The long circuitous trajectory designed to minimize PVO's arrival speed by looping more than half way around the sun was the reason for the delay. That delay allowed the spacecraft to rendezvous with Venus just as PVO reached the perihelion, the point of closest approach to the sun, of its transfer orbit between earth and Venus. A shorter flight time was possible, but would have required a retrorocket with fifty percent of the mass of the spacecraft.

Pioneer Venus 2 followed in August. The launch was set for the sixth, but a strange incident delayed the flight for two days: The truck supplying liquid helium to the booster's Centaur upper stage ran out of helium during the countdown. Liftoff was rescheduled for August 8 when a spectacular launch shattered the still Florida night at 3:33 A.M. The multiprobe would have missed Venus by 14,000 km (8700 mi), but a 2.25-m (7.4-ft)-per-sec velocity change on August 16 brought the craft back on target. The multiprobe with its cargo of atmospheric probes followed a more direct route to Venus and would arrive at the planet only five days after PVO even though it was launched three months later.

The transit to Venus was relatively uneventful except for trouble with the PVO computer's memory which experienced sporadic and temporary errors induced by cosmic radiation. Just under a month after the multiprobe left earth, both Pioneers found they were accompanied by the Russian Venera 11 and 12 spacecraft, also targeted for Venus.

As both Pioneers approached Venus, the four probes were released from the multiprobe. The first to go was the large probe, released on November 15 while still 11.1 million km (6.9 million mi) from Venus. Five days later and still 9.3 million km (5.8 million mi) from its destination, the multiprobe was spun up to 48 rpm. The three small probes were then released, spreading out like shotgun pellets to arrive at widely separated locations on Venus. The probes were all nudged forward by a spring release mechanism and slowly drifted ahead of the multiprobe bus.

PROBES RAIN DOWN ON VENUS

The first to arrive at Venus was PVO. On December 4 it passed behind the planet as seen from earth and fired its retrorocket at 11:51 A.M. PVO then entered a 1-day orbit which was slowly trimmed over the next 2 weeks to $150 \times 66,889$ km ($93.2 \times 41,565$ mi), inclined 105 degrees with a period of 24 hr. Images of the planet's cloud cover were taken every 3.5 hr near apoapsis, the high point of the orbit, when the entire planet was visible. Radar mapping was done at periapsis, the low point of the orbit, when the radar could best distinguish features on the surface.

The multiprobe and its swarm arrived on December 9 and began an exciting 2 hr of repeated planetary strikes. The large probe punched into the atmosphere first. During its 50-min descent, it streamed data to earth at 256 bits per sec until it struck the surface.

At 4-min intervals, the small probes each took their turn diving into the clouds of Venus. The free-falling probes took 53 min to reach the surface as the thick atmosphere slowed their fall to 35 km (22 mi) per hr. The probe's Kapton insulation limited their internal temperature to 50°C (112°F).

North Probe was silenced immediately on landing. Night Probe continued transmitting for 2 seconds. The Day Probe, however, proved quite hardy. After landing, it survived for 67.5 min. Once on the surface, the probe may as well have been dumped into molten lead. It was squeezed by pressure equal to that at a depth of 900 m (3000 ft) in earth's oceans and baked at a temperature of 480°C (900°F). When the signal faded because of battery depletion, the probe's internal temperature had only risen to 126°C (259°F).

The multiprobe carrier followed 1.5 hr later. Its job was finished, 63 seconds later, when it melted and burned up as a result of atmospheric friction.

LATEST LOOK AT VENUS

The probes detailed the atmospheric structure, establishing that the clouds were composed mostly of corrosive sulfuric acid droplets. During their descent into the veils above Venus, they first encountered a fine haze, a layer of nearly transparent cloud between 90 and 70 km (56 and 43.5 mi). Below this, the probes sank through three separate cloud layers between 70 and 47 km (43.5 and 29 mi). The lowest cloud layer was opaque. Breaking through the lower cloud layer, the probes encountered another haze layer extending down to 30 km (18.6 mi) altitude. Once through the lower haze layer, the probes found the atmosphere was transparent. Between 50 and 10 km (31 and 6.2 mi), little mixing was found between cloud layers, and the atmosphere was nearly stagnant.

The ratio of deuterium to hydrogen in the Venusian atmosphere turned out to be 100 times higher than on earth. This implied that in the distant past, at a time when the sun was cooler, Venus might have had large oceans. These bodies of water would have evaporated eventually as the temperature of the surface rose because of greenhouse heating.

The PVO spacecraft spent the next two Venusian years mapping 93 percent of the surface with a resolution 30 km (19 mi) across and 200 m (656 ft) in elevation. The radar indicated that Venus was surprisingly flat compared to earth with most of the planet being within 500 m (1640 ft) of mean planetary level, the overall average surface elevation. However, Venus did show some extremes. Radar scans showed a giant 10.8-km (6.7-mile) mountain dubbed Maxwell Montes and the 2.9-km (1.8-mi) deep Diana Chasma.

Other studies from orbit found the upper night side atmosphere to be 250°C (482°F) cooler than the dayside upper atmosphere, indicating that strong winds blow across the terminator, the division between the day and night side of the planet. PVO also observed a slow decline in sulfur dioxide in the atmosphere, implying a major volcanic eruption must have occurred prior to arrival. The low resolution of PVO's radar prevented any detection of fresh volcanic activity. Radio studies also found evidence of lightning on Venus.

EXTENDED MISSION CONTINUES

After two years in Venus orbit, PVO was still healthy. Only the infrared radiometer had failed. Now, an extended mission was devised to take advantage of the orbiter's unexpected longevity. Since the radar mapping was already completed, a controlled orbit was no longer required, and, to conserve fuel, the hydrazine thrusters used to maintain the precise orbit for radar studies were shut off on July 27, 1980, when only 4.5 kg (10 lb) of propellant remained. The orbiter would now investigate how the atmosphere of Venus reacted over the 11-year sunspot cycle to see if the solar phenomenon of varying numbers of sunspots caused any changes in the Venusian atmosphere.

Without the constant trim maneuvers, the orbiter's periapsis slowly rose to 2270 km (1411 mi) by mid-1986. Over the next decade, PVO made a fascinating discovery, observing that the high altitude haze layer above the Venusian clouds appeared and disappeared over a period of several years.

From a vantage point which often took it to the opposite side of the solar system, PVO became America's remote outpost observatory. The craft was particularly useful during the 1986 appearance of Halley's Comet. Congressional fiscal restraints prevented the United States from sending its own craft along with the international scientific armada which greeted the comet. However, PVO was in the right place for making unique Halley observations since both Halley and PVO were on the far side of the sun. The orbiter was commanded to flip over in order to observe Halley during its solar perihelion passage (when the comet was invisible from earth). One of the most striking discoveries made was that, when the comet was near the sun, it was surrounded by a tenuous, very rarified, but huge 12.5-million-km (7.75-million-mile)-diameter cloud of hydrogen gas, This giant hydrogen coma made Halley the largest object in the solar system, larger even than the sun.

The PVO spacecraft had been designed to last 8 months in Venus orbit. That 8-month mission lasted an amazing 14 years during which time the exceptional spacecraft continued to perform flawlessly. Eventually, the drag of the upper Venusian atmosphere slowed the orbiter slightly and gravity pulled PVO toward the planet. By 1992, the craft was skimming dangerously close to the atmosphere. Controllers began to use the hydrazine thrusters to sustain the orbit just above the cloud tops to make unique atmospheric observations.

In 90 days, the remaining hydrazine was expended and PVO again began to sink toward Venus. As the orbiter spiraled toward certain destruction, it explored previously uncharted portions of the upper atmosphere. Among the last data transmitted was an analysis of atmospheric components which gave more startling evidence that Venus may have at one time possessed a shallow ocean.

The extraordinarily long-lived Pioneer Venus mission was one of the most productive of NASA's explorations. Both spacecraft had responded to more than 2 million commands and had transmitted a staggering 10 trillion bits of data, enough to fill 700 million high-density computer floppy disks. This mass of data provided more information about Venus than all the data collected about the planet in the previous 500 years.

Finally, on October 8, 1992, PVO lost its struggle with gravity and fell into the upper atmosphere of Venus. The last transmission was received at 3:22 P.M. from an altitude of 130 km (80 mi). The orbiter then incinerated like flashpowder. It was a particularly nostalgic moment for scientists as they watched their old friend at Venus go down fighting.

CONTINUED RUSSIAN PLANETARY SUCCESS

After the brilliantly successful Venera 9 and 10 missions, the Russians passed up the 1976–77 Venus flight opportunity to modify their lander with improved instruments to reflect the latest planetary discoveries. When two Pioneer Venus probes departed in summer 1978, they were followed closely by the improved Veneras 11 and 12.

Less favorable orbital geometry between earth and Venus during the 1978 flight opportunity taxed the carrying capacity of the Proton boosters and required that engineers reduce the launch weights of Venera 11 to 4450 kg (9810 lb) and Venera 12 to 4461 kg (9835 lb). This restriction meant the craft were unable to carry enough fuel to brake into Venus orbit—they were to be fly-by craft instead of orbiters. The American PVO spacecraft following the two Veneras carried no lander and was designed from the outset to enter Venus orbit.

Externally, their design was nearly identical to Veneras 9 and 10 and, again, the spacecraft buses carried an extensive complement of instruments for studying interplanetary space. The ambitious objectives of these experiments included comparing interplanetary data with that obtained by the American Pioneer Venus probes—which would precede the Veneras by several weeks. The dual flights by both nations represented a unique opportunity to study the interaction of the solar wind with earth, interplanetary space, and Venus by a succession of spacecraft strung out between earth and Venus.

LANDERS CARRY ADVANCED INSTRUMENTS

The Venus landing craft were packed with instruments which would study the atmosphere in unprecedented detail. In addition to a panoramic camera system and gamma-ray spectrometer, the landers carried a mass spectrometer, temperature and atmospheric pressure sensors, a wind anemometer, and a 4500-to-12,000-angstrom spectrophotometer to analyze the atmosphere in addition to carrying out several new experiments.

The "Groza" ("thunderstorm" in Russian) experiment was to search for lightning in the atmosphere by listening for electrically induced static.

The new landers were designed to verify the previous atmospheric analyses made by Veneras 9 and 10 using another new instrument, a gas chromatograph. These instruments are fairly bulky devices but researchers at the Institute For Space Research devised a gas chromatograph for the Venera landers that weighed only 10 kg (22 lb). The instrument was considered more sensitive than the gas chromatograph carried by the Pioneer Venus probe.

Only Venera 12's lander carried a nephelometer to study the size of cloud particles. Also, for the first time, special filters would capture cloud particles for analysis by an X-ray fluorescence spectrometer.

Designers at the Lavochkin Association had built previous probes which succeeded in reaching the surface, but the devil's playground that is Venus still tricked spacecraft designers. Russian aerospace engineer Valery Timofeev, in 1991, retold the story of the challenge designers faced in developing a piece of instrumentation for the Venera 11 lander: "The engineers of the Lavochkin Association designed a scientific device for Venera 11 which they tested in a high-pressure chamber. It was a very big device with a mass of 300 kg (661 lb). After this test, they opened the chamber, but they could not find it. It was very strange! Why? Where was it? It was a very large device and the chamber was closed! All they found were some melted optical lenses and insulation of wires.

"The reason for this was that when we simulated the conditions of Venus: the temperature, pressure, and composition of the atmosphere; the materials that were used reacted, the device vaporized! It was made of titanium and it melted and vaporized. We learned we must use another material on the surface of Venus!"[8]

Timofeev's anecdote also shows that luck flew with the American Pioneer Venus probes. They too were made of titanium, but survived the drop through the pressurized horror that is the Venusian atmosphere.

Venus is a strange place indeed.

SUCCESSFUL TWIN LAUNCH

Venera 11 was launched from the still secret Proton launch pad at Tyuratam on September 9, 1978. Venera 12 followed on September 14. Mid-course corrections were performed by Venera 11 on September 16 and December 17. Venera 12's path was similarly refined September 21 and December 14.

The American Pioneer Venus 2 had been launched about three weeks ahead of Veneras 11 and 12. Living up to previous space cooperation agreements, data from the Pioneer Venus and Venera probes were shared.

All four spacecraft conducted complementary observations of the interplanetary medium between earth and Venus. In a further cooperative effort, Veneras 11 and 12 were commanded to make long-range observations of Venus on December 4 and 9, to provide complementary data on the days that the two Pioneers arrived at Venus.

During the flight to Venus, the Veneras recorded 27 gamma-ray bursts and 120 solar flares. During a powerful solar flare on September 23, a dramatic increase in the energy of solar-produced protons and alpha particles was detected over a 2-day period. Such bursts could have fatal consequences for unprotected human interplanetary travelers in the future.

Because of varying energy requirements on different launch dates, Venera 12 overtook and passed the lead craft, arriving at Venus 4 days ahead of its twin, even though it was launched 5 days later.

SUCCESSFUL LANDING MARRED BY INSTRUMENT PROBLEMS

As Venera 12 approached Venus, the lander's batteries were charged and its interior chilled. Then, on December 19, 2 days before planetary intercept, the descent capsule separated and the bus was directed to miss the planet by 35,000 km (21,750 mi).

After a 98-day flight, the descent capsule entered the atmosphere at 5:30 A.M., December 21. Decelerating through the atmosphere in a sequence similar to Veneras 9 and 10, the new lander sank to the surface. Venera 12's external temperature sensors failed several minutes before landing. Upon landing, the craft's soil analyzer also failed. When it was time for the surface photograph to be transmitted, engineers puzzled over the black image. At first they feared the craft had sunk into some sort of viscous fluid, with only its antenna structure still above the surface. Then scientists came to the horrifying realization that Venera had performed the same photographic error common to earth snapshooters: it had failed to jettison the lens cap!

The rest of the lander's scientific cargo performed as planned and showed the surface temperature to be 460°C (860°F) and pressure 88 atm. Data were transmitted for 110 min before the spacecraft bus, which acted as a signal relay to earth, passed below the horizon at 8:20 A.M., terminating contact.

The Venera 11 lander entered the Venusian atmosphere at 5:25 A.M. on Christmas Day and followed the same landing profile as Venera 12.

While similar in appearance to the Venera 9 and 10 landers, the new landers carried the most sophisticated analytical instruments yet dropped through the atmosphere of Venus. However, due to a common design fault, the camera covers on Venera 11 also stubbornly refused to eject after landing and the temperature probe and soil analyzer also failed. All other instruments aboard the Venera 11 lander returned data for 95 min until the spacecraft bus passed below the local horizon. Surface conditions at the Venera 11 landing site were 446°C (835°F) with a pressure of 88 atm.

CAMERA LOSS FAILS TO DETER SCIENTIFIC GAINS

Both landers carried instruments called scanning spectrophotometers which studied sunlight shining through the atmosphere. Five hundred separate spectra were gathered which showed the spectral absorption bands, the unique spectral signature, for carbon dioxide, water vapor, and gaseous sulfur.

One of the major riddles about Venus was the presence of water on the planet. Venera 11 found that the water vapor content in the atmosphere, as determined by the gas chromatograph, decreased as the craft neared the surface [from 0.5 percent at 44 km (26 mi) to less than 0.01 percent below 24 km (15 mi)]. (Water vapor was undetected by Venera 12 because the gas chromatograph instrument failed.) Water vapor readings gathered by the new Veneras disagreed significantly with those from the Pioneer Venus probes—the American instruments detected 10 times the water vapor reported by the Veneras. Russian scientists, however, stood staunchly by the Venera readings and argued that the higher amount of water could not be present unless the planet's temperature were 200°C (392°F) hotter. According to the latest Venera data, if all the water vapor in the atmosphere condensed, it would cover the planet to a depth of only 1 cm (0.4 inch). Ultimately, the Russian data proved closer to the truth: Venus is astonishingly dry.

With such low water vapor readings, the question again arose over the disappearance of Venus' water and possible past oceans. A popular theory was that solar radiation photodissociated (broke up) the molecules making up the water vapor in the planet's atmosphere early in Venus' evolution. The hydrogen would have escaped into space while the oxygen became bound with the surface minerals. Another theory suggests that the water is still there, but is bound to hydrated minerals that can survive the extreme heat. The mystery of Venus' water remains unsolved to this day.

CLOUD LAYERS INVESTIGATED

The X-ray fluorescence spectrometer performed approximately 500 scans of the atmosphere during descent. The instruments determined that above 61 km (38 mi) altitude the droplets making up the cloud particles were composed mostly of chlorine, not of sulfur as scientists had expected. (It should be noted that the later Venera 13 and 14 missions found the opposite to be true, perhaps implying massive short-term changes in the atmosphere.)

Venera 11's nephelometer indicated that the thickest cloud layer existed between 51 and 48 km (31.7 and 29.8 mi) altitude. The instrument also detected other heavy layers not seen by Pioneer Venus at 17 to 13 km (10.6 to 8 mi) and 12 to 8 km (7.5 to 5 mi) altitude.

Venera 12 confirmed past findings that the cloud veil around Venus located between 50 to 70 km (31 to 43.5 mi) altitude was composed of sulfuric acid droplets. The mean density of the clouds was determined to be about 200 particles per cm^3. Visibility within the clouds was approximately 1 km (0.6 mi), indicating that the clouds were thin but nonetheless opaque because of their depth.

It was also determined that all of the heat Venus radiates into space originates from the upper cloud layers [between 67 and 70 km (41.6 and 43.5 mi) altitude]. The Venera 9 and 10 orbiters had established the seemingly contradictory fact that nighttime cloud-top temperatures actually were higher than the daytime temperatures. Veneras 11 and 12 resolved the conflict, determining that large amounts of sulfuric acid aerosol particles, which form only during the day, block some of the planet's heat from radiating into space on the day side. Although it was reported that a sulfuric acid rain was discovered on Venus, this erroneous report resulted from a translation error.

Light-level readings showed that only 6 percent of the incident sunlight reached the surface. The light that does make it to the surface is so diffuse that the sun's location could not be determined. Only a general sky brightening in the direction of the sun was visible.

ATMOSPHERIC ORIGIN DEBATED

Ionizing mass spectrometers analyzed eleven samples of atmospheric gas between 23 km (14.3 mi) and the surface. After ionizing small samples, the instrument grouped the ions according to their masses and relayed 176 mass spectra to earth which showed isotopes of carbon, oxygen, nitrogen, neon, argon, and krypton.

The mass spectrometer showed that, while the ratios of krypton isotopes in the atmosphere of Venus and earth are similar, there are vast differences between the planets in the ratios of argon isotopes. The Venera data agreed with Pioneer Venus on its readings of equal amounts of the isotopes argon 36 to argon 40. By comparison, earth has 300 times more argon 40 than argon 36. The radiogenic isotope argon 40 is formed by the radioactive decay of natural elements, while the primordial isotope argon 36 is thought to be left over from the original gaseous solar nebula from which the planets formed. The finding that Venus had equal amounts of argon 36 and argon 40 isotopes cast doubt on the theory that the atmospheres of all the inner planets were formed by outgasing, the expulsion of gases from their interior, either by volcanic eruption or the slow release during long-term tectonic movement of the planet's crust. To explain why Venus retained so much more of the primordial argon 36 than the rest of the solar system, one theory holds that most of Venus' early atmosphere was formed from the early solar nebula, unlike the atmospheres of earth and Mars which evolved by outgasing from the planet.

The detection of the argon 40 revealed further evidence of tectonic activity on Venus. For this isotope to be present in the atmosphere, it had to be released from the planet's interior as a result of either the movements of tectonic plates or volcanism.

The overall Venusian atmospheric composition as determined by the gas chromatographs aboard the Venera 11 and 12 landers was 95 percent carbon dioxide, 3 to 4 percent nitrogen, 0.03 percent water vapor, 0.01 percent argon, 0.005 percent krypton, and 0.001 percent neon.

LIGHTNING DETECTED?

During descent through the atmosphere, the Veneras detected a radio crackle similar to that produced by terrestrial lightning on AM-band commercial radio. Venera 12 observed almost 1000 lightning pulses, in two large groups, during its descent. During its descent, Venera 11 detected thousands of pulses at rates up to 25 per sec. The precise cause of the discharges could not be determined.

Microphones on the landers also detected sounds similar to thunder with one clap reverberating for 15 min. However, the audio evidence for lightning is inconclusive as the microphones are thought to have been saturated by the sound of the atmosphere rushing past as the lander fell.

Two months after their fly-bys, both the Venera 11 and 12 spacecraft buses detected a little-understood celestial phenomenon. On March 5, 1979, the Veneras along with five other spacecraft in earth orbit, one in Venus orbit, and another in solar orbit, detected a gigantic gamma-ray burst, an extremely high-energy celestial radiation burst. This event was 100 times more powerful than any previously detected gamma-ray burst. Data supplied by the Venera's instruments were correlated with that from other spacecraft, and the source of the burst was traced to a neutron star (a massive, gravitationally collapsed star) in the Large Magellanic Cloud, one of the Milky Way's companion galaxies.

COLD WAR THAW AND VENUS COOPERATION

With America's two Pioneer Venus probes also in flight, the shadow of American competition horning in on "their" planet caused Soviet scientists to become defensive about their Venera spacecraft. America had largely ignored Venus while concentrating on the outer planets. The opposite was true of Russian planetary efforts. Their scientists considered the Americans to be upstarts in the Venus exploration field and argued the superiority of their own established Venera designs. There may well have been merit in their arguments. Previous Venera missions had already answered about a third of the questions investigated by the Pioneer Venus experiments. While the international press openly discussed which probe, Venera or Pioneer, was superior, fate would make these nationalist arguments moot because some of the most pressing scientific questions were not answered by either probe. The imaging systems and soil analysis instruments on both Venera landers failed while the Pioneer probes were not equipped to investigate these areas.

The competition between the American and Russian Venus probes made good stories for the press, but the dual missions working together presented exciting scientific opportunities for data comparison. It is fortunate that the Pioneers and Veneras flew at a time of political detente between the two superpowers, since this facilitated agreements on the sharing of Venus data. These agreements set the stage for later meetings, culminating in 1978 with the U.S.–U.S.S.R. Working Group on Near-Earth Space, the Moon, and the Planets in Innsbruck, Austria. These meetings resulted in plans for greater cooperation in future missions. However, portions of this space exploration agenda were scaled back after the 1979 Soviet invasion of Afghanistan.

At the time of the Venera 11 and 12 missions there was a growing awareness of the potential harm that the burning of hydrocarbon and fossil fuels, as well as ozone-depleting fluorocarbons, could bring to earth's atmosphere. Our worst fears were illustrated by the runaway greenhouse effect on Venus. It was rapidly becoming clear that by considering the example of Venus, we should be forewarned about the potential for environmental disaster on earth. Venera data continued to be invaluable for scientists making comparisons of Venus' and earth's atmosphere which were being made to predict models of global warming on earth.

PREPARING FOR MORE PLANETARY TRIUMPHS

When Soviet planetary scientists did not take advantage of a Venus launch opportunity, it had always been for the purpose of making major improvements in the landers. The 1980 launch window was passed over to do just that. Three major new instruments significantly upgraded the lander's design. These included a soil-sample-drilling and analysis mechanism, a penetrometer to determine the supporting strength of Venusian soil, and a new color camera for terrain photography. Designing these instruments was difficult since they had to function in an environment five times hotter than boiling water.

Previous Venera probes had landed "in the blind" below the planet's obscuring cloud layers. To help direct the Venera 13 and 14 landers toward more scientifically productive areas, Dr. Harold Masursky of the U.S. Geological Survey provided the Russians with Pioneer Venus radar data during a visit to the Soviet Union in 1980. This was the first direct American cooperation with the Soviets in Venus exploration.

The objectives of Veneras 13 and 14 were to investigate two of the four broad geological zones on Venus. Venera 13 was to investigate the rolling plains thought to be made of original crust while Venera 14 was to investigate lowland areas flooded by lava flows. The other two geological zones, the Phoebe and Beta Regio mountainous regions, already had been investigated by Veneras 9 and 10. The Pioneer radar data showed that both Veneras 13 and 14 were aimed toward the same lowland plain east of Phoebe Regio. Masursky's data allowed Venera 13's landing site to be moved ten degrees closer to Phoebe Regio, where the rolling plains were expected to be granite-like rock.

The overall configuration and instrument complement of Veneras 13 and 14 were much like their predecessors and the spacecraft buses again were used as planetary fly-by vehicles instead of orbiters. The weight of each new Venera totaled 4363 kg (9619 lb) at the time of launch.

IMPROVED INSTRUMENTS CARRIED

Each of the new 760-kg (1675-lb) landers was equipped with two cameras that jointly returned 360-degree panoramic photographs instead of a single image. Their improved contrast and smaller pixel size allowed study of details near the lander as small as 4 mm (0.167 in).

Venera 13 alone was equipped to take color photos by exposing three black-and-white images through red, blue, and green filters respectively, then combining the images back on earth. Each of the lander's twin cameras had a 37 × 180-degree field of view, centered 50 degrees below the spacecraft's horizontal axis. The color panorama took 14 min to acquire.

A new instrument carried for the first time was an X-ray fluorescence spectrometer for soil analysis. This device was much more sensitive than the gamma-ray spectrometer previously carried. It used radioactive plutonium-238 and iron-55 to irradiate soil samples, inducing secondary radiation. From this, four radiation detectors would test the soil for 22 chemical elements.

To deliver soil to the X-ray unit within the lander, a sampling mechanism used a hollow pipe containing a two-bladed drill shaft. After drilling into the surface for 12 min, the device would transfer soil and rock samples to an analysis chamber by drawing them through a series of compartments, each with progressively lower pressure to draw the sample in. Pressure in the final chamber then was pumped down to a pressure of 50 mm of mercury so that atmospheric gases would not introduce contaminating elements which would alter the spectrometer's readings.

The weight-supporting properties of the surface were to be measured by a spring-fired penetrometer that swung out from the lander on a hinged arm. The Surface Evaluation Instrument was known by the Russian acronym of "PROP."

A ROUTINE FLIGHT TO VENUS

Venera 13 was launched from Tyuratam on October 30, 1981, while Venera 14 lifted off 5 days later. Using their on-board rocket engine, mid-course corrections were performed by both craft. This time, the Russian probes flew alone. No American craft accompanied them as, once again, American Venus plans were mired by funding shortages created by the expensive development of the space shuttle. But planetary science did not suffer. The new Veneras would soon flood the scientific community with a vast amount of Venus data.

Venera 13 ejected its landing capsule February 27, 1982. The spacecraft bus then performed a course correction to ensure that it would miss the planet by 36,000 km (22,370 mi). Two days later on March 1, atmospheric entry began at 5:55 A.M. During the lander's meteor-like descent, a density profile of the upper atmosphere between 110 and 63 km (68 and 39 mi) was charted for the first time by noting the rate of deceleration using an accelerometer. At 6:57:21 A.M., the lander came to rest. It then survived a record 127 min on the surface, almost four times longer than expected.

Preparations for the Venera 14 landing culminated 2 days before its March 5 planetary encounter when the lander was ejected from the spacecraft bus. The lander impacted the surface at 10:00:10 A.M.

Venera 13 and 14 measured surface temperatures of 457 and 465°C (855 and 869°F), with pressures of 89.5 and 93.5 atm, respectively.

LANDERS PROVIDE DETAILED ATMOSPHERIC ANALYSIS

During descent, the improved mass spectrometers took 7 seconds to analyze each atmospheric sample. These measurements updated the 1978 investigations by now showing that Venus has less of the isotopic gas argon 40 than of argon 36 in its atmosphere. The isotope argon 40 is formed by the radioactive decay of potassium 40, and requires tectonic activity or volcanism to bring the gas to the surface where it can enter the atmosphere. The abundance of the element potassium in the Venusian rocks examined by the Veneras so far had been similar to that in earth rocks. Less argon 40 in the atmosphere suggests that Venus is not as tectonically active as earth. The atmospheric neon and argon readings showed that Venus and earth could not have been made from the same combinations of volatile materials from the solar nebula. The basic makeup of each planet was slightly different. These data suggest that earth formed before Venus.

Gas chromatographs carried by Veneras 13 and 14 also found the previously undetected gases carbonyl sulfide (COS) and hydrogen sulfide (H_2S). It had been assumed previously that carbonyl sulfide was present in the atmosphere of Venus and had played an important role in the formation of its atmosphere. When it was not detected by Pioneer Venus, these formation theories were re-evaluated. Now, the discovery of this gas by Veneras 13 and 14 again shook up theories about the formation of the Venusian atmosphere.

Hydrometer readings of 0.2 percent water vapor between altitudes of 50 to 46 km (31 to 28 mi) were very different from previous measurements by other probes. Instrument data suggested that water vapor was being removed from the atmosphere within the clouds and released at the cloud base. Water absorption within the clouds could be explained by the presence of sulfuric acid, but a question remained as to why the water-vapor content decreased with decreasing altitude.

During descent, the landers confirmed the fine structure at the bottom of the cloud layers when they detected layers of cloud only 100 m (328 ft) thick. As expected, sulfur was the most abundant element in the clouds, with chlorine present in smaller amounts. This was the opposite of the result received from Venera 12, which used a similar instrument.

Both landers again showed that the cloud layers were in three layers which ended at 49 km (30 mi) altitude during Venera 13's drop and 47.5 km (29 mi) during Venera 14's descent. At the base of the clouds, the solar ultraviolet radiation had been filtered out.

LANDERS DRILL INTO THE VENUSIAN SURFACE

Within 32 seconds after landing, Venera 13 began drilling for soil samples. After reaching a depth of 3 cm (1.2 in), a 1-cm^3 sample of rock chips was transferred to the analysis chamber. Sealing out the harsh

Venusian atmosphere presented the instruments with a severe environmental problem The rock analysis was done in a sealed chamber that maintained a pressure of only 1/2000th that of Venus' normal surface pressure, and a temperature of 30°C (86°F).

The Venera 13 highland rock sample contained 45 percent silica oxide, 4 percent potassium oxide and 7 percent calcium oxide. This is very similar to terrestrial leucite basalt, which is rich in potassium and magnesium. Five days later, at the Venera 14 site, rock analysis revealed less potassium. These samples were similar to earth's oceanic tholeiitic basalts.

Rocks similar to the Venera 13 and 14 samples exist in the area around Hawaii. The lowland Venera 14 samples are similar to more common basalts like the lava on the ocean floor near Hawaii while the Venera 13 highland samples are similar to the volcanic mountainsides of the Hawaiian Islands.

The following table compares the percentages of the composition of the Venera 13 and 14 sites with oceanic basalt and continental crust on earth:

Constituent	Venera 13	Venera 14	Oceanic	Continental
Magnesium oxide	10 ± 6	8 ± 4	7.56	2.2
Aluminum oxide	16 ± 4	18 ± 4	16.5	16.0
Silicon oxide	45 ± 3	49 ± 4	51.4	63.3
Potassium oxide	4 ± 0.8	0.2 ± 0.1	1.0	2.9
Calcium oxide	7 ± 1.5	10 ± 1.5	9.4	4.1
Titanium oxide	1.5 ± 0.6	1.2 ± 0.4	1.5	0.6
Manganese oxide	0.2 ± 0.1	0.16 ± 0.08	0.26	0.08
Iron oxide	9 ± 3	9 ± 2	12.24	3.5
Total	92.7	95.56	99.86	92.68

The mechanical strength of the Venusian soil was measured by a spring-powered penetrometer. Venera 13 found the soil had a resistance of 2.7 to 10.3 kg per cm^2 (38.4 to 146.5 lb per in^2). Apparently, in an unlucky break, the Venera 14 penetrometer experiment was ruined when it landed on one of the 12×20 cm (4.7×7.9 in) camera covers which had been ejected earlier.

Seismic activity was studied using a single-axis seismometer which could only study vertical movement at a resolution of 26 cycles per sec. Venera 13 found no events while Venera 14 recorded two, but the readings could have been caused by wind.

COLOR SURFACE PHOTOS HIGHLIGHT MISSION

The landing of Venera 13 was eagerly anticipated by Soviet scientists as the craft carried the first color camera to the planet. Landing in rolling foothills east of Phoebe Regio, the craft came to rest at an 8-degree angle relative to the local horizon. The panoramic views showed the surface covered with sharp rocks, partially covered with fine dust and sand. Large gray boulders also were seen.

During its unexpectedly long life, Venera 13 transmitted eight 360-degree surface panoramas. When processed into color images, these showed primarily orange-brownish rocks with an orange sky. The TASS news agency reported this to be one of the most interesting results from the mission.

Investigators examined the color of the soil in an effort to see if surface rocks were oxidized and reddish, as on Mars. They found, instead, that the surface reflected blue light as strongly as it did red, leading to the conclusion that the surface was dark gray.

The orange appearance of the surface was the effect of Rayleigh scattering, the same effect which creates earth's blue sky. On Venus however, the atmosphere is so thick that by the time light reaches the surface, Rayleigh scattering removes all the blue wavelengths. Venus therefore appears orange in the photos simply because it is illuminated by red light. If illuminated by white light, the surface would be dark gray.

The corners of the panoramas showed the horizon to be about 100 m (328 ft) away instead of the expected 1 km (0.6 mi). The near horizon was explained as possibly being a mirage caused by the thick atmosphere. It was concluded that if an observer were standing on Venus, the near-horizon illusion would give the impression of standing on a small 1-km (0.6-mi) diameter body.

Successive panoramas showed soil being blown onto the base of the lander. This was the first real-time evidence of any dynamic change on another world. (Viking landers observed slow changes on Mars, but not over several minutes.)

Venera 14 landed on a level plain covered with flat cracked rock characteristic of cooled basalt. The appearance of the site was harsher and more weathered than Venera 13's. The scene has been described as looking like the icing on a chocolate cake. Part of the view was an area of rock showing evidence of where gases had bubbled through the material while it was molten.

Overall, the Venera 13 and 14 images appear more like the Venera 10 landing site. The pictures show a surface that looks much like the ocean floor of earth and suggests that the extreme atmospheric pressure on Venus mimics the pressure of earth's oceans and the sedimentation process. Scientists concluded, from the lack of secondary soil changes, that the areas were geologically young.

After completing their lander relay task, both Venera buses continued to study solar and cosmic radiation as they sped along their heliocentric trajectories. The engine on Venera 13 was fired in deep space on June 10 and again on November 14, 1982, about four months after delivering its lander to Venus. This operation demonstrated techniques to be used for a later spacecraft rendezvous with Halley's comet in 1986.

A wealth of planetary data had been returned, but in spite of the Venera 13 and 14 missions, many mysteries remained. In light of these, it was clear that we now knew a little more about Venus than we did before, but much less than needed to understand that fierce alien world.

By now, the success of the Venera program was almost routine. Repeated scientific revelations delighted scientists who had worked for decades to achieve the well-deserved success. The old excitement of cold-war scientific competition between the U.S. and U.S.S.R. was replaced by scientific discovery and cooperation. Indeed, some Russian scientists privately grumbled that they felt "sentenced" to Venus and longed for the excitement of other explorations. Fortunately, they would not have long to wait. Exciting destinations awaited future Veneras.

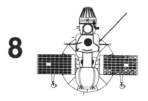

8 Balloons, Comets, and Radar Magic

RADAR TO REVEAL VENUS GEOLOGY

The 1978 flight of the American Pioneer Venus Orbiter revealed the gross features of Venusian topography by using a small on-board radar. However, the Pioneer instrument was limited to a resolution of only 20 km (12.4 mi). This was sufficient to understand the overall Venusian topography and to establish the mean level of the surface, but the geology and tectonics of the surface remained elusive.

In 1983, the Soviet Union was to fill this void in our knowledge of Venus by flying two side-looking synthetic aperture radar (SAR) payloads into Venus orbit aboard the Venera 15 and 16 spacecraft. The SAR system, using microwave signals instead of light, could penetrate clouds to produce surface images which appeared startlingly similar to visible-light photographs. The resolution of the Venera radar was not appreciably better than that of earth-based radar, but it was better positioned to cover areas of Venus not accessible from earth. Thus, for the first time in nearly 20 years, Russian spacecraft were to be sent to the inner planet without a landing probe.

The Russian ability to perform such a mission caught American space experts by surprise. The SAR concept was already being used by the Soviet military to track western maritime traffic from earth orbit, but operating such a system around Venus was a formidable task. American space exploration officials completely underestimated Russian expertise and their resolve to accomplish a radar-mapping mission at another planet. In earth orbit, Soviet military radar satellites were powered by large nuclear reactors. However, such devices would be prohibitively heavy to transport over interplanetary distances. The mass of data generated by the imaging also dictated a high-speed transmission capability. The Soviets not only overcame these obstacles, but leapfrogged American Venus radar-imaging plans by a number of years.

The Venera 15 radar probe was launched from Tyuratam at 5:38 A.M., June 2, 1983. The 4-month interplanetary cruise was punctuated by two course corrections, on June 10 and October 1. As with previous planetary missions, Venera 15 monitored solar and cosmic radiation on the way to Venus.

A twin spacecraft, Venera 16, was launched June 7. Course corrections on June 15 and October 5 permitted Venera 16 to accurately target Venus.

Following a 130-day flight from earth, Venera 15 fired its braking engine at 3:05 A.M., October 10. The craft settled into a 1000 × 65,000-km (621 × 40,391-mi) Venus orbit, inclined 87 degrees, with a period of 24 hr. Periapsis occurred at about 60 degrees north latitude, allowing the radar to target the northern hemisphere during closest approach. Venera 16 entered a similar orbit at 3:22 A.M., October 14.

Each 5300-kg (11,684-lb) spacecraft, the heaviest yet flown to Venus, carried a scientific payload which included the Polyus V ("Pole" V in Russian) side-looking radar to image the surface, a radar altimeter system to determine the elevation of the surface, an East German infrared spectrometer, a radio occultation experiment, and cosmic-ray and solar-wind detectors.

In place of the usual spherical planetary landing capsule, the craft carried a 1.4 × 6-m (4.6 × 19.7-ft) side-looking radar antenna. The huge antenna was unfolded once the craft was in space. Additionally, the orbiters carried a radar altimeter called "Omega," which used a 1-m (3.3-ft)-diameter antenna mounted next to the main radar antenna. It measured the altitude of the ground track directly below the spacecraft with an accuracy of 50 m (164 ft).

Modifications to the new Venera buses included lengthening the fuel tank by 1 m (3.3 ft), thus doubling the fuel capacity to two tons. Two rings of attitude-control gas bottles, one at each end of the spacecraft bus, were attached to the exterior instead of the usual single ring. These modifications allowed a longer, eight-month lifetime for the spacecraft during extensive attitude maneuvering in Venus orbit. Also, two additional solar panels provided extra electricity for the power-hungry radar apparatus.

The radar data were recorded and transmitted to earth during an 8-hr period between successive radar passes which occurred every 24 hr. The volumes of data were transmitted at 100,000 bits per sec, a 30-fold improvement over previous Veneras. This required enlarging the directional parabolic antenna to 3 m (9.9 ft) in diameter.

STRIPPING THE VEILS OF VENUS

The mapping mission of Venera 15 began, officially, on October 16 and Venera 16's mission began on October 20. Both spacecraft operated in shifts with one making a mapping pass while the other transmitted data to earth. The spacecraft's radar scanned a 150 × 9000-km (93 × 5592-mi) strip 12 degrees to the side of the orbital path each day during the periapsis swing over the Venusian north pole. The rest of the orbit was dedicated to recharging batteries and transmitting data.

The SAR system used complex electronics and computer wizardry to create images of the surface below Venus' obscuring clouds. The radar transmitter operated in cycles, sending out a burst of microwave signals made up of hundreds of individual pulses, then shutting off to receive the return echoes. The echoes were sorted out electronically by their frequency and by the interval between transmission and reception. These data were then transmitted to earth where powerful computers measured the interval between each pulse and its return echo. This data processing also determined each signal's Doppler-shifted frequency pitch, that is, the change in frequency of the reflected radar pulse caused by differing round-trip travel times.

The signal's travel time and Doppler shift were the key elements in recreating images of the surface. All echoes with the same Doppler shift returned from a ground track the same distance from the spacecraft, establishing where that portion of the final image should be located. The strength of the individual return echoes determined the "radar brightness" of the material from which the signal was reflected. A strong signal indicated a rough surface while a weak signal denoted a smooth surface. The signal travel time could also determine the relative depth or height of surface features. Complicating the image processing was the spacecraft's orbital motion over Venus. This motion introduced another Doppler shift for which the radar data had to be corrected to allow an accurate image to be reconstructed.

After computer processing, the radar data produced an image which looked much like a visible light photograph with one major difference: Light and dark coloration in a radar image does not necessarily correspond to actual visible light coloration on the surface. Bright areas on the radar image simply mean that area is more radar reflective, and probably rougher, than dark areas which are smoother and reflect less radar energy.

As the Veneras operated in orbit, the slow rotation of Venus allowed the spacecraft to scan an additional strip 1.5 degrees eastward from that done the previous day. The surface was mapped strip by strip until a complete image of the northern part of the planet was built up.

By the time the missions of both craft ended 8 months later in July 1984, 115 million km^2 (44.4 million mi^2) of Venusian surface from 18 degrees above the equator to the north pole had been mapped. The best images showed details 1.2 km (0.75 mi) in size.

VENERA SUPPLEMENTS EARTH RADAR DATA

The data returned from the two mapping spacecraft filled 600 km (373 mi) of magnetic tape, presenting an incredible data reduction project for Russian planetary scientists. The data were processed using sophisticated mathematics to compensate for the moving spacecraft and to create enhanced optical-like images of the surface. Two computers at the Soviet Institute of Radio Technology and Electronics spent a year reducing the data and produced an atlas of the northern latitudes containing 27 maps, each 3 m^2 (32.2 ft^2) in size.

Soviet scientists were openly criticized in the west for their slowness in releasing the results. Surface photographs were provided in sparing amounts, often without accompanying geodetic (positional) information to locate the area on Venus. These delays resulted from longer than expected computer processing and enhancement time.

At the fifteenth Lunar and Planetary Conference in Houston, Texas, in March 1984, the Venera 15 and 16 results were finally released in a gush. After studying the Venera radar images, the Russians related the following conclusions about the terrain:

- The observed geologic pattern seen on the surface is the result of volcanism and the horizontal movement of the planet's crust.

- The way that Venus' crust responds to internal planetary motions (the movement of magma within the planet) and responds to heat and chemical transformations is different from that of Mercury, earth, the moon, and Mars.

- The abundance of cometary and asteroid craters indicates that the terrain is about 200 to 400 million years old. In time, such craters are obliterated by geologic activity and weathering. Because these craters are still intact, we assume that the volcanism and tectonic activity are not recent and that the weathering process which would erase the cratering is slower than that on earth. The observed surface is thus younger than the mare of earth's moon, but older than the ancient ocean bottoms of earth.

A NEW WORLD REVEALED

Radar images from the Venera 15 and 16 missions revealed mountains, plateaus, ridges, impact craters, and manifestations of tectonic activity. By international agreement, the newly discovered Venusian features were named after mythological females and notable women. The radar mapping also revealed that 60 percent of the surface lay within 800 m (2625 ft) of mean Venusian level, making Venus much flatter than earth and our moon.

In contrast to the general flatness of the planet, the Veneras discovered an elevated continent the size of Australia near the planet's north pole. Called Ishtar Terra, the elevated terrain partially arcs around the pole. The area is bordered by escarpments that drop off several kilometers. Within Ishtar Terra stands Maxwell Montes, a giant mountain towering 1525 m (5003 ft) higher than earth's Mount Everest.

Rising a total of 11 km (6.8 mi), Maxwell Montes lies to the east of the Lakshmi Planum area, a giant, flat lava plateau located in the Ishtar region and rising 3 to 4 km (1.9 to 2.5 mi) above the low plains of Venus. Surrounding the plateau are ridge and valley mountains rising another 3 to 7 km (1.9 to 4.3 mi), containing Akna Montes to the northwest and Freyja Montes to the north. These are thought to have been created by horizontal compression in a manner similar to the North American Appalachian mountains.

Extensive solidified lava flows spread over Shegurochka Planitia and the southwest portion of the Lakshmi Planum. On the smooth lava plains of Lakshmi, a solitary 20-km (12.4 mile) diameter impact crater dominates the landscape and proclaims the young geological age of the area.

To the southwest of Ishtar, the Veneras scanned the lowland plains of Sedna Planitia and Guinevere Planitia. These proved to be lava plains containing ridges similar to the mare on earth's moon. Furrow systems hundreds of kilometers long were also observed. The differing dome-like hills and flat-topped mountains near each suggest that the two plains originated from differing volcanic events. At the same latitude as Ishtar, but on the opposite hemisphere, the spacecraft imaged another flat lowland lava plain, the broad Atalanta Planitia.

The Venera data confirmed that Beta Regio along the equator was a geologic rift system, which appeared to have been torn like the Rift Valley of East Africa. The 2500 × 2000-km (1554 × 1243-mi) area hosts the high mountains, Rhea Mons and Theia Mons, as well as an enormous north-south valley 3 km (1.9 mi) deep and 140 km (87 mi) wide. These features showed that the surface was subjected to combinations of compression and extension stresses as well as shear stresses (two land masses moving in different directions).

In other areas, horizontal tectonic deformation thought to be caused by the collision of moving land masses created a curious crisscross pattern on the surface called "tesserae terrain." The name tesserae was derived from the Greek word for "tiles" since the terrain has a similar appearance. Some geologists argue that this terrain of intersecting fractures and grooves is caused by the collapse of volcanic domes. This type of feature is common along the boundary of Ishtar Terra.

EVIDENCE OF VOLCANOES

Direct evidence of past volcanic activity shows clearly in images of the Lakshmi Planum area. Two large volcanic calderas, Colette and Sacajewea, stand prominently on the plain and may be the source of the flat lava fields of Lakshmi. Colette extends 100 × 200 km (62 × 124 mi) in area and rises less than 2 km (1.2 mi) above Lakshmi, but volcanic flows radiate several hundred kilometers away from the rim.

Other radar images clearly show volcanic domes up to 20 km (12.4 mi) in diameter, many capped by calderas, dotting the lowland lava plains. These appear individually and in groups. Larger domes, between 50 and 300 km (31 and 186 mi) in size and less than 1 km (0.6 mi) high, also are presumed to be volcanoes.

Infrared scans from orbit indicated an average surface temperature of 500°C (932°F), but also fascinating "hot spots" where the temperature exceeded 700°C (1292°F), implying the possibility of active volcanism.

Confusing the issue is the fact that Venera radar images did little to show that there was active volcanism on the surface at the time.

CRATERS HELP DATE SURFACE

A surprisingly clear record of bombardment by asteroid-sized bodies was also imaged. In the northern hemisphere about 150 evenly scattered craters were found ranging from 8 to 150 km (5 to 93 mi) in size. Because the ultradense atmosphere provides a natural defense against smaller impacting objects, the bodies creating the largest craters must have been at least 14 km (8.7 mi) in diameter.

Venusian craters were found to be similar in appearance to lunar craters. Small craters are bowl-shaped, medium-sized craters have central peaks, and large craters have multiple rims. Even the oldest and most degraded craters were still circular, implying that there was a lack of tectonic movement in these areas which would distort features over time.

The distance ejecta, the material thrown out of a crater by a meteor impact, traveled from their origin crater created something of a puzzle. The thick atmosphere theoretically limits the distance ejecta can fly, but ejecta bands were observed beyond the theoretical limits. Researchers have suggested that the ejecta traveled in a cloud or plume which collectively drifted farther than individual particles.

In addition to the classical impact craters, large circular features hundreds of kilometers in diameter called "coronae" were evident. These oval features, some up to 600 km (373 mi) in diameter, showed relatively little surface relief and consisted of a nearly circular system of low ridges and valleys. Surrounding some coronae were flowlike features. It was argued that these huge circular spots were not formed by impact, but by hot magma rising from the planet's interior.

The Venera 15 and 16 missions broke historic ground in the study of Venus by providing much detailed topographical data on the northern areas of the planet. In spite of this fact, the public perception of the mission was very low-key because Veneras 15 and 16 were poorly publicized compared to previous Soviet triumphs on the veiled planet.

BALLOONS ABOVE VENUS

The next Russian visit to Venus took yet another twist. Expanding cooperation between the Babakin Design Bureau and the French Centre National d'Études Spatiales (CNES) eventually led to the adoption of the French plan to float instrumented balloons in the atmosphere of Venus. This novel approach to planetary exploration added a horizontal dimension to the investigation of Venus and presented the first opportunity to make planetary investigations from a mobile laboratory. Instead of the headlong plunge through the atmosphere in a breakneck race with time to reach the surface, the final Soviet visit to Venus would include a leisurely adventure. Two balloons were to drift for several days, probing the planet's weather.

In the eighteenth century, balloon flight was introduced to western civilization by the French scientists Joseph and Etienne Montgolfier. It was delightfully fitting that the first balloon flight at another planet was also initiated by another French scientist, Professor Jacques Blamont of the French space agency.

The history of the Venus balloon experiment is filled with scientific twists and political turns. The concept was originally studied by the Martin Marietta Corporation under a 1966 contract with NASA's Langley Research Center. A year later, Blamont proposed the joint French-Soviet Venus balloon exploration. However, eighteen years would pass before the mission was flown.

EXCITING COMET MISSION PLANNED

The 1984 Venus mission also presented the unique opportunity to retarget the Venera spacecraft buses to intercept Halley's comet almost a year after their Venus fly-by. Scientific interest in the comet has always been high since it is believed that comets are made of primordial material which formed at the time the solar system was created.

Two spacecraft were to be launched toward Venus, but they were not called Veneras 17 and 18 as was expected. Instead, because of the secondary mission to Halley's comet, the new craft were called Vega. (This is a combination of "Venera" and the Russian word for Halley. There is no "h" in the Russian language and "g" is usually substituted. As a result, the Russian word for Halley is "Gallie.")

Preliminary plans for the Vega missions to Halley were announced in 1982. This disclosure was made much further in advance than the usual Soviet announcements about upcoming planetary probes—probably because of the international nature of the mission. The Vega spacecraft would carry 16 instruments from ten nations. Instruments were to be provided and investigations conducted by scientists from Austria, Bulgaria, Czechoslovakia, the former East Germany, France, Hungary, Poland, the former Soviet Union, the United States and the former West Germany. The American contribution was a dust detector from the University of Chicago.

Final plans for the Vega missions were approved in 1983 and called for the spacecraft to carry 145.9 kg (321.7 lb) of comet study instruments to within 10,000 km (6214 mi) of Halley's comet.

In a marvelous display of international cooperation, the Vegas would act as pathfinders for the European Giotto comet explorer. In early 1986, the Soviet craft were to chart the exact position of Halley's Comet, the environment near Halley's nucleus, and the size of the comet's nucleus. This would help maximize Giotto's chances of surviving a plunge twenty times closer through Halley's dust-shrouded coma a week after the Vegas flew by.

The collaboration on this effort between the Russian, European, Japanese, and American scientific communities came without the assistance of formal governmental relations or treaties. The bilateral space agreements between the U.S. and U.S.S.R., which were signed in 1972 and led to the famed Apollo/Soyuz mission in 1975, were not renewed in 1982 because of American displeasure with Soviet involvement in Poland and Afghanistan. International scientific success at Venus and Halley's comet was therefore the result of direct involvement between the scientists of different nations.

The dual Venus and Halley mission was the most ambitious Russian space exploration project since the lunar rover and surface-sample return missions ten years before. Additionally, the Vega missions represented the first Soviet use of a planetary gravitational assist, the gravity of Venus to boost the probes toward Halley. A lot was riding on the Vega missions and their success would greatly bolster the image of Soviet science. The Vegas were thus the crown jewel of a quarter-century of Russian planetary exploration and would cap a glorious chapter in Russian Venus exploration by becoming the first craft to make a close investigation of a comet.

FAMILIAR VENUS DESIGN ADDS COMET INSTRUMENTS

The Vegas were the last spacecraft based on the second-generation Venera probe design and carried more instruments than any previous Venus probe. Total mass of each spacecraft was 5040 kg (11,111 lb). Because they were designed to operate at greater distances from the sun during their Halley encounter, the Vegas carried two extra solar panels, bringing their total collection area to 10 m^2 (107.6 ft^2).

The landers were the familiar 1-m (3.3-ft)-diameter spheres topped by a hat-shaped atmospheric braking disk which was now supplemented by an additional tapered metal ring mounted just below the disk. This smoothed the flow of atmospheric gases around the descending lander and prevented it from wobbling during its fall. Each lander carried 117 kg (258 lb) of atmospheric and surface investigation instruments which again included a surface drilling mechanism with an X-ray fluorescence spectrometer to analyze the chemical makeup of the soil.

Attached inside the top half of the aeroshield which surrounds the landers was a 115-kg (253.5-lb) balloon package which was to be released during descent. It carried temperature and pressure sensors, a vertical wind anemometer, a nephelometer, and a light level-lightning detector.

Hardware design for the 1984 Venus balloon mission was begun in 1979.

When the French balloon experiment was originally approved, Russian space planners had not anticipated the trip to Halley. The ambitious Russian 1984 Venus exploration plan was scrambled by an almost casual comment made in 1980 by French space scientist Jacques Blamont at a cocktail party attended by Russian space scientists. Blamont mused that the trajectory of the 1984 Venus flight offered the opportunity to use the gravity of the planet to redirect the Venera spacecraft toward Halley's comet. According to Blamont, when the Russians at the party realized this, "all hell broke loose."[1]

Once this was pointed out to them, the Russians seized this golden opportunity in a rare display of flexibility led by Space Research Institute director Roald Z. Sagdeyev. By 1981, mission planning had changed to include the fly-by of Halley's comet. In order to accomplish this, the large French balloon payloads were canceled in favor of two landers that would descend on the night side of Venus while the spacecraft buses continued around the sun toward a rendezvous with the comet. However, no mission plan is carved in stone until the last possible moment. The lesser energy requirements to reach Venus and then continue toward Halley's comet allowed two smaller Soviet-made balloon experiments to be reincorporated into the Vega mission.

In their final form, the scaled-back balloon payloads were based on the French proposal, but with the Soviet Union developing the hardware. The prime French responsibility was to organize the world-wide network of radio telescopes needed to receive data from the balloon transmitters. NASA assisted in this effort by making its Deep Space Network antennae available.

The balloon payloads were designed to investigate the motions and structure of the atmosphere and clouds at the balloon's altitude. These data were to be transmitted directly to earth and did not need the Vega spacecraft to act as a relay. By directly tracking the movement of the balloons within the atmosphere of Venus, the atmospheric motion could be studied.

For the Halley encounter, a 253-kg (558-lb) scan platform was mounted at the base of the instrument section and housed a wide- and narrow-angle imaging system, an infrared spectrometer, and a three-channel spectrometer. The platform could rotate 110 degrees horizontally and 40 degrees vertically, scanning at a rate up to one degree per sec.

The dual-camera imaging system was expected to resolve Halley details only 200 m (656 ft) in size from a distance of 10,000 km (6214 mi). During the comet encounter, only one-tenth of the narrow angle frame, centered on the region of greatest brightness, would be transmitted to earth. This arrangement maximized the number of live images transmitted as there was the possibility that debris in Halley's coma might damage the spacecraft, preventing later transmission of recorded images.

Other instruments mounted on the Vega buses were to measure the mass, energy, and wave phenomena in the plasmas and gases in Halley's coma. In all, twenty separate investigations were dedicated to Halley studies.

During the encounter, data would be transmitted directly to earth via a 65,536-bit per second telemetry link. A five-megabyte tape recorder also would collect the data for later playback at a slower 3072-bit per second rate if the craft survived their plunge through Halley's debris.

To protect the Vega spacecraft during their high-speed encounters with Halley's comet, portions of their body and base were covered by 5 m^2 (53.8 ft^2) of double-layered metallic armor. In a puzzling announcement, the Soviets said that, because the work of installing the dust shields was so meticulous and exacting, it was performed by women.

SUCCESSFUL LAUNCHES UNVEIL PROTON BOOSTER

Vega 1 was launched at 12:16 P.M., December 15, 1984, from Tyuratam. The nearly identical Vega 2 probe followed at 12:14 P.M., December 21. The twin launches were a special treat for western space analysts. Visiting foreign scientists and engineers were invited to witness both liftoffs. This was the first public look at the Proton which had previously been a state secret.

The normal 4-month cruise between earth and Venus was extended to nearly 6 months because of the special trajectory required to achieve the later rendezvous with Halley's comet.

On June 9, 1985, after traveling 500 million kilometers (310 million mi) around the sun, Vega 1 had approached within 500,000 km (310,700 mi) of Venus. Two days before closest approach, it ejected its landing capsule toward Venus and then fired its onboard engine in order to miss the planet by 39,000 km (24,235 mi).

The balloon package was carried inside the upper hemisphere of the aeroshell which protected the Vega landers during atmospheric entry. The balloon package was ejected at 61 km (38 mi) and fell until its own parachute opened at 55 km (34.2 mi). At 54 km (33.5 mi), the inflation sequence of the 3.54-m (11.8-ft)-diameter balloon began with parachute separation occurring at 53 km (33 mi). The radio-transparent, teflon-coated plastic balloon was inflated with 2 kg (4.4 lb) of helium and stopped its descent at 50 km (31 mi). The atmospheric probe then settled at an equilibrium altitude of 53.6 km (33.3 mi) where the temperature is a tolerable 32°C (90°F). At this altitude, the Venusian atmospheric pressure is 535 millibars, or about half that at sea level on earth. By comparison, earth's atmosphere at the balloon's flight altitude is one-thousand times thinner.

On June 11 the Vega 1 landing capsule entered the atmosphere on the night side of Venus. This was the first nightside landing since Venera 7 touched down 15 years before. The balloon package was released at 61 km (37.9 mi), and the lander continued to the surface.

Touchdown was at local midnight, on the Mermaid Plain north of Aphrodite. The area was a smooth, low plain, typical of half the surface of the planet, but no previous lander had ever performed a chemical analysis of such territory. Unfortunately, the Vega 1 soil analysis experiment failed when the instrument's drill mechanism accidentally began its automatic sequence while at a 16-km (10-mile) altitude, still 15 minutes away from landing. By the time the lander reached the surface, the mechanism had irreversibly shut down.

The Vega 1 lander returned other data from the surface for 56 minutes after landing, however, there were no surface photos this time. The balloon experiment dictated a nightside landing so earth-based tracking could follow the balloons, therefore, no cameras were carried.

A DETAILED LOOK AT THE ATMOSPHERE

Though the loss of the X-ray fluorescence data did not classify the landing as a failure—extensive atmospheric studies were performed by the lander during its descent—the loss of rock analysis data was a bitter disappointment to geologists.

A mass spectrometer and aerosol collection package jointly developed by Russian and French scientists sampled the cloud layers. The instrument detected sulfur and chlorine, and hinted at the possibility of phosphorus in the clouds. Free sulfur, which gives the clouds their yellowish tinge, was also detected. The Sigma 3 gas chromatograph detected one milligram of sulphuric acid per cubic meter of atmosphere between 63 and 48 km (39 and 30 mi). This reading was corroborated by the mass spectrometer.

Instruments that looked at the density of cloud particles and the intensity of light levels showed significant differences from those of the American Pioneer Venus probes in 1978. Since both the Vega 1 and 2 landers showed similar readings, many believe there may have been large-scale changes in the atmosphere of Venus between 1978 and 1985.

Vega 1's instruments showed that the cloud layers were like a thin terrestrial fog with particle sizes of less than a micrometer. Vega also determined that there were two distinct cloud layers, not the three suggested by previous probes. The layers were 3 to 5 km (1.9 to 3.1 mi) thick, centered at 58 and 50 km (36 and 31 mi) from the surface. Additionally, the clouds did not clear up at 48 km (30 mi), but persisted in some fashion down to 35 km (21.7 mi).

The Vega landers, being part of a broader international mission, attracted a host of foreign scientists and journalists to Moscow. For the first time, western officials were present to experience a Soviet planetary landing. Soviet space officials, however, were not used to the gaze of international representatives. Data returned from the Vega landers at the speed of light, but the results were forwarded to the press at the Space Research Institute auditorium at a snail's pace. A single one-hour press conference was held for the journalists. While scientifically interesting, the press conference lacked the flair and air of wonder that prevails at NASA-sponsored planetary encounters.

The Venus portion of the Vega 1 mission was a success, but the mood of the Soviet researchers present was restrained in comparison to the familiar scene of jubilant western researchers during a NASA planetary encounter. One Vega experimenter, Lev Mukhin, seemed to be an exception. He excitedly showed off fresh data and openly speculated on its significance. One western journalist remarked to him that this sort of on-the-spot analysis is known in the United States as "instant science." Mukhin grinned and agreed.[2]

FINAL VENUS LANDING SUCCESSFUL

After following the same landing procedure used by its twin, the Vega 2 lander touched down on June 15. The craft came to rest about 1500 km (932 mi) southeast of Vega 1 on the northern transitional plains adjacent to the elevated Aphrodite Terra continent. The Vega 2 spacecraft bus acted as a data relay station and passed Venus at a 24,500-km (15,224-mile) altitude. The arrival of Vega 2 was timed so the first lander's balloon would have completed its two-day mission prior to the flight of Balloon 2.

Vega 2's touchdown occurred at Venus coordinates 6.5 degrees south and 181.1 degrees longitude. This area had been well explored by Pioneer Venus and was a smooth region 1.5 km above mean Venus level.

This time, the surface drilling and sample analysis experiment worked perfectly. The lander transmitted 57 minutes of data after touchdown and reported interesting geological data. The X-ray fluorescence experiment detected a rare type of rock which is found in Precambrian areas on earth and in the highlands of earth's moon. Vega's drill had scooped up anorthosite-troctolite, a type of rock rich in aluminum and silicon, but poor in iron and magnesium. The Vega 2 landing site seemed to be the oldest yet investigated by chemical analysis. A high sulphur content of 4 to 5 percent by mass seemed to indicate an interaction between the atmosphere and the surface rocks.

SPECIAL BALLOON PAYLOADS STUDY ATMOSPHERE

The Balloon 1 payload was released into the atmosphere 7 degrees north of the equator at about 180 degrees longitude near local midnight. Within 25 minutes of entering the atmosphere, the balloon's payload was transmitting data to earth. The payload relayed data for another 46.5 hr as it drifted 11,600 km (7208 mi) into the morning side of Venus.

Balloon 1 operated in the middle of the planet's most active cloud layer, which consisted of droplets of concentrated sulfuric acid. The object of the mission was to learn more about the atmospheric circulation. Observations included looking for lightning flashes and recording vertical wind gusts, cloud density, and atmospheric pressure and density. One important objective was to see if the atmospheric measurements changed with time and location.

As the balloon slowly lost helium and sank, ballast was released at 50 km (31 mi) to raise it back to its operating altitude. During its two days of life, Balloon 1 lost only five percent of its helium, maintaining a mass of 20.8 kg (45.8 lb).

Hanging on a tether 13 m (42.6 ft) below the balloon was the 1.2-m (3.9-ft) science package. This three-section apparatus was coated with a special white finish to protect it from the corrosive acid in Venus' atmosphere. The upper portion forming the attachment point to the balloon tether was a 37-cm (15-in) long, 30-degree angle cone which acted as an antenna. Suspended below this was a 40.8 × 14.5 × 13-cm (16 × 5.7 × 6.3-in) section carrying the electronics and radio. Extended from this was a carbon-fiber arm holding two temperature sensors and a four-vane anemometer propeller made of polypropylene to measure vertical wind speeds. The lower 9 × 14.5 × 15-cm (3.5 × 5.7 × 5.9-in) section carried the nephelometer for cloud-particle measurements.

Data were relayed directly to earth by a 4.5-watt transmitter operating at 1.667 Gigahertz (GHz). The payload transmitted data, stored in a 1024-bit memory, every half-hour in 270-second bursts at a transmission rate of 4 bits per second. The interval between contacts was lengthened later in the mission to conserve battery life. The signal often faded to only 2 watts, but the data link was continuous until the 1-kg (2.2-lb) 250-watt-hour lithium battery was expended after two days as expected.

To hear the faint transmitter, the Soviets built a new 70-m antenna at Ussurisk, near Vladivostok in the Far East. Additionally, five other Soviet antennas were used, including complexes at Yevpatoria and Semeiz. To secure maximum data from the balloon experiments, the French space agency assembled a very-long-baseline interferometry network around the world to supplement the Soviet antennas. By electronically linking many widely spaced antennae, they had an effective aperture equal to the distance between them, thus greatly increasing their ability to track the balloons at Venus accurately. In all, 20 antennae around the world were used.

In spite of the far-flung tracking network, data were retrieved with amazing effectiveness. A total of 25.5 hr of data was received on earth during the balloon's 46.5-hr lifetime. Although Venus was 110 million km (68.4 million mi) distant, the network was able to precisely measure the balloon's location to within 10 km (6.2 mi) and its horizontal velocity to within 3 km (1.8 mi) per hr.

As the balloon payloads were tracked by the tracking network, Andrew Ingersoll of Caltech helped interpret the signals received from Venus. As is the case with important space missions, a press conference was called at the Jet Propulsion Laboratory to publicize the American contribution. However, at the last minute, the press conference was canceled on orders from Washington. The Reagan Administration chose not to publicize that America was helping to track and support a Russian space venture.

In reality, NASA's discreet help was arranged between Caltech's Jet Propulsion Laboratory and the Soviet Space Research Institute by French scientific liaisons. This nongovernmental arrangement made the NASA tracking stations a vital partner in the Soviet Vega balloon experiment. The American member of the balloon science team, Boris Ragent of NASA's Ames Research Center, also provided the design of the balloon's nephelometer.

The world-wide radio telescope network determined that the wind speeds at the balloon's altitude were a hurricane force of 240 km (149 mi) per hr instead of the anticipated 30 to 50 km (18.6 to 31 mi) per hr. Balloon 1 confirmed that the atmosphere was moving at high velocity in a retrograde (backward) direction around the planet.

During its long drift, Balloon 1 regularly encountered downward wind gusts of 1 m (3.3 ft) per sec, with occasional 3.5-m (11.5-ft)-per-sec gusts. These bounced the balloon 200 to 300 m (656 to 984 ft) vertically. Balloon 1 encountered the roughest ride at the beginning and again at end of its flight.

After drifting 8000 km in 33.8 hr, the payload's light detector recorded a continuous increase in brightness. This was 3 hr of drift time and

7 degrees of longitude before the sunrise terminator was crossed. The light detector never conclusively established the presence of lightning flashes. The nephelometer experiment also never detected any clear areas in the clouds at the altitude where Balloon 1 drifted.

Once on the day side of Venus, solar radiation was expected to heat, expand, and burst the balloon. However, battery failure, signaled by fading signal strength, ended Balloon 1's mission before the balloon burst.

SECOND BALLOON FLOATS ABOVE VENUS

Like its twin, the Vega 2 lander also released a balloon probe into the atmosphere. Balloon 2 was released 7 degrees below the equator near local midnight. This balloon traveled 11,100 km (6898 mi) in 46.5 hr while it drifted toward the daytime side of Venus.

Balloon 2 initially found quiet sailing, but after 20 hr it also was buffeted by downdraft winds. The Vega balloons found downdrafts ten times greater than expected and established that they were as strong as those in earth's atmosphere and occur on a planet-wide scale.

The long-term direct measurement of these downdrafts provided compelling evidence that lightning detected by previous Venera missions may have been real. Previously, it was thought that volcanic activity was needed to inject temperature differences into the atmosphere to produce lightning. The Vega balloons showed that vertical mixing of the atmosphere was present without underlying volcanic eruptions.

After 33 hr, Balloon 2 encountered 8 hr of strong downdrafts which often pushed the probe 2.5 km (1.6 mi) lower, to the 0.9-atm pressure level. This period of turbulence was associated with the probe's passage over a 5-km (3.1-mi) high mountain peak in the Aphrodite area. Surprisingly, the high mountain created atmospheric waves which reached the balloon's altitude above and downwind from the mountain. These waves deflected the balloon's path as it drifted around the planet.

Atmospheric eddy currents varied the temperature at the balloon's altitude by 6.5°C (11.7°F). This indicated eddies as large or larger than those in earth's atmosphere. The temperature readings from Balloon 2 were consistently 6.5°C (11.7°F) lower than those of Balloon 1. Curiously, the atmospheric data returned by the Vega 2 lander were also similarly cooler.

As the signal from Balloon 2 faded, it marked the end of Russian Venus exploration during this century. This final, scientifically productive mission was remarkable in that it was carried out in an open and cooperative manner with the world scientific community. This refreshing candor was in stark contrast to the secretive space flights carried out at the beginning of the exploration of Venus.

FIRST TO HALLEY

After departing from Venus, the Vega 1 and 2 spacecraft began the second phase of their mission—a 708-million km (440-million mi) journey farther around the sun to Halley's Comet. The course correction to retarget the probes toward the comet was the most complex interplanetary maneuver ever attempted by Soviet spacecraft controllers.

A month before arriving at Halley, mission controllers began preparing the craft for the encounter. Vega 1 performed its final course correction on February 10, 1986, while Vega 2 performed its correction a week later. The instrument scan platforms were then unlocked from their stowed positions.

In mid-February, calibration and adjustment of the imaging system and other instruments were done by targeting the planet Jupiter, which was then some 800 million km (497 million mi) distant.

As the rendezvous with Halley approached, Russian scientists found themselves at the center of public attention as never before. The news media showed considerably more interest in the Halley encounter than in the Venus landings 8 months before. Representatives of the Planetary Society, Carl Sagan and Louis Friedman, were present as was a large contingent from NASA. In the festive atmosphere of success as the Vegas approached their target, Roald Sagdeev, head of the Space Research Institute, opened the Institute to American space journalists and school children from several nations.

At 9:10 A.M., March 4, two days before closest approach, Vega 1 sent back its first comet images. For 90 minutes, the imaging system made several dozen photographs of the comet through various filters. Distance to the comet at the time was still 14 million km (8.7 million mi). Initial images seemed to show a double nucleus, but this was later interpreted as an illusion caused by a dust structure surrounding the comet that was more complicated than expected. The next day, Vega 1 had approached within 7 million km (4.3 million mi) of Halley and a second series of long-distance images were relayed to earth.

On March 6, Vega 1 made its closest approach, briefly passing 8890 km (5524 mi) from the nucleus at 10:20 A.M. For three hours, the probe relayed images of Halley's nucleus—500 of them—before flashing by at a relative velocity of 79.2 km (49.2 mi) per sec.

NASA's 70-m (230-ft) Deep Space Network tracking antenna in Australia tracked Vega with absolute accuracy during the encounter. The craft relayed the close-up images of the comet's nucleus and critical data needed to refine its exact position in space. Giotto was scheduled to follow on March 14 and would swoop within 590 km (367 mi) of the solid surface of Halley to snap high-resolution images of the heart of the comet. Vega's positional data were vital to navigate Giotto close to the comet.

The complex dynamics involving active gas and dust jets evaporating from the nucleus constantly altered Halley's trajectory as it sped around the sun. At Giotto's encounter velocity, should the comet's calculated position be in error by just a few tens of kilometers, the spacecraft's camera would be aimed at empty space during the critical final seconds when the probe and comet zipped past each other at 70 km (43.5 mi) per sec. The timing of Giotto's closest approach to Halley had to be accurate within one second. The Vega imaging data and NASA's tracking provided the means of performing such a fantastic feat of navigation. The total effort resulted in the reduction of Giotto's initial navigational error from hundreds of kilometers down to about 40 km (24.9 mi).

During Vega 1's high-speed encounter with Halley's nucleus, the craft was sandblasted by comet dust, but was nonetheless still functional. The outstretched solar panels caught the worst of the encounter and could only produce half the electrical power previously available.

Additional comet imaging was performed on March 7 and 8 as the craft receded from Halley.

SECOND ENCOUNTER SNAPS BETTER PICTURES

The day after the first encounter, Vega 2 began its studies of Halley. One hundred images were relayed on March 7 from a distance of 14 million km (8.7 million mi).

On March 9 the mood at the Space Research Institute was lighter and less apprehensive as the second Soviet craft dove to within 8030 km (4990 mi) of the comet's nucleus. The line of diplomatic limousines outside the Institute was mute testimony to the festive atmosphere at the research center.

Vega 2 made its closest approach at 10:20 A.M., passing Halley at a relative velocity of 76.8 km (47.7 mi) per sec. At this speed, the probe took only half an hour to traverse the 100,000-km (62,140-mi) diameter dust coma surrounding the nucleus.

Vega 2, however, decided to make the Hungarian-Russian imaging team earn their keep. All seemed well with the craft until 32 min before encounter when the automatic camera pointing system failed. Photographs showed nothing but blank space. Apparently, a cometary dust particle struck and disabled the microprocessor controlling the scan platform.

Mission controllers frantically sent signals to Vega 2 ordering it to switch to a backup system. Even at the speed of light, it took ten minutes for the command to reach the craft, then nearly 160 million km (100 million mi) from earth. Yet another agonizing ten minutes would pass before earth could receive acknowledgment. Then, 24 tension-filled minutes after the malfunction was detected, images from Vega 2 clearly showed Halley. Six minutes later, the best pictures yet of the famous comet were received by the relieved science team. Seven hundred images were returned with many details as small as 200 m (656 ft).

Vega 2 survived its encounter with Halley's dust cloud in fair shape, but its solar panels were even more seriously damaged than those of Vega 1. Only 20 percent of the solar cells were still functioning after the encounter. Looking back at Halley, Vega 2 returned more views over the next two days.

WHAT DID THE VEGAS FIND?

Both Vegas had scored a resounding space exploration success, not only for the Russians, but for the international team of researchers that participated in the mission. Both probes returned nearly 12,000 comet images taken from the ultraviolet through the infrared portion of the spectrum.

But what did the Vega spacecraft find when they shot past Halley? For the first time in history, mankind looked eyeball-to-eyeball at the nucleus of a comet. Halley turned out to be an irregular object, variously described as avocado- or peanut-shaped, $16 \times 8.5 \times 8.5$ km ($10 \times 5.3 \times 5.3$ mi) in size. Vega 1 viewed Halley from its narrow end while Vega 2 viewed it broadside. Comparison of images from both spacecraft indicated that the nucleus had an apparent rotation rate of 53 hr.

The Vegas determined that the material in Halley's nucleus was very fluffy with a density of 0.1 to 0.4 g per cm³. This is less than half the density of water, implying that Halley was mostly frozen gases and water ice. Stony meteoric material and hydrocarbons were also detected.

The surface of Halley is covered with a thin, porous black crust that reflects less than 4 percent of incoming sunlight. If viewed up close, Halley's nucleus would appear as black as coal. The Vegas showed that at earth's distance from the sun, the sun side of the nucleus reaches between 27 and 127°C (81 and 261°F) while interior ices remained at −73°C (−99°F).

The gases produced by the sublimation of subsurface ices penetrates the porous crust of Halley's nucleus and causes it to crack and break. Dust particles of various sizes are then carried away with the escaping gas streams. The jets of gas are not evenly distributed since Vega images of Halley showed very localized outbursts. Vega 2 images showed a linear feature close to the middle of the nucleus which united many of the smaller gas jets. This feature was responsible for much of the dust ejected from the nucleus during the Vega 2 encounter. During Halley's closest approach to the sun, this gas escaped from the nucleus at the rate of 30 tons per sec while the rate of dust release was about 10 tons per sec.

The Vegas found that the dust particles surrounding the comet were lighter than the individual particles in cigarette smoke, being less than 0.1 microns in size, and were mostly composed of carbon, hydrogen, oxygen, and nitrogen.

As a result of the Vega studies, Halley's mass has been calculated to be 200 billion tons. As it spends most of its 76-year orbit in the deep freeze of space beyond the inner planets, Halley remains for the most part a solid, frozen object. Based on the observed mass loss, it is expected that the comet will be active for another 50,000 years before its volatile materials evaporate completely, leaving the nucleus as a cold stony object passing unseen through the solar system.

THE LONG AMERICAN ROAD BACK TO VENUS

After the Vega missions sounded the final note in the Venera explorations, both American and Russian craft had sniffed the atmosphere, scratched the surface, and created a crude map of the Venusian globe. But the gross topographical maps created by Pioneer Venus and Veneras 15 and 16 only whetted scientists' appetites for greater detail from the hidden surface.

PVO's radar provided a great leap forward in the understanding of the Venusian surface, but it was able to reveal features no larger than the city of Los Angeles. The Veneras 15 and 16 radar mapping missions only covered 30 percent of the planet at what could be called medium resolution at best. It fell to American scientists to mount a higher resolution mapping mission to attain a detailed understanding of the Venusian surface and geology.

Plans for such American radar mappers had been in the works since 1970 when the National Academy of Sciences recommended sending two radar mapping satellites into Venus orbit. NASA's Ames Research Center furthered this recommendation by initiating study of the synthetic aperture radar (SAR) technique—which had previously been used only from aircraft. Three American space radar missions eventually evolved from the Ames study: Pioneer Venus, an earth oceanographic satellite called Seasat, and another Venus mission called VOIR, which was both an acronym for "Venus orbiting imaging radar" and the French verb "to see." From the VOIR concept, the seeds of today's American Magellan Venus radar mapper were sown.

The idea of the VOIR mission following Pioneer Venus was refined through the 1970s. By 1979, a group of scientists had been chosen to participate in such a mission. The following year, NASA announced the formal start of the project under the direction of the Jet Propulsion Laboratory. Launch was scheduled for 1983, shortly after PVO's primary mission had ended.

But as with many previous planetary exploration proposals in the 1970s, NASA found Congress and the President unreceptive to initiating future explorations. The newly elected Reagan administration was initially supportive of the new radar mapper, but in early 1981 it abruptly canceled the entire project. Even proposals for a scaled down version of the project fell on deaf ears. The unexpectedly high costs of developing the space shuttle had once again crimped NASA's budget. New ventures were starved for funds while the shuttle anchored our once proud space-faring heritage into near-earth orbit.

VENUS PROBE BUILT FROM SPARE PARTS

In spite of government funding cutbacks, American planetary scientists did not give up. Instead, they set out to rethink the new Venus mission with the aim of lowering costs to acceptable levels. VOIR was expensive because the entire spacecraft was to be custom made. If a new spacecraft could be built using existing components, the cost could be cut significantly. In addition, $69 million could be saved by dropping five atmospheric experiments and "descoping" the mission to a radar mapper only. The downsized mission was now simply called the Venus Radar Mapper.

The first money-saving move was to scrap plans for VOIR's custom-made computer and substitute a spare computer developed for the future Galileo Jupiter mission. Additional equipment scavenged from Galileo included the data tape recorder, attitude control computer, and power system. Items were also adapted from the space shuttle and the joint U.S.-European Ulysses solar mission. Components built a decade before for the Viking Mars orbiters and landers were also pressed into use.

Other borrowed components included the spare antenna built for the Voyager Jupiter probes. This solid, one-piece, 3.66-m (12-ft) diameter structure would serve at Venus as both the SAR antenna and the high-gain antenna to relay data to earth. However, while the antenna was excellent for communicating, it was the wrong shape to perform radar duties. To compensate, the SAR computer was replaced by the much smarter Galileo computer which worked around the antenna's deficiency. Another smaller antenna used was originally built in the 1960s for the Mariner 9 Mars probe. Even the 10-sided 47-cm (18.5-in) high Voyager spacecraft bus was used to house equipment on the Venus mapper.

By eliminating the expensive one-of-a-kind liquid-fueled retrorocket and substituting an existing design solid-fueled rocket to enter Venus orbit, costs were further cut. This move carried a penalty however. A solid-fueled rocket could only slow the spacecraft into an elliptical orbit instead of the desired circular orbit. The radar apparatus would have to be modified to work in an eccentric orbit.

The resulting spacecraft was a strange collection of hardware, but it had at least a chance to accomplish the radar imaging needed to round out our knowledge about Venus.

INSTRUMENTS DEDICATED TO MAPPING MISSION

In 1984, NASA approved the project and the revised Venus Radar Mapper received funding. The Planetary Society, a public space advocacy group, sponsored a contest to name the spacecraft. Nicholas Cognito from Braddock, Pennsylvania, submitted the chosen entry. The radar mapper was officially rechristened Magellan in honor of the 16th-century Portuguese nautical voyager who charted our planet.

As the Magellan spacecraft took shape, it evolved into one of the more unusual-looking craft to leave earth. Below the wide white Voyager antenna was a rectangular forward equipment module containing the radar sensor subsystem and spacecraft attitude control system. Under this was the Voyager bus which housed Magellan's other electrical systems and the hydrazine-fueled liquid propulsion system. Extending from the forward equipment module just above the Voyager bus were twin movable solar panels which would produce 1545 watts of power at Venus to charge twin nickel-cadmium batteries. Protruding from under the Voyager bus was a framework with four spider-like arms to support hydrazine thrusters which could be varied from 0.1 to 45.4 kg (0.25 to 100 lb) of thrust. These would be used for attitude control and maintaining the proper orbit around Venus. Attached below this was the Star 48-B solid-fueled retrorocket. The mass of the spacecraft without fuel was 1035 kg (2282 lb), but with a fully fueled hydrazine tank and the retrorocket attached, the mass ballooned to 3449 kg (7603 lb).

The 154-kg (340-lb) radar package was Magellan's only payload. Similar in function to the SAR payload carried by the Venera radar mappers in 1983, Magellan's radar was more refined and could nominally resolve details 150 m (492 ft) in diameter. This is ten times the resolution available from Venera. The device packed an incredible 15,000 electronic parts and 22,000 other items into 37 modules housed in a box $0.3 \times 1 \times 1.5$ m ($1 \times 3 \times 5$ ft) in size. However, clever planning allowed four separate experiments to be conducted by this one device—radar imaging, measurement of surface elevation by radar altimetry, temperature measurement by radiometry, and mapping of the gravitational field.

On each mapping pass the radar system was to send out 6000 bursts of 12.6-cm wavelength microwave pulses for periods lasting 25 to 200 milliseconds, depending on the craft's altitude. The beam, at 325 watts of power, would cover 17 to 28 km (10 to 17 mi) on the surface, depending on the mapper's side-look angle, which varied between 14 and 45 degrees during each orbit. Successive 16,000-km (9942-mi) pole-to-pole swaths of radar data, called "noodles," were to be gathered on each orbit. During each swath, the radar would expose each point on the surface at least four times. The multiple radar echoes were to be stored for later transmission to earth. Intensive computer processing would then organize this electronic jumble into a single image. Since the Venusian equator rotates at 6.5 km (4 mi) per hr, adjacent noodles would overlap.

After each imaging radar burst, a one-millisecond radar altimeter burst was to measure the elevation of the surface directly below the spacecraft to an accuracy of 30 m (98 ft). This would be followed by a 50-millisecond period where the receiver would act as a radiometer and listen to the radio energy emitted by the hot Venusian surface. In this mode, the receiver would measure the planet's temperature to an accuracy of two degrees as it looked for hot spots indicative of active volcanism.

After completing surface mapping for several Venusian years, each lasting 243 earth days—known as a mapping "cycle"—Magellan would be used to map the gravitational field of Venus and search for localized mass concentrations on or below the surface. These concentrations would be detected by their effect on Magellan's orbit since the variations in the planet's gravitational pull they would produce would cause the spacecraft to dip or rise slightly.

Unlike previous Venus orbiters which were stabilized only by thrusters, Magellan was uniquely qualified to perform gravitational mapping because it would use three massive, electrically driven reaction wheels for attitude control. Thrusters not only turn a spacecraft, but their action causes the orbit to shift minutely, enough to spoil gravity measurements. By speeding up or slowing down its spinning reaction wheels, Magellan could twist and dance in its orbit without disturbing the trajectory. The reaction wheels had the added benefit of saving thruster fuel, considerably prolonging the mission.

MORE HURDLES TO CROSS

Magellan was originally scheduled to be launched by the space shuttle in April, 1988. This was to be a landmark mission for NASA since it was the first planetary probe to be launched since the Pioneer Venus craft left earth a decade before. Magellan was to break a long drought in new programs for American planetary exploration. To boost the radar probe out of earth orbit, a modified hydrogen-fueled Centaur upper stage was to propel Magellan into a six-month trajectory toward Venus. The catastrophic 1986 explosion of the space shuttle Challenger quickly scrambled that plan. A post-Challenger review of the space shuttle system revealed that carrying the hydrogen-filled Centaur stage within the shuttle's payload bay presented too many safety risks. The $1 billion, shuttle-carried Centaur concept was therefore scrapped.

This left Magellan with no booster. Although the mapper could have been launched with an expendable Titan-3–Centaur booster, NASA, through a bureaucratic decision in the early 1980s, dictated the inflexible launch policy that the space shuttle, and not expendable boosters, would be used for all NASA payloads. This edict was partly a futile attempt to lower the cost of space shuttle missions through increased usage, and partly an attempt to justify the expensive program. This policy was enforced even though an expendable booster could launch Magellan for half the expense of a manned shuttle mission.

To get Magellan to Venus, a two-stage, solid-fueled booster developed for the Air Force, the Inertial Upper Stage (IUS), was pressed into service. But the IUS was far less powerful than the Centaur and compromises had to be made. Magellan's weight had to be pared down. However, the fast trajectory possible with the Centaur—which dictated a large retrorocket to slow the probe into Venus orbit—was now not needed since the IUS was too feeble to loft Magellan into such a trajectory. The trip would now take fifteen months with the spacecraft looping 1.5 times around the sun before arriving at Venus. The slower trajectory also allowed the use of a lighter retrorocket, the spherical 1.22-m (48-inch)-diameter Star 48-B. Magellan could now get to Venus, but arrival would be delayed from October 1988 to mid-1990.

In all, the development of the spacecraft from the early 1980s, the delay caused by the 1986 Challenger tragedy, the redesign forced by booster changes in the late 1980s, and the need to operate the spacecraft in Venus orbit meant that Magellan's estimated cost would reach $530 million by the time its research is complete in 1994. This price does not include the $500 million expense of the space shuttle flight to launch the radar probe.

Development reserved one more barrier for Magellan to cross before it was ready to leave earth. In a strange incident at Cape Canaveral on October 17, 1988, the spacecraft actually caught fire. During a power system checkout, a technician accidentally connected the wrong cable to an electrical connector and shorted components of the power distribution system. Sparks, black smoke, and flames gushed from the battery connector panel and technicians subdued the fire with a Halon fire extinguisher. Fortunately, damage was localized near a temporary test battery installed inside Magellan, but the spacecraft required several days of intensive cleaning to ready it for further testing.

SPACECRAFT READIED AT LAST

By early 1989, Magellan was ready: The crucial and complex electronics were perfected, the tricky attitude control and data management techniques to be used during successive radar passes were mastered, and the daunting task of data reduction had been designed. The space shuttle Atlantis was readied for an April 28 liftoff to keep Magellan on schedule for a summer 1990 rendezvous with the Evening Star.

The launch was scheduled at the beginning of a 29-day launch window in case technical delays forced delays. However, the early launch date was not the best for Magellan. A late April liftoff would mean the spacecraft would arrive at Venus traveling too fast. The retrorocket would be unable to slow it into the proper elliptical orbit and the hydrazine thrusters would have to help slow it down. This would use fuel reserves needed to control the craft in orbit, ultimately shortening the extended mission after radar mapping was completed. A launch on May 4 or 5 would be optimal for Magellan's arrival speed and would maximize the mission's lifetime.

Strangely, the failure of a pump in Atlantis' engine compartment set Magellan up for the best launch date. The April 28 attempt was canceled and rescheduled for May 4. This is one of the few times that a launch malfunction actually improved the overall performance of a space mission.

At 2:47 P.M., the shuttle's three main engines ignited, followed quickly by the gut-shaking roar of the solid-fueled boosters bursting into life. Atlantis, with Magellan tucked inside, leaped from Cape Canaveral's Launch Complex 39 and soared into space. Six hours later, the first shuttle-launched deep space probe was gently pushed out of Atlantis' cargo bay. An hour later, after the shuttle had backed away to a safe distance, the IUS fired and accelerated Magellan into its long 1.3-billion km (806-million mi) journey around the sun. By May 21, the probe had receded 3.2 million km (2 million mi) from earth. Here, it used its hydrazine thrusters to speed up by 106 km (66 mi) per hr to ensure a proper path to Venus.

FINAL VENUS MISSION ARRIVES

After a leisurely fifteen-month trip to Venus, Magellan arrived at the planet on August 10, 1990. On the far side of the planet, out of view from earth, the retrorocket ignited at 1:31 P.M. Burning for eighty-three seconds, the rocket settled the spacecraft into an initial 294 × 8450 km (183 × 5251 mi) orbit, inclined 85.5 degrees with a period of 3 hr, 16 min. For the next six days, the orbit was trimmed while the spacecraft was checked out.

Then came a time of panic. On August 16 controllers at JPL lost contact with the spacecraft and the mission seemed doomed. For fourteen worrisome hours, Magellan disappeared before its faint signal was heard again by JPL's Deep Space Network antennas. It turned out the spacecraft had suffered a case of scrambled computer memory and had effectively lapsed into a coma. In a case like this, Magellan's computer was designed to "safe" itself automatically, or enter a hibernation state, and await instructions from earth. In this mode, the high-gain antenna's narrow half-degree beam could not aim directly at earth. Instead, the spacecraft sent out a signal over the 10-degree beam of its medium-gain antenna. To ensure that it was heard, the spacecraft "coned" (deliberately wobbled) so the beam would sweep a wide area of space and eventually cover earth.

To give Magellan the electronic equivalent of a wake-up call, the signal transmitted toward the craft was increased from the normal 18 kilowatts to the maximum 350 kilowatts available from the 70-m (230-ft) antenna at Goldstone, California. This beam was so powerful that nearby aircraft had to be warned to leave the area. Responding to the radio shout, Magellan stopped its slow wobble and fixed its gaze on earth. Control was slowly regained and prospects for mapping Venus brightened.

Five days later, Magellan's attention wandered for another 17.5 hr before the spacecraft was tamed again. Magellan possessed one of the most capable computers ever flown to the planets, but it was proving to be a temperamental system as well. It took until September 12 to regain full control of the spacecraft. The exact cause of the recurring problem was not determined for months, but by mid-September project managers were confident enough to begin the mapping program.

THE REAL VENUS UNCOVERED

From its 258 × 8460 km (160 × 5257 mi) orbit, Magellan swung around Venus every 3 hr and 15 min. During this time, the mapper became one of the busiest space probes ever launched. For 37 min as Magellan made its closest approach to Venus, it aimed the big SAR antenna toward the surface so that the radar would gather another "noodle." After the tape recorder gathered 1.8 gigabytes of data, the spacecraft used its reaction wheels to shift the big antenna's aim slowly toward earth so that more data could be transmitted—57 min at 268,800 bits per sec. As the spacecraft approached apoapsis, it temporarily broke contact with earth to locate a star selected as a navigational aid and update its attitude control system. During the return to periapsis, radar data were relayed to earth for another 57 min before the SAR antenna was again aimed downward for the next radar pass. To fully map the entire Venusian globe, Magellan needed 1852 consecutive mapping passes. This produced a staggering 3334 gigabytes of digital data requiring a superhuman computer-processing effort to reduce the data into usable images.

Once the mapping mission officially got underway on September 15, the fondest hopes of project scientists were realized. Twenty years of struggling to get a high-resolution radar mapper to Venus were worth the effort—Magellan's images were superb. Previous imaging probes had acquainted us with the unseen surface below the clouds, but now Magellan let us examine that surface as if with a microscope. The SAR images often revealed details the size of a baseball field. As Magellan unwrapped the hidden surface swath by swath, the secretive and mysterious surface was mapped in greater detail than some portions of the earth have been.

It is hard to describe briefly what Magellan saw since every orbit's-worth of data was a book in itself. The images confirmed that Venus was covered with hundreds of large volcanos and approximately 100,000 shield volcanos, low volcanos surrounded by broad lava flows, less than 15 km (9.3 mi) in diameter. Another form of intriguing volcanic activity observed was "pancake" volcanic domes. These circular features were created by thick lava flowing outward from a central vent and forming a plateau. Some of these pancakes were up to 2 km (1.2 mi) high. Other volcanic features included the curious circular "coronae." These were believed to have been formed by volcanic uplifting from the interior which deformed the surface.

Magellan found no evidence of tectonic activity such as continental drift on earth. It did, however, show that the "tesserae" terrain, areas with crisscrossed groves, were present in nearly all areas of the planet and might represent the remains of an earlier era of tectonic activity. Other images of vast lava flows, mountains, chasms, and 900 impact craters provided geologists with data that would occupy them for years. By July, 1992, 99 percent of the surface had been imaged and a quarter of the surface mapped in stereo. The imaging phase of Magellan's mission was an astounding success.

FINANCES CRITICALLY SHORT

Congressional funding for Magellan's operations only covered the initial cycle of radar mapping. Congress was unwilling to underwrite additional explorations at Venus and seemed eager to abandon the working spacecraft in Venus orbit to fund future, yet-to-be-flown planetary probes. But abandoning the $500 million Magellan mission before it was completed could be viewed as irresponsible and a slap in the face of the American public who had financed the expensive mission. The situation was analogous to killing the first-born child to make room in the crib for a second child. Since NASA had no additional monies to continue Magellan's mission, the only means of proceeding was to tap into funds earmarked for future explorations. While that made the Magellan team unpopular with other space scientists, it did allow the productive spacecraft to continue operating.

By late 1992, lack of funding was at crisis point. As Magellan began its fourth mission cycle in September 1992, operations were being conducted solely by means of money saved by frugal program administration during the initial cycles. Magellan was in danger of being the first planetary spacecraft to be shut off deliberately for lack of money to receive its data. There was more risk to Magellan from the federal budget than from the hazards of spaceflight.

The emphasis of the fourth cycle would be on mapping of the gravitational field. This activity would look for mass concentrations on Venus much the same way that satellites orbiting the moon discovered the lunar "mascons" which gravitationally altered their path. Understanding Venus' gravitational field would reveal important clues to the internal structure of the planet.

To perform the gravitational mapping, Magellan's perigee was lowered to 184.7 km (114.8 mi) on September 15. The lower the spacecraft's orbit, the more it would react to gravitational perturbations. By accurately monitoring the Doppler shift of a signal transmitted from earth, then relayed back by Magellan, changes of velocity as small as 0.1 mm per sec could be detected every two seconds. At perigee, these gravity measurements had a resolution of 200 km (124 mi). Since the surface of Venus only shifted 20 km (12.4 mi) between orbital passes, the craft only needed to be tracked on every fourth orbit, or about twice a day.

NOVEL TECHNIQUE FURTHERS SCIENTIFIC GAINS

By May 1993, one final cycle still remained before scientists would consider Magellan's mission complete. The fifth cycle called for Magellan's orbit to be circularized just above the planet's cloud tops to perform even more detailed gravitational mapping. To do this only with Magellan's thrusters would require over eight times more hydrazine than the spacecraft carried. In order to lower the orbit, a bold experiment was attempted. Magellan performed an "aerobraking" maneuver, a technique which used the atmosphere of Venus to slow the spacecraft, dropping it to a lower orbit. On May 25, Magellan used its thrusters to reduce its perigee to only 140 km (87 mi). As the spacecraft raked through the rarified upper atmosphere of Venus, the drag exerted a force of up to 9.8 Newtons (2 lb) and slowed the spacecraft slightly. By carefully maintaining the proper attitude and altitude, aerodynamic heating on the spacecraft remained within safe levels, never exceeding a design limit of 180°C (356°F) on the large radar antenna. Over the next 70 days, Magellan repeatedly dipped into the tenuous upper atmosphere and little by little reduced the apogee from 8460 km (5257 mi) to 540 km (335 mi) by August 3. The perigee was then raised to 197 km (122 mi), establishing a 94-min orbit.

Magellan's funding expired during the aerobraking maneuver and JPL was forced to budget $700,000 of its own money to finish the process. Once in its lower orbit, Magellan began precision gravitational mapping over the entire planet, not just at the equator as during cycle 4. Although Magellan had completed the historic first aerobraking maneuver, the science planned for cycle 5 required $30 million. Realizing that this funding simply was not available, program managers reduced Magellan's staff of 95 to just 32 people. The resulting group, called the "lean, mean, gravity team," had funds to last only through December 31, 1993.

For a time, it looked as if the powers that were would make Magellan the first deep space explorer to be abandoned while it was still producing unique and valuable data. Then, at the last minute, NASA's management saved the mission. Realizing that it would be years before another spacecraft approached Venus and that NASA's battered public image could not tolerate damage, enough funding was allocated in the budget for the following year to operate Magellan at Venus until October, 1994. The valuable, and essentially free, cycle 5 gravity mapping would be completed. Scientists would be able to wring every last bit of data out of the fabulously successful Magellan mission.

REFLECTIONS AND DREAMS OF VENUS

As Magellan chips away at Venusian secrets, no future American Venus projects have been seriously considered. As the next century approaches, all American planetary activities are aimed toward the outer planets and Venus has again sunk to a low NASA priority.

The 1984 flights of the Vega probes also marked the end of an era for Russian space exploration. At the time Vega 2 left the earth, Russian scientists were excited about plans for improved landers which would image the surface of Venus from below the clouds as the craft descended. These new armored landers would transmit seismological data for several days from the torrid surface of the planet. Another 1989 proposal called for use of a 1998 Venus orbiter which would fire ten penetrometers into the surface of Venus to study physical characteristics over a wide area. But, since the completion of the Vega missions, no other Russian probes have been sent to Venus. After 24 years of dogged persistence in pursuit of Venusian secrets, the highly successful Soviet Venera program seems to have been abandoned. There are no known Russian plans to return to Venus for the rest of the 20th century.

Like the American Venus withdrawal, the Venera program is not standing down for lack of scientific want or technical competence, but rather for economic reasons. One of the effects of President Mikhail Gorbachev's "perestroika," their restructuring program of the late 1980s, was that spacecraft would have to be purchased by the Russian Academy of Sciences; the government would no longer supply them. This immediately scaled back all space endeavors.

Lavochkin engineer Valery Timofeev told this author: "The politics of the Veneras is different now. Now, the problem is money. The most important question is economic, not political. Our government gives money to the Academy of Sciences and the Academy decides what is important to investigate. Now, we only have money for the investigation of the earth."[3]

Thus, after years of basking in the success of the technically difficult tasks of both delivering instruments to and operating them on the fiery surface of Venus, Russian scientific pride has been wounded by the accelerating economic and political crises in eastern Europe. It has been nearly a decade since the last Venus launch from Tyuratam. The longer the interval to the next flight, the more the scientific and industrial teams which produced the Veneras will disperse. Much of what we know about the planet is a direct result of these missions. After all that has been gained, it would be a scientific disaster to lose the Russian ability to explore Venus.

Some experts guess that it will be the year 2005 before Russian parachutes drift through the Venusian atmosphere again. In hopes of better times in the future, the Babakin Center and the Lavochkin Association have not been idle. Already on the drawing boards are designs for the third-generation Venera explorers. These new craft will weigh up to 28 tons and be launched by derivatives of the SL-17 Energia heavy-lift booster. When these giant new Veneras fly in the next century, hopefully, they will be cooperative missions flown with international participation. With such broad-based support, these missions would surely reveal astounding new secrets from earth's inner neighbor.

9 In Pursuit of the Old Mars

The planet Mars has not been kind to Russian scientists. As the history of the space age has unraveled over the past four decades, spacecraft after spacecraft bound for Mars would rise up from their launch site at Tyuratam. Early probes were to pass near the planet while later efforts were to land on the surface. However, every one of these missions would be destined to fail. In all, seventeen attempts to reach Mars were made. Some returned useful data about Mars and its moons, but no Russian craft succeeded in landing on the planet.

America was luckier. As Soviet Mars probes continued to flounder in the ocean of space between earth and Mars, NASA probes to Mars returned stunning scientific results which quickly altered our perception of the planet. Previous conceptions of the planet became the "old Mars" as waves of American Mariner probes showed the surprising "new Mars." Early photographic reconnaissance probes gave way to landers which scored an American scientific triumph. Eventually, the Russians gave up on Mars, concentrating on their more successful Venus explorations and the red planet became an American planetary playground.

But, in the 1950s, little was really known about Mars. Beyond basic information about the planet's size and orbit, most of our concepts about Mars were little removed from informed speculation. The sum of knowledge gathered about Mars from earth-based observation was in Gerard de Vaucoulers' *The Physics of Mars*, then regarded as the "bible" for Mars studies.

TO THE RED PLANET

For several years, the Mars competition was actually a one-sided race with Russia as the only competitor because America's Mars efforts were already off to a rocky start early in the space age. When Caltech's Jet Propulsion Laboratory was transferred to NASA in December 1958, JPL scientists recommended a progressive series of eighteen lunar and planetary missions over the following five years. Included in these proposals were flights to Mars at the next Martian launch window, October 1960. Rockets available to NASA in the late 1950s lacked the power to send craft carrying a heavy retrorocket required to decelerate it into Mars orbit, so initial efforts would be fly-by probes that would streak past Mars and relay information about the planet during their brief encounter. Unfortunately, President Eisenhower's administration was reluctant to fund expensive space ventures.

While American space planners debated their goals, Russian scientists decided to go *to* Mars. The huge propaganda success of Sputnik fueled Premier Khrushchev's desire for more space firsts, and he readily funded an early Soviet Mars flight.

Mars was a natural target to fire the imagination of people everywhere. In the world of science fiction, Mars was a place of tantalizing familiarity. The fictional works of H.G. Wells, Edgar Rice Burroughs, and Ray Bradbury had introduced generations to a fascinating Martian world. However, in the world of scientific fact, most of our early ideas about Mars were merely speculation, most of which proved to be wrong. Khrushchev, lured by the red planet's role as an ideal place for Soviet science to make great propaganda gains, encouraged the development of the fledgling Soviet Mars program.

In mid-1958, design work began for the first Soviet Mars exploration. By August 1959, all the theoretical research for a flight to Mars had been completed by the Applied Mathematical Division of the Mathematical Institute of the U.S.S.R. Academy of Sciences. These studies showed that the Soviet R-7 ICBM, coupled with the upper stages being developed by Sergei Korolyov and Semyin Kosberg, could launch a spacecraft with a mass of about 500 kg (1100 lb) toward Mars in September or October of 1960.

SOVIETS PREPARE FOR MARS

The principal leaders of the early Soviet Mars effort were Sergei Korolyov who built the spacecraft and academician Mstislav Keldysh who headed the scientific investigations planned for the Mars fly-by. At the same time, a small group at Moscow University led by A.I. Lebedisky began developing the scientific instrumentation for the spacecraft. The first Russian Mars craft would carry 10 kg (22 lb) of instruments to study interplanetary space and observe Mars during a brief fly-by. Though the first attempt was doomed to fail, it laid the groundwork for future flights.

The earlier Luna flights to the moon had remained in relatively close proximity to earth until their batteries gave out. Their radios could be heard with modest receivers. The Mars explorer, however, would travel millions of kilometers away from earth. Giant radio-telescope-like antennas were therefore needed to gather the probe's faint signal from such distances.

The Soviets built a receiver consisting of eight aluminum dish antennas, each 15.8 m (52 ft) in diameter, arranged in two rows of four each. The entire assembly, standing on its common rotating frame, was twelve stories high. The receiver electronics were extraordinarily sensitive, using a maser (an acronym for microwave amplification by stimulated emission of radiation) amplifier cooled by liquid helium to reduce the receiver's electronic noise which would otherwise have drowned out the Mars spacecraft's weak signal. Transmissions to the probe were to have been broadcast at a power of 100 kilowatts.

The movable part of the antenna assembly weighed more than one thousand tons. Most of its mass was support structure which prevented the eight separate dishes from sagging by even a millimeter as the antenna scanned different parts of the sky. An article in the newspaper *Pravda* later disclosed that the task of building the giant antenna "was no less than that required to launch the first Sputnik."[1] For a time the Soviets attempted to keep the antenna's location a secret, but it was eventually spotted by Air Force reconnaissance satellites on the State Farm at Yevpatoria in the Crimea.

A Soviet Mars attempt was expected during the October 1960 Mars launch window, especially as it coincided with the arrival in New York of Premier Khrushchev for the 1960 U.N. summit meeting. Khrushchev had used a Luna moon flight the previous year to his great propaganda benefit when he attended the 1959 U.N. summit. At that meeting, Khrushchev gave President Eisenhower replicas of the Soviet pennants carried by Luna 2 when it struck the moon. Khrushchev now had the opportunity to repeat that scene on a planetary scale.

A dramatic event in New York harbor reinforced the expectation of an October 1960 Mars flight. A Russian sailor who defected from the *Baltika*, the ship that brought Khrushchev to the United States, said there was a model of an advanced spaceship aboard. Apparently this was to be displayed if the anticipated Mars flight was launched successfully.

On October 14, 1960, the initial Soviet Mars probe lifted off from Tyuratam as a part of the maiden planetary launch of the SL-6 Molniya rocket. After a successful liftoff, Korolyov's ambitious planetary attempt failed at the edge of space. During the booster's third stage burn, the rocket failed. Mankind's first leap to the planets then fell back into the atmosphere and crashed—on the wrong planet.

With Korolyov's Mars probe splattered over Soviet territory, Khrushchev's spaceship model remained stowed away aboard the Baltika and was never displayed.

This Mars launch was never acknowledged by Russian space officials. However, if it had been successful, the Mars probe would have arrived at the planet in May 1961. Such a planetary success would have come a month after Yuri Gagarin became the first human being to orbit the earth, and would have given Khrushchev a stunning double space victory to celebrate in the spring of 1961.

AMERICAN INDECISION

American scientists were not allowed to begin serious Mars exploration studies until 1961, a year after the first Soviet Mars probe had failed to rocket into space. Before that, a series of plans to explore Mars were presented to NASA by JPL scientists in July 1960. They then watched in frustration as their proposed planetary explorations were canceled or scaled down by NASA and the Government.

Hopes for explorations of Mars were soon revived, however. President John Kennedy's 1961 mandate to send men to the moon by the end of the 1960s gave NASA a blank check to race to the planets as well as the moon.

NASA assumed that the first Mars probes would be heavy instrument platforms carried by early versions of the Saturn moon rocket, a booster with many times the power of NASA's early boosters. However, grand plans and reality seldom come to agreement. By 1962, the large probe was scaled back to fit the smaller Atlas-Centaur booster, then under development but expected to be ready for a 1964 Mars launch. Reality then pressed heavily again. Perfecting the hydrogen-powered Centaur upper stage proved to be a long, painstaking process, and the proposed Mars probe shrank to a simple fly-by probe. To fit the only rocket available in 1964 which could reach Mars, the Air Force's Atlas-Agena, the probe was reduced from 1000 kg (2200 lb) to 261 kg (575 lb). In November 1962, when designs for the spacecraft that were to become Mariners 3 and 4 were approved by NASA, they were mere wisps of their former selves. When preparations finally began in earnest for America's first Mars probe, JPL was again in charge of assembling the scientific instrumentation. A leading instrument candidate was an imaging system. Close-up photos of Mars would lay to rest many century-long controversies about the red planet: What was the nature of the "canals?" What caused the seasonal color changes on Mars? What was the nature of the polar caps? Could Mars possibly harbor life? From its previous lunar experience, JPL had the expertise to develop such instruments and to interpret their results.

RUSSIA TRIES AGAIN

Scientists at JPL were not the only ones busily preparing Mars spacecraft. As late 1962 approached, the fruits of Korolyov's labor were in the shops of the Assembly and Test Building at the Tyuratam cosmodrome in Kazakhstan. With the assistance of Georgi Babakin, the chief designer was completing preparations on two different types of spacecraft for the next round of Soviet Mars launches in October and November 1962.

During the 780-day interval after the last Mars launch window, Korolyov had redesigned the initial Soviet planetary probes into a unified spacecraft to carry out missions to either Venus or Mars. The resulting spacecraft, known as "Object MV" (Object Mars-Venera), had a mass of 893.5 kg (1970 lb), the heaviest interplanetary probe to date. The cylindrical spacecraft was 1.1 m (43 in) in diameter, 3.3 m (10.8 ft) in length, and spanned 4 m (13.2 ft) across its solar panels. The Object MV spacecraft also had the ability to correct errors in its trajectory with a small, on-board rocket engine.

The probe's pressurized body was divided into two sections. The orbital compartment housed the guidance, command, communications, and propulsion equipment. The planetary compartment, also referred to as the "special compartment," contained the scientific equipment, either a lander or photographic gear. Also attached to the spacecraft was a 2-m (6.5-ft) diameter parabolic directional antenna for communication with earth. At the end of both solar panels were hemispherical heat exchangers. The hemispheres were divided into two sections, each with a different finish to absorb or reflect solar heat. These were designed to supply either hot or cool liquid, as needed, to control the spacecraft's internal temperature which was increased by solar radiation on the sunward side of the craft while the shadow side experienced subfreezing temperatures.

The U.S.S.R. Academy of Sciences incorporated an array of Mars study instruments into the new probes. The "MV-4" version carried an imaging system along with the hardware to transmit close-up Mars images across the reaches of interplanetary space. In keeping with the notion of the day that seasonal color changes implied some form of Martian vegetation, a spectrometer was included to detect the spectral signature of organic matter. A spectrograph was also included to examine the Martian atmosphere for the absorption bands of ozone. What instruments were carried by the "MV-3" Mars landers were never disclosed. (MV-1 and MV-2 were dedicated to exploring Venus.)

To study interplanetary space, both the probes were also equipped with cosmic ray and meteoroid detectors. Magnetic fields were to be studied by a unicomponent magnetometer which had a threshold of 2 gammas, a fraction of a percent of earth's magnetic field strength. This was more sensitive than the one carried by the American Mariner 2. Beginning a long-standing Soviet study of solar radio waves in outer space, the 1962 Mars craft had special receivers tuned to the 150 and 1500 m bands.

TRIPLE MARS LAUNCH

In 1962, no less than three Mars spacecraft riding aboard SL-6 Molniya boosters were launched in the hopes that one would succeed. The first, launched on October 24, 1962, placed a Mars craft and its fourth stage booster into a 202×260-km (125.5×161.6-mi) earth parking orbit, inclined 65.1 degrees. Ninety minutes later, the booster exploded shortly after ignition and broke up into 24 recognizable orbital fragments.

While a Mars shot was expected because of the launch window timing, the flight was not announced by the Soviets. The failed launch was particularly awkward in that it came at the height of the Cuban Missile Crisis. When the booster broke up in earth orbit, it presented a swarm of targets to the Ballistic Missile Early Warning System (BMEWS) radar in Alaska, giving the nerve-jangling impression of a missile attack on the United States.

The second launch actually departed earth and struck out toward Mars. The probe, designated "Mars 1," lifted off from Tyuratam on November 1, 1962. Following a one-orbit loop around the earth, a successful fourth-stage ignition lofted the probe out of earth orbit and onto a 231-day trip to Mars. Arrival would occur on June 19, 1963, when Mars was 249.5 million km (155 million mi) from earth. If all went well, the Soviet Union would win the race to Mars by default as no American craft would be pacing the Soviet craft.

The third 1962 Mars launch departed November 4, 1962. Shortly after entering a 170 km (105.6 mi) circular earth orbit inclined 64.8 degrees, the fourth-stage rocket engine again exploded after ignition. Five major pieces of debris were tracked in orbit, all of which reentered between November 5, 1962 and January 19, 1963. This launch also was not acknowledged.

CRUISING TO THE RED PLANET

At 4:50 A.M., Moscow time on November 2, 1962, while Mars 1 was receding from the earth, the 102-inch reflecting telescope at the Crimean Astrophysical Observatory succeeded in photographing the probe as a 14-magnitude, star-like object. Over the next several days, more than 350 photographs of Mars 1 were taken which helped establish its trajectory very accurately. Some of the pictures were obtained with the aid of an electronic image intensifier which amplified the light gathered by the telescope, cutting the required photographic exposure by a factor of one-hundred.

The ideal distance for Mars 1's passage by the red planet was between 1000 to 11,000 km (621 to 6835 mi) altitude, but it was unrealistic to hope that the booster's aim would shoot the probe past Mars within such tight tolerances. For every 0.3 m (1 ft) per sec of velocity error or each 1/60 of a degree of error in aiming, the probe would miss Mars by an additional 20,000 km (12,427 mi). Indeed, the booster's error in direction was slightly more than hoped for as early trajectory measurements showed Mars 1 would miss the planet by 251,000 km (156,000 mi), rendering useless its scientific instruments. This error was still well within the 483,000 km (300,000 mi) correction limit and a mid-course correction rocket burn was planned to steer the probe back on course.

Speeding away from earth at 3.9 km (2.4 mi) per sec, all remained well with the spacecraft. Mars 1 slowly rotated once every four minutes to even the effects of solar heating and keep its internal temperature stabilized between 20 and 30°C (68 to 86°F). Equally important, the internal pressure held steady at 850 mm of mercury, allowing the instruments to function.

While the simultaneous American Mariner 2 Venus mission was impressive, the Mars 1 mission was seen as more ambitious. Had it been widely known that three other Soviet Mars attempts had previously failed, perhaps the success of Mars 1 would not have seemed so laudable.

The probe was not in continuous contact with earth like American deep space probes. Instead, a programming device sampled and recorded data from the scientific instruments for later replay back to earth at regular intervals over a 922.76 MHz telemetry link. During its first month in space, while Mars 1 was still close to earth, it transmitted data 37 times. For the next two weeks, the probe was interrogated every two days to transfer the scientific data stored onboard. As the distance between earth and Mars 1 widened, the interval was increased to every five days, then to every fifteen days.

Each of the 1.5- to 2-hour communications sessions began with the reception of scientific data about the space environment around the craft. Then, housekeeping data about the probe's status were sent while the signal allowed the craft's course to be determined. Finally, on command from earth, stored scientific data were played back. At the end, more housekeeping data, such as the probe's internal temperature and pressure, battery voltage, and power consumption, were transmitted.

Early data transmitted by Mars 1 yielded scientific information about space near earth. Mars 1 confirmed the presence of a third high-altitude radiation belt around the earth. While Mars 1 was still close to earth, it encountered the Taurid meteor shower at altitudes of 5950 km (3700 mi) to 40,230 km (25,000 mi). The craft encountered a heavy concentration of meteoric particles, recording one micrometeor impact every two minutes with piezoelectric sensors. The probe also showed that the intensity of cosmic rays near earth had doubled since the 1959 Soviet Luna flights to the moon.

The solar wind outside earth's orbit was continuously sampled as was the solar magnetic field in deep space. Intensities of 3 to 4 gammas were recorded, with peaks reaching 6 to 9 gammas several times. These levels were only one- to two-thousandths that of earth's magnetic field. The probe also noted a decrease in the amount of cosmic dust as it receded from earth. On November 30, 1962, the craft encountered an extremely intense stream of solar particles which reached 600 million particles per cm^2 per sec. Later, when Mars 1 was about 37 million km (23 million mi) from earth, it passed through a previously unknown meteor stream.

When contacted on March 16, 1963, Mars 1 was 98.8 million km (61.4 million mi) from earth. The Soviets claimed this as a long distance communications record, bettering that of the American Mariner 2 Venus explorer by 13.8 million km (8.6 million mi).

PREMATURE END TO THE MISSION

After giving weekly progress reports on the flight, authorities issued no reports after March 16, 1963. Soviet scientists announced on May 16, 1963, that contact had been lost with Mars 1 on March 21, 1963, when the craft was 106.2 million km (66 million mi) from earth. Up to that time, there had been sixty-one communications sessions with the probe and some 3000 commands had been sent to the craft.

The mission was lost when Mars 1 maneuvered to use its on-board rocket engine to refine its aim toward Mars. It is not known if the craft completed its rocket burn because the craft's orientation system failed at this point. Now unable to point the high-gain antenna back toward earth, no further communication was possible with the spacecraft.

The premature end of the mission had a bittersweet consolation for Soviet scientists. Mars 1 had survived five and one-half months in deep space, longer than any previous probe beyond earth orbit. It had gathered the first data between earth and Mars and established a long-distance communication record which would stand for two more years.

In spite of the Mars 1 failure, subsequent engineering reviews found no fault with the basic concept of the spacecraft. Subsystems were modified and improved, but the basic Object MV spacecraft bus proved to be a satisfactory design. It was, in fact, used for the next Soviet Mars launches and became the standard Venus probe bus up through Venera 8 in 1972.

But still, Mars 1 did not reach Mars. The American Mariner 2 had beaten no less than five Soviet shots toward Venus. Now after four Soviet launches toward Mars, American scientists were snapping at the heels of their Russian counterparts. At the next launch window, the U.S. would be ready to race the Russians to Mars.

MARINERS TO MARS

While Mars 1 looped outward from the sun, two identical, scaled-back Mars explorers were being assembled for the initial American assault on the red planet. They traced their pedigree through JPL's Mariner Venus and Ranger lunar probes. Following the modular concept started with the Rangers, the Mariner Mars craft were built around a 1.38-m (4.5-ft)-diameter, 0.46-m (1.5-ft)-high octagonal magnesium frame. Seven sides of the frame supported compartments housing scientific instruments and electronics. The eighth side housed a 22.7-kg (50-lb)-thrust, hydrazine-powered course correction rocket. The rocket was unusual in that it thrust laterally from the side of the spacecraft instead of from the bottom as in traditional designs. The motor was capable of two firings for a total velocity change of 81 m (266 ft) per sec.

The new Mariner was to communicate through an elliptical 1.2 × 0.5-m (3.9 × 1.6-ft) parabolic antenna. Transmitting with a power of 10.5 watts, it would dribble data to earth at what seems today to be an astonishingly slow rate of 8.3 bits per sec.

Almost as important as the spacecraft itself were the three receiving stations of JPL's Deep Space Network which were to listen to Mariner's radio voice. When the probe encountered Mars, it would be a greater distance from earth than the earth itself is from the sun. By the time Mariner's signal traveled twelve minutes at the speed of light to reach earth, its strength would be only one-tenth of a billionth of a billionth (0.0000000000000000001) of a watt. Each of the antennas placed around the world used the most advanced and sensitive electronics to pick out the probe's faint signal from the background static of natural cosmic radio noise.

The new Mariners would be arcing away from the sun and thus would receive less solar energy. To compensate, four solar panels were carried instead of the two flown on Ranger and Mariner 2. Each panel had 7056 solar cells and all four combined produced 700 watts of power at earth's distance from the sun. The array of panels fed a 1200 watt-hr, silver-zinc battery which would push Mariner's faint radio signal across the void between Mars and earth.

A computer using gyroscopes for attitude reference and sensors which looked for the sun and the bright star Canopus controlled the Mars explorer through twelve tiny nitrogen jets at the ends of the solar panels. In a novel scheme, Mariner also sported an adjustable solar vane at the tip of each panel. Totaling 0.65 m^2 in area, these vanes acted like aircraft trim tabs to steady the craft by using the faint pressure of solar energy. This system effectively kept the solar panels aimed at the sun, saving the limited nitrogen gas supply for more aggressive maneuvers. With its solar panels spanning 6.79 m (22.3 ft), Mariner, with all of its 138,000 interlocking parts, looked somewhat like a Dutch windmill.

The stripped-down Mariner Mars craft were to carry a total of 15.5 kg (34 lb) of scientific instruments. The premier instrument was a scan platform mounted under the spacecraft which housed a 30.5-cm (12- in) focal length f/8 Cassegrain telescope attached to a slow-scan television camera. A swath of closeup images was to be taken at 48-second intervals as the probe sped by Mars. The images were to be stored by a tape recorder for later transmission to earth. Other instruments included a meteoroid detector, magnetometer, two instruments to chart solar and cosmic rays, and two instruments to study gas composition in space and near Mars.

Another experiment was of crucial importance for understanding the nature of the Martian atmosphere: In a daring plan, JPL scientists decided to aim Mariner so that it would pass behind Mars on its swing by the planet. In doing so, the probe's radio signal would pass through deeper and deeper layers of the atmosphere before the planet blocked the signal. By studying the signal's slow fading as it passed through progressively denser portions, the first true profile of the Martian atmosphere could be established. This experiment took on added urgency when 1964 studies with the 100-inch telescope on Mt. Wilson showed that the atmosphere on Mars was much thinner than the anticipated one-tenth of earth's atmospheric pressure. Accurate information was paramount in the design of future Mars landers.

The experiment was not without risks however. The occultation would occur immediately after the important imaging session, before any photos were transmitted to earth. Because of planetary positions during the occultation, not only would Mariner be out of contact with earth, but for over an hour it would be passing through the dark shadow of Mars. The spacecraft normally relied on the sun for power and orientation reference. In the Martian darkness, batteries and gyros would have to keep Mariner alive and point the directional antenna to where earth would be when the craft re-emerged from behind Mars. If something went wrong after entering the shadow for the first time in eight months, the critical imaging data would be lost, wiping out one of the prime objectives of the mission.

FIRST U.S. LAUNCH TOWARD MARS

In November 1964, all was ready. Mars would not wait; within a month the planet would be out of range. At Cape Canaveral it was time to launch. Mariner 3 lifted off into the Florida sky from Pad 13 on November 5 at 1:22 P.M. All seemed well with the Atlas booster as it thundered upwards. Then, something went terribly wrong at the edge of space. Instead of tumbling into the Atlantic like so many other American space catastrophes, Mariner 3 made it into space, then simply tumbled.

A new light-weight fiberglass payload shroud had been built by Lockheed Aircraft to protect the Martian Mariners during their ascent through the atmosphere. The special shroud had been designed to shave precious pounds off the booster so the Mars-bound craft would have a greater chance of making it into the proper trajectory. But instead, the new shroud ended up killing Mariner 3. During ascent, the inner layer of the shroud had collapsed around the spacecraft and fatally pinned its solar panels in the stowed position. Although en route to Mars, without power from the solar panels, Mariner 3's batteries gave out 8 hr, 43 min after launch. Powerless, Mariner was unable to communicate with earth. Now both deaf and mute, Mariner 3 receded from earth as a lifeless mechanical hulk.

This was a stunning blow, but JPL quickly reacted to save the remaining Mars mission. Engineers had just three weeks to find the problem, solve it, and launch the mission for Mars before the launch window closed, trapping Mariner 4 on earth. In a perfect example of the no-holds-barred, can-do attitude which prevailed in the early American space program, JPL and Lockheed Aircraft, aided by engineers from NASA's Lewis Research Center, determined what went wrong. A new all-metal shroud was quickly built in a seventeen-day, around-the-clock effort and installed on Mariner 4's Atlas-Agena waiting on Pad 12 at Cape Canaveral.

On November 28, 1964, the booster lifted off at 8:22 A.M. and lofted Mariner 4 effortlessly into space. After a 32-minute coast in a 185-km (115-mi) earth parking orbit, the Agena rocket set its sights on Mars and refired its engine for 95 seconds. Mariner 4 was accelerated to 11.5 km (7.15 mi) per sec and flung away from earth forever.

RUSSIAN CRAFT JOINS MARINER 4

In spite of the loss of its twin, Mariner 4 would not fly alone to Mars. Half a world away from Cape Canaveral, Korolyov and Babakin had not been idle since Mars 1 had come within weeks of reaching its target. On the launch pad at Tyuratam, another Mars probe awaited the exact moment when the dance of the planets required that it lift off.

At the appointed time on November 30, 1964, a four-stage Molniya booster carried the probe into earth orbit, then pushed it outward toward Mars. Now there was a *real* race to Mars! However, it was a race the Russians could not win. Even though the Soviet probe was launched two days after the U.S. craft, the paths of Mariner 4 and the Russian spacecraft differed. The new Soviet craft was a refinement of the Object MV-3 spacecraft developed two years before and was, therefore, a Mars lander. Its path was chosen to minimize its arrival speed and make an atmospheric entry easier. Thus Zond 2 would arrive at Mars a full three weeks after Mariner 4. For victory in the race to Mars, the Soviets could only hope that Mariner would suffer a fatal breakdown en route.

The Soviets, wary of yet another Mars probe failure, were vague about the intent of the new 950-kg (2094-lb) spacecraft. Instead of calling the craft Mars 2, it was designated Zond 2 (Probe 2 in Russian) as the second in the series inaugurated by the Zond 1 launch toward Venus. TASS reports stated Zond was a "technological probe" designed to perfect equipment for more advanced vehicles and would perform experiments in interplanetary space and in the "vicinity of Mars."

However, all was not well with the Zond. Shortly after launch, it was noted that the output of the electrical power supply was half that expected. One of Zond 2's solar panels had failed. Corrective measures were attempted without success. While engineers frantically tried to troubleshoot the electrical problem, the next Zond remained in the Assembly and Test Building at Tyuratam.

As the crippled Zond 2 continued toward Mars, three course corrections were done assuring that the probe would pass within 1609 km (1000 mi) of the planet on August 6, 1965.

MARINER PROVES CONTRARY

NASA in the meantime had a healthy spacecraft en route to Mars. The only annoying hitch was Mariner's stubborn tendency to latch onto the wrong guiding star. The previous Mariner flew to Venus using the brightest object in the sky for navigation reference: the earth. Mariner 4 however was traveling beyond earth's orbit and thus could not use its home planet for reference. Instead, the craft was equipped with an electronic eye which searched for the bright star Canopus. The sensor initially locked onto the wrong star, then finally oriented itself properly.

The next order of business was to refine Mariner 4's trajectory. This was important to get the critical radio occultation data needed to study the Martian atmosphere. For the occultation experiment to succeed, Mariner needed to reach Mars after an eight-month voyage from earth, then pass through a precisely located "keyhole" in space only several thousand kilometers across at a distance only 1.5 planetary diameters above the Martian surface. If the craft missed this target, it would not pass behind the planet and the occultation would not take place. To achieve this incredible feat of celestial navigation, Mariner's on-board engine was called into play.

Precision tracking by JPL's Deep Space Network showed Mariner 4 was on a course that would pass Mars on July 17, 1965, at an altitude of 246,378 km (153,100 mi) above the wrong side of the planet. On this course, both the photography and the radio occultation data would be lost.

A week after launch, on December 5, 1964, Mariner was instructed to cock itself at a precise angle to the flight path. The craft's small course correction engine then flared into action for twenty seconds. The resulting 17.3-m (56.8-ft) per sec velocity change pushed the flight path in the proper direction. Mariner would now pass Mars late on July 14 at 9600 km (5965 mi) above the proper side of the planet, right through the keyhole needed for the radio occultation experiment.

During the rocket firing, Mariner's navigational instruments again lost their lock on Canopus. After relocating the bright star, it frustrated ground controllers three days later when it locked onto the star Gamma-Velorum. Mariner's controllers then decided to leave the spacecraft oriented on Gamma-Velorum until December 17 when the craft was ordered to lock onto Canopus once again. This time, the sensor obeyed and remained on the star for the rest of the mission. The Canopus sensor's temperamental nature was attributed to dust particles on its lens.

For the next seven months, Mariner 4 cruised toward the red planet. With the exception of the television camera, all the scientific instruments were active during the long flight. On the way to Mars, 235 micrometeor impacts were recorded and 20 solar flares were detected. Curiously, as Mariner approached the orbit of Mars, the rate of impacts decreased, as if Mars had swept clean its path around the sun.

Meanwhile, Zond 2 trailed behind Mariner. As the Russian craft sailed farther away from the sun, the crippled solar panel took its toll. In April 1965, while still three months away from Mars and its power fading, contact with Zond 2 was lost. The five-month accumulation of interplanetary data was little consolation to the Soviets. After five years of effort, the Martian prize had once again been snatched away.

The seeming predisposition for Soviet craft to fail just weeks away from a Martian rendezvous led to the creation of the mythical "Great Galactic Ghoul." John Casani, Mariner 4 deputy spacecraft manager, satirically invented the imaginary creature which lurked halfway between earth and Mars, ready to devour any passing spacecraft.[2] Its appetite satisfied with two Russian craft, the Ghoul let Mariner 4 pass unmolested. Future craft, however, would not be so lucky!

MARS AT LAST!

In July 1965, Mars loomed larger each passing day as Mariner 4 approached its rendezvous. Then, after traveling 523 million km (325 million mi) around the sun in 228 days, the probe reached its target. On the evening of July 14, the spacecraft flashed past the planet at an altitude of 9958 km (6188 mi) and flawlessly snapped 21 photographs over a period of 25 minutes. The precious close ups were dutifully stored by Mariner's tape recorder. Then 75 minutes after closest approach, Mariner slipped behind Mars. The sensitive receivers of JPL's Deep Space Network carefully measured the strength of Mariner's signal as the probe slid behind the planet, then reappeared an hour later, thankfully, still in good shape.

America was first to the red planet!

It is easy to get lost in the technicalities of spaceflight and lose sight of the marvel of this accomplishment. There is a danger that waves of impersonal numbers, statistics, and new discoveries can obscure an achievement. Mariner 4 successfully produced its share of facts and figures, but it also marked the first time mankind had succeeded in reaching Mars. What had fueled imaginations for centuries, had now become a reality.

In the half-century since Percival Lowell popularized the idea of life on Mars, humanity could only wonder and guess what Mars was really like. Now, Mariner had some rudimentary answers. Unfortunately, they were agonizingly slow in coming. Across the 215 million km (133.5 million mi) separating earth from Mars, the photographic images trickled out of Mariner's tape recorder at the rate of three pictures per day, taking nine days for all the images to arrive safely in the hands of JPL scientists.

The first Mars images were taken from a distance of 16,895 km (10,500 mi) and showed the planet's limb, or visible edge, at mid-northern latitudes in the area historically known as Phlegra, or "The Burning Plain." The swath of images extended across the equator to a point halfway to the southern pole. The photos then continued back up to the mid-northern latitudes on the opposite limb near Chryse Planitia, or "The Plain of Gold," at a distance of 9844 km (6118 mi). The strip of images did not show much of Mars. Like looking through a series of keyholes, just 1 percent of the total surface was imaged. However, their resolution was 30 times that available from earth-bound telescopes, and the photos were a scientific bonanza for Mars studies.

JPL scientists had repeatedly warned that the resolution of the Mariner photos would be too low to detect any evidence of life on Mars. At best, each photo pixel would represent about 1.6 km (1 mi) of the Martian surface. Using weather satellite photos of the earth for comparison, scientists showed how large man-made features on earth like canals, highways and cities remained unseen at a resolution comparable to the Mariner photos.

But still, the press clamored for the first close-up views of Mars. There was one problem, however, when the electronic images were received: they appeared to be blank! There was nothing to be seen! Apparently dust had collected on the television camera lens and the glare had washed out the images. JPL analysts struggled around the clock using a rudimentary form of image processing to extract recognizable features from the images. As each of the 40,000 pixels making up one image was received, it was in the form of a binary number ranging from 0 (white) to 63 (black). To form the preliminary image, scientists literally hand-colored each box of a 200×200 space checkerboard mosaic with the proper shade. Later, more detailed processing was done by giant IBM 7094 mainframe computers.

As the first images and data from Mars were slowly reconstructed, no one could foretell how Mariner's findings would alter our understanding of the red planet. So much of what we thought we knew about Mars would prove to be wrong! At the same time, so much of what we were about to learn would, in time, prove to be totally misleading. The golden era of planetary exploration was now in full bloom. New insights and discoveries would pile on each other at a frightening pace for the next two decades.

Now, the first of these insights trickled back from Mariner 4. As the data were deciphered, the rim of the planet appeared, then successive overlapping images showed dark markings. Then came the surprise on the seventh frame—the real Mars came into view. Not Percival Lowell's vision of a canal-strewn planet, not Edgar Rice Burroughs' fictional Barsoom teeming with life, but a dead world covered with craters! Big craters! Lots of craters up to several hundred kilometers in size. In all, 70 large craters were counted in Mariner 4's limited peek at the surface.

Some planetary geologists had quietly expected to see craters on Mars, but the public had not. After years of speculation, Mariner's images showed that Mars had to have been a dead world for a long, long time. On earth's moon, the geological record of cosmic bombardment has been preserved for four billion years. Lack of water and an atmosphere left the moon's cratering just as it was at the time of its creation. On earth, similar cratering has long since been erased by our weather. The sight of ancient craters on Mars instantly implied a lack of weather and any significant atmosphere.

The death knell for any hope of Martian life came when the radio occultation data were analyzed. When the craft ducked behind Mars for 54 minutes, Mariner's signals had faded and resumed abruptly. This showed there was little atmosphere to mute the signal progressively. Final analysis showed that the atmosphere is even thinner than that implied by the 1964 100-inch telescope data. Mars had a surface pressure of only 0.5 percent that of earth, equal to the atmospheric pressure at 30,000 m (about 100,000 ft) above our planet. At such low pressure, no liquid water, or even moisture in the soil, could exist. It would quickly evaporate into the near vacuum of Mars' atmosphere. Without water, life as we know it could not exist on Mars. Additionally, an atmosphere only 1/200th of the density of earth's would not shield the surface from solar ultraviolet radiation. Any exposed microorganisms surviving on the dessicated, near-vacuum terrain would be fried alive by the sun. With Mariner 4's data, it would seem that any hopes of finding life on Mars had vanished into thin Martian air.

No Martian magnetic field or Van Allen-like radiation belts were found either. A measured magnetic field only 0.1 percent that of earth implied Mars lacked a molten metallic core like that within our planet. Our molten core coupled with earth's rotation creates our powerful magnetic field. On earth, this magnetic field and our atmosphere protect us from dangerous cosmic rays and solar radiation. Mars, on the other hand, lacks both these forms of shielding, further precluding any significant form of life.

Mariner 4 had performed the most important Martian science of the century. During its rapid pass by Mars, it shed light on century-old questions about the atmosphere, surface, and interior of this now not-quite-so-mysterious planet.

Mariner's success was also a shot in the arm for the entire American space effort. The little planetary explorer did much to improve NASA's image. Coming on the heels of the Ranger's lunar successes, Mariner 4 represented a turning point in American deep space exploration. From now on, success would be the operative word for NASA planetary exploration. Never again would America play second fiddle to a Russian space spectacular.

SOVIETS REALIZE DESIGN ERROR

In mid-1965, Soviet astronomer Arkady Kuzmin was at Caltech as part of an American–Soviet scientific exchange. When the unofficial Mariner 4 results were presented at a Caltech seminar, Kuzmin took a special interest in projected slides displaying the results of the atmospheric occultation experiment. The results foretold a grim fate awaiting the Zond 2 probe when it arrived at Mars on August 8. The information on the darkened auditorium's screen was too vital to await publication in a scientific journal so Kuzmin photographed the projected images with his 35 mm camera. The film was soon on its way to the U.S.S.R. via diplomatic pouch.[3]

Back in Moscow, engineers at the Lavochkin Association looked over the results beamed back from Mariner and relayed by their colleague. If by some miracle the lost Zond 2 was still functioning and ejected an instrument package into the atmosphere of Mars, Mariner showed it was doomed to fail. In the near vacuum of the Martian atmosphere, Zond would plunge into the ground at supersonic speed. The Russian craft's parachute had been designed under the old assumption that Mars had a much thicker atmosphere. Now the Russians soberly realized that their craft would need a parachute the size of Red Square to slow its landing capsule.

Lavochkin engineers, realizing Zond could not succeed, went back to their drawing boards. Georgi Babakin, using Kuzmin's information, began designing a future lander which would use a retrorocket to slow its drop onto the unknown surface of Mars.

It was small consolation to Soviet scientists, but if an American lander had been launched in 1964, it would have also been designed assuming a thicker Martian atmosphere and would have failed as well. If the Centaur rocket had been ready on time, if Congress had authorized the money, and JPL had been lucky, an American probe would have faced the same specter of failure awaiting the Zond.

MARINER 4 LONG LIVED

On October 5, 1965, the last data from the planetary encounter were transmitted from a distance of 309 million km (192 million mi) from earth. Mariner 4 to Mars was an unqualified success, but its mission was not over yet. After looping around the sun, as the spacecraft approached the earth again, it was frequently interrogated about conditions in deep space. On September 15, 1967, it passed through a meteoroid stream while 47.6 million km (29.5 million mi) from earth, detecting an astonishingly high seventeen micrometeor impacts against the craft in fifteen minutes.

The following month, Mariner 4 was used to test spacecraft components like those to be used on the Mariner 5 mission scheduled to fly to Venus. The Venus craft was in fact Mariner 4's modified backup spacecraft, thus they shared many common systems. On October 26, 1967, Mariner 4 was commanded to fire its course correction motor once more. After 1060 days in space, the motor worked perfectly, operating for 70 seconds. Additionally, frames 16 and 17 from the Martian photo encounter two years before were retransmitted without any sign of deterioration.

On December 7, 1967, Mariner 4 ran out of gas for its attitude control jets and could no longer steady itself in space, but the hardy craft refused to die. It remained in contact until December 21. Ten days before contact with the long-lived explorer was lost for good, it reported encountering another meteoroid stream. This time, Mariner's instruments detected 83 strikes.

ADVANCED EXPLORATIONS PLANNED

As the startling 1965 discoveries about Mars were being digested, NASA began to look toward future explorations of the red planet on a much grander scale. With the single mission of the quarter-ton Mariner 4 under their belt, NASA planners envisioned a gigantic 22,680-kg (50,000-lb) robotic biological laboratory as the next step in Martian investigations. Instead of following a more conservative, step-by-step approach to Mars exploration using the newly perfected Atlas-Centaur booster, the huge multi-billion dollar craft they planned would be launched by the gigantic and expensive three-stage Saturn 5 rocket developed to send the manned Apollo landers to the moon. The incremental approach to Mars exploration was abandoned. NASA even declared the Centaur rocket unavailable for planetary exploration, although it was used for other missions. The fact that one of NASA's justifications for developing the expensive Centaur in the first place was planetary exploration only accentuated the absurdity of the plan.

The immaturity of this wild leap from the initial basic Mars mission to a colossal exploration represented one of NASA's first bouts with its obsession for building huge space systems while sacrificing many smaller, more scientifically productive ventures. This type of bureaucratic thinking would dog NASA's exploration of the solar system for the next quarter-century. Fortunately, the Budget Bureau (known today as the Office of Management and Budget) took a dim view of the Martian extravagance and killed the plan.

After the Budget Bureau provided NASA planners with a quick reality check, the Atlas-Centaur rocket was suddenly available again for planetary exploration. Having proved itself as the muscle powering the Surveyor landers to the moon, Centaur allowed a heavier, more sophisticated and capable offspring of Mariner 4 to be designed. An atmospheric entry probe was considered but rejected because of the cost and the development time needed. The resulting twin craft, designated Mariner F and G, looked superficially like Mariner 4, but were twice as heavy. NASA officially approved the new Mariners on December 22, 1965, and funded them with a $148 million budget. It was too late to ready them for the 1967 Mars launch window, so they would fly three years later, in early 1969.

While NASA re-established its Mars goals, the Russians tested their planetary spacecraft with a launch on July 18, 1965, toward the orbit of Mars. Zond 3 successfully tested the mid-course correction engine on September 16, 1965, while at a distance of 12.55 million km (7.8 million mi) from earth. The craft then validated the design of Korolyov's Object MV spacecraft as it transmitted interplanetary data all the way out to a distance from the sun equal to Mars' orbit. By March 3, 1966, the probe was still functioning at a distance of 153.5 million km (95.3 million mi) from earth.

Ironically, Zond 3 outlived its creator. Sergei Korolyov himself had died the previous January.

EXPECTED 1967 MARS MISSIONS NEVER MATERIALIZE

As the January 1967 Mars launch window approached, western observers expected the Soviets to again loft a pair of Mars probes just as they had tried on every Mars launch occasion since 1960. Some Soviet scientists had even told Czech and French colleagues that Mars flights were planned in 1967.

When Cosmos 139 and Cosmos 140 entered orbit on January 25 and February 7, 1967, speculation centered on their being failed Mars probes which were trapped in earth orbit. The timing of their launches coincided with the expected Mars launch window and little was said of their mission in official announcements. Modern evidence suggests, however, that these were not failed Mars attempts. Launching only a year and a half after Mariner 4 discovered how rarified the atmosphere of Mars really was, it is unlikely that a major spacecraft modification could have been accomplished in that short a time.

As early as mid-1965, Academician Mstislav Keldysh admitted that Russian deep space probes still faced serious problems in their power supply and long-range communications. He said at the time that Russia might not be ready to launch new probes to Mars during the next launch window.[4] Babakin Design Bureau engineers had already begun the design of the next generation of planetary explorers, and too little time remained before the next window.

American planetary plans suffered, in turn, from a political setback in 1967. As the war in Vietnam escalated, its cost placed great strain on the American government's "peacetime" budget. The space program was therefore called upon to take its share of cutbacks to ease the budget crunch. The politically motivated man-to-the-moon program was awarded the lion's share of NASA's shrinking budget, and planetary exploration took a back seat to beating the Russians to the moon. As a consequence, the ambitious planetary exploration program known as Voyager (not to be confused with the two Voyagers flown in the 1970s and 1980s) was canceled in October 1967.

NEW MARINERS TO MARS

The United States also passed up the 1967 Mars launch opportunity, concentrating instead on preparing the next generation of Mariner probes for a 1969 fly-by of the planet. Mariners 6 and 7 were able to take advantage of the Centaur's lifting power, and the probes grew to 413 kg (910.5 lb), including 59 kg (130 lb) of scientific instruments.

Mariners 6 and 7 retained the same octagonal shape of their predecessors. Mounted atop the octagon was a 1-m (3.3-ft)-diameter parabolic antenna. Below the craft was a movable scan platform, now carrying two cameras, which could swivel 70 degrees in elevation and 215 degrees in azimuth (laterally) moving up to one degree per sec. Four 90×215 cm (3×7 ft) solar panels spanned 5.79 m (19 ft). They contained 17,472 solar cells which provided 449 watts of power, at Mars' distance from the sun, to recharge a 14-kg (31-lb), 1200-watt-hr, silver-zinc battery. This provided more than enough power to operate the spacecraft as it receded from the sun.

The twin television system used a 508-mm focal-length telephoto lens and a 52-mm focal-length wide angle lens for close-up and full disc views of Mars. Based on the Mariner 4 system, the new cameras allowed the number of pixels per image to be increased by a factor of 16 to 704 scan lines of 935 pixels each, with a significant increase in image resolution. The new television system, coupled with dual photographic sessions for each spacecraft, allowed these newer probes to collect 200 times the amount of photographic information Mariner 4 had obtained. The television scan platform was controlled by a rudimentary, reprogrammable computer which had a 128-word memory, and the photos were stored on dual tape recorders.

Mariner's television cameras functioned continuously beginning about three days before planetary encounter. The cameras snapped a photo every forty-two seconds without regard to whether the image readout was recorded, transmitted, or wasted. Because of limited tape-recorder space and transmission ability, a majority of the images were left to evaporate into electronic limbo.

The orbital geometry between earth and Mars brought the two planets closer during the 1969 encounter than they were when Mariner 4 had flown four years before, thus the craft's communication distance was halved to 96.5 million km (60 million mi). Additionally, JPL's tracking station at Goldstone, California, had been upgraded with a new, more sensitive 64-m (210-ft)-diameter receiving dish antenna. Using this station, Mariner 6 and 7 would be able to relay their photos 2000 times faster than Mariner 4 by broadcasting their picture data at 16,200 bits per second through a 20-watt transmitter. When in view of the other two smaller, less sensitive 26-m (85-ft)-diameter tracking dishes at Johannesburg and Tidbinbilla, the data rate was reduced to 2000 bits per second. With this faster system, the probe's tape recorders could be played back to earth, then erased, allowing several photographic sequences to be taken during the approach to Mars.

Other instruments carried included an infrared radiometer, infrared spectrometer and an ultraviolet spectrometer. These devices were installed to study the Martian polar caps to determine their temperature and composition as well as examine the atmosphere. The only non-Mars instrument carried was a radiometer which continuously studied the energy output of the sun. This device was more of an engineering instrument—its solar data were gathered for use in the thermal control design of future interplanetary spacecraft.

MARS OUTLOOK BRIGHTENS

In early 1969, American Mars exploration plans began to look up again. Two new fly-by missions were ready to depart and work on two Mars orbiters for 1971 were underway. Additionally, a year after Congress mandated the demise of the Voyager Mars explorer, NASA approved the Viking program on December 4, 1968. This new program was to expand the Mariner investigations with twin launches in 1973. The craft were to make extensive surveys from orbit as well as from the surface where they would employ life-detection instruments.

At Cape Canaveral a crisis occurred in February 1969. The previously postulated Galactic Ghoul had played havoc with Russian Mars probes and had even tickled Mariner 4 as it passed by, but the Ghoul seemed bent on wrecking Mariner 6 before it even got off the ground. Just before Mariner 6 was to be bolted atop its Atlas-Centaur booster on the launch pad, the Atlas partially collapsed. An electrical malfunction had caused the Atlas' propellant tanks, which were little more than thin-skinned metal balloons, to vent their internal pressurization. The rocket buckled under its own weight. When it was reinflated, its metal skin was badly crinkled. Because Mars would not wait, technicians quickly made heroic efforts to substitute the booster intended for Mariner 7. A third Atlas was shipped from Convair (now General Dynamics) in San Diego to launch Mariner 7 later.

Mariner 6 rumbled into the Florida evening at 8:29 P.M., February 24, 1969. Its launch differed from previous planetary flights in that the Centaur upper stage was not placed into an initial earth parking orbit. Instead, the booster flew a direct-ascent trajectory to place Mariner 6 on course toward Mars. The Centaur also had to take a curious flight path, a yaw-like dogleg trajectory to avoid flying over Caribbean land masses during the ascent in case the rocket failed and crashed. Mariner 7, mounted atop its replacement booster, followed in similar fashion at 4:22 P.M., March 27, 1969.

1969 SOVIET MARS FAILURES

The same day that Mariner 7 lifted off from Florida, the Soviet Union also launched for Mars. The effort was not successful and the twin American Mariners sailed alone. As was the usual Soviet practice, the Russian planetary failure was not reported. This official silence hid a huge development effort which had begun many years before.

In the late 1960s, reports filtered out of the Soviet Union describing high altitude aircraft drop tests of new Soviet planetary landers. Babakin Bureau designers were trying to solve a two-pronged planetary problem; the techniques of quickly traversing the ultra-dense Venusian atmosphere as well as safely descending through the ultra-thin Martian atmosphere.

In 1967, the new Institute for Space Research (known by the Russian acronym of IKI), part of the Soviet Academy of Sciences, was founded with Georgi Petrov named as head of the Institute. This new agency was now responsible for the scientific payload of future Russian planetary explorers.

By early 1969, the evolution of the second generation Mars probe was complete and the first flight hardware was prepared for launch by

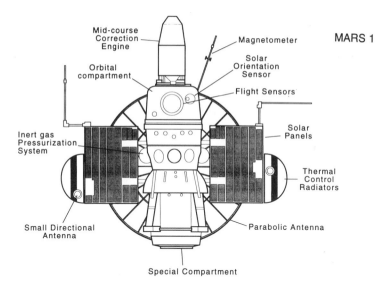

Figure 52. First to the red planet was the Soviet Mars 1 spacecraft. Intended as a photographic fly-by probe, the spacecraft reached a record-breaking 106 million km (66 million mi) from earth before contact was lost three months short of reaching Mars. (Artwork by Ron Dawes.)

Figure 53. NASA's Mariner 4 became the first probe to reach Mars on July 14, 1965. While its photos of Mars were crude by later standards, they showed that the Martian surface was a cratered desert and retired the notion that Mars might be covered by some form of vegetation. (NASA photo)

Figure 54. The eleventh of Mariner 4's nearly two dozen images of Mars left no doubt that the surface was vastly different than expected by most observers. A massive weather-worn crater dominates this 240×270 km (150×170 mi) field of view with many smaller craters also visible. (NASA photo)

Figure 55. Mariner 6 returned more evidence that the Martian surface was heavily cratered. This series of overlapping photos were taken at 84-sec intervals during the craft's July 30, 1969, pass by the planet. The images cover an area 725 by 4000 km (450 by 2500 mi). (NASA photo)

Figure 56. Mariner 7's telephoto camera imaged these frost-filled craters near the south Martian polar cap during its fly-by on August 5, 1969. The largest crater is 79 km (49 mi) in diameter. (NASA photo)

Figure 57. Selected wide-field frames from both Mariner 6 and 7 are overlaid on a Mars globe to show the area of the planet covered by the spacecraft. Mariner 6 made the two horizontal strips while Mariner 7 made the diagonal strip and the sweep over the south pole. (NASA photo)

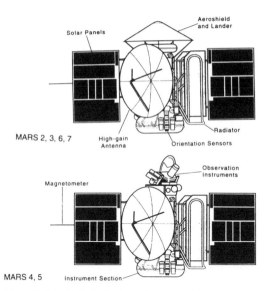

Figure 58. From 1969 to 1973 the Soviet Union launched nine of the second generation Mars probes toward the red planet. The craft, each with a mass four times greater than early Soviet Mars probes, came in two versions, one an orbiter only, the other carrying a lander. (Artwork by Ron Dawes.)

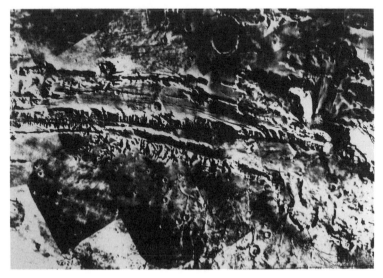

Figure 59. One of Mariner 9's most astounding discoveries was a 5500-km (3400-mi)-long canyon system in the Coprates area of Mars. The western half of this continent-spanning system is shown in this photomosaic. The feature was named Valles Marineris in honor of Mariner 9. (NASA photo courtesy of the Lunar and Planetary Institute.)

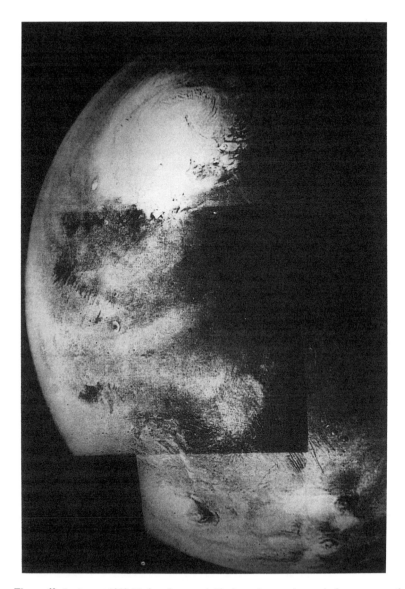

Figure 60. In August 1972 Mariner 9 snapped this three-photograph mosaic from a range of 13,700 km (8500 mi). At the top is the shrinking north polar cap. At the lower right are the volcanic peaks in the Tharsis region. (NASA photo courtesy of the Lunar and Planetary Institute.)

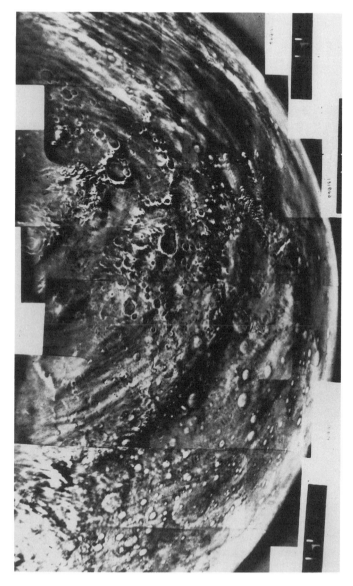

Figure 61. Mariner 9 made repeated scans of Mars looking for transient weather features. Visible in this photomosaic are frost-filled craters and wind-swept clouds which stream around the circumference of the planet. (NASA photo courtesy of the Lunar and Planetary Institute.)

Figure 62. Viking 1 lifted off from Launch Complex 41 at Cape Canaveral on August 20, 1975, aboard the most powerful American booster used for planetary exploration, the Titan 3-Centaur. After an eleven-month journey, the four-ton Viking arrived at Mars and carried out explorations until 1982. (NASA photo)

Figure 63. The Viking spacecraft was two probes in one. The upper half was an orbiter based on the Mariner spacecraft which would survey Mars from orbit. The lens-shaped lower half was the bioshield which isolates the lander from terrestrial contamination. (NASA photo courtesy of the Lunar and Planetary Institute.)

Figure 64. The Viking lander was the most complex craft ever sent to another world. Powered by nuclear generators, the lander carried a biological laboratory which searched for signs of life in the Martian soil. The boom on the right carried weather sensors. Twin cameras protruded upward on either side of the antenna and the extendable soil scoop was just below the antenna. (NASA photo)

Figure 65. Twenty-five seconds after touchdown on Chryse Planitia, the Viking 1 lander began transmitting the first image from the surface of Mars. This portion of the photo by footpad number 2 shows rocks and pebbles on the surface down to millimeters in size. (NASA photo courtesy of the Lunar and Planetary Institute.)

Figure 66. The Viking 1 lander showed that the sands of Mars, long popularized by science fiction writers, was indeed real. Sand and dust was piled into drifts around a large nearby boulder nicknamed "Big Joe." (NASA photo courtesy of the Lunar and Planetary Institute.)

Figure 67. These two photos show the soil scoop on Viking Lander 2 reaching out and digging a trench into the Martian surface. The rounded rock which was displaced by the scoop was nick-named "Mr. Badger" after a character in *The Wind in the Willows*. (NASA photos)

Figure 68. After spending one Martian year (twenty-three earth months) on the surface at Utopia Planitia, the Viking Lander 2 returned this view showing water frost on the rocks and soil. The frost is formed when water clings to atmospheric dust particles, then frozen carbon dioxide makes them heavy enough to fall to the ground. The frost layer was about a 1/40 of a millimeter (1/1000 in) thick. (NASA photo)

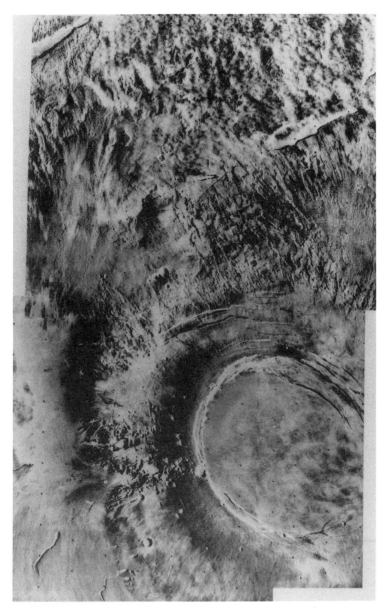

Figure 69. On July 29, 1976, the Viking 1 orbiter returned this photomosaic showing the 100-km (620-mi)-diameter caldera of Arisa Mons, a 27-km (17-mi)-high volcano in the Tharsis region of Mars. (NASA photo)

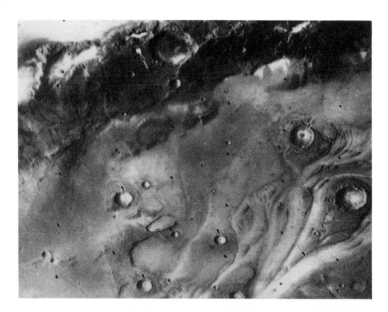

Figure 70. An exciting find by Viking was early morning fog which lay in low craters and channels in the Memnonia region of Mars. These two images were taken a half-hour apart and show that the fog quickly evaporated after being warmed by the sun. The fog suggests that there may be subsurface moisture. (NASA photos)

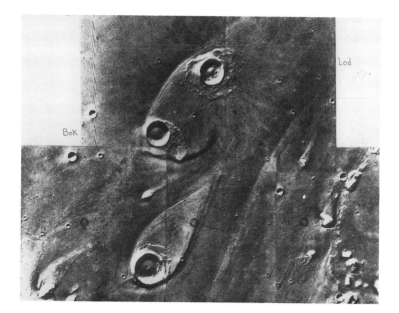

Figure 71. The crater Gold on the southern boundary of Chryse Planitia creates a teardrop-shaped "island" indicating that some sort of flow had washed over the area in times past. The craters Bok and Lod also created an obstacle causing the flow to scour terrace-like beaches in the upper center of this Viking orbiter mosaic. (NASA photo)

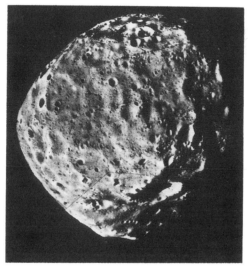

Figure 72. Viking 1 Orbiter flew within 480 km (298 mi) of the inner Martian moon, Phobos. The tiny moon, measuring 19 by 21 km (11.8 by 13 mi) shows a heavily cratered surface covered with loose granular soil. (NASA photo)

Figure 73. Argyre Planitia, the smooth impact basin to the left was imaged by the Viking 1 orbiter in July 1976. This feature is visible from earth, and Viking showed that it was surrounded by heavily cratered terrain. The haze layers on the horizon were caused by dry ice crystals at an altitude between 25 and 40 km (15 and 25 mi). (NASA photo)

Figure 74. The Viking orbiter returned this intriguing image showing an outflow channel emerging from chaotic terrain. This channel is believed to have been formed by either the sudden release of water from an aquifer or melting of subsurface ice by volcanism. (NASA photo)

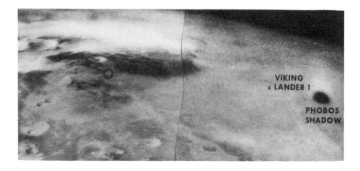

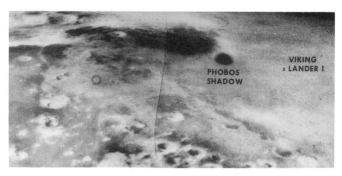

Figure 75. The exact location of Viking Lander 1 was determined to within one km (0.6 mi) by simultaneously photographing the position of the shadow of the moon Phobos from the Viking orbiter while the lander observed an eclipse of the sun by Phobos. (NASA photos)

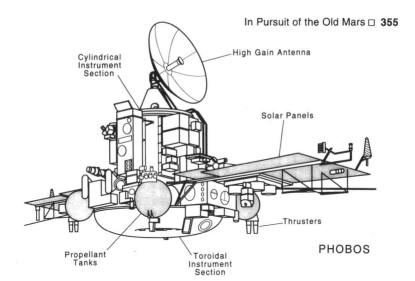

Cylindrical
Instrument
Section

High Gain Antenna

Solar Panels

Thrusters

PHOBOS

Propellant
Tanks

Toroidal
Instrument
Section

Figure 76. The Soviet Phobos 1 and 2 spacecraft represented an ambitious Russian return to the red planet after the disastrous Mars missions of the 1960s and 1970s. While the craft carried advanced scientific equipment, they lacked adequate computer control and both were lost before completing their missions. (Artwork by Ron Dawes.)

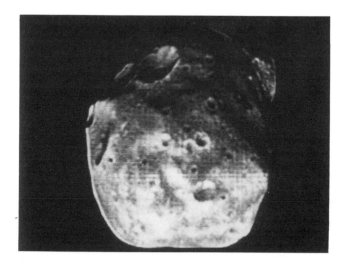

Figure 77. This unenhanced image of the Martian moon Phobos was returned on February 28, 1989, by the Soviet Mars probe Phobos 2. Taken from a range of 320 km (200 mi), the image shows features as small as 75 m (246 ft). (Photo courtesy of the Lunar and Planetary Institute.)

Figure 78. American hopes for Mars exploration centered on the Mars Observer spacecraft. Its mission was to survey Mars from orbit during 1994 and 1995 and act as a radio relay for surface probes dropped by the Russian Mars 94 mission. The Mars Observer spacecraft was lost three days prior to entering Mars orbit. (NASA photo courtesy of the Jet Propulsion Laboratory.)

the massive SL-12 Proton booster. The new probes were nearly three times heavier than their 1000-kg (2200-lb) Zond predecessors and correspondingly carried a greater scientific payload. While no figures were ever given by Russian space officials, the estimated mass of the 1969 Mars craft was 2780 kg (6129 lb). The new craft were to enter Mars orbit after a 150-day flight from earth. The 1969 Mars missions carried no planetary landing capsules. They instead were to study Mars exclusively from orbit. A film and facsimile scan imaging system was to photograph Mars while radiometers and photometers studied the planet's temperature and analyzed the atmosphere. Plasma and ion traps would study solar wind and its interaction with the planet while a magnetometer searched for Martian magnetic fields.

Academician Boris Petrov stated that engineers responsible for the design of the new Mars probes had drawn heavily on the experience of prior

Venera and Luna shots, as well as applied many new technical innovations to the construction and launch of the craft. He said the spacecraft had been developed in a relatively short time by a design team at the Babakin Bureau whose average age was less than thirty, but they were under the guidance of more experienced designers.[5] This indicated the new Mars effort was being carried out by a new team independent of those who had concentrated on Luna and Venera missions. A new push for Soviet Mars exploration was underway.

The powerful four-stage Proton booster had been used for the lunar test flights of Zonds 4, 5, and 6, but had failed catastrophically on a number of other occasions. However, the great mass of the new Mars probes dictated the use of the unreliable rocket. The 1969 Russian Mars twins were launched on March 27 and April 14, 1969. However, because of more problems with the Proton, the craft never reached their earth parking orbits. The first Proton booster exploded in flight and the second booster also failed.

Although the 1969 Mars missions failed, the design of the second generation spacecraft was so successful that it eventually became the standard bus for all Soviet solar system explorations through 1986.

MARINERS 6 AND 7 SAIL ON

In the meantime, NASA's twin Mariners sailed flawlessly toward Mars. Indeed, Mariner 6's launch was the most accurate to date. The craft fired its course correction engine for 5.35 seconds on March 1, 1969, using only five percent of its capability to adjust course to pass 3540 km (2200 mi) from Mars. A similar 7.6-sec firing by Mariner 7 on April 8, 1969, adjusted its course by 4 m (13.1 ft) per sec, placing its aim point within 190 km (118 mi) of that desired.

As the probes circled the sun on their way to Mars, Mariner 7 began to catch up to its twin. Although launched a month later, it would only be a week behind Mariner 6 in arriving at Mars.

With the exception of annoying radio problems which eventually resolved themselves, the Mariners cruised quietly toward Mars. Then, as both craft approached the planet, Mariner 6 gave ground controllers a scare. Its Canopus sensor proved to be as finicky as that of Mariner 4. When the television scan platform was unlocked, a bright piece of debris was cast off. The Canopus sensor obediently followed the bright bauble instead of keeping an eye on the star. After regaining control of the craft, engineers decided that during the Mars encounter, the attitude of both spacecraft would be under the control of a gyroscopic autopilot to prevent the possibility of the Canopus sensor pointing the cameras into blank space.

Two days before arriving, Mariner 6 began taking a series of thirty-three images beginning at a distance of 1.25 million km (775,000 mi). When the photos, taken at thirty-seven-minute intervals, were played back, they showed a rotating Mars looming ever larger. Later, seventeen more images were secured before the near-encounter photo sequence began.

Just 10 days after Apollo 11 placed Americans on the moon for the first time, Mariner shot past Mars at 17 min, 50 seconds past midnight on July 31, 1969. Passing at an altitude of 3429 km (2130 mi), Mariner 6 relayed its infrared data in real time while the photographs were recorded for later playback. The photographs were similar to those of Mariner 4, showing heavily cratered areas as well as flat desert-like terrain.

Daytime equatorial temperatures up to 16°C (61°F) were found but nighttime equatorial temperature was −73°C (−99°F) while the pole was −125°C (−193°F).

Photos of the south polar cap showed an irregular border, prompting scientists to ask for extended Mariner 7 photo coverage of the area. Infrared studies showed the polar caps were either carbon dioxide dry ice or carbon dioxide clouds. Unwelcome news to supporters of life-on-Mars theories were data showing the Martian atmosphere was 98 percent carbon dioxide.

After zipping past Mars, Mariner 6 flew behind the planet and remained out of contact for twenty-five minutes during the radio occultation experiment. The only flaw in the fly-by was that the refrigeration unit on the infrared spectrometer's detector failed to cool, degrading the instrument's data.

THE GALACTIC GHOUL STRIKES!

While Mariner 6 was beaming back precious new data about Mars, the Galactic Ghoul reached out and seized Mariner 7. The probe's signals vanished from the receivers at the Johannesburg station of the Deep Space Network. Just seven days before its Mars encounter, Mariner 7 was apparently dead!

Frantic communication between Deep Space Network stations called for an effort to locate Mariner 7. However, most DSN facilities were at the time dedicated to recovering data from the Mariner 6 fly-by. Finally, a small team of engineers was freed from Mariner 6 duties to work on the problem. Short bursts of radio signals were received from the point in space where Mariner 7 should have been, indicating the craft was alive but tumbling. Its directional radio beam was sweeping past earth like a searchlight. A powerful signal was sent toward Mariner's assumed location directing the craft to switch to its omnidirectional antenna. Eleven minutes later, about seven hours after the craft had been lost, a faint but steady signal returned from Mariner 7. The probe was alive although crippled.

Slowly, control was regained and normal communication re-established. Mariner was found to be slightly off course, as if a giant hand had swatted the spacecraft. This push had moved the probe's aim point 130 km (81 mi) southeast of where it was intended to pass Mars and had caused the probe to tumble, breaking the directional antenna lock with earth. A check of the spacecraft showed that out of 90 radio telemetry channels, 15 were dead and others were garbled. Fortunately, the scientific instruments were still functional, although positional reference for the television scan platform had been lost. The platform was quickly realigned using long-range views of Mars.

What had happened to Mariner 7? It turned out that one of the eighteen cells of its silver-zinc battery had exploded. The blast had ripped through Mariner 7 like a bursting anti-aircraft shell, tearing out part of the craft's engineering systems. The electrolyte spewing from the battery shorted out some electrical systems and also acted like a thruster, pushing the probe off course. Several hours later, another cell also exploded. Fortunately, none of Mariner's critical systems was damaged and the on-board computer was reprogrammed to bypass the damage. Soon, Mariner was in shape for a near-normal fly-by of Mars. That Mariner 7 survived such a violent incident is a tribute to the JPL engineers who designed and built the hardy craft.

A SUCCESSFUL SECOND ENCOUNTER

Two and a half days before closest approach, Mariner 7 began sending the first of 93 long-range photographs of Mars. The flexibility of having a programmable control computer aboard the explorers was demonstrated when scientists analyzing the Mariner 6 data requested that Mariner 7 extend its close-encounter photographic coverage. Instead of 25 photographs, the probe was commanded to transmit 33 reaching down to the pole.

Close-encounter photography began 4.5 hr before closest approach. All other scientific instruments also worked smoothly. At 69 seconds past midnight on August 5, 1969, Mariner 7 passed 3430 km (2131 mi) above the surface, just a single kilometer higher than Mariner 6.

Photography showed more cratered terrain. However, the Hellas plain, a vast shallow depression on the surface, was smooth and showed no craters down to the camera's 300-m (1000-ft) resolution limit. Oddly, the Hellespontus Montes area, a hilly landscape to the west of Hellas, was heavily cratered. Other photos showing the limb of Mars revealed light scattered by atmospheric dust at altitudes up to 40 km (25 mi).

Mariner 7's infrared data showed that the atmosphere is indeed carbon dioxide and that Mars is colder and more inhospitable to any potential life than anyone had suspected. Clouds in the atmosphere were found to be dust and dry ice crystals, or literally frozen Martian "air," if nearly pure carbon dioxide could qualify for that name. The Mariner determined that it never rains on Mars, but that the ground does frost a lot and it may snow dry ice.

The upper atmosphere proved to be composed of products created by the dissociation of carbon dioxide by solar ultraviolet radiation. A high altitude cloud of atomic oxygen surrounds Mars with atomic hydrogen at even higher altitudes. No ozone or nitrogen was detected.

Radio occultation studies confirmed Mariner 4's earlier determination that the atmospheric pressure was 6 to 7 millibars, or about 0.5 percent that of earth's pressure at sea level. One reading was only 3.8 millibars, but this was measured where the local elevation was 5 to 6 km (3.5 mi). A Martian ionosphere was also detected at 140 km (87 mi) altitude on the day side of the planet, but no ionosphere was detected on the night side, a reading consistent with previous Mariner 4 studies.

Both Mariners 6 and 7 continued to function after their summer 1969 Mars encounters. By December 1970, their attitude control gas was nearly depleted and their transmitters were switched off.

Together, the two fly-bys had gathered 201 photographs showing twenty percent of the Martian surface. Mariner 4 had shown the red planet to be lunar-like. Mariners 6 and 7 on the other hand had shown phenomena which were unique to Mars. Ironically, all three Mariners had flown past the bland side of Mars. This view initially gave planetologists the false impression that the Martian terrain lacked diversity. In two years when the next Mariners arrived, that impression would change dramatically.

The dual 1969 Mariner successes were America's final Mars fly-by missions. Later flights were aimed for Mars orbit. Even as Mariner 6 and 7 were completing their fly-bys, the new Mariner orbiters were being designed and readied. Approved and funded with $120 million in November 1968, the new Mariners were to carry out similar missions from different orbits around Mars. Mariner 8 was to enter a polar orbit and map 70 percent of the planet over the next three months. Mariner 9 was to enter an elliptical orbit, which dipped as low as 885 km (550 mi), and chart transient features and atmospheric phenomena such as dust storms and drifting clouds.

SOVIETS PRACTICE FOR THEIR NEXT MARS ATTEMPT

In the 1960s Soviet scientists had failed miserably at reaching Mars. From launches in 1960, 1962, 1964, and 1969, they had received not one shred of planetary information. In spite of a 4-year head start over the U.S. in the race to Mars, by decade's end their entire Mars program had struck out.

Nearly two years after the failed 1969 debut of the new Soviet Mars craft, Cosmos 379 and Cosmos 382 were launched by Proton boosters on November 24 and December 2, 1970. Both of these craft then executed extensive maneuvers in earth orbit. These two maneuvering Cosmos satellites were in fact earth orbital shakedown tests of the Proton rocket and Mars flight hardware to qualify them for the next round of Mars launches to follow five months later. Another clue to future Mars plans was seen in November 1970 when the Soviet scientists controlling the Lunokhod 1 robotic rover on the moon predicted that similar devices—"planetokhods" ("planet walkers") or "Marsokhods" ("Mars walkers")—would someday be tested on the Martian surface.

While NASA prepared to scout Mars with the ambitious Mariner 8 and 9 orbiters, the Soviets were doing everything they could to get their house in order and assure a scientific success at the red planet. The Academy of Sciences, the Institute for Space Research and the Lavochkin Association were determined to reach Mars in the 1970s. By now, American plans to orbit the planet with the next Mariners as well as plans to land life-detection instruments later in the decade were well publicized. For Soviet scientists, enough was enough. It was time to claim a Martian prize for Russia. No less than nine giant Proton boosters and associated spacecraft hardware were prepared to begin an all-out Soviet attack on Mars in the 1970s.

10  Discovering the New Mars

AMERICAN MARS ORBITER PREPARED

In 1971 the orbits of earth and Mars brought the two planets into closer proximity than at any time since the space age began. This close alignment meant that both Soviet and American scientists could fly a larger and heavier spacecraft to Mars than ever before.

The launch weight of Mariner 8 and 9 would be more than double the previous Mariner twins even though the same type of rocket would be used. The new 998-kg (2200-lb) spacecraft were very similar in structure to Mariners 6 and 7, but were to be planetary orbiters. To attain this new goal, major improvements were made to the propulsion system. Mounted atop the spacecraft were twin 76-cm (30-in)-diameter spherical titanium propellant tanks. These carried 463 kg (1021 lb) of monomethyl hydrazine and nitrogen tetroxide to fuel a 136-kg (300-lb)-thrust rocket motor. This rocket was for both mid-mission course corrections and reducing the speed of the new Mariners by 1600 m per second (5250 ft per sec) which would cause them to enter Mars orbit.

A more capable computer controlled the Mars orbiters. The 10.4-kg (23-lb), 512-word memory unit used a magnetic core memory which, unlike solid-state memory chips, was resistant to radiation-induced failures. Commands stored in the computer could be updated in flight to allow great flexibility during investigations from Mars orbit. Since Mariner 7's silver-zinc battery had exploded near Mars, Mariner 8 and 9 were equipped instead with a 600-watt-hr, nickel-cadmium rechargeable battery.

The 25.8-kg (56.9-lb) dual television imaging system was to be the primary scientific instrument. Mounted on the scan platform was a 508-mm focal-length, f/2.35 telephoto camera capable of one-km (0.6-mile) resolution on the surface. A separate 50-mm focal-length, f/4 wide angle camera was equipped with a filter wheel for color and polarization studies. Other scientific instruments included a 15.9-kg (35-lb) ultraviolet spectrometer and a 23-kg (50.7-lb) infrared spectrometer which would study the composition and profile of the atmosphere and search for water vapor. Additionally, a 3.6-kg (7.9-lb) infrared radiometer would map the surface temperature.

The total surface area of Mars is approximately equal to the non-oceanic land area of earth. Imaging this vast new area would be like exploring our home planet for the first time. Fortunately, the mapping of earth's moon in support of the Apollo project by scientists from the U.S. Geological Survey (USGS) was complete. Their unique experience with extraterrestrial geology was now available for the Mars mapping effort.

TWIN LAUNCH FAILURES

When the May 1971 Mars launch window opened, both American and Russian craft were poised to leave earth within hours of each other. Perhaps American mission planners were spoiled by the twin successes of the last pair of Mariners—or perhaps the Galactic Ghoul was hungry—but there would not be twin Mariner orbiters above Mars.

Mariner 8 departed from Cape Canaveral atop an Atlas-Centaur rocket at 9:11 P.M., May 9, 1971. The Atlas performed well and lifted the Centaur stage and its Mariner payload to the edge of space. The Centaur was to use a direct ascent trajectory to place the Mars explorer into an orbit around the sun which would intercept Mars six months later. However, a circuit chip in the Centaur's autopilot failed and the vehicle's engines lost their directional control. The Range Safety Officer, entrusted with the safety of nearby populated areas, signaled an explosive package to destroy the rocket after it drifted off course. Mariner 8 thus ended up at the bottom of the Atlantic Ocean instead of in the cosmic ocean of space. Ironically, the first Russian Mars shot in 1971, carried out in secret the next day, would also fail.

Three weeks after Mariner 8 nosed into the Atlantic and just two days after the last of the three 1971 Soviet Mars probes had departed earth, it was America's turn again. At 6:23 P.M., May 30, 1971, another Atlas-Centaur rumbled up from Cape Canaveral with Mariner 9 aboard. This time, the Centaur stage fired flawlessly for 454 sec, boosting Mariner 9 to a speed of 11.05 km (6.87 mi) per sec. Eighteen minutes after launch, Mariner 9 had opened its solar panels and was streaking toward Mars.

The launch had been deliberately aimed to miss Mars. An accidental impact on the planet by the unsterilized Centaur rocket could potentially contaminate the planet with earth microbes, possibly rendering futile the later Viking mission's search for extraterrestrial life. To put Mariner 9 back on course, the craft's engine was fired for 5.11 seconds on June 4, 1971, while 1.35 million km (839,000 mi) from earth. This 6.75-m (22.1-ft)-per-sec adjustment aimed Mariner 9 at a point 1600 km (1000 mi) from the edge of Mars. The firing was so accurate that further corrections were not necessary.

Carrying only a planetary science payload, Mariner 9 had little to do during its half-year flight to the red planet. However, with its twin at the bottom of the Atlantic Ocean, Mariner 9 mission planners were quite busy. They quickly hammered out a new mission plan to salvage most of the objectives of what was to have been a dual spacecraft mission. A compromise was devised in which Mariner 9 would observe Mars from an elliptical orbit circling the planet every twelve hours, inclined 65 degrees to the equator. This new path would cross the same ground track every seventeen days to allow study of transient features such as the advance and retreat of the polar caps and the seasonal darkening of the equatorial regions as well as mapping Mars.

STORM CLOUDS BREWING

While Mariner 9 and the two Russian Mars craft which kept it company were still in interplanetary space on September 22, 1971, a cloud appeared over the Noachis region, a cratered territory to the west of the smooth Hellas Planitia on Mars. This innocent weather feature soon ballooned into a giant planet-wide dust storm which would not only delay Mariner's investigations, but would have disastrous consequences for the Soviet explorers.

As Mariner 9 approached, the planet appeared as a red waning sphere ahead of the craft. The first long-range Mars photos were relayed on November 10 from a distance of 860,000 km (534,400 mi). The views were disappointing to say the least. The dust storm which had started two months before was still in progress and rendered Mariner's cameras useless. The planet was a totally featureless dust ball except for the south polar cap and four dark spots in the Tharsis region, a broad plain just above the equator.

Arriving at 6:18 P.M., November 13, Mariner's engine fired while 2753 km (1711 mi) from Mars. Burning 431 kg (950 lb) of propellant over 915.6 sec, Mariner decelerated into an initial 1398 × 17,916 km (869 × 11,133 mi) orbit with a period of 12 hr, 34 min. In a pleasant surprise, the rocket performed better than expected and the on-board accelerometer had to cut off the engine early.

A day later, the orbit was trimmed with a 6-sec engine burst. The 15-m (49.2-ft) per sec correction placed Mariner 9 in a 1394 × 17,144 km (866 × 10,653 mi) orbit inclined 64.34 degrees with a period of 11 hr, 57 min. This orbit synchronized Mariner with visibility from the Deep Space Network's Goldstone tracking station.

While waiting out the dust storm, Mariner 9 made an exciting find: the discovery of water vapor over the south polar cap. The two tiny Martian moons, Phobos and Deimos, were also imaged between November 26 and 30. The historic first look at non-terrestrial satellites revealed two lumpy, irregular, crater-covered moons which scientists said looked like a "diseased potato."[1] Both were thought to be gravitationally captured asteroids.

While Mariner 9 continued to loop around the featureless planet, the twin Russian Mars probes arrived and attempted to land instruments on the surface. The Galactic Ghoul dashed the Mars 2 and 3 landing attempts, but the American Mariner 9 was patient. In Martian orbit, it waited for the weather to clear.

Biding its time, Mariner 9 watched the four mysterious spots in the Tharsis region. Over a period of weeks, the dust slowly settled and the spots revealed themselves to be massive crater-like structures 65 to 80 km (40 to 50 mi) wide. Scientists thought it was strange that these craters were situated atop mountains, one which was astonishingly large, over 560 km (350 mi) across.

Mars turned out to be lumpy. The Tharsis region was a 7-km (4.3-mi)-high bulge which gravitationally altered Mariner 9's orbit. By December 30, another seventeen-second engine firing was required.

By New Year, most of the dust had settled and Mariner 9 could go to work in earnest. On January 2, 1972, routine mapping sequences began. As succeeding strips of photos were beamed back from the craft, scientists were astounded by what they saw. The "old Mars" ceased to exist. Previous Mariners had flown over a particularly moon-like portion of the red planet and had wiped out Percival Lowell's concept of an earth-like Mars. Now, Mariner 9 showed that Mars was not like the moon either.

The unfolding geological diversity marked the beginning of the "new Mars." Mariner 9 both revolutionized our understanding of the planet and presented a whole new series of mysteries. The four spots on the Tharsis region were now recognized to be giant volcanoes. The largest, Olympus Mons, towered 25 km (15.5 mi) and dwarfed any volcano on earth.

By January 12, Mariner's view included portions of the Coprates Chasma. This area, seen as a dark equatorial smudge from earth, turned out to be part of the largest canyon in the solar system. Renamed "Valles Marineris" ("Mariner's Valley" in honor of Mariner 9), this giant cleft, 6 km (3.7 mi) deep in places and 4000 km (2525 mi) long, spanned one-fifth of the Martian globe. The existence of volcanoes and massive canyons showed Mars was far from the geologically dead world portrayed earlier.

As the weeks passed, still more interesting data flowed in. The southern half of the planet was heavily cratered while the northern half was relatively smooth and covered by dust. Mariner also resolved the riddle of Martian seasonal color changes. Summer's wave of darkening was not caused by the growth of vegetation as hoped by those who clung to the belief that life might exist on Mars. Mars darkened because seasonal winds blew dust, alternately covering and uncovering dark rock.

The most intriguing finds were east of Valles Marineris and to the north on Chryse Planitia, a plain in the mid-northern latitudes. Here, sinuous channels which appeared to have been cut by flowing water crisscrossed the surface. The conditions recorded by Mariner 9, a carbon dioxide atmosphere with a pressure of between 2.8 millibars at the equator and 8.9 millibars at mid-latitudes, precluded the presence of liquid water on Mars. It simply could not exist at a pressure less than 1/100th that of earth's atmospheric pressure. However, the channels were clear evidence that water had flowed on Mars in the distant past and raised the hopes of those seeking life on Mars.

MARINER 9 LIVES ON

In early 1972 Mariner 9 continued to sail flawlessly around the planet. By February 11 scientists considered that Mariner 9 had fulfilled its primary mapping mission, charting most of the planet at a 1-to-2 km (roughly 1-mile) resolution and about two percent of the planet at a 200-to-300 m

(656-to-984-ft) resolution. The craft would now patrol Mars looking at scientifically interesting targets.

Originally designed for a 90-day lifetime in Mars orbit, Mariner 9 proved as durable as its previous sister craft. Nine months after arriving, it was still scouting Mars. Between August and October, 1972, Mars was behind the sun, as viewed from earth, rendering control of the craft impossible. Upon emerging, Mariner obediently responded to controllers and sent back more photographs on October 17. However, the craft's attitude control gas was nearly exhausted.

As part of a program to monitor long-term seasonal changes on Mars, Mariner was directed to take another series of fifteen photographs of the Syrtis Major and Tharsis regions, areas where cloud structure and color changes had been charted from earth. However, when it was time to play back these photos, Mariner 9 was unable to lock its antenna on earth. On the probe's 698th orbit, the nitrogen supply for the control jets ran out and Mariner slowly tumbled in Mars orbit, its mission now over. The last of the 45,960 commands sent to the intrepid explorer shut off its transmitter.

The irony of Mariner 9's quiet end is that it need not have happened so soon. Indeed, while the craft lasted not just 90, but 349 earth days in Mars orbit and returned 7329 photographs, at one time there was a plan which would have extended Mariner 9's lifetime another year. A scheme had been devised to tap into unused nitrogen from the retrorocket propulsion system. This involved installing a pipe and valve between the propulsion system gas supply to the attitude control system. This modification would have cost a mere $30,000. However, merciless penny-pinching by Congress, the Nixon White House, and the Office of Management and Budget eliminated the cheap modification. As a result, $150 million worth of science from Mars orbit was needlessly lost.

Mariner 9's accomplishments were still impressive. It had beaten a Soviet spacecraft into Mars orbit, no small achievement in the politically charged times of the cold war. More importantly, it had mapped Mars at a greater resolution than the moon had been charted as seen from earth. But now more Mars mysteries abounded, not because scientists knew so little about the planet, but because they had been overwhelmed by Mariner's discoveries.

NASA proudly pointed out that Mariner 9 had sent back 54 billion bits of data about Mars. This was enough information to fill the entire text of the Encyclopaedia Britannica thirty-six times! Mariner 9 had returned twenty-seven times as much Martian data as the three previous Mars

Mariners combined. It was getting progressively harder to drink in the new volumes of data about the strange world, and the Viking missions yet to come promised a greater deluge of data. New charts of Mars created from this mountain of data were put to use immediately. On November 6, 1972, five preliminary landing sites were chosen for the next American Mars venture, the Viking missions.

SOVIETS PREPARE LANDERS AND A SURPRISE

Three spacecraft were also prepared for an extraordinarily ambitious 1971 Russian Mars program which would fly at the same time as Mariner 9. However, Soviet scientists only admitted the existence of two of them, both orbiters which were to carry landers. The third probe was to be an orbiter only which carried no lander, similar to the failed 1969 Mars craft. At the time, the existence of the third Mars craft was kept a secret by government edict. The secret orbiter was to be part of a space propaganda effort.

The two Soviet landers would arrive at Mars after the planned American Mariner orbiters. The twin probes were to follow a lengthier trajectory to allow a slower atmospheric entry speed for their landers. Because of this, the Soviet government ordered the Lavochkin Association to make the third planetary orbiter capable of beating the 1971 Mariners into Mars orbit. Thus, a craft was created with a mass of just under 3000 kg (6614 lb). Being lighter without a landing capsule, its mission was to fly a faster trajectory and enter Mars orbit first for the politically motivated goal of gaining another spaceflight "first" for the Soviet Union.

The optimal 1971 planetary alignment allowed the other two orbiters to carry a Mars landing capsule similar in design to the Luna 9 moon lander. Thus the two 4650-kg (10,251-lb) probes were a new spacecraft combination. The main portion consisted of a spacecraft bus which would enter Mars orbit while a descent module carrying a sterilized planetary landing capsule entered the atmosphere.

The new Mars spacecraft bus was built around a 1.8-m (5.9-ft)-diameter cylindrical body which housed tanks for the nitric acid and amine-based propellants used by the course correction and Mars orbit insertion rocket engine. The cylindrical section provided the structural support for attaching other elements of the craft. Extending on each side were twin 2.3 × 1.4 m (7.5 × 4.6 ft) solar panels spanning a total of 5.9 m (19.4 ft). On one side of the bus was a 2-m (6.6-ft)-diameter directional, high-gain communications antenna and the omnidirectional antenna. Attached to the solar panel supports was a temperature control system which could use either radiators on the shadow side or heaters on the sun side to circulate inert gas into the instrument compartment.

The base of the spacecraft flared into a 2.3-m (7.5-ft) toroidal pressurized section which housed the command, communication and navigational equipment. This torus surrounded the KTDU-425A rocket engine used for course corrections and deceleration to enter Mars orbit. The engine's thrust could be varied between 1000 and 2000 kg (2205 and 4410 lb). Navigational sensors mounted on the instrument compartment looked for the sun, earth, and Canopus, a bright star in the southern sky. According to engineers at the Babakin Design Bureau, the design allowed for the lightest weight, best access during manufacturing and testing and the least interference with the scientific instruments.

RUSSIAN ORBITERS TO STUDY MARS

A total of eleven separate experiments were to be performed by all three Russian orbiters. Seven would look at Mars exclusively, three would study interplanetary space, and one, in conjunction with the French, would study the sun. The scientific goals of the orbiters were to measure the surface and subsurface temperature, surface relief, water vapor content of the atmosphere, the photometric properties of the surface and atmosphere, and to investigate the ultraviolet emission of the atmosphere.

All orbiters carried cameras which had both a wide-angle and a four-degree-field-of-view telephoto lens. Twelve exposures were to be taken on photographic film and automatically developed on board. The images would be transmitted by a 1000 × 1000-pixel facsimile scanner.

The infrared, visible light, and ultraviolet instruments were all located in a common housing called the photoradiometric complex. An infrared photometer would check the water vapor content of the Martian atmosphere. The instrument had enough sensitivity to measure the water vapor in one m (3.3 ft) of earth's atmosphere. This was thought to be roughly equal to the amount of water vapor along the entire thickness of the Martian atmosphere. Another infrared photometer was to measure sunlight reflected from the surface to calculate the density of the atmosphere below the spacecraft. A third infrared instrument, a one-kg (2.2-lb) palm-sized radiometer was to record the planet's temperature. Included too was a visible-light photometer that was to observe the limb and twilight areas of the planet to study the distribution of dust in the Martian atmosphere. The ultraviolet spectrometer would view parallel to the horizon to look for three dark oxygen absorption lines and a similar dark hydrogen absorption line in spectra of the atmosphere. A small radio telescope would also scan the surface in the 3.5-cm radio band to determine the subsoil temperature and density to a depth of 30 to 50 cm (1 to 1.6 ft).

The two lander-carrying orbiters were identical except that the last one launched would carry part of the French "Stereo" experiment which would study solar radio emissions at the one-m wavelength. Data from this experiment were to be compared with similar data gathered on earth to measure the direction and three-dimensional structure of the solar wind.

THE MARS LANDER

The low atmospheric density of Mars complicated the design of the lander, but Soviet scientists worked out ingenious ways to overcome this. The spherical landing capsule was nested in a torus-shaped parachute container which in turn was tucked into a 2.9-m (9.5-ft)-diameter aeroshield, a conical heat shield, which resembled a Chinese "coolie hat." When the assembly entered the atmosphere, the aeroshield would both act as a heat shield and increase the lander's cross section for additional drag in the thin Martian atmosphere. When slowed to near supersonic speed, a decelerometer would activate the parachute system. A rocket-propelled drogue chute would then stabilize the capsule and pull out the main parachute in a reefed, or partially opened, condition. After slowing to Mach 1, the 15-m (49.2-ft)-diameter chute would fully open and the aeroshield would be jettisoned.

Because the Martian atmospheric density is equal to earth's at a 35-km (22-mile) altitude, it is too thin for a parachute to slow the capsule to a safe landing speed. To solve this problem, Lavochkin engineers used a simple alternative. While still falling at 90 m (295 ft) per second at an altitude of 30 m (100 ft), a ground contact sensor hanging below the lander would trigger a 4500-kg (10,000-lb) thrust retrorocket attached to the parachute lines. Firing for one second, this would cushion the lander's impact. After landing, a smaller rocket would pull the parachute off to one side so it would not cover the landing capsule.

The lander was built to withstand an impact shock of one-thousand *g*s and was encased in a hard shell with shock absorbing material surrounding the interior instruments. The capsule had an offset center of gravity to make it roll into an upright position. The shell's upper half was designed to split open into four petals to stabilize the spacecraft on the surface. Four pop-up antennae were to send signals to the orbiter for relay to earth.

Each lander was known as an Automatic Mars Station (AMS) and was to operate for three to five days. Scientific instruments included atmospheric temperature and pressure sensors, a mass spectrometer for chemical analysis of the atmosphere, and a wind anemometer. Other devices would measure the chemical and physical properties of the Martian soil and take stereoscopic panoramic photographs of the surface. No biological or life-detection experiments were carried as Soviet scientists considered such tasks "too complex."[2]

Each lander was carefully sterilized before leaving earth to prevent contamination of Mars with earth microorganisms. Additionally, after completion of its investigations, a thermite bomb, a type of incendiary device, was to be exploded inside each lander to destroy any possible organisms which escaped sterilization.

In 1990, Dr. Alexander Kermurjian, from the Industrial Transportation Institute, revealed that the 1971 Mars landers carried the first robotic rovers to the Martian surface. For twenty years, the existence of these small tethered robots was omitted from descriptions of the lander. The small, flat, box-shaped rovers were to move on the Martian surface by means of a shuffling action between two sets of articulated skis and had a range of 15 m (49 ft). Two thin sensor bars located in front of the robot would detect obstacles. A rudimentary artificial intelligence would allow them to determine on which side the obstacle lay, then to command the craft to back up and go around the object. Each rover carried a dynamic penetrometer to measure the bearing strength of the soil and a densitometer to measure soil density.

SOVIETS REACH FOR MARS GLORY

At Tyuratam in early May, an SL-12 Proton also stood ready to launch the lightweight secret Soviet Mars orbiter to race the Mariners to the red planet. On May 10, 1971, the booster successfully carried the probe into a 134 × 187 km (83 × 116 mi) earth parking orbit. Apparently the Galactic

Ghoul was not satisfied with placing only Mariner 8 in a watery grave. When Soviet announcements identified the craft by the cover name of Cosmos 419, it was clear that their first 1971 Mars probe had failed to leave earth orbit. After fifty-one hours in space, Cosmos 419 fell back to earth from its low unstable orbit and the secret Mars orbiter burned in the atmosphere.

It was not until twenty years later that the truth was published in Russia confirming that Cosmos 419 was to be a fleet-footed Mars orbiter designed to beat Mariner. Stranger still was why Cosmos 419 never left earth orbit.

After entering orbit, the Proton booster's escape stage was to ignite 90 minutes later to propel the Mars probe away from earth. At the appointed time, this did not take place. Engineers from the Institute of Mechanics who designed the control system quickly discovered the reason. In their haste to prepare the launch, instead of setting the engine control computer timer for 1.5 hr, it had been set for 1.5 years. The otherwise healthy booster and spacecraft were obediently awaiting the timer's signal, which would not come for another 550 days. The Galactic Ghoul worked in strange ways.

Compounding the embarrassment was the fact that part of the French Stereo solar instrument was also aboard the stranded Mars orbiter. Desiring the greatest baseline separation between the twin Stereo units, the Soviets had included them on the first and last of the three planned Mars launches. Rather than admit to a launch failure, Soviet scientists told their French collaborators that the unit was aboard the next successfully launched Mars probe, but through a Soviet fault, it had not been turned on.

After the Cosmos 419 fiasco, extra care was taken with the next launch. Mars 2 lifted off at 7:22:49 P.M., Moscow time, May, 19, 1971. Making one revolution in a 137 × 172-km (85 × 107-mi) parking orbit inclined 51.52 degrees, the escape stage ignited at 8:59 P.M. and propelled Mars 2 into interplanetary space. This was the first successful planetary launch by the 1,002,000-kg (2,209,010-lb) thrust Proton booster.

Mars 3, successfully followed at 6:26:30 P.M., May 28, 1971.

INTERPLANETARY CRUISE

During their 470 million-km (292 million-mi) flight to Mars, the Soviet craft investigated the solar wind and cosmic rays while transmitting data at frequency of 928.4 MHz. More than 230 communications sessions were held and about 5000 commands were transmitted to both probes.

Mars 2 performed three mid-course corrections in flight. The first occurred at 4:30 A.M., June 17, while 7 million km (4.35 million mi) from earth. Two others followed on November 20 and November 27. The final correction, just hours before planetary encounter, was controlled entirely by the Mars spacecraft's own computers.

Mars 3 performed its initial course correction at 5:10 A.M., June 8, 1971. The craft carried out extensive studies of the earth's magnetic tail, the extended magnetic field blown away from the earth by the solar wind, and established that the earth's magnetic field disturbs the ionized gases flowing outward from the sun at distances up to 20 million km (12 million mi) from earth. This finding changed accepted concepts about the extended structure of the earth's magnetic field.

While the position of the spacecraft could be determined with great accuracy by radio tracking, the exact astronomical position of Mars was unknown by several thousand kilometers. To target the Mars lander required extreme accuracy. The Mars spacecraft had to measure the position of the planet Mars relative to itself autonomously and guide the lander toward the planet with an accuracy unobtainable from earth. The rocket burn to properly align the craft for entry into Mars orbit was done on the basis of the spacecraft performing an optical survey of Mars and comparing the planet's location with the sun and the star Canopus. Data from the survey were used for setting the angle of the navigation gyroscopes as well as to calculate the direction and duration of the course-correction engine burn.

The thin atmosphere of Mars made accuracy vital. An entry angle of ten degrees made the lander's deceleration path through the atmosphere as long as possible. If the lander entered at too shallow an angle, it would not slow down and would skip back into space. If the entry angle was to steep, it would descend too fast for the parachute to operate.

STORM DOGS RUSSIAN PLANS

Soviet planetary scientists had concluded that, since Venus was obscured by permanent cloud cover, it would be best studied by landing instruments directly on its surface. Mars on the other hand had a transparent atmosphere and thus would be open to the eyes of instruments in orbit. The irony of this assumption was that when the spacecraft arrived, the planet was still totally obscured by the largest planet-wide dust storm in modern history. Dust clouds had been kicked as high as 70 km (43.5 mi) by winds blowing at several hundred kilometers per hr.

After a 192-day flight, Mars 2 arrived on November 27, 1971. Unlike the American Viking Mars probes then under development, the Soviet spacecraft did not carry enough fuel to enter Mars orbit with its lander attached. The craft thus lacked the flexibility of waiting out the dust storm while safely in orbit. Mars 2 was committed to a go-for-broke landing no matter what the surface conditions were.

Four and a half hours before arriving, the Mars 2 lander separated using a small solid-propellant rocket. The landing capsule entered the Martian atmosphere at a velocity of 21,600 km (13,422 mi) per hr and the aeroshield heated to 1000°C (1832°F). After aerodynamic braking, the drogue parachute was released while still descending at supersonic speed. This was the first use of supersonic velocity parachutes with a spacecraft. After deployment of the main parachute, touchdown occurred three minutes after atmospheric entry at Martian coordinates 45 degrees South, 58 degrees East, in an area 500 km (310 mi) southwest of Hellas.

The Mars 2 lander was thought to have landed at a velocity of 20 m (66 ft) per sec with an impact of 500 gs. There was no contact with the capsule after landing and it is assumed that the planet-wide dust storm overwhelmed the lander and caused it to crash. While the landing was a scientific failure, the Soviet Mars 2 was the first man-made object to impact the planet and carried the usual commemorative hammer-and-sickle.

Conflicting statements have been issued about the payloads of Mars 2 and 3. Shortly after launch, it was said the two craft had identical instrumented landers. However, after Mars 2 crashed, it was said this lander carried only commemorative memorabilia celebrating the first landing on Mars.

The Mars 2 orbiter retrorocket fired at 11:19 P.M., November 27, 1971, placing the craft in an initial 1380 × 25,000-km (860 × 15,500-mi), 18-hr orbit, inclined 48.54 degrees.

MARS 3 ENCOUNTERS TROUBLE

Mars 3 reached the red planet on December 2, 1971, after 188 days of flight. During the interplanetary cruise, the craft's fuel system developed a leak and the orbiter's engine had insufficient fuel to place it in the desired orbit. After a short engine burn, Mars 3 entered a highly elliptical and nearly useless 1530 × 214,500-km (951 × 133,290-mi) orbit, inclined 60 degrees, with a period of 12 days, 16 hr.

Four and a half hours before entering Mars orbit, the Mars 3 landing capsule was jettisoned at 12:14 P.M. A small solid fuel rocket fired 15 minutes later to change the lander's course to intercept Mars. The Mars 3 orbiter's path was then adjusted to place it in the most advantageous position to relay the signals from the lander.

The second lander reached the surface at 4:47 P.M. The landing was in a 1500-km (932-mile)-diameter depression in the cratered southern hemisphere between the Electris and Phaetontis regions at coordinates 45 degrees South and 158 West. This was not far from the annual limit of the southern polar cap. Here, because of the lower altitude, the atmospheric pressure would be greater, allowing the braking parachute to work better. Soviet scientists had assumed this area of Mars was covered with "something resembling the sands of earth."[3]

SURFACE TELEVISION PHOTOS FAIL

Upon landing, a sequencer started the Mars 3 lander's instruments, tried to open the capsule's protective petals and extend the radio antennae and a telescopic sensor arm to the surface. Ninety seconds after landing, the capsule began to transmit a television photo from the surface. The signal was recorded by tape recorders aboard the Mars 3 orbiter. But the historic first photo from the surface of another planet never arrived on earth.

On December 7, the Soviets revealed that a test image was transmitted in preparation for imaging the surface, but after 20 seconds, the lander's signal inexplicably died. Only a small part of the panoramic frame was transmitted, but no image details could be seen. A spokesman stated that the clear, static-free signal was received on two channels simultaneously and the exact cause of the signal's loss was a mystery.

Likely the craft was heavily damaged by a crashlanding during the dust storm. High winds had blown the capsule's parachute as it fell and it crashed with a high horizontal velocity. After being dashed to the ground, the capsule's cover mechanisms were probably unable to open.

For a week, controllers tried to re-establish contact with the lander. Finally an announcement stated: "It is too early to say what stopped the transmission. It could be due to the local peculiarities of the landing area, which are absolutely unknown, or to the strong dust storm that was taking place at the time."[4] In an attempt to find out what happened to the Mars 3 lander, Mariner 9 photographs of the landing area were transported to Moscow via diplomatic pouch.

MARS COOPERATION BEGINS

With both Mars 2 and 3 and Mariner 9 in orbit around the red planet, a special teletype hot line was set up between the U.S. and the U.S.S.R. to share data gathered. In January 1971 the Working Group on Interplanetary Exploration was established between NASA and the Soviet Academy of Sciences. As American involvement in Vietnam was winding down, Soviet-American cold war tensions eased and scientific cooperation between the superpowers was initiated. However, the Soviets requested that their hotline data not be published.

As three orbiters shared the Martian skies, the American craft concentrated on photography of the planet while the Soviet craft used non-imaging techniques to study Mars. Mariner was capable of investigations the Soviet craft were not, and the Mars craft studied the planet in ways not possible from Mariner. The craft from both nations thus complemented each other and expanded our knowledge of Mars. Under the agreement between NASA and the Academy of Sciences, Mars 2 and 3 data would be swapped for Mariner 9 pictures and maps at a meeting in Moscow on April 15, 1973.

MARS STUDIED FROM ORBIT

Two weeks after entering orbit, both Mars 2 and 3 were taking surface photos, but because of inflexible preprogramming, all twelve exposures taken by each spacecraft were ruined by the great dust storm obscuring the planet. On January 22 three featureless pictures of Mars returned by the Mars 2 orbiter were shown on Moscow television. Only a single photo has ever been published—also a featureless view taken from a great distance by Mars 3. The Soviets later downplayed the stroke of bad luck by stating that the planetary photography was only a "secondary role" in the mission.

While the Mars 2 orbiter was in a more advantageous orbit to study Mars, its telemetry was of poor quality and most of the planetary data were lost. Mars 3, trapped in an unplanned extended orbit, spent most of its time too far from the planet for useful observations. The craft was limited to seven close passes of the planet during its useful lifetime, restricting the data-gathering period to about two hours.

SOVIET PROBES GLEAN PLANETARY SCIENCE

After a month of orbital tracking, Soviet scientists reported that Mars was fifty percent more oblate, or flattened, at its poles than the earth. Just as Mariner 9's orbit had been altered by the uneven Martian gravity, Mars 2's perigee was lowered by 150 km (93.2 mi) and Mars 3's orbit was altered by a similar amount.

Soviet infrared detectors showed that Mars was an incredibly dry place. If all the water in the Martian atmosphere precipitated onto the surface, it would produce a layer just over the thickness of a human hair.

For three orbits before the storm ended and four orbits after, Mars 3 also studied the huge 1971 dust storm which completely enveloped Mars. Soviet scientists concluded that the winds were not constant but occurred only in the initial phase of the storm. Dust particles 10 to 15 microns in size fell quickly while the smaller particles took months to fall.

Infrared photometer studies showed that transparency of the dust increased as the infrared wavelength increased. The clouds were visible in the blue (0.36 micron) wavelengths but were invisible in the red (0.7 micron) wavelengths. This indicated that most of the dust particles were about a micron in size and numbered about 100 million per square cm. Spectroscopic analysis showed the dust particles were about sixty percent silicon. The estimated total amount of dust in the atmosphere was ten billion tons.

Studies of the global cooling effects of the Martian dust storm were instrumental in understanding the concept of "nuclear winter." Data gathered at Mars led to theories about global cooling and plant life extinction on earth as a result of smoke and dust which would be suspended in earth's atmosphere after many simultaneous nuclear explosions.

During the Martian dust storm, surface temperatures dropped 20 to 30°C (36 to 54°F) while the atmosphere warmed up as the suspended dust absorbed solar heat. When the storm ended, surface temperatures in the summer southern hemisphere were 13°C (55°F) while the winter northern hemisphere was –93°C (–135°F). The north polar cap had cooled to –110°C (–166°F). Several nightside temperature anomalies were noted with areas 20 to 25°C (36 to 45°F) higher than surrounding regions.

Orbiter observations showed that the surface cooled quickly after sunset, indicating that it was covered with dry dust or sand in a rarefied atmosphere. The dark areas were warmer than the lighter areas and, in some cases, the dark areas took a longer time to cool, suggesting that these areas were rock. Other measurements showed that at a depth of 20 to 30 cm (8 to 12 in), the temperature of the soil varied little between day and night and demonstrated the low heat conductivity of the soil.

At 100 km (62 mi) altitude, the carbon dioxide of the Martian atmosphere is broken up by solar ultraviolet radiation into carbon monoxide molecules and oxygen atoms. Ultraviolet radiation also breaks up water vapor into its gaseous components and above 300 to 400 km (186 to 249 mi) the atmosphere is composed primarily of atomic hydrogen. Ultraviolet photometers on both Soviet craft showed that traces of atomic oxygen were still found between 700 and 1000 km (435 and 621 mi) in concentrations of 100 atoms per cubic cm. The same detectors showed that atomic hydrogen from the Martian atmosphere was still present above 10,000 km (6214 mi).

Photos from the Soviet orbiters showed an unusual twilight phenomenon: an air glow extending 200 (124 mi) km beyond the terminator. Some of the photos also showed a layered structure in the atmosphere caused by dust blown to high altitudes. The Martian ionosphere, as measured by repeated radio occultation experiments, was shown to be about ten times less dense than earth's ionosphere, reaching peak density at 140 km (87 mi) altitude compared to earth's 300 km (186 mi) ionospheric altitude. At 110 km (68 mi), a second ionospheric concentration was observed with a density three times less than the higher layer.

Mars 2 and 3 indicated a weak Martian magnetic field of about 30 gammas, approximately 1/1000th that of earth's, exists in the near vicinity of the planet. This is only several times the intensity of the interplanetary magnetic field.

The Mars 2 and 3 orbiters operated until August 24, 1972, when their missions were declared complete. Mars 2 made 362 orbits of the planet while Mars 3 completed only 20. Mars 2 and 3 had each traveled nearly a billion kilometers (621 million mi) and had together communicated with earth a total of 687 times, 448 of these while in Mars orbit.

The big Martian political and scientific prize, a successful landing, was still up for grabs. Funding delays had stretched the launch of the American Viking Mars landing program from 1973 into 1975, giving the Russians one more chance to reach the surface first.

A SOVIET MARS FLOTILLA

After the Mars 2 and 3 missions met with less than expected success, Soviet scientists immediately began planning new missions for 1973. They announced in advance that the new probes would again attempt a landing and would carry out much of the research attempted by Mars 2 and 3. The ambitious new missions represented a massive effort to achieve a Martian success prior to the planned 1975 launch of the American Viking probes.

The 1973 Mars launch window was less favorable than the last with earth and Mars separated by additional millions of kilometers. Because Mars was at a greater distance from the sun at launch time, the Proton booster had to accelerate its Mars probe to a higher velocity. At the time this meant that the Soviets could loft either an orbiter probe or a landing probe, but not both at the same time on the same rocket.

Four Russian probes were prepared for the red planet in 1973. The first two craft carried full propellant loads to brake into Mars orbit, but carried no landers. They were to study the planet from space and were to relay information from the landers which followed later. The second two probes carried landers but were stripped of the two-ton fuel load in order to carry the heavy landers. Rationed to only 300 kg (661 lb) of fuel, these craft would eject their landers during a planetary fly-by. The descent modules were similar to those of Mars 2 and 3, but this time data would be transmitted to earth in real time via the orbiters instead of being recorded for later playback. This would prevent the loss of atmospheric data in case the landers crashed. Soviet officials stated that the landers, as before, would not carry life-detection instruments.

Mars 4, 5, 6, and 7 were all launched within a three-week period by SL-12 Proton boosters from Tyuratam. For the first time, all Soviet planetary launches succeeded in leaving the earth during a launch window. The technical effort to launch the squadron of probes was enormous, and the final probe, Mars 7, was launched with just hours to spare.

MARS 4 ORBITER LEADS THE PACK

The 4536-kg (10,000-lb) Mars 4 was launched at 10:31 A.M. on July 21, 1973. After accelerating from an earth parking orbit, the initial launch velocity was 11,496 m (37,720 ft) per sec. Although this was about 300 m (1000 ft) per sec faster than Mars 2 and 3, transit time between earth and Mars was two weeks longer than during the 1971 flights.

Instruments carried by the orbiters were similar to those aboard Mars 2 and 3. Additionally, the new Mars craft carried a panoramic survey scanning telephotometer to image Mars, a gamma ray spectrometer, two radio instruments to study the ionosphere, instruments to study electrostatic plasma fields, and the French "Stereo 2" solar instrument.

Mars 4 and 5 also carried two film cameras. One, called "Vega," had a 52-mm, f/2.8 lens with a 35.5-degree field of view. The second, called "Zufar," had a 350-mm, f/2.5 lens with a 5.5-degree field of view. The cameras could resolve an area 1000 m (3280 ft) square and 100 m (328 ft) square respectively at 1931 km (1200 mi). Both cameras transmitted their images with a television readout called the phototelevision unit (PTU) similar to that on Mars 2 and 3. The Mars 4 cameras used a red filter while those on Mars 5 took color photographs by combining images taken through red, blue, green, and orange filters. Following the embarrassing episode in which Mars 2 and 3 automatically photographed a featureless dust storm, Mars 4 and 5 were modified to snap their pictures only by command from earth. A second imaging device was a line-scanning instrument for obtaining 30-degree-high panoramic pictures in the visible and near-infrared spectra.

On July 30, Mars 4 made a successful course correction. However, the probe's engine fuel plumbing suffered a malfunction. After a 204-day flight to the planet, Mars 4's retrorocket failed to fire upon arrival because the engine's fuel had leaked out during the interplanetary cruise. The craft sped past the planet on February 10, 1974, at an altitude of 2,200 km (1367 mi) and continued in solar orbit.

Realizing in advance that the retrorocket was useless, spacecraft controllers· programmed Mars 4's camera to photograph the planet during the unplanned fly-by. Soviet scientists were able to salvage one swath of photographs and some radio occultation data as the probe flew past Mars.

SECOND ORBITER FOLLOWS

Mars 5 left earth at 9:56 P.M., July 25, 1973, and also carried no landing capsule. At 11:15 P.M., the Proton's escape stage propelled Mars 5 toward the red planet. A week later, on August 3, the craft performed a successful course correction. Mars 5 arrived at 6:45 P.M., February 12, 1974, after 202 days in space. The probe entered a 1755 × 32,555 km (1090 × 20,180 mi) orbit with a period of 24 hr, 53 min, inclined 35.33 degrees. The craft was to act as a relay for the Mars 7 lander.

A total of sixty pictures were returned by Mars 4 and 5 in a nine-day period. All of the photos were of the same general area, from roughly 5 degrees North and 330 degrees West to 20 degrees South and 130 degrees West. A panorama released by the Soviets showed a 3200-km (1988-mi)-wide view centered on Mare Erythraeum in the planet's southern hemisphere. Flat, shallow, wind-eroded craters were visible, ranging from 8 to 160 km (5 to 100 mi) in diameter. Also visible were more of the mysterious river-like channels first charted by Mariner 9. The orbiter also relayed color photographs of the Martian terrain with resolution approximately equal to that of Mariner 9. Color photography by Mariner 9 had been curtailed by a filter wheel malfunction, and photos from Mars 5 showed the first direct evidence that the surface of Mars was bright orange.

Contact with Mars 5 was prematurely lost after only 22 orbits because of loss of pressurization in the craft's instrument section where the radio transmitter was housed.

TWO LANDERS DEPART FOR MARS

The 3495-kg (7705-lb) Mars 6 was launched into an earth parking orbit at 8:46 P.M., August 5, 1973. Eighty-one minutes later the craft was accelerated toward Mars. Mars 7 followed at 8:00 P.M., August 9, and lifted off just hours before the Martian launch window closed for the next 25 months. On August 13 Mars 6 successfully performed its course correction while Mars 7 performed a similar maneuver on August 16.

Instruments carried by the Mars 6 and 7 fly-by modules included a telephotometer to image Mars, a magnetometer, solar wind detector, micrometeor detector, cosmic ray detector, and a solar radiometer to study solar radio emissions. The landers were similar to those carried by Mars 2 and 3, and had a mass of 450 kg (992 lb). They also carried a television imaging system, a tethered minirover, and other instruments similar to Mars 2 and 3.

Having passed Mars 6 en route, Mars 7 arrived three days ahead of its twin. On March 9, 1974, after 212 days of flight, Mars 7 prepared to eject its lander toward the eastern rim of Argyre Planitia, near the crater Galle. However, a malfunction in either the attitude control system or the lander's solid propellant rocket caused the landing capsule to miss the planet by 1300 km (780 mi), rendering the mission a complete failure.

A FINAL RUSSIAN MARS LANDING ATTEMPT

Mars 6, following a slower trajectory, eventually trailed behind Mars 7 and arrived last. After 219 days in space, while still 55,000 km (34,177 mi) from Mars, it ejected its lander at 8:02 A.M., March 12. Four hours later at 12:06 P.M., as the fly-by spacecraft passed Mars at 16,000 km (9942 mi), the descent capsule entered the atmosphere at 5.6 km (3.48 mi) per sec.

By 12:08:32 P.M. the lander had slowed to 600 m (1968 ft) per sec and the automatic parachute sequence began. As it descended under the parachute for 148 sec, it returned the first direct readings from the thin Martian atmosphere. However, for the fourth time, a landing success eluded the Soviets. Telemetry ceased abruptly when the landing retrorocket fired. At the time contact was lost, the spacecraft was descending at 61 m (200 ft) per sec. High winds were thought to be a factor in the crash as over a decade later, the Soviets admitted that the lander descended with an unplanned and very high horizontal velocity. A major loss was the data from the lander's mass spectrometer which was used to determine atmospheric composition. The data were too voluminous for real-time transmission and were recorded for later playback.

The impact occurred at 24 degrees South and 19 degrees West on the southern boundary of a dark region called Margaritifer Sinus. This landing area is centered in an area from which the Soviets had requested Mariner 9 data. The Soviets had also requested Mariner 9 data about an area near 43 degrees South and 42 degrees West. Presumably this was the destination of Mars 7.

DISAPPOINTING MISSIONS YIELD LIMITED RESULTS

Of the four craft sent toward Mars, only Mars 5 completed a signifi-cant part of its mission. Only limited fly-by data were returned from Mars

4. After failing to enter Martian orbit, Mars 4, 6, and 7 continued in heliocentric orbit and returned data on solar and cosmic radiation. Instruments aboard Mars 4 and 5 studied the interplanetary medium and showed that the solar system was filled with neutral hydrogen at a density of one atom per ten cm^3 of space.

Solar plasma detectors aboard Mars 5 discovered three zones of plasma near Mars. The first was composed of the undisturbed solar wind, the second thermalized (heated) plasma behind the bow shock, and the third small proton currents in the tail of the magnetosphere. Magnetometer data coupled with the plasma detector data showed that the solar wind is deflected from the planet by a slight intrinsic magnetic field. The leading edge of the solar wind bow shock occurs at 350 km (217 mi) above the surface.

The density of the atmosphere and ionosphere were measured on both the sunlit and dark sides of Mars by radio occultation experiments during the fly-bys of Mars 4 and 6 as well as on a single orbit by Mars 5. The experiments showed Mars has a previously undetected nightside ionosphere.

Mars 5 studies compared to Mars 3 studies during the dust storm two years earlier showed four times more water vapor in the atmosphere, with two and threefold variations within several hundred kilometers. Mars 5 also showed that water loss from Mars was higher than the previously estimated 450,000 liters (125,000 gallons) per day.

Gamma ray spectrometry from orbit determined that the content of uranium, thorium, and potassium in the Martian soil was similar to terrestrial mafic rock such as pyroxenes and olivenes.

Velocity data gathered by a decelerometer aboard the Mars 6 lander and changes in the Doppler shift of the probe's radio signal allowed calculations of the structure of the Martian atmosphere between 82 and 12 km (51 and 7.5 mi). The data showed that the lander impacted the surface 3389 km (2105.9 mi) from the center of the planet. Temperature at the site was –46°C (–51°F).

SOVIET DATA INFLUENCE AMERICAN VIKING PLANS

Engineering data from the electrically driven pump which supplied atmospheric gases to the Mars 6 lander's mass spectrometer suggested something unusual in Martian atmosphere. The electrical current needed to run the pump showed an unexpected increase as the capsule descended, implying that the pump had to work harder than anticipated. This further meant that one in three molecules of the Martian atmosphere was an inert gas, not carbon dioxide. Soviet scientists assumed the reason for the current increase to be the presence of argon gas. Unfortunately, the destruction of the lander prevented transmission of the data gathered by the mass spectrometer which would have resolved this speculation.

Large amounts of argon in the Martian atmosphere would adversely affect the descent sequence and atmospheric mass spectrometer of the Viking landers. As a result of the Mars 6 argon data, changes were made in the American craft to compensate for the presence of the gas. When the Vikings finally landed two years later, they found Mars 6's calculated argon percentage to be wrong. The entire mystery had been caused by an instrument malfunction.

AN END TO SOVIET MARS ACTIVITY

If the Mars 4 through 7 missions had been successful, they would have preceded the Viking landings by two years and achieved important propaganda victories for the Soviet Union after their embarrassing defeat in the man-to-the-moon race. Because of the multiple failures, the data obtained were miniscule compared to the data obtained from Mariner 9 two years before.

The American-Soviet interplanetary cooperation begun during the Mars 2 and 3 missions was expanded during the new missions. Photographs from Mars 4 and 5 were shared almost immediately as were the unexpected argon data which had implications for the future Viking landings.

As the next Mars launch window approached in 1975, western scientists expected the Soviets to try again for Mars. Because the orbital geometry between earth and Mars was similar to the previous launch window, it was expected that the 1975 attempts would redeem the Mars quads of 1973.

The Russian attempts to land on Mars seemed to imitate the attempts to soft-land on the moon in the mid-1960s. Lunas 5, 6, 7, and 8 all failed. The fifth attempt with Luna 9 succeeded. Would the fifth Soviet attempt to reach the Martian surface succeed? French scientists said "it is practically certain" that the Soviets would try again.[5]

The optimum launch dates for Mars in 1975 were from mid-September to early October. Two orbiters were expected to be launched first, followed two weeks later by two craft carrying landers. The four were expected to arrive at Mars in the second and fourth weeks of May. American Viking Mars landing plans called for a touchdown on July 4, 1976, so even after the heartbreak of four landing failures, the Soviets still had a chance to land a working probe on the surface of Mars before the Americans.

But this was not to be. Vikings 1 and 2 left earth alone in 1975. When they arrived at Mars the following summer, no Soviet probes joined them. At the same time, Soviet lunar explorations were curtailed and plans to probe the outer planets were canceled. The cost of planetary exploration was apparently too much for the Soviet government and the Russians simply gave up on Mars for the next decade.

VIKING OPTIMISM HIDES DARK PLANETARY FUTURE

The Soviets were not the only ones backing away from Mars exploration in the mid-1970s. As the two Viking probes prepared to make America's first landing on another planet and search for life on Mars, no follow-up explorations had been approved by the government. While most scientists thought this was only a temporary situation, Viking would prove to be America's final shot at Mars for the next two decades.

Viking was born in the heyday of NASA's race to land men on the moon. As an outgrowth of the Mariner program, it was originally called the "Titan Mars 1973 Orbiter and Lander," with Titan referring to the launch rocket. By the time Congress approved the project in December 1968, it had an identity of its own—Viking.

Carried along by the political, bureaucratic, and scientific inertia of Apollo, NASA assumed that manned expeditions to Mars would follow the Apollo moon flights. Viking was seen as the vanguard of future manned expeditions to Mars just as Apollo had followed Ranger, Surveyor, and Lunar Orbiter to the moon. But NASA and the interested public underestimated how fickle Congress and the White House were with regard to expensive, large-scale space programs. Even as the first political victories were scored by the initial Apollo landings on the moon, subsequent science-oriented manned lunar landings were canceled, victims of the expense of the prolonged Vietnam war and burgeoning federal social welfare programs. Future planetary exploration programs would have to fight to avoid a similar fate.

Another complication clouded the American planetary exploration outlook. In the 1970s, NASA set its goal as achieving affordable, reliable transportation to get scientific and commercial payloads into space. This goal was to include expansion of future planetary explorations by providing routine access to space. Thus NASA placed all of its "eggs in one basket" by backing the manned, reusable space shuttle as America's only rocket transportation system for achieving space flight. On paper, the plan looked good and bureaucratic promises assured that planetary exploration dreams would be fulfilled by means of the shuttle.

But, in reality, perfecting the space shuttle was like the monster that devoured Cleveland. In time, the shuttle program turned into NASA's money pit. Cost overruns, overly optimistic development and test schedules with exotic new technology, as well as funding cuts soon changed the promise of the space shuttle into a nightmare for planetary exploration. Shuttle development swallowed major portions of NASA's shrinking budget and hopes for deep-space exploration withered. Future craft and missions, including Pioneers 10 and 11, the new Voyagers to Jupiter and Saturn, and two Pioneer flights to Venus, were already in NASA's pipeline. After these missions, there were no new missions scheduled to explore the planets for the next decade as the shuttle sponged up even NASA's loose change.

But in mid-August 1975, no one suspected the dark future facing new missions to the planets. Poised on its launch pad at Cape (Kennedy) Canaveral, America's most powerful operational space rocket, the Titan 3E-Centaur, was prepared to vault Viking 1 toward Mars. It had been six-and-a-half years since the Viking program had been approved by Congress and three years since Mariner 9 sent the last data from Mars. Now, the culmination of America's Martian dream was about to take flight.

11  Martian Glory, Heartbreak, and Hope for the Future

COMPLEX CRAFT FOR A COMPLEX MISSION

Viking was a two-part spacecraft. Like the 1971 Soviet Mars explorers, Viking consisted of an autonomous orbiter and a detachable lander. But unlike the Soviet craft, Viking would carry its lander into Martian orbit before dispatching it to the surface. The success of the first American Mars landing depended on Viking scouting out its own landing site through high-resolution reconnaissance.

With an unfueled mass of 883 kg (1948 lb), the Viking orbiter was basically an expanded Mariner 9. Still octagonal in shape, the body of the spacecraft was 46 cm (1.5 ft) high while its eight sides alternated between 51 cm (20 inch) and 140 cm (4.6 ft). Attached to the four narrow sides were solar panels. Each was made of twin 123 × 157-cm (4 × 5-ft) solar cell arrays and altogether provided 620 watts of power to charge twin 30 ampere-hr batteries. In all, the orbiter stretched 9.75 m (32 ft) across the panels.

Sixteen electronics bays housed the orbiter's components. Included were dual 4096-word-memory computers and dual tape recorders capable of storing 55 television images. Mounted atop the orbiter was the propulsion system. Twin 140-cm (4.6-ft)-long tanks fed 1406 kg (3096 lb) of propellant to a 136-kg (300-lb)-thrust rocket engine.

The orbiter was more than just a transporter and health monitor for the lander. From Mars orbit, it was to use twin television systems to map the surface at resolutions up to 35 m (115 ft) as well as search for Martian water and map the thermal characteristics of the surface. The television system, water detector, and infrared mapper were mounted on a movable scan platform as on previous Mariners. The cameras worked together, alternately gathering and reading out the 1056 × 1182 pixel images every 4.48 seconds. The initial primary task of the television system was to work in conjunction with the water detector in an effort to locate smooth, moist areas on the planet where the lander would have a greater chance of finding life. Later, the imaging system would return systematic swaths of high resolution surface photographs to map the entire planet.

The enormous technological advances in spacecraft electronics during the decade since Mariner 4's vanguard mission were hammered home by the orbiter's cameras. Each image contained nearly a million bits of data, the same amount in all of Mariner 4's images combined. Furthermore, Viking could relay that amount of data in five minutes as opposed to the week required by Mariner 4.

ADVANCED LANDERS PREPARED

Mounted under the orbiter was a 3.66-m (12-ft)-diameter, lens-shaped lander assembly composed of a bioshield to keep the lander sterilized, an atmospheric entry aeroshield, and the Viking lander itself.

The lander bore a superficial resemblance to the earlier Surveyor probes which landed on the moon. The body of the craft was a six-sided aluminum and titanium box with three extendable landing legs. The lander's body was nearly obscured by a jumble of attached equipment. Twin external propellant tanks fed 139 kg (307 lb) of hydrazine fuel to three throttleable 27.2-to-292.6-kg (60-to-645-lb)-thrust descent engines. Each engine had an unusual 18-nozzle configuration to minimize the disruption of the surface during the landing.

The lander's eyes were twin high-resolution stereoscopic facsimile cameras. Separated by 80 cm (31.5 in), they viewed the terrain from 1.3 m (4.3 ft) above the surface. The cameras used a nodding mirror to scan the surface, viewing from 40 degrees above to 60 degrees below the horizon. Differing camera sensors were used to return black and white, red, blue, green, and infrared images. The individual single-color images were combined to produce full-color pictures of the Martian surface.

Other appendages included a surface sampler arm capable of reeling out 3 m (10 ft) from the lander and scooping Martian soil for various analyzers. A meteorological station mounted on a 1-m (3.3-ft) boom measured temperature, pressure, and wind velocity. A seismometer capable of detecting a level 3 quake 200 km (124 mi) away, a gas chromatograph mass spectrometer, and an X-ray fluorescence spectrometer to analyze the atmosphere and soil were also carried.

A 76-cm (30-in) steerable dish antenna relayed data to earth at 500 bits per sec while another fixed antenna relayed data to the orbiter at 16,000 bits per sec. The lander was limited to only two hours of direct communication with earth each day so most data were relayed by the orbiter.

The weather on Mars is at times too severe to deploy a solar array so electrical power for the lander came from twin plutonium-powered radioisotope thermoelectric generators (RTGs). These provided a total of seventy watts to charge four nickle-cadmium batteries. This system was expected to power the lander into the 1990s.

To guide the landers to touchdown and then control the various instruments, they carried two computers which, by the standards of the time, were extremely powerful. Each possessing a 18,400-word, plated-wire memory, the computers could store up to sixty days worth of commands. Other electronics included a recorder with 198 m (650 ft) of magnetic tape capable of storing forty megabits of data for later transmission to earth.

BIOLOGICAL LABORATORY CARRIED

The main purpose of the Viking landing was to search for life on Mars. To do this, an instrument was prepared that had never been carried by a spacecraft before, a miniaturized biological laboratory. Measuring only 0.03 m^3 (1 ft^3), this amazing laboratory was to use three different methods to analyze the Martian soil for signs of life.

Two decades later, the Viking biology laboratory proved still to be a scientific wonder. Within its tiny confines were three automated chemical laboratories, a computer, sample ovens, analytical equipment, 40 thermostats, 43 valves, 22,000 transistors, and 18,000 other electronic parts. To test the Martian soil for microbial life, the laboratory was to perform multiple investigations called the pyrolitic release, labeled release, and gas-exchange release experiments. Samples would be placed into the laboratory by a scoop on the surface sampler arm.

The pyrolitic release experiment involved incubating a soil sample for five days under a xenon lamp in an atmosphere of carbon dioxide labeled with (i.e., containing) radioactive carbon-14. If life were present, scientists thought the carbon 14 would be taken in by the organisms. Subsequently, the soil sample would be heated to drive out the carbon-14 ingested by any living organisms. Instruments would detect this carbon-14, indicating that some form of biological activity had been present.

The labeled release experiment fed water and nutrients labeled with carbon-14 to a soil sample. Any bacteria present should consume the nutrients and release detectable radioactive gases.

The final test, the gas-exchange experiment, was to feed unlabeled nutrients to a soil sample in a humid helium-krypton-carbon dioxide atmosphere. Detectors would then search for signs of water, oxygen, and methane produced by biological processes.

Two other instruments aboard the lander, an X-ray fluorescence spectrometer and a gas chromatograph mass spectrometer were to examine the elemental make up of soil samples and search for organic material.

For the trip to Mars, the lander was cocooned inside a bioshield which isolated the entire sterilized spacecraft and aeroshell from earthly contamination. Transporting earth microbes to Mars would render the multibillion-dollar mission a biological failure, so extra care was taken to prevent contamination of Mars with earth germs.

VIKINGS OFF TOWARD MARS

The launch had been scheduled for August 11, but one of the Viking spacecraft's batteries failed on the launch pad. The second Viking was swapped atop the launcher and was given the identity of Viking 1. On August 20, 1975, at 5:22 P.M., the Titan 3 lofted the Centaur stage into space where it entered a circular 185-km (115-mi) parking orbit. After 30 minutes, the rocket fired again and propelled Viking 1 on its way to Mars.

NASA was relieved that there were no further delays in launching Viking. A cosmic coincidence had allowed a happy circumstance. If Viking was away on time, the historic first American landing on another planet would occur on the July 4, 1976—America's second centennial. Massive nation-wide celebrations were planned for the bicentennial. What better day for America to claim the Mars landing prize?

Once in space and freed from its Centaur booster, Viking 1 opened its solar panels, ejected the bioshield cover, and settled into a 10-month cruise to Mars. A week after launch, the trajectory was corrected with a

12-second engine firing to bring the probe within 5500 km (3417 mi) of Mars ten months later, in June 1976.

In the meantime, the original Viking spacecraft had been repaired and was readied for launch. Liftoff came at 2:39 P.M., September 9. The Centaur propelling Viking 2 was less accurate, placing the craft on a trajectory which would miss Mars by 279,259 km (173,532 mi). A correction ten days after launch placed the probe back on course.

The cruise to Mars was fairly uneventful, but as Viking 1 closed in on its target, the potential for a propulsion system failure became a real concern. A leaking nitrogen valve threatened to overpressurize the propellant tanks with possibly disastrous consequences. After seven years of hard work by NASA, the American Martian landing was about to fall victim to the old planetary nemesis, the Galactic Ghoul.

A simple means was devised to outwit the Ghoul and lower the propulsion system pressure to safe levels—just fire the engine! While Viking 1's initial correction of 3 m (10 ft) per sec was all that was required to reach Mars, two more engine firings of 80 and 60 m (262 and 197 ft) per sec were performed nine and five days before arrival to bleed off dangerously high propulsion system helium pressures. These safety maneuvers delayed Viking 1's arrival at Mars by six hours, but placed operations safely back on track.

FIRST LANDING DELAYED

On June 19, 1976, Viking 1 arrived at Mars and fired its engine for 38 min. Consuming 1063 kg (2343 lb) of propellant, the probe decelerated into a 1500 × 50,300-km (932 × 31,256-mi) orbit with a period of 42.6 hr. Two days later, the apogee was lowered to 32,800 km (20,382 mi) to trim the orbital period to 24 hr, 39.5 min, thus matching the length of the Martian day.

The first reconnaissance photos of the primary landing site were returned June 22. The target was in the Chryse region which Mariner 9 had shown to be a smooth area where the curious dry, river-like channels seemed to flow. This evidence of past water raised hopes that some form of life lingered in the area. Years had been spent carefully selecting the landing site on the basis of Mariner 9 photography. Now, to the shock of mission scientists, Viking's own higher resolution imaging showed the target was far from the smooth, safe area planners had imagined. It was, in fact, so rough that the bicentennial day landing was immediately postponed. It was better to select a delayed but safer landing site than to keep a convenient public relations date.

Continued reconnaissance from orbit mapped the Chryse area searching for a suitable touchdown site. On July 12, it was decided to land at Martian coordinates 22.5 North and 47.5 West on the western slope of Chryse Planitia. The landing was now scheduled to occur on a more modern anniversary date, July 20, seven years after Americans first set foot on the moon.

On July 20, Mars was 360 million km (223.7 million mi) from earth. At that distance, signals from Viking took 19 minutes to reach earth. There was no way that ground controllers could guide the craft when the round-trip time for their commands was nearly 40 minutes. Viking had to land autonomously while controllers helplessly watched events transpire 19 minutes after they had actually happened.

At 4:51 A.M., the lander separated from the orbiter. Eight hydrazine thrusters fired for nearly 23 minutes to push the Viking 1 lander toward the upper Martian atmosphere. Three hours later, at 8:03 A.M., the lander streaked into the atmosphere at a 16 degree angle, protected from heat by the aeroshell which would reach a temperature of 1500°C (2732°F). The lander traversed 3000 km (1864 mi) of thin Martian atmosphere as it decelerated. During the fiery descent, a mass spectrometer housed in the aeroshell analyzed the atmosphere from 230 to 100 km (143 to 62 mi) and deduced that nitrogen composed 2.5 percent of the atmosphere. Maximum deceleration was 8.7 gs at 27 km (16.8 mi).

TOUCHDOWN!

At 5.9 km (3.66 mi) altitude, the lander's 16.2-m (53.1-ft) parachute opened. The aeroshield fell away seven seconds later and the landing legs extended. At 1400 m (4600 ft) the descent speed had slowed to 53 m (173 ft) per sec and the parachute was jettisoned. The lander's terminal descent engines were fired and the lander continued to decelerate as it sank to the surface.

At 8:12 A.M.—touchdown! The lander gently dropped onto the sands of Mars at 2.4 m (8 ft) per second. America's first landing attempt had succeeded. Upon landing, the telemetry rate to the orbiter automatically jumped from 4000 to 16,000 bits per second, alerting jubilant mission controllers to the success. After traveling to the far side of the solar system, Lander 1 had settled onto Chryse Planitia at 22.46 degrees North and 47.82 degrees West, only 28 km (17.3 mi) from its target.

Twenty-five seconds after landing, Lander 1 began to relay the first photograph from the Martian surface. Over the next five minutes, a live nation-wide television audience shared in the exciting event as the image was formed scan line by scan line. The picture showed footpad number 2 firmly resting on pebble-strewn loose soil. After decades of fantasy and scientific speculation, Mars became a very real, almost tangible place.

What happened over the next several weeks became the most documented space exploration endeavour since Neil Armstrong set foot on the moon seven years before. Nightly television specials unfolded the Martian exploration drama in American living rooms. It was prime-time science and everyone was a co-investigator!

Panoramic views revealed a barren desert landscape covered with stony rubble which looked like broken-up lava flow. In a surprise, the Martian sky was pink, an effect caused by sunlight scattering off airborne dust. The surface was reddish, its color stained by rust.

After a day, the lander issued the first Martian weather report: A predawn low of −86°C (−123°F), an afternoon high of −33°C (−27°F), winds of 29 km (18 mi) per hr with gusts of 51 km (31.7 mi) per hr, pressure steady at 7.6 millibars.

MARS UNDER ANALYSIS

Soil gathered by the sample arm on July 28 was deposited into the X-ray fluorescence analyzer which determined it to be iron-rich clay. In all, thirteen minerals were identified with silicon and iron being the most abundant. The composition was 5 percent magnesium, 3 percent aluminum, 20.9 percent silicon, 3.1 percent sulfur, 0.7 percent chlorine, less than 0.25 percent potassium, 4 percent calcium, 0.51 percent titanium, and 12.7 percent iron. Traces of rubidium, strontium, ytterbium, and zirconium were also detected while the remainder consisted of elements the spectrometer could not identify.

The Martian soil was firm except in the area of the left footpad which had completely submerged in soft dirt. A magnet on the sample scoop showed that about ten percent of the soil was magnetic.

Later, soil samples placed in the gas chromatograph mass spectrometer failed to reveal organic matter. The instrument then sampled the atmosphere of Mars and found it was composed of 95 percent carbon dioxide, 2.7 percent nitrogen, 1.6 percent argon, and 0.13 percent oxygen.

A week after landing, the biological experiments began. Soil samples placed in the detection laboratories soon began to show strange results. The pyrolitic release experiment reported positive results, but investigators suspected a chemical reaction, not life, was involved.

The labeled release experiment also showed encouraging results initially, but the behavior of the sample was inconsistent with growing microbes. It was suspected that an oxidizing agent in the soil produced a false reading because a sterilized sample returned similar data.

When both natural and sterilized samples returned positive results in the gas-exchange experiment, it was again suspected that some form of chemical reaction was producing false positive reports. When all was done, scientists could not agree about what had happened inside the biological laboratory. Some thought life had been detected, others were not sure.

EXPLORATIONS CONTINUE

While scientists tried to sort out the life-detection puzzle created by the Lander 1 data, Viking 2 arrived at Mars on August 7, and slipped into orbit. Following the same reconnaissance routine as its predecessor, Viking 2 found its Cydonia landing site at mid-northern latitudes along the Martian meridian to be too rough. The craft soon identified a new landing site on Utopia Planitia. This area, one-third the way around the globe from the original site and 6460 km (4014 mi) from Lander 1, was located at 47.9 degrees North and 225.9 degrees West. It was hoped a site further north would have more moisture and offer a greater chance of finding life.

The second lander touched down at 6:58 P.M., September 3. The Viking 2 lander had given controllers a scare when it fell silent 26 seconds after separating from its orbiter. However, the craft executed a flawless automatic landing and re-established communications.

Lander 2's biological experiments disappointed investigators when they repeated the inconclusive results of the first lander. Again scientists simply could not say for sure whether or not the instruments had detected life.

The meaning of the strange biological results forwarded by both landers was debated for years afterward. Ultimately, the most widely accepted explanation centered on the reaction of substances known as superoxides, or peroxides, in the Martian soil. Scientists currently think that solar ultraviolet radiation had bound oxygen to minerals in the soil. When water from the nutrient solutions was added, it released the bound oxygen, imitating the biological response sought by the test apparatus.

Further meteorological investigation, soil analysis, and surface photography by Lander 2 supplemented the findings from the first lander. Later in the Martian winter, a low of −118°C (−180°F) was reached. Also during the winter, the surface pressure dropped 30 percent as the carbon dioxide atmosphere became part of the polar cap.

The first lander's seismometer had failed to function, but Lander 2's worked perfectly. The instrument was sensitive enough to detect the movement of the craft's internal tape recorder, but during the lander's lifetime, only one small quake, 2.8 on the Richter scale, was detected.

EXTENDED MISSION CONTINUES MARS STUDIES

The four Vikings, two orbiter and two landers, proved long-lived at Mars. Each of the Viking's primary missions lasted 90 days after arrival. However, both craft continued to return data for one Martian year (each 2 earth-years long), and Lander 1 lasted three Martian years. But in time, machines break down or run out of fuel and, one by one, the orbiters and landers died.

The Viking 2 orbiter developed attitude control gas leaks in the spring of 1978, and finally tumbled out of control in July 1978. The longer-lived Viking 1 orbiter scanned Mars until August of 1980. Together, they returned 51,539 images and mapped 97 percent of the planet to a 300-m (1000-ft) resolution and 2 percent to a resolution of 25 m (82 ft) or less. Eventually, the orbiter's minimum altitude above Mars was reduced to 300 km (186.4 mi) where image resolution was 7.5 m (25 ft).

Lander 2 expired on April 12, 1980. However, Lander 1 was still functional and sent new data from Mars for almost three more years. Ultimately, both landers returned 4587 images from the surface, many in color. Lander 1 even photographed a solar eclipse by the moon Phobos, allowing the lander's position to be determined to within one km (0.6 mi).

Sadly, though Viking's extended mission proved long-lived, NASA's budget crunch, caused by the space shuttle, began to strangle the effort to collect Mars data. Overall, Viking's search for life on Mars had cost $2.5 billion (1984 dollars), making it the most expensive planetary mission to date. Running the Deep Space Network cost money—money NASA did not have. Now, late in the Viking mission, after spending billions to get to Mars, NASA did not have the mere pocket change required to listen to what Viking was saying. To continue the exploration, public space advocacy groups actually funded part of the extended Viking research program by passing the hat for cash donations.

Ultimately, Lander 1 also ceased to function. After receiving a weekly weather report on November 13, 1982, an inexperienced spacecraft controller accidentally sent a command which permanently shut down the lander. Unsuccessful efforts to revive the lander continued until the following May.

The accidental loss of Lander 1 was particularly sad in light of the fact that no future American Mars explorations were planned. Instead of being a building block for future exploration or manned expeditions to Mars, the Vikings became the final chapter in American Martian explorations for nearly two decades. Like the Soviets after 1973, American governmental leaders had lost the political will to go to Mars.

But that which slumbers will eventually awake; the Soviet Mars initiative revived. In the late 1980s, Mars would be within reach again, but the Galactic Ghoul also lay waiting for its next victim.

A NEW BEGINNING FOR SOVIET MARS EXPLORATION

In 1983 the Phobos missions were adopted as the next major Soviet solar system exploration project. Buoyed by the success of the Venera spacecraft and the cooperative international Vega missions to Halley's Comet, Soviet technicians put past Mars failures behind them and prepared a pair of advanced missions for a 1986 launch toward the red planet.

Continuing the scientific openness started with the Vega missions, Roald Sagdeyev, head of the Space Research Institute, revealed in 1984 that the missions would study three specific areas: the sun, Mars, and the moon Phobos.

The Phobos project was the first wave of a planned, new, all-out Russian assault on Mars which was to culminate in the year 2000 with a surface-sample return mission leading to later manned landings. The

Phobos spacecraft, Russian scientists reasoned, were the pride of Soviet space technology and would at last defeat the Galactic Ghoul!

By far the mission's most intriguing scientific target was the irregularly shaped Martian moon, Phobos. Spectroscopic studies from earth as well as investigation by the Viking orbiters showed that Phobos, and the other Martian moon, Deimos, were Type 1 carbonaceous chondrites, similar to carbon-rich, stony meteorites which strike earth. This means they are probably gravitationally captured asteroids. These are the most primitive of planetary bodies. Their elemental make-up has remained unchanged since the birth of the solar system, making them an inviting scientific target.

Phobos' small size, only $27 \times 21 \times 19$ km ($16.8 \times 13 \times 11.8$ mi), limits its gravity to only 1/1000th of earth's. This weak gravity allowed the new Phobos missions to tackle the technically challenging project of overflying Phobos at an altitude of only 50 m (164 ft) and dropping three probes onto its surface. One of these probes was to be an ingenious mobile device which would move across the surface of the moon in a series of spring-powered jumps, and was thus known by the names of "Hopper" or "Kangaroo." It is interesting to note that the overflight altitude above Phobos would actually be closer to the moon than the spacecraft was to the earth when it sat atop its Proton launcher.

INTERNATIONAL COOPERATION EXPANDED

The capabilities of the 6220-kg (13,684-lb) Phobos spacecraft rivaled those of advanced NASA planetary explorers and represented a new generation of planetary probe for the Soviet Union. The latest in hardware and computer software were incorporated to make Phobos the most complex Russian interplanetary spacecraft ever flown. To support the new Mars venture, even a new ground control center was built.

Expanding the precedent started with the highly acclaimed Vega missions to Halley's Comet, equipment was assembled from thirteen different countries for the Phobos project. Contributors included Austria, Bulgaria, Czechoslovakia, France, Finland, former East and West Germany, Hungary, Ireland, Poland, Sweden, Switzerland, and the former U.S.S.R. The European Space Agency's (ESA) European Space Operations Center (ESOC) and the French space agency's tracking facility at Toulouse assisted the NASA/JPL Deep Space Tracking Network in tracking and data acquisition. Ten American scientists also informally participated in science investigations. The Phobos Project represented the first truly international space venture to another planet.

As the project progressed, the complexities of designing and integrating state-of-the-art experiments from a dozen different countries proved to be more challenging than anticipated. Even when the planned launch date slipped from 1986 to 1988, final integration of all the experiment packages was not completed until after both spacecraft were delivered to the launch site at Tyuratam in March 1988.

Soviet confidence in this new Mars mission was high. This optimism, coupled with the international nature of the Phobos project and a new openness in Soviet reporting about their space program activities, provided the western world with much greater insight into the design and development of Russian spacecraft than they had gleaned from previous missions.

NEW GENERATION EXPLORERS

The Phobos spacecraft consisted of two separate modules; the Phobos probe and its autonomous propulsion module. The probe's base was a pressurized toroidal instrument compartment which housed the major electronics. Above this was a cylindrical pressurized instrument section. The craft was topped with a dish-shaped, directional high-gain communications antenna. Two solar panels attached to the toroidal section provided power. Radar and altimeter antennae were mounted under the solar panels. In addition to stabilizing the Phobos spacecraft in space, the probe's control system would use an intricate electronic system to navigate the Phobos spacecraft during the critical close encounter session with the inner Martian moon.

Below the spacecraft was the autonomous propulsion system which was an outgrowth of the earlier rocket system used on Venera spacecraft. It consisted of eight spherical tanks which supplied 3000 kg (6614 lb) of propellants to a rocket engine. This propulsion system was to lift the probe into a trans-Martian trajectory from an earth orbit, perform two mid-course corrections, slow the probe into a Mars orbit, then place the spacecraft into an orbit just outside the path of the moon, Phobos.

AMBITIOUS SCIENTIFIC GOALS

The Phobos spacecraft fairly bristled with scientific instruments. Twenty-five scientific packages and two Phobos landers were distributed around the outside of the spacecraft as launch-vehicle-shroud and center-of-gravity restrictions allowed. The total scientific payload carried was approximately 450 kg (992 lb).

Originally, each of the two Phobos spacecraft were to be identical. However, the realities of experiment integration and weight constraints eventually forced the deletion of several duplicate experiments. Consequently, while each spacecraft was basically the same, only Phobos 1 carried the extreme ultraviolet (EUV) solar detector and the Terek solar X-ray telescope and coronagraph, while only Phobos 2 was equipped with an infrared spectrometer-radiometer and the Hopper mobile landing probe.

Innovative scientific investigations were to be performed during the 15-min, 50-m (164-ft)-altitude close encounter with Phobos. The most exciting of these would be carried out by the 76-kg (167.5-lb) LIMA-D laser which was to fire 150 laser shots at the surface of Phobos. Every five to ten seconds, a 0.5-joule laser blast would vaporize a one-millimeter diameter spot. A mass spectrometer would collect and analyze about a million liberated ions to reveal their atomic weights and determine the composition of the moon.

Simultaneous observations would be performed by the 22-kg (48.5-lb) DION ion gun. By focusing a stream of krypton ions onto Phobos, the instrument would dislodge ions deposited by the solar wind. Analysis of these ions by a reflectron would tell what elements have been placed into Phobos' chemistry by the sun.

Also during the Phobos encounter, the moon's surface relief and subsurface structure to a depth of 200 m (656 ft) would be studied by radar and the composition of the surfaces of Mars and Phobos would be obtained by a gamma ray spectrometer. The 50-kg (110-lb) FREGAT television and spectrogram system would image Mars and resolve details as small as 6 cm (2.4 in) on the the moon Phobos.

LANDERS FOR PHOBOS

Studies from the moon Phobos were also to be carried out by landers dropped from the spacecraft as they cruised past at a relative speed of 2 to

5 m (6.5 to 16.4 ft) per second. Phobos 1 carried one fixed-site lander while Phobos 2 carried both a fixed-site and mobile lander.

Known as the Longterm Automated Lander (LAL), the 40-kg (88-lb), three-legged, flat-bodied, fixed-site lander was to stand a little over a half-meter (20-in) above the surface of the moon. A harpoon-like penetrometer was to extend from the underside of the lander and anchor it to the surface. A windmill-like, three-panel solar array topped by a helicodial (spiral-shaped) antenna was to extend from the lander's top. Experiments were to measure seismic noises on Phobos caused by Mars' gravity, thermal expansion, and meteor impacts. An X-ray fluorescence spectrometer, television camera, and a temperature sensor in the penetrometer were to study the surface composition, structure and mechanical properties of the moon's crust. The lander was to have a lifetime of 12 months and communicate with earth for 30 minutes on every other 7.5-hr orbit.

One of the fixed landers also carried an unusual momento from earth: an aluminum plaque containing a photographic etching duplicating the page from Asaph Hall's telescope log book from the night he discovered Phobos with the 26-inch refractor at the U.S. Naval Observatory in 1877. Below Halls' notes, the plaque read "U.S.S.R. Phobos Mission, 1988."

The other lander carried by Phobos 2 was the 40-kg (88-lb) PROP-F (a Russian acronym for Mobile Robot for Evaluating the Surface of Phobos), affectionately known as the "Hopper." The Hopper was to take advantage of Phobos' weak gravity to repeat its hopping maneuver ten times. The lander, with each jump, was to travel 20 m (66 ft). At each new position the Hopper was to roll upright and activate its experiments to study the moon.

Following a 15- to 20-minute close encounter and the deployment of the landers, the spacecraft were to back off from the moon to a distance of a few kilometers and continue investigations using radar. After studying the moon, the craft would concentrate on the planet Mars for the following six months.

PHOBOS PROJECT BECOMES A REALITY

The launch of Phobos 1 by an SL-12 Proton booster occurred at 9:38 P.M., July 5, 1988. Phobos 2 lifted off from Tyuratam soon after on July 12. Because each Phobos spacecraft had a mass of more than 6000 kg (13,228 lb on earth), the Proton, powerful as it was, could not supply enough energy to push the probes into an interplanetary trajectory. At the completion of the Proton fourth-stage burn, the Phobos craft was still in a highly elliptical earth orbit. The final 500-m (1640-ft)-per-second velocity needed to escape earth's pull came from the Phobos' own autonomous propulsion system. This was the first time this unusual method for escaping earth had been used for Soviet planetary exploration.

Following a perfect launch, the two spacecraft quickly passed through the shock wave created by the solar wind colliding with earth's magnetic field. The craft used this phenomenon to test some of their instruments.

Phobos 1 caused controllers some initial worry when, soon after launch, internal temperatures climbed to 46°C (115°F) and threatened some sensors. When the craft was properly reoriented toward the sun, the temperatures returned to design levels. With the mission now proceeding normally, preplanned course corrections took place for Phobos 1 and 2 on July 16 and 21, respectively.

PHOBOS 1 IS LOST

Through the end of August 1988, all was well with the two Phobos spacecraft and a total of 39 communications sessions were held with Phobos 1. In an international cooperative solar observation program during the month of September, the Terek X-ray telescope aboard Phobos 1 was to perform simultaneous observations with the American Solar Max satellite which was in earth orbit. This was to produce 3-dimensional X-ray images of the sun.

On August 31, the day before the cooperative solar venture was to begin, a major disaster occurred when a ground technician's error resulted in the accidental loss of the Phobos 1 spacecraft at a distance of 17 million km (10.6 million mi) from earth.

All control commands transmitted to the Phobos spacecraft were supposed to be tested for validity by running them through a special computer program to make sure they would not inadvertently cause any undesirable actions by the spacecraft. On the upload August 31, this checking routine was omitted by spacecraft controllers and an improper command was sent to the spacecraft.

During the transmission, a single character of computer code was skipped which resulted in the command to Phobos 1 to permanently shut off the guidance sensor for its attitude control system. Without this sensor, the spacecraft began to tumble slowly and power from the solar panels was lost. The error was not immediately noticed as the spacecraft were only contacted every three days. Eventually, battery power aboard Phobos 1 dropped to the point where contact was permanently lost.

During September, commands to revive Phobos 1 were broadcast at high power through Soviet RT-70 radio telescopes. However, the spacecraft could not respond. Phobos 1 had settled into a gravity-gradient-stabilized attitude, that is, the most massive part naturally oriented toward the sun's gravity. This attitude permanently placed the solar panels facing away from the sun, killing the spacecraft.

PHOBOS 2 CARRIES ON

The loss of the lead spacecraft left only Phobos 2 to carry out the Martian investigations. By November the second craft was 60 million km (37.3 million mi) from earth. Tests were conducted on the various scientific instruments to calibrate them for the upcoming Martian rendezvous at the end of January.

By the end of the year, Phobos 2 was having serious problems of its own. Temporary malfunctions with the television system were resolved by ground technicians; however, the mission experienced a serious setback with the loss of the craft's high-speed 50-watt transmitter. This left only the 5-watt backup transmitter to return data to earth at a slower rate.

On January 23, 1989, Phobos 2 made the final correction to its approach path. At 4:55 P.M., January 29, the craft fired it's retrorocket for 201 seconds and entered a highly elliptical 850 × 79,750-km (528 × 49,557-mi) orbit with a period of 76.5 hr. Phobos 2 then became the first spacecraft to explore Mars since the Viking 1 lander was accidentally shut down six years before. The craft remained in this orbit for three weeks while performing close studies of Mars from the low point of its orbit.

On February 12, Phobos 2 fired its engine to raise the low point of its orbit to 9600 km (5965 mi). Six days later, its orbit was circularized at 9670 km (6009 mi), inclined 0.5 degrees. The propulsion unit was then jettisoned. At this altitude, the spacecraft was about 300 km (186 mi) above the orbit of the moon Phobos and passed it at close range about once a week.

The first nine photographs of the moon Phobos were returned on February 21, from as close as 860 km (534 mi). Subsequent passes returned highly detailed photographs from a distance of several hundred kilometers.

Up to this time the position of Phobos was known only to within 200 km (124 mi), a figure much too rough for a rendezvous. Data from the spacecraft were used to determine an orbital ephemeris of the moon to be used for the close approach in a few weeks time. By early March the moon's position was known to within 30 km (18.6 mi).

SECOND PROBE LOST

By March 14 the distance between Phobos and the spacecraft had been reduced to 100 km (62 mi). But sadly, the rendezvous with Phobos on April 9 was not to be. The Phobos 2 spacecraft failed in Martian orbit before completing it's close approach to the moon. At 3:59 P.M., March 27, the Phobos spacecraft began an imaging session of the moon which required slewing its antenna away from earth. At the completion of the session, between 6:59 P.M. and 7:05 P.M., the spacecraft failed to point its high gain antenna back toward earth.

Emergency procedures were implemented and at 8:50 P.M., signals from the omnidirectional antenna were received for thirteen minutes before they were lost for good. Technicians reported that it was as if the signals were "sweeping by" the earth. Another engineer reported the signals gave him the impression that he was "tracking a spinner," a tumbling spacecraft.

A failure in Phobos 2's attitude control system left the spacecraft tumbling uselessly in an orbit just outside that of the moon Phobos. The spacecraft had come within two weeks of completing its primary mission of landing probes on Phobos. After continuous efforts to re-establish contact, the Soviets gave up on April 18 and declared the mission lost.

LIMITED SCIENCE FROM SHORTENED MISSION

Soviet officials, while obviously disappointed at the loss of both spacecraft, did not consider the Phobos missions a total failure. The primary objectives were not accomplished, but many data were returned during the interplanetary cruise and early Mars encounters. But, even putting the best possible face on the mission, the fact still remained that the Phobos project only accomplished about 15 percent of its objectives.

Solar studies by the Terek X-ray telescope aboard Phobos 1 yielded 140 high-quality images of the sun, some showing plasma erupting nearly

800,000 km (500,000 mi) into space. Also, more than 100 bursts of gamma radiation originating from other stars were recorded. These gamma-ray bursts ranged from events less than 1 millisecond in duration to the most intensive gamma-ray burst ever detected on October 24, 1988.

Infrared and visible light imaging of Phobos and Mars also provided new data. Thirty-seven pictures of Phobos were returned, showing 80 percent of it, including areas missed by the Viking orbiters. The images, with resolutions up to 40 m (131 ft) showed that Phobos was a uniform gray color. The mean density of Phobos was determined to be 2 g per cm^3, slightly less than expected for its carbonaceous chondrite material. The minerals of the moon Phobos had less water than expected and the daytime temperature reached 27°C (80°F). These readings were surprising since it was thought that Phobos' low density implied internal ice.

Measurements of weak gamma radiation from Mars allowed scientists to determine the soil's elemental makeup. In addition to uranium, thorium, and potassium, the gamma-ray spectrometer detected the signatures of iron, aluminum, silicon, calcium, and titanium. These results were consistent with earlier Viking and Mars 5 data.

The liquid-nitrogen-cooled TERMOSKAN radiometer also returned many 1500-km (932-mi)-wide infrared panoramas of Mars with a 1.8-km (1-mi) resolution. The instrument showed that the entire surface of Mars was covered with a fine layer of dust with a thermal inertia two to three times lower than exposed rock. Often the shadow of the moon Phobos appeared in the images and left a thermal trail across the Martian surface where the dust had cooled 4 to 6°C (7 to 11°F) from the shadow's passage.

Phobos 2 also determined that the atmosphere of Mars was losing 1 to 2 kg (2.2 to 4.4 lb) of matter into space every second. Considering the rarified Martian atmosphere, this is a significant amount of material. The rate of loss is equal to losing a uniform surface depth of 1 to 2 m (3.3 to 6.6 ft) of liquid water over the lifetime of Mars.

WHY DID PHOBOS FAIL?

The Phobos project was conceived and implemented in the pre-glasnost U.S.S.R. However, the mission failures occurred after the advent of glasnost and international cooperation. The failures thus spawned some unusually frank public discussion and interagency discord in the Soviet scientific community.

Earlier Venera designs also suffered failures, but eventually evolved into successful spacecraft. Phobos, the first of a new breed, not only suffered technical problems associated with a new design, but also suffered because investigating scientists were excluded from the design process and delays in project approval left little time for testing.

The Soviet system of designing spacecraft differed from that of NASA in that no single administrator was accountable for the entire project. Engineering and industrial groups were funded and managed separately by the Academy of Sciences. These groups independently conceived and manufactured the spacecraft, then negotiated its use with scientists. This system often left investigating scientists at odds with Lavochkin's current Designer General, Vyacheslav Kovtunenko, who actually built the spacecraft.

Roald Sagdeyev, Phobos mission scientific director, expressed the opinion that the mission's eventual loss was a near certainty. Sagdeyev believed that the primary cause of the dual failures was the fact that designers at Lavochkin had less than three and a half years to design and complete the spacecraft. When the Vega missions to Venus and Halley's Comet were launched in 1984, the Phobos project had yet to gain official approval. Sagdeyev said at least six to seven years were required to prepare such a complex project and the rush to complete the spacecraft placed the Lavochkin Association under enormous pressure. The design of the craft therefore suffered. The spacecraft builders suggested that a meteor or damage from solar radiation caused the failure. Sagdeyev however, was blunt in his assessment, stating "On Project Phobos, we were at odds with General Designer Vyacheslav Kovtunenko, who blames the breakdown on extraneous factors, whereas we are taking a different view."[1]

Recriminations aside, the fact remained that the Phobos craft, while the most advanced Russian space probes yet, still lacked adequate backups for their computer control systems. Indeed, by American standards, Phobos carried a very primitive computer. Had Phobos 1 carried added computer oversight which would reset the spacecraft in a "safe" condition in case of a system failure, the mission could have been saved. Additionally, in hindsight the addition of a steerable earth-pointing antenna or a movable camera scan platform might have saved the Phobos 2 mission. The previous Vega spacecraft had used a moving scan platform to image Halley's comet, but, inexplicably, such a device was omitted from the Phobos design.

PURSUING UNANSWERED QUESTIONS

Phobos had been billed as the opening volley in a new Soviet assault on Mars. But hard political reality also frustrated the Soviet as well as the American space program. By the end of 1988, only their 1994 Mars mission was close to approval by their government. The untimely demise of the Phobos missions dealt a serious blow to the fulfilment of the Soviet Mars dream. The prematurely terminated Phobos mission represented, in the Soviet economy, the equivalent of a $480-million investment.

After two generations, Soviet hard luck and tough breaks continued to foil attempts to complete a fully successful Mars mission. As the Soviets tried to resolve their planetary exploration problems, they experienced first hand the same effects of poor governmental planning and leadership which had crippled the American planetary exploration program in the late 1970s.

When the Phobos missions were launched, the Soviet Martian exploration program was the planetary envy of the world. A year later, the harsh realities of skimpy budgets, weak management, and technical setbacks had shown no special preference for either Soviet or American projects. As America's next Mars venture would show, both were fair game for the Galactic Ghoul!

Vikings 1 and 2 had sent back an incredible amount of data about Mars and analyzed two landing sites in detail, but still the overall Martian geological makeup remained unknown. To fully understand the red planet, scientists needed a broader investigation to answer questions in key areas. What is the Martian surface made of, how much water was once on the planet and where is it now? They also needed to know the Martian weather patterns, how they changed over the year and what triggered the great dust storms. Even such basic questions as the nature of the Martian magnetic field, whether the interior was still molten and the activity or non-activity of volcanoes still needed to be answered.

It was not until a decade after Viking that serious plans were undertaken to find answers to these and other basic, yet critical unknowns about Mars. While Soviet scientists were preparing the Phobos missions, American scientists were not idle with their Martian endeavours. The Mars Observer project promised to return American science to Mars 15 years after the Vikings. However, mercurial fortunes, politics, and threadbare budgets all combined to make America's return to the red planet a struggle.

America's next step to Mars had its genesis in 1977 when the Mars Science Working Group recommended a follow-on to Viking be flown as early as 1984. However, as cost overruns in the development of the space shuttle began to squeeze NASA's budget, no new planetary missions were planned beyond the twin 1978 Pioneer Venus probes. Additionally, the Reagan Administration's early 1980s freeze on Federal spending killed all future planetary exploration.

The Government's gutting of the scientifically productive and relatively inexpensive planetary exploration program enraged the scientific community. By 1982, a compromise between the government and scientists was struck in the form of NASA's newly formed Solar System Exploration Committee. This group recommended a modest, cheaper approach for future Mars explorations.

POLITICS HINDERS SCIENCE

Following the committee's recommendation, a new generation of cheaper spacecraft utilizing existing technology were to be built. The plan was to adapt off-the-shelf, proven earth satellite components into a probe which would allow an inexpensive return to Mars. The initial mission was to be a combined Martian weather satellite and mineral prospector. Appropriately, it was given the name of Mars Geochemical-Climatology Orbiter. A decade after the Viking missions left earth, Congress finally approved this project. When funded in 1985, it was given the name of Mars Observer.

This new mission was originally conceived as a dual spacecraft effort with one probe concentrating on atmospheric studies while the other analyzed the surface. To hold down development costs and increase reliability, Mars Observer was to be based on the design of RCA's Satcom K communications satellite and use subsystems from the TIROS and the Defense Meteorological Satellite Program (DMSP) weather satellites.

Soon, the dual mission was reduced to a single spacecraft. The budget also dictated that there would be no back-up spacecraft. Just a one-shot, winner-take-all mission would perform a two-year survey of Mars. Emphasis would be on Martian meteorology and climate, and analysis of atmospheric chemistry and surface composition. No lander or exotic life detection experiments were planned. Mars Observer was thus well named: It was not a true explorer but rather an observer, studying a known world to fill in the gaps in our knowledge. A launch in 1990 would be a natural follow-on to the international Phobos missions.

By August 1986 the fledgling Mars Observer program had received its first setback from the repercussions following the explosion of the space shuttle Challenger earlier in the year. As the realization dawned that a major review and redesign of the shuttle's booster rockets would halt shuttle flights for several years, the launch of Mars Observer was delayed from 1990 to 1992. The scientific community was appalled. After planetary exploration was rendered financially still-born by the shuttle in the 1970s and early 1980s, the rebirth of new explorations were again stifled by the shuttle. NASA administrators would not even consider switching Mars Observer to an expendable booster to keep the project on track. America's return to Mars was delayed two more years because of NASA's seemingly unbreakable rule of shuttle-only launches for NASA payloads.

Compounding Mars Observer's woes, the cost of the two-year delay was underestimated. It would have been impractical to disband the industrial and scientific team assembled for Mars Observer, then expect them to reconvene two years later, so the payroll continued. The cost of the two-year delay turned out to be more expensive than bypassing the shuttle and switching to an expendable booster.

The project continued to suffer from bureaucratic shortsightedness: it seemed the Mars Observer need not have feared the Galactic Ghoul in space for it had greater enemies right here on earth. Instead of switching the mission to a Titan 34D booster, commercially available from the Martin Marietta Corporation and avoiding the delay, NASA administrator James Fletcher raided the project's hard-earned reserves and transferred $50 million to support the troubled space station.

The reason for steadfastly retaining the shuttle as Mars Observer's transport was based in NASA's bewildering method of accounting. To NASA, a ride aboard the shuttle was "free" while money to purchase a Titan booster would have to be appropriated from other sources.

MARS OBSERVER TAKES SHAPE

Public space advocacy groups like the Planetary Society along with the scientific community lobbied NASA to reconsider using an expendable booster. Astonishingly, NASA agreed and reinstated the 1990 launch date using a Titan 3. Then, an incredible bureaucratic about-face occurred; on April 15, 1987, NASA ordered preparations for a 1990 launch to be stopped. Mars Observer was delayed until 1992 even with a launch by a Titan 3.

It is ironic that on that same day that work was halted on Mars Observer, Secretary of State George Schultz and Soviet Foreign Minister Eduard Shevardnadze signed a new space cooperation agreement which emphasized Mars missions. In spite of contradictory actions by NASA and the Government, Mars Observer was still stuck with a 1992 launch date.

In time, Mars Observer finally came into being. However, the plan to hold down the mission's cost by adapting existing spacecraft components evaporated. Built by a commercial contractor instead of being assembled in-house by JPL, the probe's cost ballooned to $510 million. Another $280 million was earmarked for the Titan 3 booster and its newly designed Transfer Orbit Stage (TOS) upper stage. The mission's overall cost finally grew to $1.01 billion (1993 dollars). Politics, funding delays, flip-flop management decisions, and the horror of the Challenger disaster all combined to change the original plan for a modest return to Mars into another of NASA's billion-dollar space systems.

INSTRUMENT ARRAY TO EXPAND MARS KNOWLEDGE

With a fully fueled mass of 2450 kg (5401 lb), the new Mars Observer was a box-shaped spacecraft measuring 1.5 by 2.1 m (5 by 7 ft). Eight scientific instruments were carried. Extending from the body were four booms supporting instruments and spacecraft housekeeping equipment. One short boom held a high-gain antenna which would transmit data at a maximum rate of 85,300 bits per second over a frequency of 8.4 Ghz. Another boom supported a massive solar array which gathered 1130 watts of power. Two other 6-m (20-ft) booms carried several scientific instruments while the rest were mounted beneath the probe. An internal propulsion system was fueled by nitrogen tetroxide and monomethyl hydrazine. Mid-course corrections and entry into Mars orbit would use combinations of four 50-kg (110-lb) thrusters or four 2.3-kg (5-lb) thrusters.

Two instruments were carried which would determine the chemical composition of Mars: a high-resolution gamma ray spectrometer and a thermal emission spectrometer. A thorough analysis of the atmosphere was to be done by a device called the pressure modulator infrared radiometer. Other studies of the atmospheric structure would be performed by the radio scientific experiment which would monitor the distortion and fading of the spacecraft's radio signal as it passed through the atmosphere when Mars Observer passed behind the planet eight to ten times a day.

Although it had been 30 years since the first probe reached Mars, the planet's magnetic field was still poorly understood. A magnetometer and electron reflectometer would attempt to remedy this by making the most detailed studies yet conducted of the Martian magnetic field.

The precise elevations of most Martian features were still not accurately known, complicating any mapping effort. To fill this gap, Mars Observer's laser altimeter would profile the topography with an accuracy of several meters.

By far the most exciting instruments were the dual cameras. The imaging system would map the entire planet and scan the changing weather patterns on a daily basis, returning gigabytes of electronic image detail. The wide-angle camera used an 11-mm focal-length fish-eye lens and was capable of resolving ground details of 7.2 km (4.5 mi) at the horizon and a respectable 243 m (800 ft) below the spacecraft. The narrow-angle camera would view random areas of the surface at an incredible resolution of 3 m (10 ft) through a 14-inch (355-mm) aperture, f/10 telescope.

Another item carried by Mars Observer was not an experiment, but was to play a crucial role in later Mars explorations. Installed aboard the spacecraft in a cooperative venture with Russian scientists was the Mars Balloon Relay, a device designed to receive data from four surface probes to be released by the Russian Mars 1994 mission. Mars Observer, in its polar orbit, would be in a more advantageous position than the Russian orbiter in its equatorial orbit, and was to help relay the Russian probe's data to earth. Hopefully, if Mars Observer was still functional two years later, it would also relay data from the planned Franco-Russian Mars 1996 balloon probe.

HURRICANE HALTS LAUNCH

In the summer of 1992, Mars Observer was prepared for its departure. However, the Galactic Ghoul had other plans. A frustrating series of minor glitches plagued the spacecraft's checkout, followed by a more serious fault—an elusive short circuit in the electrical system of the Transfer Orbit Stage. Just as the technical problems were solved, more trouble arose. Summoning help from the winds of earth, the Galactic Ghoul aimed a hurricane at Cape Canaveral as Mars Observer's launch preparations were being completed.

As it turned out, Hurricane Andrew spared the Florida space center, instead veering south and devastating Miami. However, as a precaution, Cape Canaveral declared a hurricane alert and braced for the storm. Mars Observer, atop its Titan 3 booster on the launch pad, was sealed and "hurricane-proofed." Part of this process included a dry nitrogen purge of the booster's shroud which cocooned the spacecraft. Unfortunately, instead of protecting the spacecraft, this process accidentally contaminated the laser altimeter with fine white particles. Mars Observer had to be taken off the booster, returned to its checkout shop and cleaned, delaying the launch by nine days.

Finally, Mars Observer's seven-year struggle to survive came to climax on September 25, 1992. At 2:05 P.M., the Titan 3 lifted off and bounded into space atop twin columns of flame from its solid rocket boosters. Performing perfectly, they placed the spacecraft and its Transfer Orbit Stage (TOS) into earth orbit ten minutes later. After a 30-minute coast, the TOS aimed for Mars and fired for 150 sec.

However, it was not smooth sailing. Mission controllers got a scare during the rocket burn when telemetry from the Transfer Orbit Stage failed. No one knew if the craft had left earth, had blown up, or was still stuck in earth orbit. Fortunately, all was well with the mute booster. Now en route to Mars, the spacecraft activated itself 90 minutes after launch and signaled its success to anxiously waiting controllers.

America was at last returning to the red planet. Ahead lay an eleven-month cruise which would carry Mars Observer to the far side of the sun. There was little for the craft to do except report its status to mission controllers as it sped toward its destiny.

Breaks in the monotony came during three scheduled course corrections. The first occurred on October 10, at a distance of 4.5 million km (2.6 million mi). This maneuver used two of the high-power thrusters during a 133-second burn which altered the craft's speed by 50 m (164 ft) per second. Accurate second and third corrections in February and March 1993 made a fourth correction unnecessary.

After calibrating its instruments, Mars Observer recorded its passage through earth's geomagnetic tail on December 9, at 25 million km (16 million mi) from earth, the greatest distance yet for spacecraft observations of this magnetic phenomenon. All seemed well with the spacecraft except for an annoying tendency for Mars Observer to loose orientation, thus causing the directional antenna to temporarily lose its fix on earth.

In July 1993 the red planet was in sight, looming closer and closer each day. By the twenty-eighth long-range images taken from 5.8 million km (3.6 million mi) revealed a half-illuminated, cloudless disk showing details too small to be seen from earth.

The mission plan called for arriving on August 24 and entering an initial 3-day elliptical orbit. During the flight from earth, mid-course corrections had been particularly frugal with their allocated fuel. With the additional fuel still available, mission controllers planned to lower the craft aggressively into its final Mars mapping orbit 21 days earlier than planned.

In the first 75 days after arrival the spacecraft would perform seven braking maneuvers to settle into a circular 390-km (242-mi) "sun-synchronous" polar orbit circling Mars every 117 min. From such a path, the craft would pass over each part of the Martian terrain when it was about 2 P.M., local Mars time, on the surface path below. This mid-afternoon sun angle was chosen to provide a good shadow angle for discriminating surface features. The two-year-long scientific mission was scheduled to begin on November 22, 1993.

THE GHOUL'S FINAL STRIKE!

But in the wink of an eye, the bold plan for new Mars science evaporated. Just three days away from ending its 724-million-km (450-million-mi) journey, Mars Observer was lost! After three decades of stalking American Mars probes, the Galactic Ghoul pounced and caught the hapless spacecraft.

The disaster occurred on August 21, 1993, at the beginning of a sequence of events leading up to the propulsion system's 29-minute-long Mars orbit insertion burn. At 2:21 P.M., both of the spacecraft's transmitters were turned off to protect the filaments in their traveling wave tube amplifiers from the shock of the pyrotechnic control valves used to pressurize the fuel system. Nothing further was ever heard from Mars Observer.

At 2:26 P.M., the valves should have opened to allow a 4300-psi helium source to pressurize the fuel tanks to 250 psi. After the fuel tanks were pressurized, the transmitters were supposed to turn back on at 3 P.M. When no signal was received, ground controllers sent commands to Mars Observer to switch on its wide-beam, low-gain antenna. It was suspected that the craft had simply lost orientation as it had on occasion during the cruise to Mars. However, the spacecraft never responded.

Time was critical. Mars Observer had to enter Mars orbit in just three days. If communications were recovered too late, the craft would overshoot Mars and uselessly orbit the sun. Numerous theories were evaluated and tested on simulators to determine what had gone wrong. But nothing controllers did would revive the spacecraft. Initially it was feared that the craft had exploded during the fuel-tank pressurization sequence, but attention soon turned to a possible computer malfunction which might have caused Mars Observer to fall mute just as it was to enter orbit around Mars, a particularly unfortunate time.

Contingency plans had been incorporated into Mars Observer's computer which controllers hoped would allow the spacecraft to enter Mars orbit autonomously. The craft was also preprogrammed to call earth automatically if no commands had been received for 120 hr. If Mars Observer was ever going to contact earth, it would do so 11:56 A.M., August 25. Controller's anxiously awaited the blip from across the solar system which would show that their half-billion-dollar probe was alive. However, the unchanging computer screens at the JPL control center grimly confirmed the death of the spacecraft.

The mission's loss was a particularly bitter blow. Not only was Mars Observer a very expensive mission, costing every American man, woman, and child $4 apiece, its very existence had been a hard-fought political battle. The public, and NASA, were not used to losing deep-space missions. JPL mission controllers had a long history of saving spacecraft from some particularly harrowing situations. The last time JPL had a mission go completely defunct was 26 years before when contact was lost with the Surveyor 4 lunar lander just two minutes before touchdown on July 17, 1967.

Speculation about the cause of Mars Observer's loss soon centered on the failure of a device called the redundant crystal oscillator, or "RXO." It would be ironic if the RXO did fail because, having been adapted from existing spacecraft, it was a feature designed to increase Mars Observer's reliability. Instead, it may have killed it. This device was the spacecraft's master computer clock. Without it, the computer could not function and without the computer, Mars Observer was nothing but a giant, gold-foil-covered paper weight.

As 1994 arrived, JPL concluded its investigation into the loss of Mars Observer. With no physical evidence to study, engineers finally concluded that the propulsion system had indeed malfunctioned just as the craft reached Mars. Suspicion now centered on a slow leak in the fuel system which may have caused a small explosion which would have sent the half-billion-dollar spacecraft tumbling uselessly past Mars.

However, the exact cause of Mars Observer's demise may never be known. Even the whereabouts of the spacecraft are a mystery. Did it enter orbit or mutely sail past the red planet? Perhaps a meteor strike crippled the spacecraft, or the computer failed, or possibly the propulsion system did explode. No one knows for sure except the Galactic Ghoul.

RUSSIAN MARS HOPES STILL ALIVE—BARELY

As the path of Mars in 1994 again brought it within range of probes launched from earth, the Martian torch passed back to the Russians. Their high-profile "Mars 94" mission was prepared at the Lovochkin Association for a launch in October, 1994. While the Russian economy was in turmoil following the collapse of the U.S.S.R., the Mars 94 mission progressed at the rate of 17 billion rubles ($15 million) per year with financial help coming from France and Germany.

This time, American instruments would ride with twin landers destined to thump down on the dusty surface of the planet. Plans call for the launch of a single Phobos-class spacecraft carrying two small landers and two spear-like surface penetrator probes. After an 11-month voyage, the Russian spacecraft was scheduled to eject its landers and penetrators, then enter a 900 × 18,200-km (560 × 11,310-mi) orbit, circling Mars every 12 hours.

The penetrators would slam into the surface at 480 km (300 mi) per hr. Their lower parts were to penetrate several meters below the ground while the upper half was to remain above the surface so a camera and weather sensors could scan the terrain.

The two landers would touch down more gently than the penetrators, but still with an impact of 200 *gs*. Similar to the Luna and Mars landers of the 1960s and 1970s, the probes were designed to split open with four petal-like panels unfolding to stabilize the lander on the surface. An international complement of instruments would then survey the Martian environment. A Russian camera would show us the surrounding terrain while meteorological sensors from Finland checked the weather. A French magnetometer was to measure the local magnetic field while a German X-ray spectrometer investigated the composition of the surface soil and rock. The American contribution was the the one-kg (2.2-lb) Mars Oxidant

Experiment (MOX) which was to test soil reactivity and composition. The experiment may shed some light on the strange soil reactions which led to the inconclusive Viking life-detection experiments in 1976.

One item to be carried by the landers is not an experiment, but a tribute to the 100,000 members of the Planetary Society, the American space advocacy group which not only pushed for further Mars exploration, but actually funded part of the testing of Russian Mars spacecraft. A microdot, inscribed with the names of all Planetary Society members (including this proud author), will be attached to the new Mars landers and carried to the surface of Mars.

While preparations for the Mars 94 mission progressed in early 1994, a follow-up mission planned for two years later was officially delayed by the ongoing economic crisis in eastern Europe. In March 1994 the Russian space science and technology council reluctantly recommended that Mars 96 be rescheduled for 1998. Complicating the delay is the unfavorable alignment between earth and Mars which will tax the limits of the powerful Proton booster. In order to reach Mars, the 1998 launch will have to carry a less massive spacecraft. This will force the elimination of some scientific instruments. The international nature of the Mars 98 mission makes the choice of which experiments to eliminate a particularly painful decision.

In April of 1994, the Russian space agency was forced to make another agonizing decision: The Mars 94 mission was itself delayed until 1996. Fiscal realities had delayed assembly of the Mars spacecraft until it was impossible to adequately test the probe before launch. Fearing the possible loss of another international Mars exploration venture, Russian space officials prudently chose to delay the mission to assure its future reliability. Thus the red planet will circle the sun one more time before Russian-built mechanical emissaries arrive.

With Mars Observer's loss, both the United States and Russia had lost high-profile Mars missions during the post-cold-war era. Now that cooperative science was a primary goal, instead of political propaganda and space "firsts," both nations mourned each other's scientific losses. Perhaps one of the underlying morals of the mutual Russian and American Mars failures in the past decade is that large-scale technical undertakings in planetary exploration are still expensive and risky. Half-billion-dollar losses are tough for any country to take. As the Mars 96 and 98 missions progress, the lessons of Phobos and Mars

Observer dictate that it is time for the Russians, Americans, Europeans, and Japanese to seriously promote planetary exploration as a cooperative world-wide activity. After all, the eventual goal will be for human beings, not nations, to go to Mars!

Endnotes

CHAPTER 1

1. Taken from Michael Stoiko, *Soviet Rocketry: Past, Present, and Future* (New York: Holt, Rinehart and Winston, 1970), p. 135.

2. Quoted in Martin Caidin, *War for the Moon* (New York: E. P. Dutton & Co., Inc., 1959), p. 206.

3. R. Cargill Hall, *Lunar Impact, NASA SP-4210* (Washington, D.C.: U.S. Government Printing Office, 1977), p. 5

4. Ibid., p. 6.

5. Caidin, p. 49.

6. "A Spaceship at Any Time," *Missiles and Rockets*, July 28, 1958.

7. "Soviet Moon Play," *Aviation Week*, August 25, 1958.

8. Caidin, p. 129.

9. Curtis Peebles, *Guardians* (Novato, CA: Presidio, 1987), p. 29.

10. Steven J. Zaloga, *Target America* (Novato, CA: Presidio, 1993), p. 141.

11. "Soviet Moon Rocket Has Half-Ton Payload," *Missiles and Rockets*, November 17, 1958.

12. "Cosmic Challenge," *Time*, January 12, 1959.

13. Ibid.

14. Evert Clark, "Soviet Moon Success Follows Failures," *Aviation Week*, January 12, 1959, p. 26.

15. "Moon—Direct Hit," *Newsweek*, September 21, 1959, p. 80.

16. "Moon Blow," *Time*, September 21, 1959.

17. Dr. A. C. Bernard Lovell, "Here Is the Evidence That the Moon Was Hit," *Life*, September 28, 1959, p. 54.

18. "A Closer Look at the Moon," *Time*, October 5, 1959.

19. "Lunar Probe Cloud," *Aviation Week*, October 29, 1959.

20. Evert Clark, "Soviets Hit Moon; Data Flow Improves," *Aviation Week*, September 21, 1959, p. 28.

CHAPTER 2

1. "Lunik III," *Time*, October 12, 1959.
2. Evert Clark, "Soviets Plan Series of Lunar Vehicles," *Aviation Week*, October 12, 1959, p. 28.
3. Yegor Lyssov, "Soviet Moon Probes," *Spaceflight*, October, 1992.
4. "Old Devil Moon," *Newsweek*, April 8, 1963, p. 62.
5. Ibid.
6. R. Cargill Hall, *Lunar Impact, NASA SP-4210, (Washington, D.C.: U.S. Government Printing Office, 1977), p. 153.*
7. Russian space exploration legend retold by the Russian-English translator present for an interview with Valery Timofeev, Lavochkin Association, conducted at Ft. Worth, Texas, August 31, 1991.
8. "Old Devil Moon," *Newsweek*, April 8, 1963, p. 62.
9. Ibid.
10. Brian Harvey, *Race into Space* (New York: John Wiley & Sons, 1988), p. 76.
11. Hall, p. 285.
12. Ibid, p. 309.
13. "Industry Observer," *Aviation Week and Space Technology*, June 21, 1965.

CHAPTER 3

1. "Triumph of Luna 9," *Spaceflight*, March, 1966, p. 131
2. "Luna 9 Sends More Pictures from the Moon," *San Antonio Light*, February 7, 1966, p. 2A.
3. Harvey, 1988, p. 104.
4. "Russia Tells Luna Findings, Hits British Photos," *San Antonio Express and News*, February 6, 1966, p. 1A.
5. Walter Sullivan, "Scale of Features Poses Problem in Moon Photos," *San Antonio Express and News*, February 5, 1966, p. 4A.
6. William J. Normyle, "U. S. Intercepts, Translates Luna 9 Signals," *Aviation Week and Space Technology*, February 14, 1966, p. 33.
7. "Russians Launch Luna 10," *San Antonio Express*, April 1, 1966, p. 14A.

CHAPTER 4

1. Nicholas Daniloff, *The Kremlin and the Cosmos* (New York: Alfred A. Knopf, 1972), p. 165.

2. Interview with Alexie Milovanov, Lavochkin Association, conducted at Fort Worth, Texas on June 29, 1991.

3. "Reds Imply Luna 15 to Stay in Orbit," *Newport News Daily Press*, July 17, 1969.

4. Boris Petrov, "The Case for Space Automation," *Pravda*, September 24, 1970.

5. "Dangerous Mission," Washington Outlook, *Aviation Week and Space Technology*, October 5, 1970, p. 13.

6. Charles Sheldon, *Soviet Space Programs, 1966–70* (Washington, D.C.: U.S. Government Printing Office, 1971), p. 204.

7. "Empty Victory," Washington Outlook, *Aviation Week and Space Technology*, December 14, 1970, p. 15.

8. "Off the Shelf," Washington Outlook, *Aviation Week and Space Technology*, September 6, 1970, p. 13.

9. Peter Smolders, *Soviets in Space* (New York: Taplinger Publishing Co., Inc., 1971), p. 213.

10. Sheldon, p. 202.

11. "Luna 18 Crashes in Landing Attempt," *Aviation Week and Space Technology*, September 20, 1971, p. 16.

12. "Back to the Moon," *Time*, January 29, 1973.

13. Sheldon, p. 202.

14. Marty Sabota, "'Stunning' Moon Photos to Be Released," *San Antonio Express-News*, March 2, 1994, p. 1-D.

15. Jeffrey Lenorovitz, "Clementine to Search for Ice at Lunar Poles," *Aviation Week and Space Technology*, April 11, 1994, p. 28.

16. Jeffrey Lenorovitz, "Low-Cost Spacecraft Begins Mapping the Moon," *Aviation Week and Space Technology*, March 7, 1994, p. 20.

CHAPTER 5

1. Dr. Albert Parry, "The Soviet Space Shot toward Venus," *Missiles and Rockets*, February 20, 1961.

2. Ibid.

3. Phillip S. Clark, "Launch Failures in the Soviet Union's Space Probe Program," *Spaceflight*, July/August, 1977, p. 275.

4. Telephone interview with University of Texas astronomer Dr. Gerard de Vaucouleurs conducted on February 10, 1994.

5. Bruce Murray, *Journey into Space* (New York: W. W. Norton & Company, 1989), p. 84.

6. Telephone interview with University of Texas astronomer Dr. Gerard de Vaucouleurs conducted on February 10, 1994.

7. "Soviets Launch Venus Probe from Orbit," *Aviation Week and Space Technology*, February 20, 1961.

8. "Soviets Launch New Space Probe from Satellite," *San Antonio Express and News*, February 12, 1961.

9. "Soviets Launch Venus Probe from Orbit," *Aviation Week and Space Technology*, February 20, 1961.

10. Interview with Valery Timofeev, Lavochkin Association, conducted at Ft. Worth, Texas, August 31, 1991.

11. "End of a Saga." *Time*, March 27, 1961.

12. R. Cargill Hall, *Lunar Impact, (NASA SP-4210)* (Washington D.C.: U.S. Government Printing Office, 1977), p. 160.

13. Charles Sheldon, *Soviet Space Programs, 1966-70* (Washington D.C.: U.S. Government Printing Office, 1971), p. 164.

14. "Russ Space Shots Fail," *San Francisco Chronicle*, September 6, 1962.

15. "U.S. Reveals Soviet Failures in Policy Shift," *Aviation Week and Space Technology*, September 10, 1962.

16. "Space Failures by Soviets Told," *San Francisco Examiner*, September 7, 1962.

17. "A Myth Exploded," *Newsweek*, September 17, 1962.

18. Dmitry Martinov, "New Facts about Venus," *Spaceworld*, November, 1967, p. 20.

19. "Russians Launch New Space Probe," *San Antonio Express and News*, April 5, 1964.

20. "Planetary Flight Gloom," *Aviation Week and Space Technology*, August 3, 1964.

21. "Double Pass for Venus," *San Antonio Light*, November 28, 1965.

22. "Soviets Launch Two Venus Probes," *Aviation Week and Space Technology*, November 22, 1965.

23. "Double Pass for Venus," *San Antonio Light*, November 28, 1965.

24. "Soviet Venus Probes," *Spaceflight*, May, 1966, p. 163.

25. "Venus 3; Hit or Miss Attempted?" *Spaceflight*, August, 1966, p. 297.

26. "Venus Rendezvous," *Spaceflight*, November, 1966, p. 392.

CHAPTER 6

1. "Early Cut of Transmissions from Venus 4 Unexplained," *Aviation Week and Space Technology*, November 6, 1967, p. 17.

2. "Soviet Venus Probe Nears Target," *Newport News Daily Press*, October 18, 1967, p. 1.

3. "Soviet Spaceship on Venus," *San Antonio Express and News*, January 26, 1971, p. 1.

4. Bruce Murray, *Journey into Space* (New York: W. W. Norton & Company, 1989), p. 83.

5. Interview with Valery Timofeev, Lavochkin Association, conducted at Ft. Worth, Texas, August 31, 1991.

6. Eric Burgess, *Venus an Errant Twin* (New York: Columbia University Press, 1985), p. 43.

7. Michael Stoiko, *Soviet Rocketry: Past, Present, and Future* (New York: Holt, Rinehart and Winston, 1970), p. 24.

8. Murray, p. 112.

CHAPTER 7

1. Interview with Valery Timofeev, Lavochkin Association, conducted at Ft. Worth, Texas, August 31, 1991.

2. Harry A. Taylor, Jr., "Auroras at Venus?" *Planetary Report*, July/August. 1987, p. 4.

3. Brian Harvey, *Race into Space* (New York: John Wiley & Sons, 1988), p. 254.

4. "Venus Unveiled," *Spaceflight*, January, 1976, p. 20.

5. Hunten, Colin, Donahue and Moroz, eds., *Venus* (Tucson: The University of Arizona Press, 1983), p. 147.

6. Ibid., p. 153.

7. "Pioneer Venus," Public relations release HSC932294/02-93, Hughes Space and Communications Company, El Segundo, California 90245.

8. Interview with Valery Timofeev, Lavochkin Association, conducted at Ft. Worth, Texas, August 31, 1991.

CHAPTER 8

1. John Noble Wilford, *Mars Beckons* (New York: Alfred A. Knopf, 1990), p. 123.

2. J. Kelly Beatty, "Interplanetary Explorations from Afar." *Planetary Report*, January/ February, 1987, p. 6.

3. Interview with Valery Timofeev, Lavochkin Association, conducted at Ft. Worth, Texas, August 31, 1991.

CHAPTER 9

1. Kenneth Gatland, *Robot Explorers* (London: Blandford Press, Ltd., 1972), p. 171.
2. Bruce Murray, *Journey into Space* (New York: W. W. Norton, 1989), p. 38.
3. Ibid., p. 43.
4. "Russians May Skip Mars Probe in 1966," *Aviation Week and Space Technology*, August 30, 1965.
5. Gatland, p. 212.

CHAPTER 10

1. John Noble Wilford, *Mars Beckons* (New York: Alfred A. Knopf, 1990), p. 77.
2. Kenneth Gatland, *Robot Explorers* (London: Blandford Press, Ltd., 1972), p. 217.
3. Reginald Turnill, *Spaceflight Directory*, (London: Frederick Warne, 1978), p. 280.
4. Martin Caidin, *Destination Mars* (Garden City: Doubleday & Company, 1972), p. 268.
5. Heikki Oja, "New Starts to the Planets," *Spaceflight*, June, 1975, p. 216.

CHAPTER 11

1. William E. Burrows, *Exploring Space* (New York: Random House, 1990), p. 374.

SUGGESTED READING

The present book deals with the history, spacecraft hardware, and nuts and bolts of planetary exploration. The flights of discovery made by these machines were, however, conceived and guided by real people, dedicated men and women with powerful visions, personalities, and colorful stories to tell. For an insight into the people behind these exciting voyages, I highly recommend two additional books:

Exploring Space by William E. Burrows, Random House, New York, 1990

Journey into Space by Bruce Murray, W. W. Norton, New York, 1989

Index